RULE BY LAW: THE POLITICS OF COURTS IN AUTHORITARIAN REGIMES

Scholars have generally assumed that courts in authoritarian states are pawns of their regimes, upholding the interests of governing elites and frustrating the efforts of their opponents. As a result, nearly all studies in comparative judicial politics have focused on democratic and democratizing countries. This volume brings together leading scholars in comparative judicial politics to consider the causes and consequences of judicial empowerment in authoritarian states. It demonstrates the wide range of governance tasks that courts perform, as well as the way in which courts can serve as critical sites of contention both among the ruling elite and between regimes and their citizens. Drawing on empirical and theoretical insights from every major region of the world, this volume advances our understanding of judicial politics in authoritarian regimes.

Tom Ginsburg is Professor of Law and Political Science at the University of Illinois. He is the author of *Judicial Review in New Democracies* (Cambridge University Press, 2003), which won the C. Herman Pritchett Award from the American Political Science Association for the best book on law and courts in 2004. Ginsburg serves as co-director of the Comparative Constitutions Project at the University of Illinois and runs the Program in Asian Law, Politics and Society.

Tamir Moustafa is Associate Professor of International Studies and Jarislowsky Chair in Religion and Cultural Change at Simon Fraser University, British Columbia. He is the author of *The Struggle for Constitutional Power: Law, Politics and Economic Development in Egypt* (Cambridge University Press, 2007) and a number of articles on comparative law and society, religion and politics, and state-society relations in the Middle East.

Rule by Law: The Politics of Courts in Authoritarian Regimes

Edited by

TOM GINSBURG

University of Illinois

TAMIR MOUSTAFA

Simon Fraser University, British Columbia

CAMBRIDGE UNIVERSITY PRESS

CAMBRIDGE UNIVERSITY PRESS
Cambridge, New York, Melbourne, Madrid, Cape Town, Singapore, São Paulo, Delhi

Cambridge University Press
32 Avenue of the Americas, New York, NY 10013–2473, USA

www.cambridge.org
Information on this title: www.cambridge.org/9780521720410

First published 2008

Printed in the United States of America

A catalog record for this publication is available from the British Library.

Library of Congress Cataloging in Publication Data

Rule by law : the politics of courts in authoritarian regimes / edited by Tom Ginsburg,
Tamir Moustafa.
   p. cm.
Includes bibliographical references and index.
ISBN 978-0-521-89590-3 (hardback) – ISBN 978-0-521-72041-0 (pbk.)
1. Courts – Political aspects.   2. Justice, Administration of – Political aspects   3. Political
questions and judicial power. 4. Judicial process. 5. Authoritarianism. I. Ginsburg,
Tom. II. Moustafa, Tamir. III. Title.
K2100.P66   2008
347′.01 – dc22   2007048073
ISBN   978-0-521-89590-3 hardback
ISBN   978-0-521-72041-0 paperback

I am therefore convinced that the prince who, in presence of an encroaching democracy, should endeavor to impair the judicial authority in his dominions, and to diminish the political influence of lawyers, would commit a great mistake: he would let slip the substance of authority to grasp the shadow. He would act more wisely in introducing lawyers into the government; and if he entrusted despotism to them under the form of violence, perhaps he would find it again in their hands under the external features of justice and law.

– Alexis de Tocqueville, *Democracy in America*, Book I, Chapter 16

Contents

Contributors

Robert Barros is Professor of Political Science at Universidad de San Andrés, Argentina. He is the author of *Constitutionalism and Dictatorship: Pinochet, the Junta, and the 1980 Constitution* (Cambridge University Press, 2002).

Lisa Hilbink is Assistant Professor of Political Science at the University of Minnesota. She is the author of *Judges beyond Politics in Democracy and Dictatorship: Lessons from Chile* (Cambridge University Press, 2007).

Pierre F. Landry is Assistant Professor of Political Science at Yale University. His research focuses on Chinese politics and comparative local government. He is currently writing a book titled *The CCP and Local Elites in Post-Deng China.*

Beatriz Magaloni is Professor of Political Science at Stanford University. She is the author of *Voting for Autocracy: Hegemonic Party Survival and Its Demise in Mexico* (Cambridge University Press, 2006). She is the recipient of the Gabriel Almond Award for the Best Dissertation in Comparative Politics from the American Political Science Association.

Karen May is completing her Ph.D. in economics at Claremont Graduate University, focusing on the political economy of international development. She holds a B.A. from Pomona College and an M.S. in community economic development from Southern New Hampshire University School of Business.

Anthony W. Pereira is Professor of Political Science at Tulane University. His work focuses on Latin American politics, and he is the author of, most recently, *Political (In)Justice: Authoritarianism and the Rule of Law in Brazil, Chile, and Argentina* (University of Pittsburgh Press, 2005). He received Fulbright and Fulbright-Hays fellowships in 2005–6 to carry out research on the reform of public security policy and policing in contemporary Brazil.

Hilton L. Root   is Professor of Public Policy at George Mason University. He is the author of many books on political economy, most recently *Capital and Collusion: Political Logic of Global Economic Development* (Princeton University Press, 2006) and the forthcoming *Alliance Curse: How America Lost the Third World* (Brookings Institution Press, 2008).

Daniel Scher   is Associate Director, Institutions for Fragile States, Princeton University.

Hootan Shambayati   is Assistant Professor of Comparative Politics and International Relations at Bilkent University, Turkey. His research is focused on judicial politics in Iran and Turkey and has appeared in top political science and area studies journals such as *Comparative Politics*.

Martin Shapiro   is the James W. and Isabel Coffroth Professor of Law at the University of California, Berkeley. He is the author of *Law and Politics in the Supreme Court; Freedom of Speech: The Supreme Court and Judicial Review; Supreme Court and Administrative Agencies; Courts: A Comparative and Political Analysis; Who Guards the Guardians: Judicial Control of Administration; and On Law, Politics and Judicialization* (with Alec Stone Sweet) in addition to dozens of chapters and articles. He is past president of the Western Political Science Association, past vice president of the American Political Science Association, a trustee of the Law and Society Association, and a member of the American Academy of Arts and Sciences. In 2003 Shapiro received a Lifetime Achievement Award from the Law and Courts section of the American Political Science Association.

Gordon Silverstein   is Assistant Professor of Political Science at the University of California, Berkeley. He is the author of *Imbalance of Powers: Constitutional Interpretation and the Making of American Foreign Policy* (Oxford University Press, 1997) and *Law's Allure: How Law Shapes, Constrains, Saves and Kills Politics* (Cambridge University Press, 2008).

Peter H. Solomon, Jr.,   Professor of Political Science at the University of Toronto, specializes in Soviet and post-Soviet politics with a focus on law and politics. He is the author of *Soviet Criminologists and Criminal Policy* (Columbia University Press, 1978) and *Soviet Criminal Justice under Stalin* (Cambridge University Press, 1996) in addition to a number of other books and articles on law and courts in the Soviet Union and Russia.

Jennifer Widner   is Professor of Political Science at Princeton University. She is the author of the highly regarded book *Building the Rule of Law* (W. W. Norton, 2001) and a number of scholarly articles dealing with constitution writing, the development of judicial institutions, and African politics.

Introduction: The Functions of Courts in Authoritarian Politics

Tamir Moustafa and Tom Ginsburg

Two decades ago, Martin Shapiro urged public law scholars to expand their horizons and begin studying "any public law other than constitutional law, any court other than the Supreme Court, any public lawmaker other then the judge, and any country other than the United States" (Shapiro 1989). Shapiro recognized that American public law scholarship stood at the margins of political science because it did not adequately engage the broad questions in the field. Perhaps more importantly, Shapiro recognized that judicial institutions had become important political players in a number of countries and that a "judicialization of politics" was on the advance across much of the world.

Since Shapiro's first call for more comparative scholarship, there has been an explosion in the judicial politics literature focused on a variety of regions and themes, including the role of courts in democratizing countries, the relationship between law and social movements, and the judicialization of international politics. However, there has been relatively little research on the dynamics of judicial politics in non-democracies.[1] This gap in the literature is likely the result of a long-standing presumption among many political scientists that courts in authoritarian regimes serve as mere pawns of their rulers, and that they therefore lack any independent influence in political life.

Note: This introduction includes material from *The Struggle for Constitutional Power: Law, Politics, and Economic Development in Egypt* by Tamir Moustafa (Cambridge University Press, 2007). For a more detailed elaboration of the theoretical framework undergirding this introduction, see Chapter 2, "The Politics of Domination: Law and Resistance in Authoriatarian States."

---

[1] This is somewhat puzzling given the longstanding view among some scholars that judicial policymaking is antidemocratic (Dahl 1957, Hirschl 2004). The normative debate over judicial governance in democratic theory indirectly suggests certain affinities between governance by judiciary and nondemocratic regimes. After all, if courts constrain majorities, perhaps they may be useful for regimes that have no interest at all in democracy.

Yet, as many of the contributors to this volume have demonstrated elsewhere (Barros 2002, Hilbink 2007, Moustafa 2007, Pereira 2005, Solomon 1996), the empirical reality in many authoritarian regimes cuts against this conventional wisdom.

Through a range of case studies and more general chapters, this volume explores the conditions under which authoritarian rulers delegate decision-making to judiciaries and the political consequences of that choice. The approach is institutionalist in character in that it does not presume the reach of law and courts, but views the scope of judicial authority and power as a target for inquiry (Ginsburg and Kagan 2005). This introduction raises some issues related to understanding courts in authoritarian politics, themes that are elaborated in the chapters that follow.

WHY STUDY COURTS IN AUTHORITARIAN REGIMES?

Our project should be viewed as a contribution to the burgeoning literature on the judicialization of politics (Tate and Vallinder 1995; Shapiro and Stone 2002; Sieder, Schjolden, and Angell 2005). In many different countries, the scope and impact of judicial authority are expanding, and judges are making decisions that were previously reserved for majoritarian institutions. But while the focus to date has been on democracies, we should not assume that judicial institutions are irrelevant to political life in authoritarian polities.

Our inquiry is, alas, particularly timely. The 1990s notion of the Washington Consensus, namely that democracy, markets, and the rule of law all would develop in unison, looks hopelessly naïve a decade later. At this writing, leftist populism is on the rise in Latin America; Russia and most of the former Soviet republics are best characterized as illiberal democracies, if not openly authoritarian; "Market-Leninism" is alive and well in China and the rest of socialist Asia; most of the Middle East remains unfree; and most African states alternate between unconsolidated democracy and soft authoritarianism. Yet, as we demonstrate in the chapters to come, many of these states exhibit an increasingly prominent role for judicial institutions. Courts are often used to advance the interests of authoritarian regimes, and yet paradoxically, they are also sometimes transformed into important sites of political resistance. In a surprising number of cases, courts become the focal point of state-society contention, resulting in a "judicialization of authoritarian politics" (Moustafa 2003, 2007). Simply put, courts should be studied in authoritarian states because they matter to political life. With more than half of all states categorized as authoritarian or semi-authoritarian and more headed in that direction, it is crucial for us to get a grip on the reality of judicial politics in nondemocratic environments.[2]

A second reason for taking courts in authoritarian regimes seriously is that they provide a useful lens through which to examine a variety of political dynamics in an environment that is otherwise distinguished by a lack of transparency. The public nature of judicial process and the paper trail that courts provide opens a point of access into internal regime dynamics and state-society contention, even if the legal process requires some interpretation. For example, in his study in this volume (see Chapter 8), Pierre Landry uses surveys of court use to illustrate general patterns of norm diffusion in post-Mao China. The Chinese regime has made the rule of law a central component of its legitimation strategy (Peerenboom 2002) and was supportive of Landry's research. What we learn is that political resources like party membership matter with regard to propensities to use government institutions, even in a formally neutral setting such as courts.

A third reason to examine courts in authoritarian regimes is to learn more about the expansion and contraction of judicial power generally. Robert Barros (Chapter 6) argues that the weakness of judicial institutions in the face of rising authoritarianism in 1970s Chile and Argentina illustrates the general problems that courts face when exercising their functions in contexts in which rulers centralize previously separated powers or remove matters from ordinary court jurisdiction. In those military dictatorships, courts were scarcely able to serve as the last bastion for upholding rights when the rest of the constitutional order had been marginalized. Courts need specific institutional configurations and social support to fulfill their missions. By looking at the extreme environment of a dictatorship, then, we may better understand the limited ability of courts to safeguard individual rights and the rules of the political game in democracies facing extraordinary circumstances. Similarly, several of our chapters address the question of whether we are witnessing a "convergence" between authoritarian and democratic regimes in the post-9/11 world. Although our contributors come down on different sides of this debate, the rich discussion underlines the fact that courts in authoritarian regimes provide a useful testing ground for hypotheses on the expansion and contraction of judicial power generally.

---

[2] Freedom House, Freedom in the World 2006. Twenty-four percent of all countries comprising 36 percent of the world's population were categorized as "not free." An additional 30 percent of all countries comprising 18 percent of the world's population were categorized as "partly free."

THE FUNCTIONS OF COURTS IN AUTHORITARIAN REGIMES

What motivates state leaders to establish judicial institutions with varying degrees of autonomy? Following Moustafa (2007) we identify five primary functions of courts in authoritarian states. Courts are used to (1) establish social control and sideline political opponents, (2) bolster a regime's claim to "legal" legitimacy, (3) strengthen administrative compliance within the state's own bureaucratic machinery and solve coordination problems among competing factions within the regime, (4) facilitate trade and investment, and (5) implement controversial policies so as to allow political distance from core elements of the regime.[3] This section describes each function in turn.

Social Control

The most obvious role played by courts in authoritarian systems is that of exercising social control (Shapiro 1981). The core criminal law function is the central mechanism for this task, but there are a variety of parallel instruments that can be used to accomplish these goals – for example, the ordinary or secret police, paramilitary units, and other components of the security apparatus. One dimension on which authoritarian regimes differ is which of these organizations are relied upon to maintain order and to sideline political opponents.[4] Thus, a crucial variable is the scope of judicial involvement. The common technique of establishing special security courts shows that authoritarian regimes exercise control over scope by channeling different types of cases to different arenas (Toharia 1975).

Even when courts are used for social control, they vary a good deal in the extent to which they enjoy real autonomy. Stalinist show trials – though a tiny part of the criminal caseload of Soviet judges – utilized courts for political education and the statement of regime policies, employing the form of law without any autonomy given to courts. But other regimes may be less willing or able to dictate outcomes in individual cases. One might categorize the levels of autonomy of courts involved in implementing regime policies, ranging from pure instruments in which outcomes and punishment are foreordained to situations of relative autonomy in which courts can find defendants innocent.

---

[3] These are in addition to the routine and universal function of conflict resolution in low-level disputes (Shapiro 1981).

[4] Perlmutter's (1981) typology of authoritarian regimes highlights this in its threefold structural categorization: single authoritarian party, bureaucratic-military complex, and parallel and auxiliary structures of domination, such as police and paramilitary. Perlmutter believes that all authoritarian leaders rely on one or another of these mechanisms as the primary instrument of control.

The contribution here by Anthony Pereira (Chapter 1) highlights these dimensions of scope and autonomy. Pereira examines three contemporaneous military dictatorships in Latin America, which varied widely in their willingness to use the regular judiciary to sideline political opponents. Where courts showed deference to the regime, political cases were routed through the regular judiciary and repression was therefore routinized and somewhat domesticated. Where judicial-military relations were poor, on the other hand, violence was extralegal in character, with much more lethal and arbitrary consequences. Brazil, and to a lesser extent, Chile, fit the first pattern; judicial autonomy was reduced significantly, but courts were used extensively to sideline regime opponents. In Argentina, on the other hand, courts retained a greater degree of autonomy, but their scope of action was sharply reduced and state violence took on an extrajudicial dimension. The degree of judicialization matters for *how* power is exercised in authoritarian regimes, and for the fate of regime opponents.

Courts are also used to maintain social control in a broader, more political sense. Hootan Shambayati's contribution to this volume (Chapter 11) illustrates how regimes with a mixture of elected and unelected bodies use judicial institutions to check the popular will. Turkey and Iran, two countries that are in one sense diametric opposites of one another (the first being a fiercely secular regime and the latter a self-proclaimed theocracy), share a core political dynamic. In Turkey, the secular power elite used unelected judicial institutions to check the Islamist AK Party, which controls the Turkish Grand National Assembly. In Iran, the religious power elite similarly used unelected judicial institutions to effectively check majoritarian institutions that were controlled by reform-oriented politicians. In both cases, courts served as the linchpin of regime control over the popular will.

Legitimation

Legitimacy is important even for authoritarian regimes, if only to economize on the use of force that is also a component of maintaining power. Without the possibility of legitimation at the ballot box, authoritarian rulers often seek to justify their continued rule through the achievement of substantive outcomes, such as income redistribution, land reform, economic growth or political stability in post-conflict environments. But to various degrees, authoritarian rulers may also attempt to make up for their questionable legitimacy by preserving judicial institutions that give the image, if not the full effect, of constraints on arbitrary rule. In Pakistan, for example, judges have reluctantly, but repeatedly, legalized the right of military leaders to rule after coups

(Mahmud 1993). Similarly, after seizing control and declaring martial law in the Philippines in 1972, Ferdinand Marcos cracked down on political opponents and attacked civil society, but left the courts open. Marcos reassured the public that "the judiciary shall continue to function in accordance with its present organization and personnel" and that his new government would have effective "checks and balances," which would be enforced by the Supreme Court in a new framework of "constitutional authoritarianism" (Del Carmen 1973: 1050). The veneer of legal legitimation is valuable to authoritarians, and may in fact bolster their image among certain constituencies.

Sometimes the target of legitimation is external rather than internal. When confronted with the threat of Western colonialism in the late nineteenth century, Japan's rulers engineered a program of forced modernization that was phenomenally successful. Since the Western powers had forced unequal treaties on Japan through a characterization of Japan's legal system as barbaric, nationalist elites made law the very center of their reform efforts. But in practice, with the political economy organized around state intervention and late development to catch up with the West, law received much less emphasis as a means of social ordering – instead it provided a kind of formal legitimacy to demonstrate to other nation-states that Japan was a member of the club of modernity. Similarly, authoritarian regimes in postwar Korea and Taiwan, dependent like Marcos on the security relationship with the United States, kept an appearance of formal constitutional legality. Courts were relatively autonomous, but the scope of their activity was carefully circumscribed. This staged deference to liberal legality was essential in the Cold War environment.

In many cases, authoritarian regimes switch to the rule of law as a legitimizing narrative only after the failure of their initial policy objectives or after popular support for the regime has faded. Tamir Moustafa's contribution here (Chapter 5) highlights how Anwar Sadat used rule-of-law rhetoric in Egypt to overcome a tremendous legitimacy deficit left by the failures of Nasserism. In his study in this volume, Pierre Landry (Chapter 8) similarly illustrates how the legal system in post-Mao China has been used to build regime legitimacy for the central government. For such legitimizing functions to succeed, however, judicial institutions must enjoy some degree of real autonomy from the executive, and they must, at least on occasion, strike against the expressed will of the regime. As E. P. Thompson (1975) famously noted, "the essential precondition for the effectiveness of law, in its function as ideology, is that it shall display an independence from gross manipulation." Otherwise, legal institutions "will mask nothing, legitimize nothing." However, the more a regime relies on rule-of-law rhetoric, the greater the opportunity for litigants and judges to expose the shortcomings of the government. This creates a core tension between empowerment and control of courts.

Controlling Administrative Agents and Maintaining Elite Cohesion

Another reason to empower courts is to discipline administrative agents of the state. As elaborated in this volume by Tom Ginsburg (Chapter 2), all rulers face the problem of controlling their inferiors, who have superior information but little incentive to share it. These problems may be particularly severe in authoritarian states. Although authoritarian bureaucracies may not have such niceties as civil service protections to insulate them from direct political pressure from above, accurate information on bureaucratic misdeeds is even more difficult for authoritarian regimes to collect because the typical mechanisms for discovery, such as a free press or interest groups that monitor government behavior, are suppressed to varying degrees. Courts can provide a useful mechanism by which rulers gain information on the behavior of their bureaucratic subordinates.

These dynamics are clearly at play in a number of the cases here. Ginsburg describes how the Chinese Communist Party turned to administrative law as ideology waned and conventional tools of hierarchical control became less effective (see also Solomon 2004). Jennifer Widner (2001; Chapter 9) observes the same dynamic in several East African countries both before and after the region's democratic transitions, illustrating the utility of administrative courts for enhancing bureaucratic compliance in both democratic *and* authoritarian regimes. According to Widner (2001: 363), "opportunities to develop judicial independence arose as leaders grew concerned about corruption within the ranks of the ruling parties or with arbitrariness and excess on the part of lower officials whose actions they could not supervise directly. The ability of private parties or prosecutors to bring complaints against wayward civil servants and party members in independent courts helped reduce the need for senior politicians to monitor and cajole." Similarly, Beatriz Magaloni's contribution here (Chapter 7) describes how, during the seven-decade stretch of single-party rule in Mexico, citizens were encouraged to use the judicial mechanism of *amparo* to challenge arbitrary applications by individual bureaucrats without threatening the underlying policy. Finally, Moustafa (Chapter 5) traces how the administrative court system was vastly expanded by the Egyptian regime beginning in the 1970s in order to restore discipline to a rapidly expanding and increasingly unwieldy bureaucracy. In all of these cases the ruling parties did not provide recourse to judicial institutions out of benevolence. Rather, regimes structured these mechanisms to better institutionalize their rule and to strengthen discipline within their states' burgeoning administrative hierarchies.

A variant of this logic is found in situations in which judicial institutions are used to formalize ad hoc power sharing arrangements among regime elites. Maintaining cohesion within the ruling coalition is a formidable challenge, and elite-level cleavages require careful management to prevent any one faction from dominating the others.[5] As with control of administrative agents, judicial mechanisms can be employed to mitigate fragmentation within the ruling apparatus.

Pinochet's Chile provides the most lucid example of how constitutions have been used to formalize pacts among competing factions within authoritarian regimes and how judicial institutions are sometimes used to balance the competing interests among those factions. According to Barros (2002), the 1980 Chilean Constitution represented a compromise among the four branches of the military, which were organized along distinct, corporatist lines with strong, cohesive interests, whereas the 1981 *Tribunal Constitucional* provided a mechanism that enabled military commanders to arbitrate their differences in light of the 1980 document. This institution, perhaps in unanticipated ways, therefore played a major role in maintaining cohesion among the military and in consolidating the 1980 Constitution.

Credible Commitments in the Economic Sphere

The central dilemma of market-based economies is that any state strong enough to ensure protection of property rights is also strong enough to intrude on them (Weingast 1995). Governments must therefore ensure that their promises not to interfere with capital are credible and that they will not renege when politically convenient later on. Establishing autonomous institutions is a common strategy to ensure credible and enduring policies in the economic sphere – in monetary policy, securities regulation, and other areas. Autonomous courts are one variant of this strategy. As elaborated by Hilton Root and Karen May in this volume (Chapter 12), by establishing a neutral institution to monitor and punish violations of property rights, the state can make credible its promise to keep its hands off. Autonomous courts allow economic actors to challenge government action, raising the cost of political

---

[5] O'Donnell and Schmitter (1986: 19) observe that "there is no transition whose beginning is not the consequence – direct or indirect – of important divisions within the authoritarian regime itself." Similar arguments can be found in a number of other studies including Haggard and Kaufman (1995), Huntington (1991), and Rustow (1970).

interference with economic activity. Root and May emphasize that there is no necessary connection between the empowerment of the courts and the ultimate liberalization of the political system.

Different regimes may be differently situated with regard to the ability of courts to provide credibility. Authoritarian judiciaries vary in their initial endowment of quality, and utilizing courts to make commitments credible may be easier in postcolonial Hong Kong than in, say, Cambodia or Vietnam. Ceteris paribus, there may be a greater incentive to utilize courts when preexisting levels of judicial quality are already high.

At the same time, a global trend toward economic liberalization in recent decades has encouraged and facilitated the establishment or reform of more robust judicial institutions. Courts provide transparent, nominally neutral forums to challenge government action, and hence are useful for foreign investors and trade. The WTO regime explicitly requires states to provide judicial or quasi-judicial institutions in trade-related arenas; a network of bilateral investment treaties promises neutral dispute resolution to reassure investors; and multilateral institutions such as the World Bank and Inter-American Development Bank expend vast resources to promote judicial reform in developing countries. In the age of global competition for capital, it is difficult to find any government that is **not** engaged in some program of judicial reform designed to make legal institutions more effective, efficient, and predictable. While the challenges of globalization are formidable for many developing countries, the option of opting out is increasingly one of economic suicide.

This suggests that there are secular pressures toward judicialization of economic activity. However, this does not mean that all state leaders have the equal ability, incentive, or desire to utilize courts in this fashion. Root and May emphasize that there is no reason to think that authoritarian rulers will always pursue broad-based growth – indeed, for many regimes, broad-based growth would undermine the ruling coalition. Similarly, authoritarian regimes in resource-rich states, such as Myanmar or Saudi Arabia, need not develop broad-based legal mechanisms to shelter investment and growth, but can instead rely on narrow bases of regime finance. For such regimes, the potential costs of judicial autonomy may outweigh any benefits, and they will seek to utilize other mechanisms to establish whatever levels of credibility are needed.

The Delegation of Controversial Reforms to Judicial Institutions

Authoritarian rulers also find great advantage in channeling controversial political questions into judicial forums. In democratic settings, Tate and others describe this process as "delegation by majoritarian institutions" (Tate 1995: 32). Several studies observe that democratically elected leaders often delegate decision-making authority to judicial institutions either when majoritarian institutions have reached a deadlock, or simply to avoid divisive and politically costly issues. As Graber notes (1993: 43), "the aim of legislative deference to the judiciary is for the courts to make controversial policies that political elites approve of but cannot publicly champion, and to do so in such a way that these elites are not held accountable by the general public, or at least not as accountable as they would be had they personally voted for that policy." Seen from this perspective, some of the most memorable Supreme Court rulings are not necessarily markers of judicial strength vis-à-vis other branches of government; rather they might be regarded as strategic modes of delegation by officeholders and strategic compliance by judges (with somewhat similar policymaking preferences) who are better insulated from the political repercussions of controversial rulings.

Perhaps the best example of this phenomenon is the continued postponement of urgently needed economic reforms in postpopulist, authoritarian regimes. Authoritarian rulers in these contexts are sensitive to the risks of retreating from prior state commitments to subsidized goods and services, state-owned enterprises, commitments to full employment, and broad pledges to labor rights generally. They rightly fear popular backlash or elite-level splits if they renege on policies that previously formed the ideological basis of their rule. However, if authoritarian leaders can steer sensitive political questions such as these into "nonpolitical" judicial forums, they stand a better chance of minimizing the political fallout. Moustafa (2007) examines how dozens of Egyptian Supreme Constitutional Court (SCC) rulings enabled the regime to overturn socialist-oriented policies without having to face direct opposition from social groups that were threatened by economic liberalization. SCC rulings enabled the executive leadership to claim that they were simply respecting an autonomous rule-of-law system rather than implementing sensitive reforms through more overt political channels.

Complementarities among the Functions

The above list is hardly exhaustive, but does capture several common circumstances that motivate authoritarian leaders to empower courts. It is worth noting that these functions are not exclusive, but complementary. For example, two of the great threats to security of investment are low-level corruption and bureaucratic arbitrariness. An administrative law regime that reduces agency costs in administration is also likely to enhance credible commitments to property rights. In turn, economic growth and administrative quality are likely to enhance a regime's claims to legitimacy. Pereira's study here and Chaskalon's (2003) discussion of South Africa both suggest that even harsh regimes may be relatively legitimated if the social control function is domesticated through legal means. In short, the functions of courts are likely to be mutually supportive.

TIME HORIZONS AND THE DOUBLE-EDGED SWORD

To this point, we have catalogued a number of reasons why regimes may wish to rely on judicial forms of governance. Some of these functions are likely to be particular to authoritarian regimes, whereas others represent more general dilemmas of states. Yet not every authoritarian regime chooses to utilize courts to perform these functions. Under what circumstances are regimes more likely to resolve these dilemmas with courts?

A crucial issue is the time horizon of the regime. Entrenched regimes with long time horizons are more likely to turn to courts for core governance functions for several reasons. First, relatively secure regimes have the opportunity to experiment with more sophisticated forms of institutional development. In the economic sphere, for example, secure regimes are more likely to prioritize institutional reforms such as courts that maximize long-term economic growth and tax revenues. In contrast, regimes with a precarious grip on power are generally less concerned with the long-term payoff of institutional reform and are more likely to engage in predatory behavior (Olson 1993).

The same logic holds for the administrative functions that courts perform. The principal-agent problems associated with bureaucracies are likely to become more severe over time and in step with the degree of bureaucratic complexity of the state. Ginsburg's contribution in this volume (Chapter 2) ties the shift toward administrative law to a decline in ideology as a basis for regime legitimation and control of agents. Once again, relatively mature regimes have the luxury of experimenting with more sophisticated forms of institutional development and administrative discipline.

Third, there is also reason to believe that the longer a regime survives, the more it is likely to shift its legitimizing rhetoric away from the achievement of substantive concerns to rule-of-law rhetoric. For example, Nasser (1954–1970) pinned his legitimacy to the revolutionary principles of national independence, the redistribution of national wealth, economic development, and Arab nationalism. However, when the state failed to deliver, Anwar Sadat (1970–1981) explicitly pinned the regime's legitimacy on *"sayadat al-qanun"* (the rule of law) to distance himself from those failures. Ginsburg notes a similar transformation to rule-of-law rhetoric in China. Mao Zedong almost completely undermined judicial institutions after founding the People's Republic of China in 1949, but rule-of-law rhetoric is being increasingly used by the regime to distance itself from the spectacular excesses and failures of its past, and to build a new legitimizing ideology.[6]

Note that the timing of judicialization outlined here contrasts with that found in democratic environments. Hirschl (2004) argues that judicialization results when "departing hegemons" seek to extend their substantive policies after prospective electoral loss. Similarly, Ginsburg (2003) views the establishment of judicial review as a strategy of political insurance by parties that foresee themselves out of power in the near future. In both accounts, ruling parties that will soon be displaced by their opponents have an incentive to empower the judiciary, because they believe the regime and its institutions will continue without them. In authoritarian environments, by contrast, entrenched regimes (i.e., authoritarian regimes with *longer* time horizons) are more likely to empower the judiciary, precisely to extend the life of the regime and guard against a loss of power.

While the electoral logic of judicialization in democracies clearly does not apply in authoritarian settings, our findings are broadly consistent with the Ginsburg-Hirschl argument in the following sense. The electoral story hinges at bottom on the disaggregation of interests within a governing regime. The presence of two competing groups with different views of policy facilitates the empowerment of the judiciary in democracies. Similarly, many of the dilemmas that prompt authoritarian regimes to empower courts are intensified by disaggregation within the regime. For example, the need for courts to resolve internal coordination problems, as identified by Barros (2002), arises from a degree of fragmentation within the ruling coalition. The need for control of administrative agents is exacerbated by state fragmentation, as Ginsburg's account of China here suggests. Thus, when we expand the focus from a simple electoral model to a broader one of state fragmentation, authoritarian and democratic regimes may not be as dissimilar as first appears in terms of the timing of judicial empowerment.

The decision to accord autonomy to courts depends on the particular configuration of challenges faced by authoritarian regimes, but in an astonishing array of circumstances, limited autonomy makes sense. The strategy, however, is hardly risk-free. Once established, judicial institutions sometimes open new

---

[6] For Nasser, these included the failure to deliver economic development, defeat in the 1967 war, and the collapse of the United Arab Republic with Syria. For Mao Zedong, these included the Great Leap Forward, which resulted in the largest famine in human history with 30 million deaths, the chaos of the Cultural Revolution, and the failure to deliver economic growth.

avenues for activists to challenge regime policy. This is perhaps an inevitable outcome, because, as Moustafa has previously noted, the success of each of these regime-supporting functions depends upon some measure of real judicial autonomy (2007). For example, commitments to property rights are not credible unless courts have independence and real powers of judicial review. Administrative courts cannot effectively stamp out corruption unless they are independent from the political and bureaucratic machinery that they are charged with supervising and disciplining. The strategy of "delegation by authoritarian institutions" will not divert blame for the abrogation of populist policies unless the courts striking down populist legislation are seen to be independent from the regime. And finally, regime legitimacy derived from a respect for judicial institutions also rings empty unless courts are perceived to be independent from the government and they rule against government interests from time to time.

Not all regimes will empower courts to capitalize on these functions, but those that do create a uniquely independent institution with public access in the midst of an authoritarian state. This provides one venue for what O'Brien and Li (2005) call "rightful resistance," defined as "a form of popular contention that operates near the boundary of authorized channels, employs the rhetoric and commitments of the powerful to curb the exercise of power, hinges on locating and exploiting divisions within the state, and relies on mobilizing support from the wider public." Even when activists do not win particular cases, courts can facilitate rightful resistance by providing publicity about government malfeasance, deterring future abuses and developing skill sets for activist leaders. Together, courts and activists can form what Moustafa (2007) calls "judicial support networks," namely institutions and associations, both domestic and transnational, that facilitate the expansion of judicial power by actively initiating litigation and/or supporting the independence of judicial institutions if they come under attack. In authoritarian contexts, the fate of judicial power and legal channels of recourse for political activists is intertwined.

Halliday, Feeley, and Karpik (2007) similarly find that the nature of the relationship among the various elements of the "legal complex" is a key variable in curbing excessive state power. The bench, bar associations, prosecutors, and nongovernmental organizations can work together to bolster judicial autonomy even in the face of authoritarian political systems. In Taiwan, for example, the alternative bar association became a key site of organizing resistance to the KMT regime, and both Korea and Taiwan had lawyer-activists as presidents in the early twenty-first century (Ginsburg, 2007). Legality in the authoritarian period provided the seeds for a complete institutional transformation once democratization began. Similar dynamics seemed to potentially be underway in Pakistan in mid 2007 when Chief Justice Muhammad Chaudhry relied on the support of the bar association to resist an attempt by General Musharraf to remove him from office. Ultimately, the bar and the courts were subjected to attack when Musharraf suspended the constitution; still, the courts have provided some space for regime opponents, and may do so again once political circumstances are less charged.

HOW REGIMES CONTAIN COURTS

Given the potential use of courts as a double-edged sword, a central challenge for authoritarian rulers is to capitalize on the regime-supporting roles that courts perform while minimizing their utility to the political opposition. Courts in authoritarian states face acute limitations, but the most serious constraints are often more subtle than tightly controlled appointment procedures, short term limits, and the like. Direct attacks on judges, such as the crude campaign of physical intimidation of the judiciary in Zimbabwe documented here by Jennifer Widner in Chapter 9, are also rare. More typically, regimes can contain judicial activism *without* infringing on judicial autonomy. Following Moustafa (2007), we outline four principal strategies: (1) providing institutional incentives that promote judicial self-restraint, (2) engineering fragmented judicial systems, (3) constraining the access to justice, and (4) incapacitating judicial support networks.

Judicial Self-Restraint

The assumption that courts serve as handmaidens of rulers obscures the strategic choices that judges make in authoritarian contexts, just as they do in democratic contexts.[7] Judges are acutely aware of their insecure position in the political system and their attenuated weakness vis-à-vis the executive, as well as the personal and political implications of rulings that impinge on the core interests of the regime.

Core interests vary from one regime to the next depending on substantive policy orientations, but all regimes seek to safeguard the core legal mechanisms that undergird their ability to sideline political opponents and maintain power. Reform-oriented judges therefore occupy a precarious position in the legal/political order. They are hamstrung by a desire to build oppositional credibility among judicial support networks, on the one hand, and an inability to challenge core regime interests for risk of retribution, on the other hand.

---

[7] A classic account in the American context is Murphy (1962).

Given this precarious position, reform-minded judges typically apply subtle pressure for political reform only at the margins of political life.

Core regime interests are typically challenged only when it appears that the regime is on its way out of power. In most cases, reform-oriented judges bide their time in anticipation of the moment that the regime will weaken to the extent that defection is no longer futile, but can have an impact on the broader constellation of political forces (Helmke 2002, 2005). Strategic defection in such a circumstance is also motivated by the desire of judicial actors to distance themselves from the outgoing regime and put themselves in good stead with incoming rulers. The more typical mode of court activism in a secure authoritarian regime is to apply subtle pressure for political reform at the margins and to resist impinging on the core interests of the regime.

The dynamics of "core compliance" with regime interests are noted in dozens of authoritarian states. In the Egyptian case, the Supreme Constitutional Court issued dozens of progressive rulings that attempted to expand basic rights and rein in executive abuses of power, but it never ruled on constitutional challenges to the emergency laws or civilian transfers to military courts, which formed the bedrock of regime dominance. Similarly, in the early days of the Marcos regime, the Philippine Supreme Court did not attempt to resist the decree of martial law, the imposition of a new constitution, or decrees placing new constraints on the jurisdiction of the courts. Rather, the court yielded to Marcos's seizure of power, and it continued to submit to the regime's core political interests for the next fourteen years of rule. Philippine Justices Castro and Makalintal candidly acknowledged the political realities that undoubtedly shaped the court's unwillingness to confront the regime, stating in their ruling that "if a new government gains authority and dominance through force, it can be effectively challenged only by a stronger force; no judicial dictum can prevail against it" (Del Carmen 1973: 1059–1060). Similar dynamics are noted in Pakistan, Ghana, Zimbabwe, Uganda, Nigeria, Cyprus, Seychelles, Grenada, and other countries (see, e.g., Mahmud 1994).

In such circumstances, formal judicial independence can clearly exist within an authoritarian state. One can also understand why an authoritarian ruler would find it politically advantageous to maintain formal judicial independence. Del Carmen's (1973: 1061) characterization of judicial politics under Marcos is particularly illuminating:

> While it is true that during the interim period . . . the President can use his power to bludgeon the Court to subservience or virtual extermination, the President will most probably not do that – ironically, because he realizes that

it is in his interest to keep the Court in operation. On the balance sheet, the Court thus far has done the President more service than disservice, more good than harm.

The important dynamic to note in each of these instances is that authoritarian regimes were able to gain judicial compliance *and* enjoy some measure of legal legitimation without having to launch a direct assault on judicial autonomy. The anticipated threat of executive reprisal and the simple futility of court rulings on the most sensitive political issues are usually sufficient to produce judicial compliance with the regime's core interests. An odd irony results: the more deference that a court pays to executive power, the more institutional autonomy an authoritarian regime is likely to extend to it.[8]

The internal structure of appointments and promotions can also constrain judicial activism quite independently of regime interference. The judiciary in Pinochet's Chile is a good example of a court system that failed to act as a meaningful constraint on the executive, despite the fact that it was institutionally independent from the government. According to Hilbink (chapter 4), this failure had everything to do with the process of internal promotion and recruitment, wherein Supreme Court justices controlled the review and promotion of subordinates throughout the judiciary. The hermetically sealed courts did not fall victim to executive bullying. Rather, the traditional political elite controlling the upper echelons of the court system disciplined judges who did not follow their commitment to a thin conception of the rule of law.[9]

The case of Singapore, discussed here by Gordon Silverstein in Chapter 3, provides a further example. Silverstein documents how Singapore's courts do very well on formal measures of independence, yet despite having a good deal of autonomy in economic and administrative matters they do not constrain the government politically. With its commanding majority in the Parliament, Lee Kuan Yew's People's Action Party easily issued new legislation and even constitutional amendments to sideline political opponents, all the while respecting

---

[8] This observation should also call into question our common understanding of the concept of "judicial independence." If we understand judicial independence to mean institutional autonomy from other branches of government, then we must conclude that more than a few authoritarian states satisfy this formal requirement. In both democratic and authoritarian contexts, formal institutional autonomy appears to be a necessary condition for the emergence of judicial power, but in both cases it is insufficient by itself to produce effective checks on power.

[9] Hilbink finds that the independent Chilean Supreme Court ironically became a significant obstacle to democratic consolidation, challenging the assumption in the vast majority of the political science literature that independent courts provide a check on executive or legislative abuses of power and that courts consistently work to protect basic rights that are essential for a healthy democracy.

formal judicial independence. All of these cases suggest that formalist conceptions of the rule of law are not enough to ensure substantive notions of political liberalism.

Alternatively, one can imagine courts that have a very broad scope of activity, but have relatively little autonomy. Scope is a distinct issue from autonomy (see Guarnieri and Pederzoli 2002). Magaloni's account in this volume (see Chapter 7) of the Mexican judiciary under the PRI seems to illustrate the model of a judiciary with a wide scope of formal authority but little autonomy. Judicial appointments were highly centralized, and the judicial process was used to suppress the opposition.

Fragmented versus Unified Judicial Systems

Authoritarian regimes also contain judicial activism by engineering fragmented judicial systems in place of unified judiciaries. In the ideal type of a unified judiciary, the regular court hierarchy has jurisdiction over every legal dispute in the land. In fragmented systems, on the other hand, one or more exceptional courts run alongside the regular court system. In these auxiliary courts, the executive retains tight controls through nontenured political appointments, heavily circumscribed due process rights, and retention of the ability to order retrials if it wishes. Politically sensitive cases are channeled into these auxiliary institutions when necessary, enabling rulers to sideline political threats as needed. With such auxiliary courts waiting in the wings, authoritarian rulers can extend substantial degrees of autonomy to the regular judiciary.

Examples can be found in a number of diverse contexts. In Franco's Spain, Jose Toharia (1975: 495) noted that "Spanish judges at present seem fairly independent of the Executive with respect to their selection, training, promotion, assignment, and tenure." Yet Toharia also observed that the fragmented structure of judicial institutions and parallel tribunals acted "to limit the sphere of action of the ordinary judiciary." This institutional configuration ultimately enabled the regime to manage the judiciary and contain judicial activism, all the while claiming respect and deference to independent rule-of-law institutions. Toharia explains that "with such an elaborate, fragile balance of independence and containment of ordinary tribunals, the political system had much to gain in terms of external image and internal legitimacy. By preserving the independence of ordinary courts . . . it has been able to claim to have an independent system of justice and, as such, to be subject to the rule of law."

All other things being equal, there is likely to be a direct relationship between the degree of independence and the degree of fragmentation of judicial institutions in authoritarian contexts. The more independence a court enjoys, the greater the likely degree of judicial fragmentation in the judicial system as a whole. Boundaries between the two sets of judicial institutions also shift according to political context. Generally speaking, the more compliant the regular courts are, the more that authoritarian rulers allow political cases to remain in their jurisdiction. The more the regular courts attempt to challenge regime interests, on the other hand, the more the jurisdiction of the auxiliary courts is expanded.

In authoritarian states, the regular judiciary is unwilling to rule on the constitutionality of parallel state security courts for fear of losing a hopeless struggle with the regime, illustrating both the core compliance function at work and the awareness among judges that they risk the ability to champion rights at the margins of political life if they attempt to challenge the regime's core legal mechanisms for maintaining political control. Returning to the Egyptian example, the Supreme Constitutional Court had ample opportunities to strike down provisions that denied citizens the right of appeal to regular judicial institutions, but it almost certainly exercised restraint because impeding the function of the exceptional courts would result in a futile confrontation with the regime. Ironically, the regime's ability to transfer select cases to exceptional courts facilitated the emergence of judicial power in the regular judiciary. The Supreme Constitutional Court was able to push a liberal agenda and maintain its institutional autonomy from the executive largely because the regime was confident that it ultimately retained full control over its political opponents. To restate the broader argument, the jurisdiction of judicial institutions in authoritarian regimes is ironically dependent on the willingness of judges (particularly those in the higher echelons of the courts) to manage and contain the judiciary's own activist impulses. Judicial activism in authoritarian regimes is only made possible by its insulation within a fundamentally illiberal system.

Constraining Access to Justice

Authoritarian rulers can also contain judicial activism by adopting a variety of institutional configurations that constrain the efforts of litigants and judges. At the most fundamental level, civil law systems provide judges with less maneuverability and less capacity to create "judge-made" law than enjoyed by their common law counterparts (Merryman 1985; Osiel 1995). The rapid spread of the civil law model historically was not merely the result of colonial diffusion, in which colonizers simply reproduced the legal institutions of the mother country. In many cases, the civil law model was purposefully adopted independent of colonial imposition because it provided a better system through which rulers could constrain, if not prevent, judge-made law. Although the differences between civil law and common law systems are often overstated and even less meaningful over time as more civil law countries adopt procedures for judicial review of legislation, civil law judges may be relatively more constrained than their common law counterparts as a formal matter.[10] More important than any legal constraints is the norm that judges in civil law systems are to apply the law mechanically, resulting in a tendency toward thin rather than thick conceptions of the rule of law.

Regimes can engineer further constraints on the *institutional structure* of judicial review,[11] the *type* of judicial review permitted,[12] and the *legal standing* requirements. For example, a regime can constrain judges more effectively by imposing a centralized structure of judicial review in place of a decentralized structure. Centralized review yields fewer judges who must be bargained with, co-opted, or contained, resulting in predictable relationships with known individuals. It was precisely for this reason that the Turkish military imposed a centralized structure of judicial review in the 1982 Constitution.[13] Another technique, recounted here by Peter Solomon in Chapter 10, is to under-enforce judicial decisions.

Most regimes also limit the types of legal challenges that can be made against the state. In Magaloni's account of Mexico under the PRI, citizens could only raise *amparo* cases, radically constraining the Mexican Supreme Court. Similarly, article 12 of the Chinese Administrative Litigation Law empowers citizens to challenge decisions involving personal and property rights, but it

---

[10] Shapiro explains that the role of the civil law judge as simply applying preexisting legal codes is a myth because it assumes that codes can be made complete, consistent, and specific, which is never fully actualized in reality. The result is that civil court judges engage in judicial interpretation, a fundamentally political role, just as judges do in common law systems (Shapiro 1981).

[11] In a centralized system of judicial review, only one judicial body (typically a specialized constitutional court) is empowered to perform review of legislation. In a diffused system of judicial review, on the other hand, any court can decide on the constitutionality or unconstitutionality of a particular piece of legislation.

[12] Courts with provisions for concrete review examine laws after they take effect, in concrete legal disputes. Courts with provisions for abstract review examine legislation as part of the normal legislative process and can nullify legislation before it takes effect.

[13] In the 1961 Turkish Constitution, courts could practice judicial review if the Constitutional Court had not issued a judgment within a defined period. This procedure was abolished in the 1982 Constitution, and a number of other constraints were put in place to narrow the scope and standing requirements of judicial review (Belge 2006).

does not mention political rights, such as the freedom of association, assembly, speech, and publication. These select issue areas speak volumes about the intent of the central government to rein in local bureaucrats while precluding the possibility of overt political challenges through the courts.

Incapacitating Judicial Support Networks

Finally, authoritarian regimes can contain court activism by incapacitating judicial support networks. In his comparative study, *The Rights Revolution*, Epp (1998) shows that the most critical variable determining the timing, strength, and impact of rights revolutions is neither the ideology of judges, nor specific rights provisions, nor a broader culture of rights consciousness. Rather, the critical ingredient is the ability of rights advocates to build organizational capacity that enables them to engage in deliberate, strategic, and repeated litigation campaigns. Rights advocates can reap the benefits that come from being "repeat players" when they are properly organized, coordinated, and funded.[14] Although Epp's study is concerned with courts in democratic polities, his framework sheds light on the structural weakness of courts in authoritarian regimes.

The weakness of judicial institutions vis-à-vis the executive is not only the result of direct constraints that the executive imposes on the courts; it is also related to the characteristic weakness of civil society in authoritarian states. The task of forming an effective judicial support network from a collection of disparate rights advocates is all the more difficult because activists not only have to deal with the collective action problems that typically bedevil political organizing in democratic systems but authoritarian regimes also actively monitor, intimidate, and suppress organizations that dare to challenge the state. Harassment can come in the form of extralegal coercion, but more often it comes in the form of a web of illiberal legislation spun out from the regime. With the legal ground beneath them constantly shifting, rights organizations find it difficult to build organizational capacity before having to disband and reorganize under another umbrella association. Given the interdependent nature of judicial power and support network capacity in authoritarian polities, the framework of laws regulating and constraining the activities of judicial support networks is likely to be one of the most important flashpoints of clashes between courts and regimes.

---

[14] The advantages enjoyed by "repeat players" in the legal system were first examined by Marc Galanter in his classic 1974 article, "Why the 'Haves' Come out Ahead."

The story of courts in authoritarian regimes is likely to involve a dialectic of empowerment – as regimes seek the benefits only judicial autonomy can provide – and constraint, as regimes seek to minimize the associated costs of judicial autonomy. The latter reaction is more likely as courts build up their power, and as activist networks expand their links within and outside of society so as to become a plausible alternative to the regime (Moustafa 2007). Yet, in certain rare cases, the wheels of justice may simply have too much momentum to stop.

CONCLUSION

Judicial politics in authoritarian states is often far more complex than we commonly assume. The cases reviewed in this volume reveal that authoritarian rulers often make use of judicial institutions to counteract the many dysfunctions that plague their regimes. Courts help regimes maintain social control, attract capital, maintain bureaucratic discipline, adopt unpopular policies, and enhance regime legitimacy. However, courts also have the potential to open a space for activists to mobilize against the state, and synergistic alliances sometimes form with judges who also wish to expand their mandate and affect political reform. Authoritarian rulers work to contain judicial activism through providing incentives that favor judicial self-restraint, designing fragmented judicial systems, constraining access to justice, and incapacitating judicial support networks. However, those efforts may not be completely effective. Instead, a lively arena of contention emerges in what we typically imagine to be the least likely environment for the judicialization of politics – the authoritarian state.

We conclude with an expression of modesty. We recognize that our findings in this volume are only a first step, and there is far more work to do to expand the geographic and institutional scope of inquiry into authoritarian regimes. The contributors to this project hope, however, to have collectively identified avenues of inquiry and particular dynamics that will inform future work in this area. Unfortunately, it appears that work on authoritarian regimes will be needed for many years to come.

The chapters in this volume came out of a meeting held at the University of Pennsylvania Law School, August 30–31, 2006. Our sincere thanks to Dean Michael Fitts and Professor Jacques DeLisle of Penn Law for facilitating our meeting there, as well as Anna Gavin for providing excellent logistical support. We thank Matt Ludwig and Seyedeh Rouhi for research assistance. We also gratefully acknowledge the support of the Raymond Geraldson Fund and the Program in Asian Law, Politics and Society at the University of Illinois College of Law, the University of Wisconsin, and Simon Fraser University for support of the conference and production of the book. Finally, special thanks to Robert Barros, Terence Halliday, Anthony Pereira, and Peter Solomon for very helpful comments on this introduction.

1

Of Judges and Generals: Security Courts under Authoritarian Regimes in Argentina, Brazil, and Chile

Anthony W. Pereira

INTRODUCTION

As Ginsburg and Moustafa point out in the Introduction to this volume, few academic studies have taken the law and legal institutions under authoritarian regimes seriously. Most studies of authoritarianism assume that regimes that come to power by force cannot rely on the law to maintain control of society or to legitimate themselves; their unconstitutional origins are seen as making such an effort contradictory and impossible. When analysts do consider the law, they often assume that authoritarian rulers wield it in a direct, unmediated way, relying on their agents to impose their will through consistently compliant courts. Yet even a cursory glance at actual authoritarian regimes, past and present, should lead us to question these assumptions. In fact, authoritarian regimes use the law and courts to bolster their rule all the time, in ways that a simplistic distinction between *de facto* and constitutional (or *de jure*) regimes obscures. Furthermore, this use of the law can be complicated and ambiguous, furnishing regime opponents and activist judges with venues in which to challenge the prerogatives of the regime and to liberalize authoritarian rule.

It might be thought that a security court would be the last place where such contestation might take place. However, such an assumption would also be incorrect. This chapter examines the use of security courts to prosecute political dissidents in three South American military dictatorships – those of Brazil (1964–1985), Chile (1973–1990), and Argentina (1976–1983). It first

This chapter includes material from *Political (In)justice: Authoritarianism and the Rule of Law in Brazil, Chile, and Argentina* by Anthony W. Pereira, © 2005. Reprinted by permission of the University of Pittsburgh Press. I would like to thank Robert Barros, Jacques de Lisle, Tom Ginsburg, Elizabeth Hilbink, Tamir Moustafa, Gordon Silverstein, Peter Solomon, and Martin Shapiro for comments on an earlier draft of this paper. Responsibility for the remaining errors of commission and omission are mine alone.

shows the wide variation in the use of security courts for purposes of political repression under these regimes. In the next section, it argues that this variation can be accounted for by examining the different histories of military-judicial collaboration before and during the establishment of the regimes. Section three examines the way that defense lawyers in the Brazilian security courts were able to push the boundaries of regime legality in a liberal direction. Section four considers whether the framework developed to explain variation in the security courts of Brazil, Chile, and Argentina can help us to understand other authoritarian regimes. In section five, the case of the United States after 9/11 is used to ask whether contemporary democracies might be converging on authoritarian regimes with regard to certain institutional mechanisms. Finally, the conclusion recapitulates the overall argument.

SECURITY COURTS IN BRAZIL AND THE SOUTHERN CONE

The military regimes of Brazil, Chile, and Argentina used security courts in three very different ways. The regimes were attempting to address three of the five problems of authoritarian regimes identified by Tamir Moustafa – elite cohesion, the tendency toward regime fragmentation, and legitimacy (Moustafa 2007). By channeling politically sensitive cases into security courts, the military regimes could engage in political theater that created a dangerous, subversive "other," thus unifying the regime and its supporters. Such a solution also allowed some degree of independence for the rest of the court system. The security courts, however, did not address the first problem identified by Tamir Moustafa, that of property rights. Furthermore, the security courts were of limited use as a means of control over lower level officials, in the way that administrative courts functioned, as described by Tom Ginsburg in Chapter 2. While the transcripts of the security court trials could have been used by higher regime officials as a source of information on the behavior of lower level officials, they tended not to be so used. Instead, regime officials were mainly interested in using the trials to demonstrate the perfidy and antinationalism of those being prosecuted, and what the trials supposedly revealed about their own commitment to the rule of law. Paradoxically, information from the security court trials was most useful to oppositional groups. Important human rights reports published after the end of military rule in both Brazil and Chile drew heavily from the records of the security court trials (see Table A.1 in the appendix).

Of the three cases described in this chapter, the security courts in Brazil had the slowest and most public proceedings, and gave the widest latitude to defendants and their supporters in civil society to maneuver within the system. These courts were peacetime military courts that had existed before the creation of the military regime. The regime never suspended the prior constitution *in toto*, but instead selectively overrode it by issuing institutional acts that were exempt from judicial review. Torture was widespread, but disappearances were relatively rare, and trials in military courts involved civilian participation on the bench and at the bar. A civilian judge trained in the law passed judgment along with four military officers who were rotated in and out of the courts for three-month stints, and defense lawyers were usually civilian lawyers. Prosecutors were civilian lawyers who worked for the military. The deck was stacked against defendants, but some room for the defense of the accused was possible. Courts issued death sentences in only four instances, and these were never carried out because they were reversed on appeal. During the period of military rule in Brazil it was always possible to appeal convictions in the military courts to the civilian Supreme Court. Cases took years to wend their way through the system. In a sample of cases from the lowest level of the security court system under military rule, the acquittal rate was about 50 percent, with a slightly higher acquittal rate at the two levels of appeal courts (the Superior Military Tribunal and the Supreme Court).[1]

The Chilean military regime, created nine years after its Brazilian counterpart, was draconian in comparison. The Chilean military suspended the constitution, declared a state of siege, and executed hundreds of people without trial. Torture was common, and most prosecutions that did take place occurred in "wartime" military courts, insulated from the civilian judiciary, for the first five years of the regime. These military courts were more autonomous from the regular judiciary, and more punitive, than their Brazilian counterparts. They were made up of seven military officers, none of whom were required to be trained in the law. The defendants faced rapid verdicts and sentences that were usually issued within a few days. Sentences included the death penalty, and defendants enjoyed few procedural rights and no effective right of appeal. The Chilean Supreme Court refused to review any military court verdicts.[2] In

---

[1] The sample comes from the *Brasil: Nunca Mais* collection in the Leuenroth archive at the State University of Campinas, Sao Paulo, Brazil. From a total of 707 cases involving 7,367 defendants, I compiled quantitative information on 257 cases (36 percent of the total) with 2,109 defendants (29 percent of the total). While the acquittal rate of 50 percent squares with other accounts of the trials, it should be emphasized that this is not a random sample and therefore may not exactly reflect outcomes in the entire universe of cases. For more on the Brazilian security court trials, see Pereira (2005: 63–89, 201–203).

[2] For the Chilean case, I concentrate only on the period of "wartime" military courts from 1973–1978, due both to a lack of data from the period after that and to clarify the comparisons of types of authoritarian legality made in this chapter (Catholic Church 1989). The great bulk of the material is on trials in the 1973–1978 period. However, these are lawyers' summaries of cases and are not comparable in richness and detail to the cases I examined in the *Brasil: Nunca Mais* archive.

a sample of cases, the acquittal rate in Chile's wartime military courts averaged about 12 percent, well below the Brazilian average.[3]

Both the Brazilian and Chilean military regimes were able to attract international investment and achieve considerable economic success despite their use of security courts and gross violations of human rights. While the claims of either regime to have even a thin rule of law were weak, these regimes, like the People's Action Party regime in Singapore described by Gordon Silverstein in Chapter 3, were able to reassure investors that they would play by the rules of the international capitalist system, despite lacking a genuine separation of powers, constitutional review, or other trappings of a liberal democratic rule of law. The Brazilian "miracle" of double-digit annual economic growth rates occurred exactly in the period of the greatest political repression, 1969–1973. In Chile, the 1973–1978 period saw the military regime engage in both sharp political repression and wholesale economic restructuring along neo-liberal lines; this restructuring paved the way for high economic growth in the late 1980s and 1990s.

The repressive strategy of the last military regime in Argentina, instituted three years after the Chilean coup, was the most drastic of all. In it, courts were largely uninvolved in the repressive system, except to deny writs of habeas corpus[4] and serve as a cover for state terror. Some 350 people were convicted in military courts during the 1976–1983 period, but almost all of these defendants had been arrested prior to the 1976 coup (Nino 1996: 80). After the coup, the modus operandi of the security forces was largely extrajudicial. Police and military personnel picked up people, took them to secret detention centers, interrogated and tortured them, and then "disappeared" them without explanation or record. In such a system, the ability of victims to maneuver within the system was very small, and family members were not even given the consolation of the right to grieve over the body of the victim. Lawyers for political detainees were also targets for repression. About 90 defense lawyers were disappeared between March and December of 1976, something that did not happen in Brazil or Chile (Argentine National Commission on the

---

[3] The Chilean sample is of 406 cases with 2,689 defendants from 31 military courts throughout the country during military rule. This represents about 45 percent of the roughly 6,000 defendants believed to have been tried in military courts in the 1973–1978 period. As with the Brazilian data, this is not a random sample.

[4] Writs of habeas corpus are legal orders from courts to prison officials ordering that prisoners be brought to the courts so that judges can decide whether prisoners have been lawfully imprisoned and whether or not they must be released. The Latin term means "you have the body" (Black, Nolan, and Connolly 1979: 638). The inoperability of writs of habeas corpus was one of the features of the military regimes in Brazil and the Southern Cone that made them so repressive.

Disappeared 1986: 413). In institutional terms, the Argentine regime was the most innovative and the most daring of all three military dictatorships. It was the only one of the three that accomplished the rare political feat of creating something truly new.[5]

Although all of the regimes that created these institutional complexes were broadly similar, their use (and nonuse) of security courts was markedly different. The regimes varied in the degree to which their authoritarian legality broke with pre-authoritarian legal forms, as well as the extent to which the treatment of political prisoners was regulated by law, or judicialized. As Table 1 in the appendix shows, the ratio of those prosecuted in courts to those killed by the state varied across regimes. In Brazil the ratio was 23 to 1, or 23 political prisoners prosecuted for every one extrajudicially killed or disappeared. In Chile the ratio was 1.5 to 1, exhibiting a rough parity between judicialized and extrajudicial repression. In Argentina, only one person was put on trial for every 71 people who were disappeared.

It is important to point out that the judicialization of repression in Brazil and Chile took place in the context of very limited independence for courts.[6] In Brazil, the military regime did not engage in widespread judicial purges, but abolished judges' traditional rights to tenure and irremovability, putting all judges and prosecutors on notice that they could be punished if they made decisions against the regime's interests. Furthermore, in 1965 the Brazilian military regime packed the Supreme Court, increasing its membership from eleven to sixteen judges, and then reduced the number to eleven judges again in 1969. In the latter reform some Supreme Court justices were also forcibly retired. These maneuvers were sparked by important decisions by the Supreme Court that went against the military regime (see Osiel 1995). In Chile, the regime's pressure on the judiciary was more indirect. Judges formally retained security of tenure, but as Elizabeth Hilbink explains in Chapter 4, the Supreme Court's ability to punish lower-ranking judges kept the judiciary in check (Hilbink 1999). In 1997 a Supreme Court justice admitted that if the court had

---

[5] These distinctions between the modes of political repression under the three regimes are not absolute. Disappearances, summary executions, and trials took place under all three regimes. The regimes also frequently ignored their own laws. Nevertheless, the proportion of one form of repression to the others varied considerably across regimes, and I have used the available data as the basis for my classification.

[6] It is important to point out that by judicialization of repression I mean the subjection of political prisoners to some kind of court proceedings. This is therefore a narrower concept than Tamir Moustafa's definition of the judicialization of politics: "the process by which courts and judges come to make or increasingly dominate the making of public policies that had been previously made (or, it is widely believed, ought to be made) by other governmental agencies, especially legislatures and executives" (Moustafa 2007: 26–27).

challenged the Pinochet government's prerogatives, it could have been closed down, as was the Congress from 1973 to 1980.

PATTERNS OF MILITARY-JUDICIAL COLLABORATION

The military regimes of Brazil, Chile, and Argentina are good candidates for comparison. They were all founded in opposition to left-populist movements that had much in common, and they are strongly connected by historical epoch, geographic proximity, common external influences, and roughly equivalent internal dynamics. The three cases are also comparable in terms of level of economic development, position in the global economic system, and cultural traditions of authoritarian rule. They thus allow for a structured, focused comparison that controls for several factors and allows for the exploration of particular explanations for their differing uses of security courts (George 1979: 43–67, 61–63; Laitin 2002: 630–659).

It might be thought that the regimes' various strategies vis-à-vis security courts can be accounted for simply by the strength of the opposition faced by each. The Brazilian coup was preemptive, and the opposition to the military regime very weak; the Chilean coup was a "rollback" coup (Drake 1996: 32–33),[7] but armed opposition to the military regime was relatively insignificant; and the Argentine regime faced what was probably the strongest armed left in Latin America at that time.[8] However, the scope and intensity of regime repression should not be confused with its form. The strength of the opposition does not account for the distinctive institutional matrix of each regime, and the different organizational arrangements for dealing with "subversion" in each case.[9] Why did the Argentine military regime not prosecute more suspected guerrillas in security courts? Why were so few members of the Brazilian armed left "disappeared"? Why were Chile's security court trials so insulated from the civilian judiciary? These questions are important, because the institutional form of authoritarian repression can influence its breadth and intensity and, in particular, how open it is to resistance, challenge, and modification by victims

---

[7] A preemptive coup is one that occurs before extensive mass mobilization by the incumbent government and is intended to forestall feared or incipient mobilization. A rollback coup is less conservative in that it seeks to reverse the reforms of the deposed regime and to crush high levels of prior mass mobilization.

[8] Some authors contest this, arguing that the armed left had been largely annihilated by the time of the 1976 coup in Argentina. See Andersen (1993).

[9] Another example of the point being made here is that the Tupamaros in Uruguay were one of the strongest armed movements in Latin America in the 1970s, but the Uruguayan military regime did not resort, as did its Argentine counterpart, to a large-scale dirty war.

and their supporters. Furthermore, the institutional form of repression may influence post-transition attempts to engage in transitional justice in important ways.

This chapter argues that a key factor in understanding the different uses of security courts in Brazil and the Southern Cone is the timing and sequence of institutional changes in the realm of political repression. Specifically, differing degrees of integration and consensus between judicial and military elites prior to those regimes, as well as the interaction between the legal system and defense lawyers and civil society groups, produced the different outcomes described above.

Judicial and military elites constitute corporate status groups, each with its own powerful organization within the state apparatus, and these status groups strongly influence the development and application of law under authoritarian regimes.[10] Consensus is defined here as substantial elite agreement about the overall design, goals, and tactics of policy (Melanson 1991: 1–12). Key factors in the formation of consensus between the groups are the organizational contours of the military justice system, the dominant military factions' and their supporters' perceptions of threat, the history of relations between military officers and the judiciary, and the degree of conflict between these groups over interpretations of national security law. My contention is that this kind of integration and consensus was highest in Brazil and lowest in Argentina, with Chile occupying a middle position.[11] The argument is historical because conditions before the formation of each authoritarian regime were important in shaping subsequent decisions by regime leaders. While the selection of policy options that shaped the legal system under military rule all took place after military coups, these prior conditions shaped attitudes among and relations between judicial and civilian elites. The subsequent policy decisions that occurred after regime change were decisive because they formed systems that endured for a relatively long period of time. It is striking that, once established, the basic legal orientation of the regimes examined here did not fundamentally change during the course of military rule.

It might be objected that it is difficult to measure judicial-military integration and consensus independently of the variable they are supposed to explain – the legal strategy adopted by the military regime. It is difficult, but

---

[10] A status group is a collection of people who share an effective claim to social esteem – and perhaps also status monopolies – based on lifestyle, formal education or training, or traditions. See Weber (1978).

[11] While I agree with Gerardo Munck that overall, the elite consensus was probably higher in Chile's military regime than it was in Brazil's, I argue that, in the specific area of authoritarian legality and judicial-military cooperation, Brazilian consensus was higher. See Munck (1998).

not impossible. I have used two indicators to gauge the degree of consensus and integration between military officers and judicial elites. First, the organizational architecture of the security court system is a key variable. The degree of formal connection between military and judicial elites in the application of national security law matters. Where security courts are part of the civilian justice system, with the participation of civilian judges and prosecutors, as in Brazil, military and judicial elites are compelled, through their common participation in the same hybrid system, to construct and maintain a cross-organizational understanding of the concrete meaning and applicability of national security law. Where security courts at the first level are completely separate from civilian justice, as in Chile, the military can more easily act upon its own view of "political justice," without regard for the ideas of civilian judges and lawyers. This variable can be discerned in the formal architecture of the security court system, but its significance goes beyond the architecture itself and affects the attitudes, dispositions, and mutual understandings of military and judicial elites.

Consensus is harder to measure. Consensus refers to the extent of agreement across status groups about key national security ideas and how to apply them. The opinions of both civilian legal experts and military officers on national security legality can reflect consensus or dissensus. These views can be found in newspapers, memoirs, academic studies, legal decisions, and specialized journals dealing with the military, the law, and military justice. This is a qualitative judgment, but consensus between military officers and civilian judicial elites can be adduced to be high, medium, or low, depending on the harmony between the military and civilian views expressed in these sources. Brazilian sources reflect a high degree of consensus, Chilean sources indicate medium consensus, and materials from Argentine exhibit signs of low consensus. It is important to point out that this is a relative judgment, and that there was conflict within and between the military and judiciary in all three cases. In many instances in Brazil, for example, the military regime imposed changes on an intimidated judiciary. However, my claim is that there was more judicial-military consensus at the heart of the system that tried political prisoners (the lowest level of the security courts) in Brazil than there was in Chile and Argentina.

Consensus between and integration of military and civilian elites on national security issues do not imply "hegemony" or some other term connoting consensus beyond these elite groups. Many divergent views of the security courts prevailed in all three of the countries analyzed here and can be found in the historical record. Defendants in the security courts certainly held their own views, and when they indicated that they accepted the legitimacy of the courts and the national security legality under which they were being prosecuted, this was usually done for tactical reasons and was unlikely to have been completely heartfelt. Evidence also suggests that defense lawyers who exalted the legitimacy of security courts during trials then publicly questioned them and the national security legality they enforced in other venues.

Some scholars might prefer the more inclusive term "legal culture" to my terms consensus and integration. However, legal culture connotes many aspects of the judicial sphere that I do not examine; therefore, I prefer to focus on institutions in the sense used by Douglass North, as the formal and informal rules regulating behavior, including both consciously created rules and those that evolve gradually over time (North 1990: 4). These rules include the internal rules of organizations such as the military and judiciary.

Studying judicial-military consensus and integration prior to and during military rule reveals new insights into the issue of regime legality. In Brazil, the 1930 revolution involved civilian-military cooperation that resulted in the organizational fusion of civilian and military justice in the 1934 Constitution. Civil-military cooperation and integration remained a hallmark of the Brazilian approach to political crime. The repression initiated by the 1964 coup was highly judicialized and gradualist; the regime slowly modified some aspects of traditional legality, but did not unleash widespread extrajudicial violence, even after the hardening of the regime in the late 1960s.

In Chile, in contrast, the military was much less closely associated with a civil-military political project in the interwar years. Instead, it disdained civilian politics, and gained a reputation for a "Prussian" degree of professionalization and autonomy. Military justice in the first instance was strictly separated from civilian courts. When the military occasionally intervened in local areas at times of conflict, it temporarily usurped judicial authority rather than, as in Brazil, working within civil-military institutions established by consensus. This pattern can be seen again after the 1973 coup. The legality of the Pinochet regime was more radical and militarized than Brazil's, even after the adoption of "peacetime" military courts in 1978 and the ratification of the 1980 Constitution.

Argentina represents yet another path – a radical break with previous legality and a largely extrajudicial assault on regime opponents. If the Chilean military tended to usurp judicial authority, its Argentine counterpart periodically rejected and overrode it altogether. Mediating conflict in a highly polarized polity, the Argentine military was prone to use force directly, and then induce a dependent judiciary to ratify its *de facto* power. Here we see the least amount of civil-military cooperation and integration in the judicial realm.

During military rule from 1966 to 1973, regime leaders tried to build authoritarian legality along the lines of their Brazilian and Chilean counterparts. The *Camarón* or National Penal Court was a special court created under military rule in 1971 to prosecute political prisoners. It convicted more than 300 defendants over a two-year period, but it was abolished in 1973 when the Peronists returned to power, and all of the prisoners who had been convicted were given amnesty and released. Military officers saw this failure to judicialize repression as requiring new tactics in the struggle against "subversion," and dirty war practices subsequently escalated. When the military seized power again in 1976, the dirty war became national policy. Prior failure to institutionalize security courts thus helps explain the Argentine case.

Political trials in security courts "worked" for the Brazilian and Chilean military regimes that used them. That is, they stabilized expectations on both sides of the repression-opposition divide, gave the security forces greater flexibility in dealing with opponents, helped marginalize and de-legitimate the opposition, purchased some credibility for the regimes both at home and abroad, and provided regime leaders with information about both the opposition and the security forces, thus facilitating the adaptation and readjustment of repressive policies. It is also plausible that the political trials in both Brazil and Chile helped consolidate and prolong authoritarian rule. It may not be a coincidence that the shortest-lived military regime of the three examined here, the Argentine, was also the one that engaged in the most extrajudicial repression.

My argument therefore makes distinctions among authoritarian regimes based on their approach to the law. I contend that, under authoritarian rule, military/judicial consensus and integration moderate political repression by allowing for its judicialization. Under judicialized repression, defense lawyers and civil society opposition groups can defend democratic principles to some degree, even if this space is highly constricted. Where the military views the judiciary with suspicion or outright hostility, on the other hand, it is likely to usurp judicial functions and engage in purely military court proceedings, as in Chile, or completely ignore the law altogether, and treat defense lawyers and sometimes even judges as subversive "enemies," as in Argentina. The scope for the defense of democratic principles is more limited in the former, and almost impossible in the latter. The danger in military regimes is that the military will bypass or even destroy the judiciary and engage in an all-out war against its perceived opponents; in such an outcome, defense lawyers and civil society groups can only demand justice with any hope of success after the end of the authoritarian regime.

Pushing the Envelope in Brazil's Security Courts

Brazil's relatively conservative authoritarian legality led to a series of political trials that preserved more elements of traditional legal procedures and doctrine than did the repressive tactics of the later Chilean and Argentine military regimes. Of these three cases, it was only in Brazilian security court trials that defense lawyers were able to gradually roll back some of the most draconian interpretations of national security law. Brazilian defense lawyers successfully won the recognition of certain individual rights from the military court judges, including the right to express certain political beliefs, to criticize government officials, to possess (if not distribute) "subversive" materials, and to disseminate such material to small, elite audiences. Brazil's defense lawyers shifted the boundaries of national security legality in the courts.

Brazilian national security law, like national security law in Chile and Argentina, was notoriously broad and vague. In political trials judges were forced to interpret the concrete meaning of such terms as "subversion," "offense against authority," "subversive propaganda," "psychosocial subversion," and the like. Military court judges had to decide which thoughts and actions were actually proscribed by national security laws and which were not. These decisions involved complex political, ideological, and legal judgments. In making them, judges transformed formal or paper laws into an evolving system of norms. This system of norms redrew boundaries between licit and illicit behavior and ideas, creating a new, more repressive legal system, but one that was not as severe or as discontinuous with the past as those of the other authoritarian regimes in the region. For example, Brazilian security courts were more likely than their Chilean counterparts to acquit certain categories of defendants, especially priests and defendants accused of recently created national security crimes. Perhaps most importantly, the boundaries shifted, toward greater leniency, in part because the perceived threats to the regime diminished in the 1970s, but also because the arguments of defense lawyers and critics of national security legality hit home.

A civilian-military consensus about the trials and the judgments made in them posed formidable obstacles to defense lawyers in Brazil's military courts. The defense faced judges who generally believed that the country was in a dire political emergency that required an extraordinary judicial response. The judges were not constrained by the need to be consistent, and they deliberately considered the political ideas of the accused as relevant to their rulings. Furthermore, the existence of an armed left made them relatively intolerant of criticisms of the regime, because they saw such criticisms – even if unaccompanied by any actions – as potential psychosocial subversion that was antinational.

On the other hand, legally recognized detainees were spared extrajudicial execution, and the workings of the military courts, while procedurally stacked against the defense, were closer to ordinary criminal justice than were most systems of military justice, including that of Chile. Furthermore, repudiations of oppositional political views and expressions of remorse were taken seriously by the judges and tended to result in leniency. Defense lawyers were able to take these slight opportunities and use them to their advantage.

Most defendants accused of political crimes in Brazil's security courts did not make impassioned defenses of their political views – describing their revolutionary beliefs and denouncing the military regime – before the judges. These kinds of defenses were punished harshly, usually with the maximum sentence, because the judges viewed them as proof of the dangerousness and incorrigibility of the defendant, even if he or she had not participated in violent actions.

Defense lawyers usually persuaded their clients to avoid political defenses and make one of two other kinds of defenses. The judicial defense involved the defendant abjuring any belief in so-called subversive ideas and denying that he or she had committed any violation of the national security laws. The mixed defense was a combination of a purely juridical defense and a political one. The defendant might defend some of his or her ideas and actions, but deny that they were subversive. Or the defendant might appeal more directly to the political sympathies of the judges, claiming that he or she had abandoned political activity, was remorseful, and/or disagreed with revolutionary ideas.

By mounting defenses of these kinds, defense lawyers found ambiguities and loopholes in the national security laws and argued for favorable interpretations in ways that sometimes achieved benefits for their clients. Defense lawyers' legal strategies were shaped by the courts. The political trials were not really the triadic conflicts between a prosecutor, defense attorney, and independent and neutral judge depicted in classic courtroom drama and legal theory (Shapiro 1975: 321–371). Instead, their proceedings were dyadic and inquisitorial, with the defense on one side, and the prosecution and the judges together on the other. Four of the five judges were active-duty military officers, making them members of one side of the military regime's antisubversive campaign. The civilian judges in the military courts were generally known for their pro-regime views. The judges' presumption was therefore usually that the prosecution's case had merit. Furthermore, the judges could actively question witnesses. Judges were thus at the same time active participants in the construction of the case against the defendants, arbiters of the court's proceedings, and signatories of the final verdict and sentence in the case.

This delicate situation presented special challenges to defense lawyers. If they were too aggressive in the defense of their clients, they risked alienating the judges. If they were too passive, they might allow the judges to taint their defendants and create the legal justification for a stiff punishment. The situation therefore called for tact, guile, finesse, and knowledge of the personal and political predilections of the judges, especially the civilian judges. Some lawyers appealed to judges to apply the national security laws according to the dictates of government – this was an appeal to the aspirations of some judges for a new "revolutionary" legality. Others appealed to the conservative image that some judges held of themselves as defenders of the traditional rule of law, urging them to fulfill the liberal function of an independent judiciary (de Matos 2002: 93–95).

Overall, lawyers achieved important victories in several areas of national security law. Defense lawyers stretched the boundaries of permissible activity and speech within national security law and served to lay the foundations for a proto-civil society, one that demanded fuller respect for human rights. Analysis of a sample of court cases reveals that defendants accused of newer crimes created by the most recent national security legislation and crimes such as offenses against authority that did not necessarily involve "subversive" intent were convicted at lower rates than defendants accused of crimes involving violence, such as armed robbery. Furthermore, certain categories of defendants – such as clerics – were treated more leniently than others, such as journalists, reflecting the courts' deference to traditional institutions such as the Catholic Church.[12]

Furthermore, defense lawyers were able to move the boundaries of legal interpretation over time, rolling back some of the most repressive interpretations of national security law. For example, in 1979 the Superior Military Tribunal, the appeal court within the military justice system, acquitted a defendant because of evidence that he had been tortured into confessing while in detention, a concession to human rights norms that had been routinely violated by judges in the early years of military rule.[13]

Defense lawyers not only changed the application of national security law but they also served as interlocutors between regime authorities and the opponents of the regime, serving as a kind of "loyal opposition" when that role was extremely limited for elected representatives in the national Congress. The lawyers also played a part in the opposition's reevaluation of armed struggle

---

[12] In a sample of 220 of the roughly 700 cases at the first level of Brazil's military courts in the 1964–1979 period, defendants accused of offenses against authority were acquitted at a rate of 80 percent, compared to 25 percent for robbery. In a sample of 193 cases from the same period, clerics were acquitted at a rate of 93 percent, compared to 40 percent for journalists. See Pereira (2005: 83–85).

[13] See the written judgment in STM case number 41,264 in the *Brasil: Nunca Mais* archive. Information about this case comes also from the author's interview with former STM judge Júlio Sá Bierrenbach, Rio de Janeiro, November 17, 1996.

and its evolution into a group of legal political parties based in grassroots social movements.

Tamir Moustafa writes that the judicialization of politics in authoritarian regimes can create a synergy between activists and judges, pushing the boundaries of regime legality (Moustafa 2007). The synergy in Brazil was primarily between a few dozen defense lawyers for political prisoners, on one hand, and defendants and social movement activists, on the other. Social movements such as the campaign for political amnesty and various domestic organizations such as the peace and justice commission and the Brazilian Bar Association, as well as international NGOs such as Amnesty International, were engaged in these synergistic relationships. All of the actors in these networks shared a critical view of authoritarian legality and a commitment to a more liberal, democratic approach to the law.

The military court judges were part of this synergy in a much more indirect way. While they ruled in favor of defendants in individual cases, and may even have expressed views that civilians should not be tried in military courts, or that the national security laws should be liberalized, they were generally staunchly pro-regime compared to the rest of the judiciary. They would probably have denied that their rulings were antiregime in any sense. After the end of military rule, several publications written by military court judges and prosecutors extolled the performance of the security courts under authoritarian rule, indicating that these officials did not see themselves as reformers, but rather as faithful servants of the military regime (da Costa Filho 1994; Fernandes 1983: 7–50; Ferreira 1984/85: 23–88).

Neither in Chile from 1973 to 1978 (under wartime military justice) nor in Argentina from 1976 to 1983 did the type of jurisprudence in Brazil's security courts exist. In these latter two countries, defense lawyers were "communities of memory," recording and protesting vainly against the machinations of an authoritarian legal order based on violence and intimidation (Lobel 2004). In Brazil, defense lawyers were also this but something more. They were active shapers of national security legality.

Nevertheless, the very characteristics of the military justice system that made it flexible and amenable to changes in interpretation – thus offering some relief to political prisoners – were also beneficial to the regime. They allowed the regime to collect information about opinion in society, facilitated cooperation within and between the legal and military establishments, and allowed the regime to modify its rule incrementally. (A controlled Congress fulfilled much the same function.) While flexible and malleable on the margins, the institutions of the Brazilian legal order were "sticky" with respect to their essential features. The hybrid civil-military nature of the system and its broad sharing of responsibilities across an array of officials, including civilian prosecutors and judges as well as military officers, gave many figures in the state apparatus a vested interest in the continuation of the near status quo. The defense lawyers' actions produced concrete results in sparing political prisoners from treatment that could have been worse. They created a record that enabled the lawyers and their supporters to accurately and thoroughly condemn the legality of the authoritarian regime. But they created little foundation for the overhaul of the legal system under democracy. The Brazilian self-amnesty of 1979 closed the book on the political trials and the authoritarian manipulation of the law far more conclusively than a similar Chilean amnesty of 1978 or the attempted self-amnesty in Argentina in 1983.

Otto Kirchheimer wrote, "Justice in political matters is the most ephemeral of all divisions of justice; a turn of history may undo its work" (1961: 429). The jurisdiction of security courts can be quickly reduced when political circumstances change, but the legacies of their authoritarian legality can endure. Each form of authoritarian legality leaves a distinctive legacy with which democratic reformers must grapple. In Argentina, the law was skirted, violated, and broken under military rule, and the rule of law had to be reconstituted. In Brazil, the law was manipulated, bent, and abused, and had to be reformed. The first challenge was probably met better than the second, in part because in Argentina there was broad consensus that reform was necessary. Brazil experienced the least transitional justice after democratic transition of all three cases, in part because the gradualist and conservative authoritarian legality of its military regime involved the participation of much of the legal establishment and continued to be legitimized under democracy. Thus Brazil did not witness the kind of reformist backlash that occurred in Argentina and Chile, in which coalitions with significant political support were able to overturn key aspects of authoritarian legality. In particular, Brazil did not replicate the sustained and serious judicial reform that took place in Chile. This chapter therefore suggests a paradox. Conservative legal systems such as the Brazilian system may prevent some excesses on the part of the security forces, but they are far more intractable once authoritarian rule ends.

EXTENDING THE ANALYTICAL FRAMEWORK

Analyzing the nexus between military and judicial elites can help explain the judicialization of repression and its absence elsewhere. In particular, the pattern we see in Brazil and the Southern Cone appears to hold in other cases: a radical approach to the law and the deployment of extrajudicial violence are more likely in regimes without much judicial-military cooperation, integration, and consensus. On the other hand, more conservative, incremental approaches to the law and judicialized repression are more common in regimes with a high degree of such cooperation, integration, and consensus.

It is easy to see why this pattern might apply to military regimes.[14] When militaries control the executive and seek to judicialize their repression, they are likely to rely on some elements of the traditional judiciary to do so. This is important, because the most ubiquitous type of authoritarian regime in the twentieth century was the military dictatorship (Brooker 2000: 4). Even today, when military regimes are less common than in the past, the threat of military coup remains a political factor in many countries.[15]

However, Booker argues that the real innovation in twentieth-century dictatorship was the dictatorship of a political party (Brooker 2000). Especially in the interwar years, new authoritarian regimes with powerful new ideologies emerged in Europe. The framework developed here can help explain the authoritarian legality of some of these regimes. A focus on military and judicial elites sheds light on the legal dimension of regime repression in three well-known dictatorships: the Nazi regime in Germany (1933–1945), the Franco dictatorship in Spain (1939–1975), and the Salazarist regime in Portugal (1926–1974). Each of these regimes closely resembles one of our three cases in its approach to legality: the Nazis with the Argentine *proceso*, Franco's Spain with Pinochet's Chile, and Salazar's Portugal with the Brazilian regime.[16]

A comparison of this type has many potential pitfalls, not least because of the widely differing life-spans of these dictatorships, ranging from seven years in Argentina to forty-eight years in the Portuguese case. The longer running regimes, especially, were subject to complicated transformations. Furthermore, each of the European regimes – which were part of an interwar authoritarian wave that predated the Brazilian and Southern Cone cases by

---

[14] I define military regimes here broadly as regimes in which the executive is controlled by a military junta or cabinet, as well as regimes with military presidents who to some degree control or represent the armed forces. Regimes with civilian presidents in which real power and control lie with the armed forces should also be included in this category, although such regimes can be difficult to evaluate. (An example is the Uruguayan regime headed by civilian President Bordaberry from 1972–1976.) See the discussion in Brooker (2000: 44–52).

[15] Strikingly, there are few military regimes in the contemporary world; one source lists only four (Burma, Libya, Syria, and Sudan) with Pakistan classified as a military-led "transitional government." From Central Intelligence Agency (2004) *World Fact Book*, accessed in August 2004 at http://www.cia.gov/cia/publications. More recently, Bangladesh and Fiji could be added to this list.

[16] For purposes of this discussion, I do not place Nazi Germany in a distinctive category of totalitarian regimes. For some types of analysis in comparative politics, the totalitarian label is no longer seen as useful; see Brooker (2000: 8–21).

forty years – clearly had important idiosyncrasies.[17] For example, Nazi repression had a strong ethnic and racial dimension lacking in most of the other cases, and the Nazi regime was engaged in a total war for half of its existence. The Franco regime emerged from a full-blown and heavily internationalized civil war absent in the other cases. Similarly, Salazar's Portugal was smaller and more rural than any other regime analyzed here, and the only one that managed a long-standing and extensive colonial empire. Such differences undoubtedly affect patterns of regime repression. Nevertheless, a focus on judicial-military relations can shed light on variation in the use of security courts by these regimes.

Nazi Germany

The Nazi regime in Germany was radical in its approach to the law and, especially in the last few years of its rule, resorted heavily to the extrajudicial extermination of large numbers of people. As in Argentina, the Nazi case seems to have been marked by a low level of integration and consensus between military and judicial elites, and purges of both corporate groups. The German case goes well beyond the Argentine in that the Nazi party hierarchy led by Adolph Hitler eventually made an end-run not only around the judiciary (as in Argentina) but largely the military as well. The extermination policy that came to be known as the "Final Solution" was carried out largely by the SS, a special political-military body, rather than the army or another conventional branch of the armed forces.

Less well known than the Final Solution is the Nazis' use of courts. A large number of political trials took place in the People's Court (*Volksgerichtshof*, or VGH) in Nazi Germany between 1934 and 1945. The People's Court was a security court created by the Nazis to try cases of treason and terrorism. However, the Nazis created a large area of extrajudicial repression alongside and completely beyond the purview of the People's Court. It was not uncommon, after 1936, for the Gestapo to rearrest people acquitted in the People's Court and send them to concentration camps (Köch 1989: 3–6). And after November of 1942, Jews were not subject to the People's Court or any other kind of legal procedure. At that time the Ministry of Justice confidentially instructed state officials that "courts will forego the carrying out of regular criminal

---

[17] I am not the first to make a connection between the authoritarian regimes founded in interwar Europe and the Brazilian and Southern Cone military regimes. The "bureaucratic-authoritarian" label that O'Donnell applied to the latter was borrowed from Janos's analysis of Eastern European regimes in the 1920s and 1930s. See Janos (1970).

procedures against Jews, who henceforth shall be turned over to the police"
(Miller 1995: 52).

The grotesque perversion of justice represented by the People's Court was
created by what Miller calls the Nazi regime's "legal atheism" and its specific
measures to distort and manipulate the law for its own ends. For example,
roughly one-fifth of the legal profession was purged under Hitler; Jewish,
socialist, and democratic members were removed (Müller 1991: 296). Furthermore, the 1933 Law for the Restoration of the Professional Civil Service
allowed the executive branch to dismiss judges for any reason – an effective
instrument for keeping those who had not been purged in line, and one also
used by the Southern Cone military regimes. In 1939, Nazi prosecutors were
allowed to appeal acquittals (Miller 1995: 52).[18] The Nazi regime encouraged
jurists to prioritize the political needs of the regime and to attempt to see
the spirit, not the letter, of the law, leading to artful constructions of laws
that completely gutted them of specificity and justified extreme harshness by
the state.[19] And using special courts could reduce the uncertainty of trusting
political cases to the ordinary judiciary. In this way the People's Court gained
almost complete jurisdiction over crimes of terrorism and treason, while over
time treason itself was defined in ever-expanding ways. The court's judges
were handpicked for their devotion to National Socialism and their expertise
in espionage and national security.

However, the political trials in the People's Court were also shaped by the
politics of the pre-Nazi Weimar regime and the Second Reich (1871–1918).
The legal bases of VGH judgments were two long-standing definitions of
treason. Köch writes "neither the legal basis for, nor the legal procedure of, the
VGH differed significantly from treason trials of the past" (Köch 1989: 3). The
prohibition of the right of appeal in treason trials was promulgated in 1922,
eleven years before the Nazis took power. The artful interpretations of the
spirit rather than the letter of the law favored by the Nazi regime reflected
an authoritarian and predemocratic legal ideology prevalent among German
jurists since at least the late nineteenth century (Müller 1991: 296). Criminal
trials under the Second Reich had been inquisitorial and heavily biased in favor
of the state. For example, the prosecutor addressed the court while located on

---

[18] The Brazilian military regime also used this tactic in cases involving national security.

[19] Scholars of Nazi legality seem to agree that rigid adherence to legal positivism was not a
characteristic of Nazi justice and not responsible for the horrors of the regime. Köch (1989),
Miller (1995), and Müller (1991) all agree that the problem was the opposite – that judges
engaged in politically motivated searches for the "fundamental idea" of the laws and often
disregarded statutory language.

the same level as the judge, whereas the defense attorney sat at a lower level with the accused. The bench and bar posed no opposition to Hitler when he assumed power in 1933 (Miller 1995: 44).[20]

For Köch, the roots of the People's Court "lay in the Weimar Republic, when the judiciary had become politicized" (1989: x). Many in the judiciary shared the widespread belief that Germany had lost World War I due to treason and revolution (it had been "stabbed in the back"). In 1924 Hitler in *Mein Kampf* had advocated the creation of a special court to try tens of thousands of people responsible for this treachery (Müller 1991: 140). However, even in a regime as ruthless and as ambitious as the Third Reich, political justice was shaped by conditions inherited from previous political regimes. Nazi legality was a distorted and intensified version of existing tendencies within the law, rather than an entirely new creation. For that reason, it proved to be highly resistant to feeble attempts at "de-Nazification" after World War II. While under Allied occupation the political trials described above came to an end, Müller shows how the mentalities and decisions of many judges did not change. Even in 1985, the German Parliament could not bring itself to take the symbolic action of declaring convictions in the People's Court and Special Courts under Nazi rule null and void (Müller 1991: 284–292).

Of our Latin American cases, Argentina comes closest to the Nazi experience. As in Argentina, the lack of a consensus within and between judicial and military elites contributed to the extrajudicial horrors of the Nazi regime. As Gordon Craig shows in his study of the Prussian Army, Hitler was able to purge and Nazify the Army and to effectively subject military officers to his control (1955: 468–503). But even this subjugated army was not completely reliable as an instrument of repression from the Nazis' point of view, and neither was the judiciary.

When it came time to implement the Final Solution, the Third Reich did not entrust the main tasks either to the courts or to the army. Even a court that executed half the defendants that came before it, such as the People's Court, was too restrained for the Nazi leadership's plan, and even an army that had already proved its willingness to massacre civilians was deemed unprepared for the systematic mass slaughter that was to be perpetrated. Instead, the responsibility was entrusted to the Economic and Administrative Main Office (*Wirtschafts und Verwaltungshauptant*, WVHA) of a special political-military body, the SS. The SS was controlled by the Armed Forces High Command or

---

[20] Miller reports the acquittal rate in Germany's criminal trials in 1932 as 15%, similar to that in the People's Court.

OKW (*Oberkommando der Wehrmacht*), directly under Hitler. The concentration and labor camps of the SS in Germany and the occupied territories, managed by the WVHA from 1942 to 1945, imprisoned roughly ten million people, killing millions of them.[21] As bad as the People's Court was, the number of victims of its lethal "justice" – 13,000 – was small compared to the camps run by the SS.[22] Nazi political repression was thus largely extrajudicial and radical with respect to preexisting legality.

It was thus not trust and consensus between judicial and military elites that led to the Nazis' particularly perverse form of dual state, but its absence, and in particular a reluctance on the part of Hitler and his inner circle – including military officers – to entrust the highest political goals of the regime to either judges or fellow generals. For example, Hitler himself assumed command of the army between 1941 and 1945. And only an inner circle of Nazi party officials was allowed to direct and profit from the horror of the death camps.

Franco's Spain

If Argentine repression bears some resemblance to that of Nazi Germany, Chile's repression looks more like that of Franco's Spain (1939–1975). As in Chile, Franco's forces were involved in a "rollback" military action, in this instance trying to undo the extensive mass mobilization of Republican rule. Similarly, the initial repression was quite violent, was led by a highly insulated military that had declared martial law throughout the whole national territory, and was only partially judicialized. However, despite Franco's declaration that his regime was "based on bayonets and blood" (Mathews 2003), the regime judicialized its repression over time, as did the Pinochet regime in Chile.

During the Spanish civil war of 1936–1939, *consejos de guerra* (military courts) tried people for political crimes. These military courts operated during a ferocious conflict marked by the "red terror" of the Republicans and the "white terror" of the Nationalists.[23] Shortly after the July 17, 1936, military rebellion that began the war, on July 28, the forces of General Francisco

---

[21] From the Harvard Law School Library Nuremberg Trials Project (A Digital Document Collection): "Introduction to NMT Case 4, *U.S.A. v Pohl et al*" at http://nuremberg.law.harvard.edu accessed on July 7, 2007.

[22] The People's Court was not the only venue for judicialized repression under the Nazis. From 1933 to 1945, German military courts sentenced about 50,000 people to death, most of them after 1942. See Stölleis (1998: 151–152) and Müller (1991: 194).

[23] This is not to imply that there were an equal number of killings on each side. Payne concludes that more people belonged to leftist organizations than to identifiably right groups, so the Nationalists had more perceived enemies to eliminate, and their executions probably exceeded those on the other side. See Payne (1967: 415).

Franco y Bahamonde declared martial law throughout Spain. All civilian and military crimes were thenceforth regulated by the Military Code. Civilian jurists were supposed to play an auxiliary role in military court trials, but apparently this was done only when conservative jurists were available and military commanders were willing to employ them.

The military court trials took place in a climate of intense reprisals and repression. Executions without any sort of judicial procedure were common. From July 1936 until roughly July 1937, mass killings occurred all over Spain, conducted by the army, the Civil Guard, the Falangists,[24] and right-wing militias. In Payne's words, "the various elements on the Nationalist side were, in effect, free to kill almost whomever they chose, as long as it could be said that the victim had supported the [Republicans'] Popular Front" (1967: 416). Peasants and workers who were found with trade union cards, people suspected of having voted for the Republicans, Freemasons, officeholders in the Republic, or people with "red" or even liberal political views were shot after two-minute hearings by military courts or no hearings at all. The mass executions even bothered the German attaché, a Nazi, who reportedly met with General Franco twice to urge him to stop them, to no avail (Payne 1967: 411–412).

As in Chile, the uncoordinated and largely extrajudicial violence of this early period was later replaced by a more centralized, judicialized type of repression. This shift occurred during the course of 1937. On October 31 of that year, the new chief of internal security, public order, and frontier inspection decreed that executions could not take place without a military court passing a sentence. This decree does not seem to have slowed down the rate of executions, but it did provide a legal cover for the killings. On February 9, 1939, less than two months before the end of the war, the Franco forces promulgated the Law of Political Responsibilities to regulate and civilianize the prosecution of political crimes. This law extended the liability for political crimes back to October 1, 1934 (almost two years before the military rebellion that initiated the Franco regime) and included as a political crime "grave passivity." This measure meant that people who had lived in Republican zones and who had not been members of the government or leftist groups, but who could not demonstrate that they had actively fought against the Republicans were liable for prosecution. Special Courts of Political Responsibilities were established, composed roughly equally of Army officers, civilian judges, and Falangist representatives (Payne 1967: 418).

---

[24] The Falangists were members of a fascist political party, called the Falange Española, founded in 1933 by José António Primo de Rivera, son of a former Spanish dictator.

Spanish political "justice" under Franco was extremely violent; on a per capita basis, it was much more violent than Pinochet's Chile. According to official figures of the Spanish Ministry of Justice, 192,684 people were executed or died in prison in Spain between April 1939 and June 30, 1944. (Gallo gives the figure of those executed as around 100,000. The total population of Spain in 1935 was 24 million [1974: 21].) This number included 6,000 school-teachers and 100 of 430 university professors. The total dead in the civil war is estimated at 560,000, including combatants, victims of bombing raids, those executed, and those who died in prison. Gallo calls Spanish justice in the immediate aftermath of the war "a ruthless machine for dealing death," and lists as some of its features confessions extracted by torture and perfunctory trials. Like the leaders of other authoritarian regimes, the Spanish nationalists were capable of ignoring their own laws when it suited them, as when a defendant was officially reprieved, released by authorities, but then picked up again and shot (Gallo 1974: 67–70).

As in Chile, Spanish political trials began as a settling of scores by the new regime, and then evolved into a mechanism of social control. While less active in later years, Francoist courts still executed opponents up to the last days of the regime in 1975. Once again, institutional pathways proved hard to reverse – political trials continued throughout the course of the regime, although at a much less intense level than they had in the 1930s. In addition, state institutions were not on a synchronous path – inquisitorial political trials of the early 1970s coexisted with the liberalization of other state institutions. As with other cases of authoritarian legality, the political trials were not ended until the demise of the regime, in this case in a transition negotiated by key figures both within and without the regime.

The course of Spanish legal repression involved a changing relationship between military and judicial elites. In the early days of the regime during the civil war, integration of and cooperation between both sets of elites were practically nonexistent. Courts had largely stopped functioning during the war, and the military took it upon itself to mete out punishments, with or without hastily conducted legal proceedings. As in Chile, the military usurped judicial authority; this phase of the repression resembles Chilean "wartime" military justice between 1973 and 1978 (even though there was no real war in Chile at that time). Subsequently, after the civil war's end in 1939, Spanish authoritarian legality incorporated civilian judges into the special courts, making this phase roughly comparable to peacetime military justice in Chile from 1978 to 1990. Again, judicial-military consensus was a key component of the judicialization of repression represented by this transformation.

Salazar's Portugal

Another important example of authoritarian legality is that of the Salazar regime (1926–1974) in Portugal.[25] Unlike Nazi and Francoist repression, Salazarist repression can be characterized as dictatorial, aimed primarily at containing, rather than exterminating, declared opponents of the regime.[26] Unlike General Franco in neighboring Spain, Salazar was a civilian. While Franco obtained power through force in a civil war, Salazar was granted power by military officers several years after a coup in 1926. In contrast to the Nazis and the Franquistas in Spain who enjoyed staging theatrical demonstrations of mass support, the Salazar regime – like the 1964–1985 military regime in Brazil – was content with a depoliticized, passively acquiescent population.[27] And like the Brazilian military regime's repression, Salazarist repression came in two distinct waves, the first at the beginning of the regime in 1926, and the second in the middle of its rule, between the electoral campaigns of 1949 and 1958.

In 1933 the Salazar regime created special military tribunals to judge political crimes. Subversion of the "fundamental principles of society" was one of those offenses (Braga de Cruz: 1988: 87). As in other cases, the roots of these political prosecutions lay in the immediate past, in this case in the conflict between the Communist left and the fascist right in the interwar years. Defendants in political trials could be imprisoned prior to sentencing under the law. The *Polícia de Defesa Política e Social* (Police for Political and Social Defense, or PVDE) was in charge of all phases of the political trials and could determine whether a defendant could remain at liberty during his or her trial or be imprisoned. The PVDE was not overly scrupulous about the law; between 1932 and 1945, 36 percent of the political prisoners that it held in special prisons were incarcerated for more time than their sentences stipulated (Braga de Cruz 1988: 88). This is similar to the way in which the Brazilian military regime frequently violated its own laws that restricted the detention of political prisoners to a fixed period of time.

---

[25] From 1968 to 1974 Portugal was ruled by Salazar's successor Caetano, but I refer to the whole period of authoritarian rule as the Salazar regime.

[26] This distinction comes from Manuel Braga da Cruz (1988: 84).

[27] After the 1926 coup d'etat that ended the Portuguese Republic, Salazar, formerly an economics professor at the University of Coimbra, became Minister of Finance in 1928 and Prime Minister in 1932 (Bermeo 1986: 13–14). In many ways, the Salazar regime is a better approximation of Juan Linz's ideal-type of a nonmobilizing authoritarian regime than is Franco's Spain; see Juan Linz (1975).

In 1945 the special military courts for dealing with political crimes were abolished and replaced with the *Tribunais Criminais Plenários* (Plenary Criminal Courts), special civilian courts located in Lisbon and Porto. Unlike the military courts, these courts were presided over by judges trained in the law. At the same time, the PVDE was reorganized and renamed the PIDE (*Polícia Internacional de Defesa do Estado*, or International Police for the Defense of the State).[28] A 1956 decree gave the PIDE the authority to detain politically "dangerous" individuals for six months to three years, renewable for up to another three years (Braga de Cruz 1988: 92). After the early 1960s, the PIDE also ran notoriously harsh special prisons for political prisoners in the colonies of Angola and Cape Verde. The PIDE had huge administrative discretion, enabling its officials to run a virtual state within a state, without court power to intervene. Deaths during interrogation by the political police sometimes occurred, and even the PIDE sometimes ignored writs of habeas corpus issued by the Supreme Court. In this sense Portuguese repression was somewhat less judicialized than Brazilian repression under military rule. Furthermore, defendants' right to a lawyer were not guaranteed in political trials. As in Brazil, defendants were routinely convicted solely on the basis of confessions extracted by torture.

Despite the lack of accountability of the Portuguese repressive apparatus, Salazarist political justice was not radical in comparison to prior legality. According to Braga da Cruz, the repression was "paternalistic" and not aimed at the extermination of opponents. The main target was the Communist Party. As in Brazil from 1964 to 1985, the death penalty was not used (the special courts did not issue death sentences), and sentences were comparatively light (only 9 percent of those convicted in political trials between 1932 and 1945 were sentenced to more than five years in prison; Braga de Cruz 1988: 83–85).[29]

Salazar's authoritarian legality ended dramatically with the collapse of the regime, in this case in the 1974 revolution. As in Brazil, the personnel of the special courts were not subject to a widespread purge, but merely transferred to other parts of the bureaucracy. While the institutions responsible for political trials changed in Portugal, the intensity and scope of political trials rose and fell in line with the political contingencies faced by the regime. Once the

---

[28] Under Salazar's successor, Caetano, the PIDE was again renamed, this time to DGS (*Direção Geral de Segurança*, or General Directorate of Security). After the revolution of April 25, 1974, the DGS was abolished.

[29] The trials were aimed primarily at the lower strata of society; 48% of political prisoners between 1932 and 1945 were workers, while only 14% were middle-class professionals (Braga de Cruz 1988: 95).

machinery of political prosecution was established, it was not dismantled until the regime itself was overthrown by revolution.

The Portuguese case illustrates the effect of a relatively high degree of integration of and consensus between military and judicial elites. As with some of the other cases, political repression became more judicialized and more civilian over time. For most of the regime, political trials were presided over by civilian judges in special courts, rather than by military officers themselves. While this institutional configuration was different from military courts in Brazil, in both systems civilian judges trained in the law were pivotal in administering a highly judicialized form of repression, unlike the repression of the other two types of authoritarian legality.

It seems likely that gradual and judicialized authoritarian legality – the type represented by military Brazil and Salazarist Portugal – is the most common legal form among authoritarian regimes. This is because few authoritarian rulers even aspire to the ruthlessness of the Nazi or Spanish fascists, let alone achieve it. Most authoritarian regimes muddle along with slightly modified versions of previously created legal systems.

Can the judicial-military framework used here help explain the use of security courts in other authoritarian regimes, particularly recent and contemporary ones? The widespread use of military courts to prosecute dissidents and opponents in such countries as Egypt, Nigeria, Pakistan, and Peru indicates the relevance of the question, which can only be answered by examining new research of the kind presented by other chapters in this volume. An equally important question is whether the use of security courts by democratic regimes, especially those confronting new and serious political threats, might follow some of the same dynamics as those in authoritarian regimes described earlier.

THE UNITED STATES AFTER 9/11: AUTHORITARIAN COURTS IN A DEMOCRACY?

Is it possible that twenty-first-century democratic regimes, by modifying their legal systems to cope with the threat of terrorism, are partially converging with authoritarian regimes? Is it possible to speak of the existence of authoritarian practices under a democratic regime? If so, what makes courts authoritarian – the procedural rules, organizational forms, and belief systems that operate within them, or the wider political environment of which they are a part?

The case of the United States after September 11, 2001, raises these questions. Before exploring the issue, however, some basic parameters should be recognized. First, the terrorist threat is genuine and complex, and it justifies new security measures of some kind. The essential disagreements concern how and how much to adapt traditional constitutionalist compromises and understandings of civil liberties, not whether to adapt them or not. My focus here is very limited and is not an attempt to describe all of the many legal changes in intelligence gathering and other areas of homeland security as part of an authoritarian convergence. Second, criticisms of the institutional innovations described later come not just from the left, but from the libertarian right, including Republicans, and even from states-rights-oriented Southern nostalgists. Third, we might be able to learn from history, because many of the institutional mechanisms being proposed as solutions to the terrorist threat have been tried before, albeit under different conditions. Carefully drawing lessons from these experiences could be a worthwhile exercise.

The overall political context under which new antiterrorist measures are adopted is important. Citizens in the contemporary United States live under a political regime that bears little resemblance to the authoritarian regimes of Brazil and the Southern Cone. Nevertheless, it is not necessarily inappropriate to compare political measures taken against presumed enemies in authoritarian regimes with those adopted in democracies. Democratic governments have certainly engaged in political trials, especially in wartime. For example, Barkan points out that some 2,000 political dissidents were prosecuted in the United States during World War I, mainly for violating laws that forbade most forms of criticism of U.S. involvement in the war (1985: 1).

A new type of security court was created in the United States in response to the attacks of 9/11. President Bush signed an emergency order on November 13, 2001, that established military commissions to try noncitizen "unlawful enemy combatants" accused of terrorism. The Military Commissions Act passed by Congress and signed by President Bush in 2006 ratified the existence and procedures of these courts. As in Brazil and Chile under military rule, the executive in the United States decreed that a terrorist "war" necessitated the use of a special court system, controlled by the executive and insulated from the civilian judiciary. Unlike Brazil and Chile, in the U.S. case this system did not consist of preexisting military courts, but a new institution that was in many ways more severe than ordinary military justice.[30]

In addition, the Bush administration created a new legal regime to deal with suspected terrorists. For citizens, it invented the designation "enemy combatant," and claimed the right to apply this label to anyone it suspected of

---

[30] As a precedent, the Bush administration cited the military tribunal that tried and sentenced to death German spies captured on U.S. soil during World War II. But this case occurred before the United States signed several major treaties, including the Geneva Conventions.

terrorist activity. These suspects were then detained in military facilities, without access to a lawyer and without charges initially being brought ("Detention Cases," 2004).[31] As for noncitizen terrorist suspects, the Department of Defense decided in early 2002 to call them "unlawful combatants" and to place them outside the purview of both U.S. justice and the Third Geneva Convention dealing with prisoners of war. Captured in Afghanistan and incarcerated on the Guantánamo naval base in Cuba, these detainees are subject to the jurisdiction of the military commissions created by President Bush's 2001 order.[32]

These two features of the legal response to the terrorist attacks constitute an extraordinary change in traditional U.S. legality as it relates to political crime. As in Brazil and the Southern Cone, the policies have produced a debate between their supporters, who feel that they are measured responses to a severe threat, and their critics, who fear the erosion of constitutional rights by the executive.[33] It seems plausible that the conventional legal order and judicial procedures might be ineffective against small cells of determined, politically motivated killers ready to attack civilian targets. The question is whether new institutions created to deal with this problem create costs, in terms of curbs on and threats to civil liberties, that outweigh their presumed benefit of increased security. Another related issue is to what extent the executive can be trusted, in the absence of conventional checks and balances, not to use its emergency powers for institutional self-aggrandizement against other branches of government, political opponents, and dissident members of the citizenry (Arato 2002: 470).

It is striking that the military commissions established to try the Guantánamo detainees are similar to the military courts employed against the opposition by the Brazilian and Chilean military regimes. When it comes to presidential control over the courts, they are more draconian than the Brazilian military courts under military rule. As described in the order, they are constituted ad

---

[31] At the time of writing – August 2007 – the best-known detainees in this category were Yaser Esam Hamdi, a U.S.-born Saudi Arabian who fought for the Taliban and was captured in Afghanistan in late 2001; and the alleged "dirty bomber" José Padilla, arrested in Chicago after a trip to Pakistan in the spring of 2002 ("Detention Cases," 2004). Hamdi was subsequently turned over to Saudi Arabian authorities and released. Padilla was detained for three and a half years before being put on trial in a Federal court in Miami. See "After 9 weeks, U.S. rests in Padilla terror trial" at CNN.com accessed at www.cnn.com/2007/ on July 13, 2007.

[32] The detainees in Guantánamo, alleged Taliban and al-Qaeda combatants from more than forty countries, numbered 370 in August of 2007 ("Brown Quer Soltos Cinco de Guantanamo,"2007). In response to the Supreme Court decision of June 2004 discussed later, some pretrial screenings of detainees have taken place to determine their status. At the time of writing (August 2007) no judgment in the military tribunals had taken place.

[33] For different views of these and other post-9/11measures, see Amitai Etzioni and Jason Marsh (2003) and Schulz (2003).

hoc by the Secretary of Defense – in other words, the executive branch directly controls their composition and procedures. The identities of judges and prosecutors are apparently kept secret, as with the "faceless courts" sometimes used in Latin America. Defendants are not allowed any right of appeal to a civilian court, either in the United States or abroad. (Appeals can only be made to panels named by the Secretary of Defense.) Judges in the tribunals are given the leeway to close the trials to the press and public for almost any reason.[34] In all these respects the courts afford fewer procedural rights to defendants and more zealously guard executive privilege than the Brazilian military courts of 1964–1979. They also involve judges who as active-duty military officers in a chain of command lack independence and simultaneously fight the defendants as well as judge and sentence them, as in the Southern Cone military courts.

The commissions are authorized to sentence defendants to death with a unanimous vote of their members (Mintz 2002). Federal officials, including President Bush, have publicly suggested that the defendants are guilty. Lawyers complain of an inability to adequately represent their clients. Charges in the commissions involve membership in particular organizations as much as specific actions. Evidence presented by prosecutors is likely to include statements made under duress or even torture (Dodds, 2004).[35] And then-Secretary of Defense Donald Rumsfeld said that acquittals in the military commissions would not necessarily lead to the release of defendants – the executive could continue to detain them (Scheuerman 2006: 119). Because those tried in the military commissions seem to lack rights, and the executive claims to be able to deal with them in what seems to constitute a legal vacuum, this particular institution seems to resemble a rule by law more than it does a rule of law.[36]

The order creating the commissions constitutes a major reform of the judiciary, accomplished by presidential decree. In the proposed special court system, there is little separation between executive power, on one hand, and the judicial power on the other. In classic military style, defendants are first

---

[34] For an argument against this provision of the regulations, see Klaris (2002).

[35] This article claims that several former prisoners at Guantánamo have said that they made false confessions after interrogations.

[36] It is important to point out that the Bush Administration's claims with regard to its treatment of noncitizen "unlawful combatants" and citizen "enemy combatants" are not at all similar to the changes in criminal law and procedure described by Martin Shapiro in his conclusion to this volume, Chapter 13. The latter changes are modifications of clearly understood and enforced rules. The Bush administration's claims are to absolute discretion unbounded by law – the kind of discretion that when wielded by regimes outside the United States is often labeled "authoritarian."

and foremost "enemy combatants," and only secondarily bearers of rights as in the civilian court system. The emergency order therefore represents a potentially serious inroad into the U.S. constitutional tradition, and a significant militarization of the judiciary.[37]

If, as Andrew Arato writes, "Constitutionalist self-limitation of elected power . . . [is] the one truly American achievement" in the political realm, then it is not clear that this achievement will entirely survive the onslaught of the "war on terrorism" (2000: 328).[38] U.S. law professor Laurence Tribe invoked a Southern Cone military regime when he talked about the treatment of citizens accused of being "enemy combatants." He said that in these cases the government is "asserting power akin to that exercised in dictatorships like Argentina, when they just 'disappeared' people from their homes with no access to counsel, no list of the detained or executed" (Benson and Wood 2002).

The fact that a prominent expert on U.S. constitutional law invoked a Southern Cone dictatorship in describing the treatment of "enemy combatants" should not go unnoticed. Professor Tribe's comment is part of a much larger body of criticism that is too scholarly to be dismissed as mere "rhetoric," "clichés," and "banners and slogans," as does Martin Shapiro in Chapter 13, when he argues that the notion of authoritarian convergence actually serves authoritarianism.[39] The parallel being drawn here between Southern Cone security courts and the U.S. military commissions is based on a careful historical examination of the institutional architecture and procedures of each set of courts. Readers may find the analogy implausible, but the argument that it is politically inconvenient should be irrelevant to the scholarly debate about how to interpret post-9/11 legal changes in the United States.

---

[37] For these and other insights into the military commissions I am indebted to the participants in the symposium "The Judiciary and the War on Terror" held at the Tulane University Law School on February 21, 2003, especially Robin Shulberg, a federal public defender; Eugene Fidell, the president of the National Institute of Military Justice; Edward Sherman, a professor of Tulane Law School; Jordan Paust, of the University of Houston Law Center; and Derek Jinks, of the St. Louis University School of Law.

[38] Arato suggests that there is a general tendency for U.S. presidents to seek a way out of the gridlock inherent in the U.S. presidential and federal system by invoking emergency powers. However, the open-ended nature of the "war on terrorism," and the unconventional nature of the presumed war, makes this particular push for emergency powers particularly dangerous from a constitutional point of view.

[39] It is difficult to understand the logic of Shapiro's position. He seems to be saying that those who criticize the indefinite detention of a U.S. citizen on suspicion of terrorism and compare it to the actions of an authoritarian regime are –somehow, mysteriously – fomenting authoritarian rule. At this point we seem to have entered a world that resembles Lewis Carroll's *Alice through the Looking Glass*, in which the conventional relationship between cause and effect has been turned upside down.

A review of the record of the use of military courts in Brazil and Chile alerts us to the fact that such courts are often a convenient tool of executives anxious to avoid compromise, dialogue, and the give-and-take of democracy. The expansion of security court jurisdiction, invoked in response to specific, seemingly unique emergencies, is often gradually ratcheted upward to encompass more people and circumstances. Over time, its pro-prosecutorial bias allows investigators, prosecutors, and judges to become sloppy about evidence and procedures, violating rights and giving the executive branch the benefit of every doubt. The result can sometimes be the emergence of an unaccountable state within a state.

However, considerable conflict over the executive branch's legal response to terrorism has occurred, and is likely to continue. A small band of commentators in the news media has criticized the creation of the military commissions.[40] Some of this criticism may have had an effect, because in addition to modifying the original order, the administration placed the accused terrorists Richard Reid and Zacarias Moussaoui, as well as the "American Taliban" John Walker Lind, on trial in civilian, federal courts. Perhaps more importantly, scholars and judicial elites – law professors, legal commentators, military lawyers, and some prosecutors and judges – have criticized the executive's claims to be able to indefinitely detain prisoners, both citizens and noncitizens.[41] One such critic characterized the architects of the federal government's detention policies as "executive power absolutists" (Taylor 2004).[42] And in an editorial, the *New York Times* called the 2006 act that consolidated the commissions "a tyrannical law that will be ranked with the low points in American democracy, our generation's version of the Alien and Sedition Acts."[43]

[40] The outpouring of commentary on the military commissions is too great to list here. For significant criticisms of the tribunals see Arato (2002), Safire (2001), Lewis (*New York Times* 2001), Butler (2002), and Nieer (2002). For a defense of the commissions see Gonzales (2001) and Wedgwood (2002).

[41] For some examples of this work, see Gathii (2003), Lugosi (2003), and Amann (2004).

[42] Other commentators have criticized the Bush administration's military commissions and treatment of citizen "enemy combatants." Law professor Sanford Levinson (2006: 67–68) writes, "I believe the Bush Administration threatens the American constitutional order – and for that matter, the edifice of world order built in the aftermath of World War II – more than any other administration in my lifetime." Political scientist Bill Scheuerman (2006: 118) declares that "In the spirit of Carl Schmitt, influential voices in the [Bush] administration interpret the executive branch's authority to determine the fate of accused terrorists along the lines of a *legal black hole* [emphasis in the original] in which unmitigated discretionary power necessarily holds sway." And law professors Neal Katyal and Laurence Tribe declare (2002: 1259–1260) that "the President's Order establishing military tribunals for the trial of terrorists is flatly unconstitutional" because it violates the principle that the powers that define the law, prosecute offenders, and adjudicate guilt should be three separate entities.

[43] "Rushing Off a Cliff," *New York Times*, September 28, 2006 at http://www.nytimes.com/2006/accessed on July 20, 2007.

If our analysis is correct, the most significant conflicts over these issues will involve judicial elites, on the one hand, and the military and the civilian proponents of militarized law on the other, with groups of activists across the ideological spectrum playing an important role as well. Already, judges have ruled against the executive branch in several high-profile cases. For example, in October 2003, a federal judge ruled that accused 9/11 terrorist Zacarias Moussaoui should not face the death penalty because the government would not allow his defense lawyers to question al-Qaeda prisoners. In this case, the court upheld the right of defense to have the same access to witness testimony and other forms of evidence. The government lawyers had claimed that the right had to be restricted in the interests of national security (Bravin 2003).[44]

In June of 2004 the U.S. Supreme Court partially rejected the Bush administration's positions in three cases involving the rights of detainees held in the war on terrorism. The most important, and the biggest reversal for the government, was *Hamdi v. Rumsfeld*. In it, the court ruled that a U.S. citizen held as an "enemy combatant" in the United States has a right to a hearing to determine the legality of his incarceration. While the court did not rule that a U.S. citizen could not be tried by a military tribunal, it did uphold the right of detainees to a notice of the charges against them, an opportunity to contest those charges, and the right to appear before an ostensibly neutral authority. In *Rasul v. Bush* and *al Odah v. the United States*, the court ruled that prisoners being held in Guantánamo Bay had the right to present legal objections to their detentions in federal courts ("Detention Cases," 2004).

Perhaps most sweepingly, in June 2006 the Supreme Court ruled that the military commissions created by President Bush's 2001 executive order were unconstitutional (Goldberg 2006). These rulings suggest that the extraordinary powers claimed by the executive after 9/11 will be at least partially rolled back by the U.S. judiciary on a case-by-case basis.

The U.S. case is an important one for understanding the use of security courts. If we can recognize the occasional existence of a limited "judicial space" and some procedural rights for defendants under an authoritarian regime, as we have in the Brazilian case, we must also be alert to the possibility of authoritarian legality in a democracy. Put another way, democracies can modify their legal systems in ways that undermine their rule-of-law characteristics and unshackle military and security forces. However, when that occurs,

---

[44] Government lawyers responded to the ruling by saying that they would appeal it, and if they lost the appeal, would designate Moussaoui as an "enemy combatant" so that he could be held without charges indefinitely or tried in a military commission. This shows how the creation of a special court can change the impact of legal decisions in the civilian judiciary, in effect giving the prosecution an entirely new and highly favorable jurisdiction.

judicial-military conflict – not consensus – is the mechanism by which individual rights are protected.

The open question about the U.S. case is to what extent judicial elites will
challenge the prerogatives claimed by the executive branch and rule that some
powers – such as the right to detain citizens deemed to be "enemy combatants"
indefinitely – are unconstitutional.[45] After both World Wars I and II, the U.S.
judiciary rolled back some of the emergency powers claimed by the executive
during those conflicts. Such a scaling back of executive privilege has begun
to take place during the "war on terrorism," but it is also far too early to make
a definitive judgment on how the "war" will reshape the legal treatment of
opposition and dissent in the United States.[46] This is an extremely important
conflict in which both the unique constitutional tradition and extraordinary
protection of basic rights in the United States are at stake.

CONCLUSION

Why do authoritarian regimes bother with trials of political opponents in
security courts? If they come to power by force, why don't they continue to
rule by force and force alone, dropping all pretenses to legality? Given that
most of them do not, and instead use security courts to some extent, why do
some regimes get such courts' verdicts and sentences to "stick" more effectively
than others?

Some existing approaches to these questions are unsatisfactory. For example, the strength of the opposition facing the regime does not seem an adequate
explanation for variation in the use of security courts by authoritarian regimes.
Similarly, broad generalizations about differences in political culture do not
appear to easily fit the cases analyzed here. Nor can variations in authoritarian legality be easily ascribed purely to ideological or attitudinal differences
among military officers or judicial elites in each country. Expressions of an
exterminationist dirty war mentality by military and judicial elites can be found
in the historical record of all three authoritarian regimes in Brazil, Chile, and
Argentina.

---

[45] Andrew Arato takes the optimistic view that resistance to "the illegitimate and dangerous
expansion of emergency government" after 9/11 will succeed (2002: 472).

[46] Interestingly, the former Supreme Court Chief Justice, the late William Rhenquist, wrote a
book on civil liberties in wartime. His measured conclusion might give hope to both supporters
and critics of the executive's claims: "It is neither desirable nor it is remotely likely that civil
liberty will occupy as favored a position in wartime as it does in peacetime. But it is both
desirable and likely that more careful attention will be paid by the courts to the basis for the
government's claims of necessity as a basis for curtailing civil liberty. The laws will thus not
be silent in time of war, but they will speak with a somewhat different voice" (Rehnquist 1998:
224–225).

Instead, our cases suggest that attempts by judicial and military organizations to impose institutional solutions to the problem of "subversion" succeed and bind them together, or fail and drive them apart. The degree of military and judicial consensus, integration, and cooperation is a key, neglected variable in unlocking the puzzle of variation in authoritarian legality.

This chapter therefore suggests a two-part answer to the question, why do authoritarian regimes bother to use security courts? First, in the modern world (and all other things being equal), there are advantages to not dropping all pretenses and to continue to legitimate authoritarian rule with some kind of appeal to the law. Legal manipulations and political trials are useful for an authoritarian regime because they can demobilize popular oppositional movements efficiently, reducing the need to exercise force; garner legitimacy for the regime by showing that it "plays fair" in dealing with opponents; create positive political images for the regime, and negative ones for the opposition; under some circumstances, help one faction gain power over another within the regime; and stabilize the repression by providing information and a predictable set of rules around which opponents' and regime officials' expectations can coalesce.

The second part of the answer is that authoritarian regimes use security courts because they can. Given that trials as a means of repression have advantages for authoritarian regimes, those regimes are able to rely on "trustworthy" security courts – courts, either civilian or military, that will produce verdicts in line with their conception of legality, and not challenge the fundamentals of regime rule. However, such trustworthy courts have to be produced by trial and error, over time. That is not easy, and the courts must be flexible enough to adapt to new exigencies of regime rule. Traditional legal establishments may also resist them. Sometimes the attempts to create trustworthy courts succeed, building up a consensus across military and judicial elites, and at other times they fail.

Where judicial-military consensus, cooperation, and integration were high, regime repression relied heavily on security courts, and the legal system was modified conservatively and incrementally. This can be seen in the Brazilian case. Where the military broke with judicial elites, as in Argentina, repression was a radical, largely extrajudicial assault on traditional legal procedures. Where the military and judiciary were quite separate, and cooperation limited, repression took a form that was midway between these two poles. This outcome can be seen in Chile.

The analysis of Argentina suggests that when regimes resort to extrajudicial violence and an all-out assault on traditional legality, they will do so because their prior attempts to manipulate the law and courts to their advantage failed. Behind a dirty war may lie an organizational failure – the collapse of a trustworthy security court that was ready to prosecute regime opponents with authoritarian laws. Regimes therefore resort to widespread terror and force when they lack the organizational means to institute more legalized forms of repression.

Finally, recent political events should compel scholars to ask whether contemporary democratic regimes, in modifying their legal structures to cope with political emergencies, might be converging with authoritarian regimes in some respects. These modifications can parallel each other even if the overall political context under each type of regime is different. Leaders of democracies in the age of the "war on terrorism" seem to be tempted to create fortress-like protections of the state's national security interests, making extravagant claims of executive privilege and eroding the very civil liberties that they claim to defend (Arato 2002: 457–476). Specific institutions that these leaders create, such as the military commissions authorized by President Bush and the ad hoc treatment of citizen "enemy combatants," can bear a striking resemblance to the practices of authoritarian regimes. At the present time, studying security courts in defunct authoritarian regimes is not just an academic exercise. Similar courts may begin operating tomorrow in the most unlikely places.

APPENDIX

TABLE A.1. *Lethal violence by state forces and other indices of political repression in Argentina, Brazil, and Chile, 1964–1991*

Category	Brazil	Chile	Argentina
Period	1964–79	1973–89	1976–83
Period of heaviest repression	1969–73	1973–77	1976–80
Deaths and disappearances	300+	3,000–5,000	20,000–30,000
Political prisoners	25,000	60,000	30,000
Exiles	10,000	40,000	500,000
Number of people tried in military courts for political crimes (estimates)	7,367+	6,000+	350+
Amnesty	8/28/79	4/19/78	9/23/83 later annulled by Congress
Main human rights Report	Nunca Mais (1985) Secret project supported by the Archdiocese of São Paulo and the World Council of Churches	Rettig Report (1991) Rettig Commission appointed by President Aylwin	Nunca Más (1984) Sabato Commission appointed by President Alfonsín
Population (1988)	144 million	13 million	32 million

Sources: Argentine National Commission on the Disappeared (1986) *Nunca Más.* New York: Farrar Straus Giroux; National Commission on Truth and Reconciliation (1993) *Report of the Chilean National Commission on Truth and Reconciliation.* University of Notre Dame Press; Paul Drake (1996) *Labor Movements and Dictatorships: The Southern Cone in Comparative Perspective.* Baltimore: Johns Hopkins University Press, pp. 29–30; Carlos Nino (1996) *Radical Evil on Trial.* New Haven: Yale University Press, p. 64, 80; Nilmário Miranda and Carlos Tibúrcio (1999) *Dos Filhos Deste Solo (Mortos e Desaparecidos Políticos Durante a Ditadura Militar: A Responsibilidade do Estado).* São Paulo: Editora Fundação Perseu Abramo/Boitempo Editorial, pp. 15–16.

2

Administrative Law and the Judicial Control of Agents in Authoritarian Regimes

Tom Ginsburg

Authoritarian regimes, like all governments, face the need to control lower level officials who work for the regime. But authoritarian and democratic governments differ in the sets of tools and constraints they bring to the problem, and even within the category of authoritarian governments there are substantial differences in regime capabilities in this regard. This chapter examines the causes and consequences of a decision by an authoritarian government to turn to administrative law as a tool for monitoring government officials.

Administrative law is a notoriously fluid area of law, in which national regimes vary, and there is substantial divergence even over the conceptual scope of the field, much more so than, say, in corporate law or tort law. Part of the confusion comes from the fact that administrative law regimes address three different but fundamental political problems. The first is the problem of coordination among the large number of governmental actors that compose and serve the regime. This problem is addressed by the formal conception of administrative law as encompassing the organization of government; that is, the organic acts establishing and empowering government agencies. This was the definition of administrative law in the former Soviet Union, for example. Administrative law in this conception was not at all about constraint of government but about empowerment of government within a framework of legality, and ensuring that the agency has been properly granted powers from the lawmaker. By defining the scope of authority, the law resolves potential coordination problems among governmental actors.

A separate function of administrative law in some regimes is social control. In the socialist legal systems, administrative law included in its scope law enforced by administrative authorities rather than by judicial authorities. In China today, for example, there are a wide range of violations subject to administrative punishments from police or executive authorities without judicial supervision (Biddulph 2004; Peerenboom 2004a). Administrative law statutes contain the substantive rules as well as the procedures for punishment, which can include significant periods of detention of the type normally considered criminal in Western conceptual architecture. In practice, "administrative" punishments are implemented by the police. This type of scheme really reflects the inability or unwillingness of the regime to delegate crime control functions to the judicial system, which may lack capacity to achieve the crucial core task of social control.

In this chapter, I focus on the third political function of administrative law regimes, namely the resolution of principal-agent problems (McCubbins, Noll and Weingast 1987; McNollgast 1998, 1999). In the Western legal tradition, administrative law concerns the rules for controlling government action, for the benefit of both the government and the citizens. From the government point of view, the problem can be understood as one in which a principal (the core of the regime, however it is composed) seeks to control agents. All rulers have limited physical and organizational capacity to govern by themselves. Government thus requires the delegation of certain tasks to administrative agents, who have the expertise and skill to accomplish desired ends. The agents' specialized knowledge gives them an informational advantage over their principals, which the agents can exploit to pursue different ends and strategies than desired by the principal. This is the principal-agent problem, and it is one that is ubiquitous in modern administration. To resolve the problem and prevent agency slack, all rulers need mechanisms to monitor agents' performance and to discipline agents who do not obey instructions.

Administrative litigation can help resolve these problems. As is described in more detail later, a lawsuit by an aggrieved citizen challenging administrative action serves the important function of bringing instances of potential agency slack to the attention of the rulers. The courts thus function to a certain degree as a second agent to watch the first. Being a court, of course, requires a commitment to certain institutional structures and practices, which sometimes may create new types of challenges for rulers; indeed, sometimes rulers will lose on particular policy matters to achieve the broader goal of controlling their agents. We should thus not expect that every ruler will adopt an administrative law regime of this type, designed to control government action on behalf of the rulers and the citizenry.

The scope of the agency problem and the tools available to rulers may vary across time, space, and type of organization of the regime itself. This sets up a problem of institutional choice for rulers, of how to choose the most effective mechanism or combination of mechanisms to resolve the particular agency problems they face. The first part of this chapter considers some of the factors that may affect this choice.

THREE DEVICES TO SOLVE AGENCY PROBLEMS

I conceptualize three categories of mechanisms that rulers can choose from to reduce agency costs (Ginsburg 2002): ideology, hierarchy, and third-party monitoring. As with any typology, there are shades of gray in between the categories. Nevertheless I find it a useful framework for categorizing regimes as well as for providing some insight into the changing pressures for judicialization of administrative law.

Internalization and Ideology

Perhaps the most desirable method of reducing agency costs from the perspective of the principal is to convince the agent to internalize the preferences of the principal. Perfect internalization of the preferences of the principal eliminates the need for monitoring and enforcement. Internalization can occur through professional indoctrination and training or through promulgation of a substantive political ideology that commands the loyalty of the agent. Leninist systems, for example, relied on a mix of internalized ideology and externally imposed terror to keep their agents in line, although the Chinese variant of that ideology has not seemed to prevent extensive corruption and severe agency problems (Root 1996). The Chinese Communist Party's conceptual contortions around the ideal of a "socialist market economy" illustrate the lengths that regimes will go to maintain ideological cohesion, which at least in part is designed to minimize agency costs.

It would be a mistake, however, to think that ideologies are the exclusive prerogative of socialist or authoritarian regimes. Internalization can also involve procedural rather than substantive values, so that the agent internalizes a way of acting that will serve the interests of the principal. For example, by requiring that all senior civil servants be trained in law (formerly a legal requirement in Germany and still largely true in Japan), rulers might discourage their agents from departing from the text of statutes. Legal education that emphasizes fidelity to text serves the interest of the coalitions that enact statutes. Indeed scholars have often noted the compatibility of legal positivism with authoritarian rule (Dyzenhaus 1991).[1] The notion that law should serve as the faithful agent of the "political" sphere is a form of ideology that can serve to uphold whatever government is in power.

---

[1] At least two accounts of important authoritarian regimes dispute this connection. Ingo Muller's classic study of courts in Nazi Germany (1991) illustrated how legal actors betrayed their positivist heritage. Similarly Hilbink (2007) and Couso (2002) emphasize that positivist ideology does not explain the behavior of the Chilean courts during the Pinochet regime, when they upheld regime interests even when the law would seem to require otherwise.

All modern political systems utilize indoctrination through legal education. Educational requirements also help the principal select among potential agents who are competing for employment. By requiring potential agents to undergo costly training *before* selection, the principal allows the agents to signal that they have internalized the values of the principal. Those potential agents who do not share the values of the principal may pursue other careers rather than undertake the training. Furthermore, preselection training reduces the need for postselection indoctrination, the cost of which must be borne directly by the principal. Nevertheless, highly ideological authoritarian systems tend to utilize postselection training, such as the system of Central Political Schools (CPS) found in China and other Communist countries. Indeed, China is currently expanding CPS training to county-level bureaucrats (Whiting 2006: 16).

It seems quite likely that democracies, with their structural commitments to pluralism, have a more difficult time producing substantive ideologies of the power of, say, Leninism. We periodically hear of the end of ideology (Bell 2000), but in an era of new, rising challenges to democracy, it is clear that these eulogies only refer to the industrialized West. One therefore might think that the internalization strategy is to be preferred by authoritarian regimes, and to be avoided by democracies. Even for authoritarians, successful internalization is difficult to observe directly. Any system of governance over a certain scale must therefore utilize other mechanisms as well.

Hierarchy and Second-Party Supervision

By hierarchy, I have in mind a decision by the principal to monitor the agent directly. Rulers may be able to influence bureaucratic agents, for example, through direct manipulation of incentive structures. As mentioned earlier, agents compete against other potential agents to be hired; once hired they compete to advance. By rewarding loyal agents and punishing disloyal agents in career advancement and retirement decisions, rulers provide bureaucrats with an incentive to perform. As has been observed since Weber's classic work (1946), hierarchical structures help reduce monitoring costs, as more senior agents help monitor and discipline junior ones.

Rulers can also manipulate the incentive structure of the bureaucracy as a whole. They can, for example, reduce the budget of an agency; impose process costs such as performance reviews, which utilize scarce staff time; and force the agency to promulgate internal rules that constrain discretion. They can create "internal affairs bureaus," which are essentially external monitors within the agent itself. They can create multiple agencies with overlapping jurisdictions that then compete for budget and authority (McNollgast 1998:

51; Rose-Ackerman 1995). When there are overlapping authorities, agents can monitor each other and prevent any one agent from becoming so powerful as to displace the principal.

Hierarchical control requires monitoring, and this can involve the creation of a specialized agent whose exclusive task is to seek out instances of agent malfeasance for punishment. The imperial Chinese Censorate is one such example, as is its successor, the Control Yuan of the Republic of China.[2] Similarly the Chinese Communist Party relies on a set of institutions to structure incentives for its cadres. For example, its Organization Department provides evaluation criteria for local party secretaries based on performance targets, and these have been adjusted over time (Whiting 2004, 2006).[3] An array of other mechanisms, including horizontal evaluation through so-called democratic appraisal of other colleagues, involve monitoring of the bureaucracy by itself. And both the party and government have internal monitors, the Central Discipline Inspection Commission and the Ministry of Supervision, respectively (Whiting 2006: 19–21).

Socialist legal systems featured a distinctive form of administrative legality (though not formally identified as such) that essentially relied on this strategy of hierarchical supervision. That was the so-called function of general supervision by the Procuracy. The institution originates in imperial Russia, when Peter the Great needed to improve the efficiency of government and tax collection (Mikhailovskaya 1999), and it eventually became quite powerful, known as "the eyes of the ruler." Under the concept of general supervision, maintained today in Russia, China, and some of the postsocialist republics, the prosecutor is empowered not just to serve as an agent for the suppression of crime, but as a supervisor of legality by all other government agents as well. This puts the procurator at a level equal to or superior to judges, and empowers it to take an active role in what would conventionally be characterized as civil or administrative law as well as criminal law.

The procuracy has a bad name in the West because of its association with Stalinism. Viewing the matter from a positive rather than normative perspective, general supervision is an undeniably effective technique for reducing agency costs.

In terms of the distinction between authoritarian and democratic regimes, a key factor is the time horizon of the ruler. Hierarchical mechanisms of control will be easier to undertake for a ruling party with a longer time horizon than for

---

[2] Republic of China Constitution, Arts. 90–106 (1946).
[3] Whiting notes that the party has engaged in "adaptive learning," for example by replacing raw production targets that created distorted incentives with more nuanced criteria.

a party with a short time horizon. If bureaucrats' time horizons are longer than the expected period of rule by the political principal, bureaucrats may not find rulers' threats of career punishment to be credible. If the punished bureaucrat anticipates that a new ruler will come to power with preferences that align more closely with his own, he may actually reap long-term gains for being disloyal to the present regime (Helmke 2005). Bureaucrats can also exploit their informational advantages to create delay, waiting until a new political principal comes into office. Authoritarian rulers *may* have longer time horizons than those associated with democracy because of the institutionalized turnover in power. This is especially true for party-based authoritarian regimes, and may be less true of military dictators.

Another important distinction between authoritarians and democratic regimes is the type of sanctions they can impose on wayward agents. In a democracy, a corrupt or politically unreliable agent can be fired or, in extreme cases, jailed in relatively good conditions. The sanctions available to authoritarians are far more severe. Thus hierarchy, like ideology, may be preferred by authoritarians.

Judicial Control and Third-Party Supervision

Judicially supervised administrative procedures, such as a right to a hearing, notice requirements, and a right to a statement of reasons for a decision, are a third mechanism for controlling agency costs. By creating a judicially enforceable procedural right, rulers decentralize the monitoring function to their constituents, who can bring suits to inform rulers of bureaucratic failure to follow instructions (McCubbins and Schwartz 1984). Rulers also create a mechanism to discipline the agents and can use the courts as a quality-control system in judging whether the monitors' claims have merit. Although administrative procedures may be accompanied by an ideology of public accountability, their political function is primarily one of control on behalf of rulers (Bishop 1990, 1998; McCubbins, Noll, and Weingast 1987, 1989).

The distinctive feature in judicial supervision is that it relies on the logic of what McCubbins and Schwartz (1984) call fire alarms. The dispute resolution structure of courts is one in which cases are brought from outside – courts are not typically equipped to proactively identify violations. They are thus truly fire alarms rather than police patrols. The institutional structure of courts facilitates upward channeling of decentralized sources of information, for which the costs are paid by private litigants.

Of course, courts are not the only type of fire alarm mechanism available to rulers. The PRC, for example, has maintained a structure for citizen

	General	Specialized
Proactive	Censorate, procuracy	Internal affairs bureau
Reactive	Ordinary court	Administrative court; ombudsmen

FIGURE 2.1. Types of Monitors.

complaints, the Letters and Visits Office, at all five levels of the Chinese government hierarchy (Leuhrmann 2003). Similarly, the Confucian tradition featured a gong whereby citizens could raise complaints before the administration (Choi 2005).

The Scandinavian countries have the additional device of the ombudsman. The ombudsman is a special government officer whose only job is to protect citizens' rights. He or she can intervene with the bureaucracy and in some countries bring court cases to force the government to take certain actions. Unlike the procurator, the ombudsman is reactive, relying on the citizenry to bring cases to his or her attention. This model has also been very influential abroad, but is not typically desired by authoritarian regimes. It is more designed for human rights protection than for ensuring the routine use of administrative procedures. Ombudsmen's legal powers vary across regimes, but generally rely on publicity, which in turn relies on a media independent enough to publicize instances of administrative and political malfeasance.

An additional design choice is the level of specialization, such as may be found in a designated administrative court or even subject-specific monitors. Specialization can improve the quality of monitoring, though it might increase agency costs if judges are themselves "captured" by the technical discourse of the bureaucrats. The range of mechanisms can be arrayed in the following two by two figure (Figure 2.1), in which the top row corresponds to certain types of hierarchical controls and the lower row corresponds to varieties of judicial control that rely on third-party monitoring.

Whereas agents who have internalized the principal's preferences are self-monitoring, and hierarchical supervision involves second-party monitoring and discipline by the principal, administrative law requires passive third parties to monitor and discipline administrative agents. It is therefore the most institutionally complex of the three mechanisms (as well as the last to develop historically). Most systems of administration utilize a combination of the three mechanisms, and the next section examines some considerations that influence the particular choice.

Under what conditions will political principals rely on third-party, legal mechanisms for supervising agents? As a mechanism of controlling agency costs, judicially enforced administrative law has costs as well as benefits. Extensive administrative procedures entail costs in the form of slower, less flexible administration. In addition, generalized administrative procedures carry some risk for rulers. As Morgan (2006: 220) notes, administrative law is a

> contingent opportunity structure – it shapes who wins and who loses but not necessarily in predictable ways. The outcomes that flow from the application of administrative law (or law-like) doctrines to particular situations can in some circumstances bolster the powerful, in others they provide openings for the disempowered or more vulnerable.

By their nature, procedural rights may extend to rulers' opponents as well as their supporters, and so may lead to policy losses. Rulers can try to tailor the procedures so as to limit access by opponents, but nevertheless will likely be faced with some losses caused by opposition lawsuits. There are also agency problems associated with the use of third-party monitors such as judges. In many systems the factors that give rise to judicial agency costs are likely to be the same as those that produce bureaucratic agency costs. The extent of judicial agency problems will depend on the mechanisms available to rulers for controlling judges, which also include hierarchy and internalization. For example, professional norms of fidelity to law function as an internalized ideology, reducing the agency costs of judicial monitoring. Hierarchical structures within the judiciary are important modalities of control as well. Civil law judges, for example, are typically appointed at a young age and serve in hierarchical structures much like the bureaucrats themselves.

Whether or not rulers want to adopt a strong administrative law regime depends in part on the other mechanisms available for controlling bureaucrats, and in part on rulers' perceptions of judicial agency costs. If rulers believe they can control bureaucrats with other mechanisms, such as indoctrination or control over careers, a system of judicially enforceable administrative law is undesirable.

There may, of course, be exogenous factors that exacerbate agency problems in particular settings. One of the most important may be economic and regulatory complexity. As economies become more complex, they are less amenable to central control and require more complicated and flexible regulatory schemes. This means empowering regulatory agents relative to political principals. In contrast, regimes of state ownership essentially utilize hierarchical control over the agents to direct the economy. We might thus expect a secular trend toward judicialization simply because of increasingly complex regulation, and a particular shift in economies formerly characterized by state ownership.

We can conceptualize the decision about the mix of judicial monitoring and hierarchical controls in simple economic terms. Rulers will evaluate the benefits of judicially monitored administrative proceduralization and will choose a level of procedural constraint where marginal costs are equal to marginal benefits in agency cost reduction. To do so, they need to consider not only "pure" bureaucratic agency costs but also process costs that come in the form of slower bureaucracy. The former decline with proceduralization, while the latter rise. Furthermore, the political principals must also consider agency costs associated with a third-party monitor, reflected in the proverbial problem of "who guards the guardians" (Shapiro 1986). Choosing the level of proceduralization that minimizes the sum of these costs will set the "price" of the legal solution. Political principals will then evaluate this price against hierarchical and ideological alternatives to choose an agency cost-reduction strategy. Since the costs of monitoring and suing the government under administrative law are borne by private litigants, rulers may be liberal in granting procedural rights.

The relative cost of administrative law as opposed to hierarchy and internalization depends in part on the structure of politics itself. For example, strong political parties help political leaders because they provide a group of committed persons who can assist in the monitoring and discipline of bureaucrats. They also can provide qualified and motivated personnel to staff the bureaucracy. Political parties utilize internalization and hierarchy to help reduce administrative agency costs.

In democracies, principals who govern for an extended period have less need to rely on independent courts as monitors. A disciplined political party that is electorally secure, for example, can easily utilize first- and second-party solutions to the problem of agency cost. Where parties are weak, however, they may want to use courts to protect their policy bargain from repeal by later coalitions because they anticipate electoral loss (Cooter and Ginsburg 1996). Furthermore, weaker and more diffuse parties will be less able to motivate agents ideologically and discipline them through hierarchical mechanisms.

My main claim is that administrative procedures are one mechanism for controlling agency problems. They feature some distinct disadvantages relative to internalization and hierarchy for an authoritarian regime, namely the possibility of agency costs in the monitor and, more problematically, the open nature of procedural rules, which means that regime opponents may be able to use the mechanisms in ways that are not desirable. Furthermore, the availability of severe punishments for wayward agents under dictatorship, where such niceties as procedural rights for civil servants may be minimal, may bias authoritarians away from judicialized administrative law.

Still under some circumstances, shifts in cost structures among the available substitutes may generate pressures for an administrative procedures regime. If hierarchy or internalization becomes less effective, either because of exogenous reasons or because of factors internal to the regime, we should see greater legal proceduralization. Conversely, if hierarchy or internalization becomes cheaper, we should see less proceduralization. The level of administrative proceduralization will thus reflect the following factors: the severity of the agency cost problem; the process costs of proceduralization, such as slower administration; the costs associated with third-party monitors; and the availability of lower cost mechanisms to reduce agency costs, such as internalization and hierarchy.

AN ILLUSTRATION: THE CASE OF CHINA AND THE SHIFT FROM HIERARCHY TO ADMINISTRATIVE LAW

The theory can also be illustrated by examining administrative litigation in China. China adopted an Administrative Litigation Law (ALL) in 1989, replacing a transitional regime first adopted in 1982 (Pei 1997; Wang 1998; see Landry, Chapter 8). Prior to the passage of this law, citizens' rights of appeal against illegal administrative acts were extremely limited, despite the presence of constitutional guarantees providing for such rights. The new law expanded appeals both within the administration and to the judiciary. This law has been used to generate thousands of administrative complaints for the courts. China's citizens have made use of the system with increasing frequency, with rates increasing more than 20 percent a year throughout the 1990s, though analysts note that the law did not extend to cover rulemaking activities nor, of course, to decisions of the Communist Party. Still, this rate of litigation growth outpaced economic disputing even in the red-hot economy (Clarke, Murrell, and Whiting 2006: 14, 41).

The caseload seems to now be stable at roughly 100,000 cases per year, with a typical "success rate" for plaintiffs of around 15–20 percent (Mahboubi 2005: 4). Virtually every government office has been subject to some suit, save the State Council itself. In addition, accompanying the new procedural mechanisms have been institutional reforms to support the shift toward the

courts. Each judicial district now has a division for administrative cases, and
government offices have established offices for monitoring compliance with
the new legal framework (Mahboubi 2005: 2).

Why did China formalize administrative procedures and facilitate review
by courts? Unlike countries in Eastern Europe, China did not experience
a change in political structure during the 1980s, as the Communist Party
remained the sole legitimate political party. However, the available modalities
of controlling agents changed. In particular, with the ascent of Deng Xiaoping,
China ended a period where ideology was the primary mechanism for internal
control of agents. Indeed, many of the decision makers in the early Deng era
had themselves been victims of ideological zealousness in the Cultural Revolution, and quite self-consciously sought to provide a sounder institutional
basis for governance. China's ideological drift is well documented, and continues to be reflected in euphemisms, such as the "Three Represents," that
help provide an increasingly thin "socialist" ideological cover for a market
economy with a large state sector.

The decline of ideology paralleled an increased reliance on decentralization
and deregulation, which reduced the possibility of direct hierarchical control
and increased the discretion of lower officials (Shirk 1993; Wang 1998:253–
58; but see Tsui and Wang 2004). Local networks of entrepreneurs and party
officials collaborated to enhance local economies. In doing so, however, they
undermined the party hierarchy that might have otherwise served as an effective means of controlling bureaucratic agents.

Regulatory complexity is also a background factor. As China's market economy developed, the traditional mechanisms of command and control over
the economy were less available. A market economy requires a regulatory
approach, which in turn depends on complex flows of information between
government and the governed. The limited ability of any party structure, even
one as elaborate as the Chinese Communist Party, to internalize all the expertise required seems to necessitate enhanced delegation.

We have observed, therefore, a shift toward external forms of monitoring
(as well as intensification of the internal forms of party control described earlier.) Multiple monitoring strategies are necessary in an environment wherein
agency costs are rampant. The regime relies on a mix of second- and third-party
monitoring, reflecting not only the long-term time horizon of the Communist
Party but also its increasing need for monitoring mechanisms. Formalizing
appeals can be seen as a device to empower citizens to monitor misbehav-
ior by the Communist Party's agents in the government. Some third-party
monitoring is acceptable because courts are not yet independent of Communist Party influence in administrative matters. Consistent with the theory, it

is generally understood that administrative law in China is used to constrain low officials but not high officials (Jiang 1998). Predictably for a one-party state, there has not been any move to formalize public participation in the rulemaking process.

Scholarly analysis of the Administrative Litigation Law (ALL) ranges from quite optimistic to more pessimistic about its real impact (Lubman 1999; Mahboubi 2005). In my view, there is at least some evidence that the availability of these mechanisms has resulted in particular agencies modifying their behavior. Creative lawyers who are bent on using the administrative litigation regime to constrain the state have been able to do so. In part this is because of the open nature of the legal process, and the availability of procedural mechanisms to any member of the public with standing. In addition, the possibility of shifting the burden of proof under the Administrative Litigation Law means that activists can impose costs on the state.

Furthermore, a sophisticated understanding of the role of law in social change would acknowledge that the impact of the law is not to be found merely in success rates. O'Brien and Li (2006), in their recent account of "rightful resistance" in China, emphasize how administrative litigation is one among many channels used by citizens to raise awareness of abusive policies.[4] Even if unsuccessful in court, administrative litigation can raise attention in the media and help generate internal pressures in the government for policy change. Beyond its impact on policies, the use of administrative litigation as a form of "rightful resistance" has led many "to reconsider their relationship to authority, while posing new questions, encouraging innovative tactics, and spurring thoughts about political change" (O'Brien and Li, 2006: 103).

In one example, a group of law professors from Sichuan used the administrative litigation process to bring attention to an issue of great concern to them, gender discrimination in employment (He 2006). There is no general law prohibiting gender discrimination in China, and private advertisements in the labor market frequently make references to gender, age, physical appearance, and height. The law professors sought to change the norms regarding discrimination in China. Unable to sue private employers, they sued a state agency for gender discrimination, based on a provision of the Chinese Constitution.

As any lawyer in China knows, the Chinese Constitution is not judicially enforceable. There was thus little chance for the lawsuit to succeed, and it

---

4 Rightful resistance is defined as "a form of popular contention that operates near the boundary of authorized channels, employs the rhetoric and commitments of the powerful to curb the exercise of power, hinges on locating and exploiting divisions within the state, and relies on mobilizing support from the wider public."

failed on the merits. However, the lawsuit was successful in changing internal policy at the Central Bank of China, the agency that was sued. The law professors had combined the lawsuit with an extensive strategy of media awareness and public education. This is one of many examples in which sophisticated social activists use the courts to try to influence norms, independent of the particular details of the case at hand. Other examples of impact litigation have included the attempt by lawyers to have the National People's Congress (NPC) repeal the system of "custody and repatriation," following the death of a young man in police administrative detention (Hand 2006). Though not filed under the ALL, the suit challenged administrative regulations as exceeding limits on power specified in the Chinese Constitution. While the NPC did not provide the legal relief desired (in part for fear of setting a precedent for constitutional litigation), the system was reformed in response to the challenge.

The Chinese Communist Party did not adopt the Administrative Litigation Law to undermine its own power. Instead, it did so to extend its power and legitimacy. The party gains control over potentially wayward bureaucrats but also gives up some control over the direction of social and economic change in the society. It seems to have found the bargain a successful one. This is all the more remarkable given that the Chinese Communist Party has a long-term horizon and is quite disciplined. But the unique problems of scale and complexity of governance in post-Mao China, and the distrust of ideological solutions, have rendered administrative law quite attractive and perhaps necessary. At the same time, the hierarchy solution continues to be utilized, as China seeks to reform the system of civil service recruitment and control[5] and promote internal review of decisions within the bureaucracy.[6]

What if administrative procedures regime become costly relative to other mechanisms of control? Administrative procedures regimes do have a built-in mechanism for disuse – namely tighter control over courts. Should courts become too activist in challenging core interests of the regime, politicians can shift to greater reliance on hierarchical mechanisms by simply rationing the supply of administrative relief available through courts. This process is easier for regimes that are not democratic, but it can also occur in countries such as the United States (McNollgast 1999). Politicians can change the structure of review or influence judicial selection to ensure more favorable outcomes. In such circumstances the extent of formal proceduralization may not capture

---

[5] A new law took effect in January 2006. *China Embarks on Civil Service Reforms*, CHINA DAILY, accessed Sept. 23, 2003 from http://www.chinadaily.com.cn/en/doc/2003-09/23/content_266501.htm.

[6] The 1999 Administrative Review Law details procedures for this form of review (Ohnesorge 2007).

actual incentives to litigate, which depend on the practical ability of courts to provide effective relief.

It is probable, of course, that principal-agent problems are more severe in a democracy than in a dictatorship because civil servants in democracies have certain rights preventing arbitrary dismissal. Democracies also tend to proscribe the use of violence in punishing malfeasance, so the relative costs of using coercion are higher. In other words, the relative price of a coercive substitute for administrative law may be lower under dictatorship than under democracy, so administrative law is likely to become more attractive with democratization. However, there is a corollary defect in terms of information generation. The usual problems of obtaining high-quality information on which to base governmental decisions are more severe when government agents themselves are afraid of the consequences of revealing information. Authoritarian systems of a more totalitarian bent may find that governing by terror means governing in the complete absence of information (as recent accounts of the Khmer Rouge regime seem to illustrate, for example.) More mild authoritarians need to provide incentives to produce good information for policy decisions, and an administrative litigation regime can complement other such incentives.

CONCLUSION

The approach taken in this chapter and volume more generally is consistent with treating courts as simply one alternative mechanism for governance (Rubin 2002; Shapiro 1964: 6). Courts have particular institutional features that affect the relative desirability of using them for the core governance task of monitoring officials and reducing agency costs. I conclude with a few remarks concerning these institutional qualities.

First, courts are *reactive*. Whereas auditors, designated monitors, and internal affairs boards can take an active role in seeking out instances of malfeasance, courts rely in their very institutional design on a quasi-adversarial process that is initiated from outside the government. Doing so enhances the courts' ability to draw in information that would otherwise be unavailable to the governance system broadly conceived – no official would voluntarily report his or her own exercises of slack.

Reactiveness requires a procedural structure to encourage "good" lawsuits that advance the goal of the regime and to discourage "bad" ones. The nature of law requires that this procedural structure be stated in *general* terms, and this is a second institutional quality that deserves mention. Generality means that regime opponents, or even constructive critics, have access to pursue strategies through the courts. We should thus anticipate the creative use of the litigation scheme by some who have different policy goals from those of the regime (O'Brien and Li 2006).

The dynamics of how this plays out vary. Sometimes, the administrative litigation scheme can become an effective arena of political contestation. However, the regime may also seek to tighten control over the courts to inhibit them from becoming a major locus of social and political change. Authoritarian governments, even more than democracies, have many tools for "Guarding the Guardians" (Shapiro 1988).

Regardless of the result of these dynamics of interaction among multiple agents, administrative litigation and procedural rules will tend to constrain the government, even if regime opponents are not successful in their particular lawsuits. Bureaucracies will become more "rationalized" in response to the threat of exposure of errors; they will seek to enhance their obedience to legality and their internal procedures.

In conclusion, it is clear that the decision by an authoritarian regime to utilize administrative law can be a rational one and need hardly be at odds with other regime goals. Indeed, by enhancing legality, the authoritarian regime can more effectively implement policy goals through state agents. However, the choice has significant consequences, namely the judicialization of governance, with all the issues that raises.

3

Singapore: The Exception That Proves Rules Matter

Gordon Silverstein

"The foundations for our financial center were the rule of law, an independent judiciary, and a stable, competent, and honest government that pursued sound macroeconomic policies."

–Lee Kuan Yew (2000: 73)

Unlike many authoritarian systems, the Republic of Singapore holds regular elections; Western media circulates widely; the Internet has deep penetration; and even Lee Kuan Yew – Singapore's paramount leader, who served as prime minister for more than 30 years – insists that adherence to the rule of law and a scrupulous, efficient, consistent judicial system are and have been essential to Singapore's spectacular growth and development. An island without adequate fresh water to serve its population, Singapore has risen to be a robust international commercial center that consistently outranks rivals ranging from Hong Kong and Japan to its own former colonial master, Great Britain, and, even in some years, the United States itself on measures of international competitiveness, economic vitality,[1] and its efficient, effective, and

---

[1] In 2000, 2002, and 2004, Singapore led the world in GDP growth, with the United Kingdom coming in third and the United States fourth (the United States rose to second in 2004); Singapore also led the world in 2003, 2004, 2005, and 2006 with an unemployment rate ranging from 4% (in 2003) to 2.9% (in 2006). Singapore's infant mortality rate also was the lowest in the world in 2000, 2001, and 2002, whereas the United Kingdom finished fifth and the United States sixth. On measures of competitiveness, Singapore has been ranked as one of the world's two most competitive economies by the World Economic Forum (WEF) in Davos, Switzerland, in each of the WEF's rankings from 1996 through 2000. In 2005, the Swiss Institute for Management Development ranked Singapore third in the world for competitiveness, behind the United States and Hong Kong. though the WEF in Davos had Singapore down a bit, falling to sixth in the world, while the United States climbed to number two. Nevertheless, Singapore continued to rank far ahead of Japan (at 12) the United Kingdom

reliable judicial system.[2] And yet, unlike so many other authoritarian systems, Singapore has avoided the pitfalls of judicialization that arise in so many other states considered in this volume. Singapore seems to offer glimmering, shimmering proof that a government can construct a rule-of-law system sufficient to satisfy the demands of a global economy and maintain domestic support in regular elections for more than forty years without being forced to tolerate the tradeoff of uncontrolled, independent judicial power, or significant political opposition.

Unraveling four apparent puzzles about Singapore will help us understand why, despite the fact that Singapore is in some ways an anomalous exception – a city-state-nation of just 4.5 million inhabitants, with a land mass of just 692 square kilometers – it is an exception that proves that, when it comes to the rule of law and judicialization, rules matter. Singapore forces us to recognize the error so many Western politicians, pundits, and academics make in conflating liberal democracy – and its maximization of individual liberty – with the rule of law. The rule of law may be a necessary precondition for liberal democracy, but liberal democracy is not necessarily the product of the rule of law.

The four puzzles, briefly stated are these:

1) With an explicit due process clause in the Singapore Constitution, clear court precedent, and your own judges ordering the government to stand down in a sensitive national security case, can you terminate the application and exercise of judicial review, without undermining your claims to adhere to the rule of law? Without paying a price in terms of international investor confidence? You can if you follow the rules.

2) Can you collapse the wall between the legislature (and executive) on one side and the judiciary on the other, and build a judicial system with very little if any insulation from the executive and legislative branch without undermining

---

(at 13), Germany (at 15), France (at 30), and China (at 49). See the tables in the Appendix, as well as World Bank (2006).

[2] The Davos-based World Economic Forum rankings, for example, include a measure of "the soundness of legal and social institutions that lay the foundation for supporting a modern, competitive market economy, *including the Rule of Law and protection of property rights*" (WEF 1997 Annual Report). Singapore's legal system actually ranked first in the Institute for Management Development 1997 list, a measure of the degree to which a country's legal system was detrimental to that country's economic competitiveness. By contrast the United States ranked 31st in that category in the same year. The same survey saw Singapore ranked six notches above the United States in response to a survey question asking if respondents had full "confidence in the fair administration of justice in the society." And Singapore's leading newspaper was proud to disclose that a 1998 survey of 400 American senior executives working in Singapore (conducted by the Political and Economic Risk Consultancy of Hong Kong) revealed that Americans themselves believed that "Singapore's judiciary and police force [are] better than those in the United States" and that the Singapore justice system "is better than that in their own country" (*Straits Times*, Sept 14, 1998).

your claims to adhere to the rule of law? Without paying a price in terms of international investor confidence? You can if you follow the rules.

3) Can you use your highly regarded, widely respected judicial system and civil law to shape international perceptions about your country through civil suits for defamation and libel combined with strict controls not on what foreign media write or say, but rather on their access to your market – all without undermining your claims to adhere to the rule of law? Without paying a price in terms of international investor confidence? You can if you follow the rules.

4) Can you use your highly regarded, widely respected judicial system and civil law, combined with strict campaign rules and parliamentary qualifications, to stifle dissent and undermine the growth and entrenchment of domestic political opposition parties and political opposition leaders without undermining your claims to adhere to the rule of law? Without paying a price in terms of international investor confidence? You can if you follow the rules.

UNPACKING THE RULE OF LAW

These puzzles force us to grapple with often unspoken assumptions about the rule of law. Singapore's leaders understand the critical importance of maintaining a judicial system that is efficient, effective, consistent, and reliable, one where laws are general, where they are known and generally available, where they are not retroactive but clear and consistent, and where laws are plausible, embodying requirements that can be accomplished and have some lasting power, and where officials have to abide by the rules they pass. These are, in fact, the eight criteria legal scholar Lon Fuller articulated in 1964 as the baseline requirements of the rule of law (Fuller 1964).

Fuller's conditions certainly had no specific national or cultural boundaries, but as Judith Shklar argues, "One may guess that he had not thought very deeply about any polity other than the United States" (Shklar 1987: 13). Fuller argued that these eight conditions knit together to form an "inner morality" to the law. And while he made no claim that these conditions, having been met, would inevitably lead to an Anglo-American system of limited government and guarantees for individual rights, there was an unspoken assumption that once in place, these conditions would knit together and that the inner morality of the law would take on something of a life of its own. But there is no clear reason why these conditions would necessarily or even likely lead to that result. These conditions, combined with a particular set of normative commitments and social conditions, might well do so. But these conditions, the criteria of the rule of law as most lawyers have come to understand it, could as easily be satisfied in an authoritarian as in a liberal democratic state.

"In its many academic manifestations," Allan Hutchinson and Patrick Monahan write, the rule of law "has been connected, to greater and lesser extents, to an individualistic theory of political justice and jurisprudence. Ostensibly, there have been two versions of the rule of law, but they both represent a commitment to liberalism; it is simply that one tends to be more explicit and marked than the other" (Hutchinson and Monahan 1987: 100). Joseph Raz supports this realistic view, noting that "[a] non-democratic legal system, based on the denial of human rights, of extensive poverty, on racial segregation, sexual inequalities, and religious persecution may, in principle, conform to the requirements of the rule of law better than any of the legal systems of the more enlightened Western democracies" (Raz 1979: 211). "In itself," Judith Shklar writes, "Fuller's inwardly moral law not only may, but has been, perfectly compatible with governments of the most repressive and irrational sort. The very formal rationality of a civil law system can legitimize a persecutive war-state among those officials who are charged with maintaining the private law and its clients" (Shklar 1987: 13).

This is not to say that the rule of law, even in this stripped-down, or "thin" formulation, is not important.[3] It very well may facilitate a move to a thicker, more rights-laden rule of law with a more robust separation of powers. But Singapore provides a brisk reminder that one *can* have a thin rule of law, build a stable and prosperous nation on a robust economy, and never veer too close to a full-blown Lockean-liberal system with firm limits on government governed by a strict separation of powers *a la* Montesquieu.

SINGAPORE AND THE RULE OF LAW

On August 9, 1965, the people of the island of Singapore were asked to remove themselves from the Federation of Malaysia. This request came from the

---

[3] The meaning of "thick" and "thin" in discussions of the rule of law is, unfortunately, highly confused. In its first incarnation, these terms were used as they are used here – a thin rule of law is one in which the basic principles Fuller articulated are present but, unlike Fuller (and more like Hart 1961), these rules are both the beginning and the end of the matter. A "thick" conception suggests far more is wrapped in with these basic assumptions – Fuller's inner morality of law, for example, or normative assumptions such as those advocated by writers such as Ronald Dworkin. Peerenboom (2004b: 2) nicely summarizes this distinction. Alan Hutchinson and Patrick Monahan (1987: 100–102) discuss this distinction as well. Conversely, and more recently, Tushnet (1999) and Graber (2001) refer to a "thick" and "thin" constitution – where the thin constitution suggests the powerful strands of fundamental commitments tracing back to the Declaration that animate and undergird the Constitution, whereas the "thick" constitution refers to the complex and specific rules and requirements of the document (how a bill becomes a law; how old one has to be to run for president).

Malaysian government, fearful that Singapore's dominant ethnic Chinese population along with the city-state's economic advantages as an international trading port would allow the tiny island to be the tail that wags the dog. With virtually no natural resources – just 1.4 percent of Singapore's 692 square kilometers of land is arable,[4] and to this day Singapore has to import much of its drinking water – Singapore had to build an outward-looking economy and engage in globalization long before the word was invented. "We inherited the island without its hinterland, a heart without a body," said Singapore's preeminent leader, Lee Kuan Yew (Lee 2000: 1). Singapore, in fact, had but two vital resources – one of the world's greatest natural seaports and a strategic location bestride some of the world's most important shipping lanes. From those humble beginnings, the Republic of Singapore rose "from third world to first,"[5] becoming a leading manufacturing, transportation, shipping, and financial services center in the global economy of the early twenty-first century. "In 1965," Lee Kuan Yew noted in one interview, "Singapore ranked economically with Chile, Argentina and Mexico," but by 1997, the city-state's per capita GNP placed it among the top eight nations in the world (Zakaria 1994).

Lee Kuan Yew is not alone in believing that the rule of law plays an essential role in Singapore's ability to attract foreign capital and to maintain the confidence of foreign investors who are essential to Singapore's prosperity and economic growth. As Singapore's then-Chief Justice, Yong Pung How noted,

> Singapore is a nation which is based wholly on the Rule of Law. It is clear and practical laws and the effective observance and enforcement of these laws which provide the foundation for our economic and social development. It is the certainty which an environment based on the Rule of Law guarantees which gives our people, as well as many [multinational corporations] and other foreign investors, the confidence to invest in our physical, industrial as well as social infrastructure (Thio 2002: 29).

Indeed, international corporations and investors seem to have confirmed this over and over again (see the Appendix). But Singapore's rule of law is not quite the individualistic, liberty-maximizing democracy most in the West conjure when they hear that term.

---

[4] See https://www.cia.gov/cia/publications.
[5] This is the subtitle of Lee Kuan Yew's book, *From Third World to First: The Singapore Story, 1965–2000.* (Lee 2000).

Puzzle 1 . . . De-Linking Globalization and Judicialization

Singapore has a long-established, written constitution. It has regular and transparent elections, in which opposition candidates often run and even, on occasion, win a couple of seats in Parliament. (Since 1968, when Lee's People's Action Party [PAP]) swept every seat in Parliament, opposition candidates have held between one and four seats in Parliament.[6]) And, as did many of the countries analyzed in this volume, Singapore experienced a burst of judicial power, despite huge cultural, social, educational, institutional, and political pressures. But unlike so many others, Singapore was able to stop this cold, and all without violating the basic requirements of the rule of law – all well within the rules, written in the constitution and enforced in the courts. And all without jeopardizing Singapore's reliability and dependability among international investors and corporate decision makers.

Singapore has a well-paid, well-educated judiciary to interpret and enforce its constitution, a constitution that explicitly incorporates British common law.[7] In fact, until 1989 the Judicial Committee of Her Britannic Majesty's Privy Council served as Singapore's final court of appeal. And Singapore's Constitution explicitly guarantees fundamental individual rights, including due process: "No person shall be deprived of his life or personal liberty save in accordance with law" (Singapore Constitution, Part IV, Article 9).[8] But, when the Singapore judiciary *did* move to expand individual rights under that due process clause, ruling against the government on an internal security case and in favor of a broad reading of fundamental individual rights,[9] the government – strictly and precisely following the provisions of Singapore's Constitution to

---

[6] The greatest threat to the dominance of the People's Action Party (PAP) came in a general election in 1991 when four opposition candidates were elected, and the PAP's share of the vote tumbled to 61%. But they recovered two of those seats in the 1997 election, and – rebounded in the shadow of terrorism threats in 2001 to a more robust 75.3%.

[7] High Court Judges are paid about US$630,000 a year, and receive a luxury government car along with access to far-below market-rate luxury accommodations in a government house. The Chief Justice receives about US$1 million a year along with a government-provided residence, chauffeur-driven car, and other perks. As Francis Seow notes, Singapore's Chief Justice "receives more than the combined stipends of the Lord Chancellor of England, the Chief Justices of the United States, Canada and Australia" (Seow 1997b).

[8] Part IV, Article 11 bans *ex post facto* laws; and Part IV, Article 12 guarantees that "all persons are equal before the law and entitled to the equal protection of the law." Other articles provide for freedom of speech, assembly and association (subject to legal restrictions Parliament "considers necessary or expedient in the interest of the security of Singapore," and those that "provide against contempt of court, defamation or incitement to any offense" (Singapore Constitution, Part IV, Art 14) and the freedom to "profess and practice" one's religion among others.

[9] *Chng Suan Tze* 1998; developing doctrine outlined in *Lee Mau Seng* 1971 and *Ong Ah Chuan* 1980–81.

the letter – was able to terminate judicial review, and eliminate the Privy Council as a court of final review, and all without any cost to the economic system or Singapore's standing in the international investment community.[10]

Four dissidents were arrested and detained without trial in December 1988, for what the government said was their role in a Marxist plot to undermine the government. Chng Suan Tze asked the Singapore Court of Appeal to order their release, arguing that the government had not followed the rules set out in the Internal Security Act (ISA) – a law left over from the British colonial era. And, shockingly, the court agreed. "All power has legal limits and the Rule of Law demands that the courts should be able to examine the exercise of discretionary power," the court ruled, concluding that "the notion of a subjective or unfettered [government] discretion is contrary to the Rule of Law" (*Chng Suan Tze* 1988).

But the court then went beyond the case itself, building its argument on a foundation that combined its own case law with long-standing interpretations of British common law as well as precedent set by the Judicial Committee of the Privy Council in London (which then continued to serve as the final court of review for Singapore). The Singapore court held that judicial review could and should be triggered when the government exercised illegal, irrational, or procedurally improper power, insisting that government action that is arbitrary or irrational must be considered *ultra vires* – an act beyond law and therefore, by definition, an act in violation of Singapore's written constitution (*Chng Suan Tze* 1988). This sort of substantive due process argument is quite familiar to any student of American constitutional law, of course. Once unleashed in the United States, substantive due process became the foundation on which a wide array of fundamental rights were built, ranging from property and economic rights in the era before the New Deal to rights of personal autonomy in the Warren Court era and beyond.

Here the Singapore court turned to precedent laid down by the Privy Council in *Ong Ah Chuan v. Public Prosecutor*, a drug case from 1980, in which the Privy Council ruled that the presumption of innocence "is a fundamental human right protected by the [Singapore] Constitution and cannot be limited or diminished by any Act of Parliament" other than a full-scale constitutional amendment. "Although nowhere expressly referred to in the Constitution," the Privy Council held that the presumption of innocence is "imported into" Singapore's Constitution through that document's due process and equal protection clauses (*Ong Ah Chuan* 1980). "References to 'law' in such contexts as 'in accordance with law,' 'equality before the law,' 'protection of the law'

---

[10] This section is more fully developed in Silverstein (2003).

and the like," the judges wrote, "refer to a system of law which incorporates those fundamental rules of natural justice that had formed part and parcel of the common law of England that was in operation in Singapore at the commencement of the Constitution."

Much like *Marbury v. Madison*, however, the judges wrapped their assertion of strong judicial review in a tolerable package – *Ong Ah Chuan* asserted the power of judicial review and the foundation for substantive due process, but did so in a case that actually found in favor of the government. *Ong Ah Chuan* asserted judicial power, but found that the government had not, in fact, violated the fundamental rights that the court had discovered in the constitution. But, like *Marbury*, the assertion of judicial review would now seemingly be available should a future court choose to build upon this foundation. And indeed, that is precisely what the court tried. Ruling against the assertion of broad discretion under the Internal Security Act in *Chng Suan Tze*, the Singapore Court of Appeal held that "giving the executive arbitrary powers of detention" would be "unconstitutional and void" under the precedent set by *Ong Ah Chuan*. "In our view," the Singapore Justices concluded,

> The notion of a subjective or unfettered discretion is contrary to the rule of law. All power has legal limits and the rule of law demands that the courts should be able to examine the exercise of discretionary power. If therefore the executive in exercising its discretion under an Act of Parliament has exceeded the four corners within which Parliament has decided it can exercise its discretion, such an exercise of discretion would be *ultra vires* the Act and a court of law must be able to hold it to be so (*Chng Suan Tze* 1988).

The judges in Singapore seemed ready to follow a familiar pattern of judicial empowerment. But in this case, the ruling was no longer wrapped in a pleasing package; instead it directly challenged the government in a most sensitive area – national security. The court ordered the prisoners released. And the government complied, driving the prisoners through the gates of the Whitley Road jail, and down the street where the prisoners got out of the car. But another car pulled up immediately, the prisoners were arrested again, and returned to prison. But unlike the last time, the government now followed the statutory procedure with precision, securing the formal authority that was required (Seow 1994).

This was not, however, the end of the story. Far from the start of a storied growth of judicial power, the national security case spurred the government into action. Not against the judges, nor against dissidents. It spurred the government to move in Parliament a bill to amend the constitution. No longer would the constitution leave room for judges to assert their authority to exercise this sort of judicial review. Further, the government amended the constitution to roll back the law to the doctrine that was in place before the court's recent ruling.[11] In addition, the constitution was also amended to foreclose appeals under the Internal Security Act, which ended the use of the Privy Council in security cases.[12]

Constitutional amendment is, of course, a perfectly viable option for most constitutional democracies displeased with court rulings. In the United States, the Sixteenth Amendment, providing for a progressive income tax, was passed explicitly to reverse the Supreme Court's ruling in *Pollock v. Farmers Loan & Trust Co.*, whereas the Thirteenth and Fourteenth Amendments reversed the Court's decision in the infamous *Dred Scott v. Sandford*. Constitutional amendment is a very difficult process for Americans unhappy with Court rulings. In Singapore it is not. Constitutional amendment in Singapore requires only the support of a super-majority in Parliament (two-thirds of the Parliament). And since, in 1989, the People's Action Party held 80 of the 81 seats, the amendment was quite easily passed. The basic premise is the same in the United States and Singapore, and the European Union, for that matter – court rulings are ultimately subject to constitutional amendment (or, in the European case, treaty revision). But American judges have a great deal of space and time in which to work before their rulings are likely to trigger the sort of political will needed to counter them with amendment. European judges may have the greatest constitutional space of all, since an amendment there requires unanimous consent of the sovereign Members of the European Union and ratification of a new treaty. Singapore's judges, by contrast, have very little constitutional space in which to work.

Little wonder then that the Singapore government has become somewhat enamored of the option of constitutional amendment as a means of responding to any hint of an aggressive judiciary. A Nominated Member of Parliament[13] once suggested that though the government is able to amend the constitution, and though such amendments certainly can make government more efficient, it is not a wise policy. If the court has acted within its powers, Simon S.C. Tay suggested, "this House should recognize this is the constitutional

---

11 Restoring the far more deferential standard the court had articulated in a 1971 case called *Lee Mau Seng v. Minister for Home Affairs*.

12 Later in the year, additional constitutional amendments were adopted that narrowly circumscribed appeals to the Privy Council. The few paths that remained to Privy Council appeal were eliminated in 1993 when Singapore established its own Court of Appeal (Lee 1999: 51–52).

13 Singapore has a number of Nominated Members of Parliament. They have highly limited voting rights, and are named by the dominant political party to represent alternative views in a body where there is virtually no elected opposition (see below).

scheme of things and give serious pause before overriding that decision by amendment of new laws and limiting judicial review."[14] Tay's has not been, however, the dominant view.

The Singapore experience suggests serious flaws with the assumptions of Western policymakers that the rule of law somehow will trigger the development of an independent court willing and able to build the economic rights and rulings essential to globalization into individual, domestic liberties, and face the governing regime with the stark choice of all (economic opportunity driven by international investment combined with the slow, but steady expansion of individual liberties) or nothing (strict limits on individual liberties at the cost of the benefits of globalization). Singapore untied the knot – by following the rules. By maintaining Fuller's eight formal criteria for the rule of law, Singapore made clear to investors that what they valued was safe and protected, and that their investments were secure. The swift constitutional revisions including the termination of appeals to the Privy Council sparked no capital flight. No corporations denounced Singapore for jeopardizing the rule of law, or undermining the foundation for investment, intellectual property rights, or the obligation of contracts. In one 1997 survey, Singapore's legal system was ranked first in the world in a measure of the degree to which a country's legal system was seen as least detrimental to its economic competitiveness.[15] And Singapore also outpaced the United States in the same survey on the question of whether people had "confidence in the fair administration of justice in the society." A year later, Singapore's *Straits Times* reported a survey in which American executives in Singapore indicated that they felt that "Singapore's judiciary and police force [are] better than those in the United States" and that the Singapore justice system "is better than that in their own country" (Tan 1998).[16]

Of course, these surveys are focused on competitiveness, on the impact of various factors on a country's economic standing. One survey, from the World Economic Forum in Davos, focuses on contract enforcement, and the ability of private firms to "file lawsuits at independent and impartial courts" if there is "a breach of trust on the part of the government." But these are precisely the aspects of the rule of law that are vital to attracting and holding international financial investment.

---

[14] Simon S.C. Tay, Nominated Member of Parliament, *Parliamentary Debates of Singapore: Official Report*, January 14, 1998, column 93.

[15] World Economic Forum's 1997 Annual Report (emphasis added).

[16] The newspaper was reporting on a survey conducted by the Political and Economic Risk Consultancy of Hong Kong.

Lee Kuan Yew told Parliament in 1995 that when the government is taken to court by a private individual, "the court must adjudicate upon the issues strictly on their merits and in accordance with the law. To have it otherwise is to lose . . . our standing and . . . our status as an investment and financial centre. The interpretation of documents, of contracts in accordance with the law is crucial. Our reputation for the rule of law has been and is a valuable economic asset, part of our capital, although an intangible one" (*Singapore Parliamentary Debates*, Nov. 2, 1995: col. 236). The rule of law is among other things the law of rules, and Singapore follows the rules.

Was there an economic price to be paid for this wrench in the globalization machine? Not at all. No corporations fled the country. Singapore's competitiveness rankings held strong and capital continued to flow in. Singapore therefore presents countries like China with the possibility of an alternative model: while economic reform and prosperity demand the rule of law, the rule of law does not necessarily mean that judicialization – and the expansion of individual rights – necessarily will follow. It is possible to de-link economic and political/social reform (Silverstein 2003).

Puzzle 2 . . . De-Linking Separation of Powers and the Rule of Law

The court that ruled against the government in *Chng Suan Tze* certainly should not have been surprised that the government would not meekly accede to a judicial order, particularly in a sensitive area such as national security. In fact, Singapore's legal judicial community had been sent a very clear message about what might happen to judges whose rulings were not finding favor with the government just months before the ISA ruling. Senior District Judge Michael Khoo acquitted one of the only opposition Members of Parliament (J.B. Jeyaretnam) on two charges involving the alleged misappropriation of contributions to his political party – the Workers' Party – and convicted him on a third, lesser charge, imposing a fine that fell below the statutorily significant threshold of S$2000. The amount of the fine "was crucial because, under Singapore law, a member of Parliament who has been convicted of a criminal offense and fined more than S$2000 is automatically disqualified from parliament" and barred from running for office for five years (thus guaranteeing that he could not run in the next parliamentary election, since elections are required to be held no more than five years apart (Lydgate 2003: 119).

Under Singapore law, prosecutors are allowed to appeal district court rulings. And while the appeal was pending, coincidentally (as the government would insist) or as direct retaliation for failing to impose a sufficiently high penalty on Jeyaretnam (as opponents concluded), Senior District Court Judge

Michael Khoo was transferred to a far less prestigious post as a prosecutor in the Attorney General's Office. "Judges in Khoo's position were usually promoted to the High court, or at least to more senior posts. But Khoo was made a prosecutor and [was] replaced by a man two [civil service] grades below him" (Lydgate 2003: 122). The sudden transfer certainly looked suspicious, and the government was quick to appoint a review panel that concluded that the transfer was perfectly proper, noting that transfers between the Attorney General's office and the Bench (and back again) were far from unusual at the lower levels of the judiciary. Lower court judges do not have tenure, and do tend to move between the courts and public service. In fact, lower court judges are "part of the executive branch of government," and "district court judges are routinely shuffled between the executive and judicial branches" (Thio 2002a: 22). Serving as a district court judge or magistrate "is simply one of a number of postings for officers within the Singapore Legal Service" (Worthington 2001: 496).

Khoo's case was an extreme reminder that the hard lines between the judicial and legislative branches that are the norm in Britain and the United States are not at all the norm in Singapore, and yet, Singapore maintains a formal constitutional guarantee of an independent judiciary. The Singapore Constitution, for example, clearly provides for a separate and independent judiciary, with Supreme Court judges guaranteed that their office cannot be abolished; they are guaranteed tenure in office until the age of sixty-five. But judges can be hired on a contract basis after age sixty-five. Chief Justice Yong Pung How, who retired in April, 2006, reached that personal milestone in 1991, and remained Chief Justice under sequential three-year contracts for fifteen more years. The new Chief Justice, Chan Sek Keong, was sixty-nine when he took over as Chief Justice in 2006 and will likely continue to work under three-year contracts.

And while Singapore's Supreme Court judges are protected by tenure in office once appointed, the Singapore Constitution also provides for the appointment of temporary judges to Singapore's top courts:

> In order to facilitate the disposal of business in the Supreme Court, the President, if he, acting in his discretion, concurs with the advice of the Prime Minister, may appoint a person qualified for appointment as a Judge of the Supreme Court to be a Judicial Commissioner of the Supreme Court in accordance with Article 95 for such period or periods as the President thinks fit; and a Judicial Commissioner so appointed may, in respect of such class or classes of cases as the Chief Justice may specify, exercise the powers and perform the functions of a Judge of the High Court. Anything done by a Judicial Commissioner when acting in accordance with the terms of his

appointment shall have the same validity and effect as if done by a Judge of that Court and, in respect thereof, he shall have the same powers and enjoy the same immunities as if he had been a Judge of that Court. (Singapore Constitution, Part VIII, Article 94).

The same powers and immunities, except for tenure in office, since the appointment's term is determined by the president. But despite the reversal in the ISA cases discussed above, and Judge Khoo's demotion, the Singapore courts have maintained a reputation for independence, even ruling (albeit rarely) in favor of individuals and against the government – an acquittal in an Official Secrets Act case in one example and, in another, a case of wrongful dismissal.[17] Li-Ann Thio notes that while in the realm of commercial law "efficiency, certainty and procedural fairness" are valued and observed, the high value placed on social order and "state stability" leads to "less attention given to civil liberties" with the rule of law strengthening state institutions and "marginalizing rights protections" (Thio 2004: 200–201, 209).

To understand why Singapore's judicial system so consistently ranks so highly, one needs to have a fuller picture of the courts. While Chief Justice Yong Pung How left legal practice to move into a business career long before his appointment to the Supreme Court, he did make "an exemplary contribution to the judiciary, not by way of legal expertise or by developing [the courts] as a constitutional bulwark against executive excess, but as chief executive officer of the courts through modernization and impressive gains in efficiency in support of a range of policies for developing Singapore's services sector" (Worthington 2001: 499) – areas that may be of far more central concern to the executives who are surveyed for rankings such as those by the *World Competitiveness Yearbook* (produced by the Institute for Management Development – IMD) or the World Competitiveness Report (from the World Economic Forum (WEF) – Davos) in which Singapore's judicial system consistently ranks among the top five in the world. In 1993, the *Straits Times* proudly announced that Singapore had moved from ninth to first place in the World Competitiveness Report, and in 1997, it noted that these reports focus on assessments of "several areas related to the quality of law," including the WEF's evaluation of "payment of bribes, tax evasion, reliability of contracts with a government; ability to rely on police for physical security and the extent to which business costs are raised by organized crime"

---

[17]   *Christopher Bridges v. Public Prosecutor*, 1 *Singapore Law Report* 406, (High Court, 1997) and
    Stansfield Business International v. Minister for Manpower 3 *Singapore Law Report* 742 (High Court, 1999).

(Tan 1997). In 1998 when Singapore was again ranked number one in the world for its legal system, the newspaper reported that "94 per cent of the respondents had full confidence in the administration of justice in Singapore" (Lim 1998).

Singapore has been able to develop an effective and efficient legal system that wins high praise from global business even as it is attacked by those concerned with the maximization of individual liberty. But Singapore clearly provides an object lesson that an authoritarian regime can gain the global benefits of a reputation for the strict enforcement of the rule of law without risking undue judicialization by following the rules explicitly. And while some measure of judicial independence is required, it would appear that the strict separation of powers is not. Singapore reminds us that the tendency in the West to conflate thick and thin versions of the rule of law, and to layer notions of separation of powers, limited government, democratic participation, and liberal norms onto the foundational requirements of the rule of law, or even the more limited rule by law of the *Rechtsstaat* is far from a foregone conclusion.[18]

Puzzle 3 . . . Law, Courts, and the Shape of International Opinion

A classic complaint about authoritarian governments and the courts is that they will avoid or ignore the courts when faced with direct threats to their regime, or even with perceived slights. Dissidents are rushed to jail without trial, reporters arrested and deported, newspapers closed down, and publications banned. But Singapore has another set of lessons for entrenched liberal democracies and soft-authoritarian republics alike – courts (and the rule of law) are effective tools not only to build and secure a stable economy but also as the method and means to shape international perceptions and formally, transparently, and within the rules, unsettle and unseat domestic political opposition. Singapore accomplished these objectives through a combination of strict statutes on the printing, publishing, and distribution of newspapers and magazines – tested and enforced by the courts – and a very strict application and interpretation (again, by the courts) of libel and defamation in civil suits.

---

[18] Randall Peerenboom (2004b: 47, ft nt 1) notes, "As with rule of law, *Rechtsstaat* has been interpreted in various ways. While some interpret it in more instrumental terms similar to rule of law, others would argue that the concept entails at minimum the principle of legality and a commitment on the part of the state to promote liberty and protect property rights, and thus some limits on the state. In any case, the concept *Rechtsstaat* has evolved over time in Europe to incorporate democracy and fundamental rights. Accordingly, it is often now used synonymously with (liberal democratic) rule of law."

Singapore's statutory tools to deal with the press began with a 1920 British law – the Printing Presses Ordinance – that required a license for anyone owning a printing press. This was supplemented in 1939, again by the British, with the additional requirement of a permit not just to own a press, but for printing and publishing a newspaper. Jumping ahead to the early 1970s, there was a flurry of activity in the Singapore journalistic community with the arrival of a new, independent, English-language paper, the *Singapore Herald*, funded by foreign investors. In his memoirs, Lee Kuan Yew makes clear his acute understanding of the power of the press: "A newspaper influences the politics of a country," Lee writes, and "I did not want a foreigner not rooted in Singapore to decide our political agenda." A year later, Lee ordered the cancellation of the *Herald's* printing license just hours before flying to Helsinki where he would explain his views of press freedom at a meeting of the International Press Institute (Lee 2000: 189–190). Saying that he "did not accept that newspaper owners had the right to print whatever they liked," Lee noted that unlike Singapore's government ministers, newspaper owners "and their journalists were not elected." He closed his speech by noting that "freedom of the press, freedom of the news media, must be subordinated to the overriding needs of Singapore, and to the primary purpose of an elected government" (Lee 2000: 190).

But on his return he didn't close any other newspapers, or have anyone arrested. Instead, he promulgated laws, openly, following the constitutional process carefully, to amend the Newspaper and Printing Presses Act (Chapter 206), which had replaced the earlier British laws. The new rules not only banned foreign ownership of local newspapers, they banned anyone from owning more than 3 percent of a newspaper company's shares, and created a two-tiered stock plan, with "managerial shares" assigned by the government to four local banks. These shares would have a voting power of 200-to-1 compared with ordinary shares in the hope that the bankers would be more likely to "remain politically neutral and protect stability and growth because of their business interests" (Lee 2000: 190).

This was not the last reform of the newspapers law. The early 1980s saw a significant growth in regional and global media, which discovered in Singapore a highly educated, mostly English-speaking audience with increasingly attractive economic demographics, not to mention an international trade and financial services hub. Newspapers such as the *International Herald Tribune* and the *Asian Wall Street Journal*, as well as magazines like the *Far Eastern Economic Review* (wholly owned by Dow Jones & Co) and *AsiaWeek* (wholly owned by Time-Life Inc.), were rapidly becoming genuine alternative news sources for Singaporeans who found the upbeat and relatively vapid coverage of the government-approved *Straits Times* less than satisfying.

The government could not, of course, so easily control these outlets. They could be banned – but that would be a blunt weapon that could backfire on Singapore, undermining its pitch to global multinationals and investors as a stable, open, and increasingly modern, First-World democracy. Instead, the government passed a new law that would allow the government to restrict circulation of any "newspaper published outside Singapore" that was "engaging in the domestic politics of Singapore." Not only that, but the law provided that the reproduction and distribution of "gazetted" newspapers (offending publications would be listed in the country's official *Gazette*) would be allowed, on a nonprofit basis, with all advertising stripped out. In effect this meant that offending publications *would* be allowed to be sold and read in Singapore, but only a very few copies. This meager circulation (which would be sufficient to provide copies to public libraries and government offices) would be further undercut by the printing of nonprofit versions of the publications that, the law clearly stated, "shall not constitute an infringement of copyright" (Newspaper and Printing Presses Act, Chapter 206, 25 (5)).

These provisions were used extensively from the late 1980s to great effect. The first "gazetted" publication – *Time* magazine – saw its circulation slashed from 18,000 to 9,000 and then to 2,000 after *Time's* editors refused to publish an unedited response from Prime Minister Lee to an article titled "Silencing the Dissenters" concerning Lee's political nemesis, J.B. Jeyaretnam (see below and Lydgate 2003). But the resistance crumbled. "Within a fortnight, *Time* magazine capitulated, and printed the reply in full, adding, by way of an exculpatory editorial footnote, that it did 'not agree with all the corrections cited … but prints this letter in the spirit of full discussion of issues'" (Seow 1998).

The next incident came in the midst of the *Time* struggle when the *Asian Wall Street Journal* (AWSJ) – edited and published in Hong Kong – ran an article on December 12, 1986, questioning the government's motives and objectives in setting up a new secondary securities market.[19] Stephen Duthie, the AWSJ's Singapore-based correspondent, quoted government critics suggesting that the government wanted to use the market to "unload state-controlled and government-backed companies." When a Singapore official wrote a thunderous denunciation, the *Journal* refused to print it, arguing that it constituted a personal attack and alleged errors the editors were "confident don't exist" (Seow 1998). This action led to the gazetting of the AWSJ, with circulation cut from 5,100 copies a day to just 400. The *Journal* challenged the law in Singapore's court – and lost.

[19]   SESDAQ (Stock Exchange of Singapore Dealing and Automated Quotation Market System).

The *Journal* argued that this law violated Singapore's constitutional guarantee of free speech. But Article 14 of the Singapore Constitution provides for freedom of speech for Singapore citizens, and not for foreign newspapers. The court was not impressed with the arguments for an indirect application of this provision (Singapore citizens as consumers of speech rather than providers). Appellants, the court ruled, "are trying to argue indirectly a point which they cannot argue directly, as article 14(1) does not guarantee freedom of speech and expression to them; they have no *locus standi* on this point" (*Dow Jones v. Attorney General* 1989).

Using the law to limit circulation allowed Lee to score significant points. The *AWSJ* offered "to distribute its journal free of charge to all paying subscribers" if Singapore lifted its circulation controls, telling the government that it was willing to "forego its sales revenue in the spirit of helping Singapore businessmen who had complained of lack of access to the journal," an offer Lee was willing to take up, provided the public-service-minded publisher was willing to leave out any advertisements. The government even "offered to defray one-half of the additional costs of removing the advertisements" but the *AWSJ* refused, leading Lee to note that the publisher was "not interested in the business community getting information," and arguing that this proved they simply wanted the "freedom to make money selling advertisements" (Lee 2000: 192–193).

By not banning the publications altogether, Singapore was able to exercise financial pressure on the magazines and newspapers while avoiding charges of direct censorship – the limited copies were, after all, readily and immediately available in all public libraries. This was the statutory route. The other route ran through the courts as well – but this time, through civil litigation.

Singapore's treatment of defamation is built on a British foundation, where the burden of proof lies more heavily with the accused than it does with the person alleging the defamation. One important variation in Singapore, however, is in how the law treats accusations of defamation against public figures in general, and political leaders in particular. In the Anglo-American tradition, public figures are presumed to have surrendered some measure of protection, and this is particularly true of elected political figures. But Singapore takes a very different view. The concept of proving actual malice in a case involving a public figure, Chief Justice Yong Pung How noted, is foreign to Singapore's legal tradition:

> Our law is not premised on the proposition that the limits of acceptable criticism of persons holding public office or politicians in respect of their official duties or conduct are wider than those of ordinary persons. Persons holding

public office or politicians are equally entitled to have their reputations protected as those of any other persons. Criticisms in relation to their official
conduct must respect the bounds set by the law of defamation. The publication of false and defamatory allegations, even in the absence of actual malice
on the part of the publisher, should not be allowed to pass with impunity
(*Jeyaretnam v. Lee Kuan Yew* 1992).

In a 1998 case, the court observed that "there is an equal public interest in
allowing those officials to execute their duties unfettered by false aspersions"
(*Goh Chok Tong v. JB Jeyaretnam*). The court here emphasized the critical
value of the "intangible qualities of good character, integrity and honesty," ruling that "the plaintiff's high standing could be a factor in raising the quantum
of damages awarded" (Thio 2002a: 72).

This strict liability standard, combined with sometimes stunning damage
awards running to S$2 million (US$1.45 million), has played out on two
fronts – the government's effective campaign to bring the foreign media to
heel (Puzzle 3) and its even more effective campaign to limit and constrain
political opposition in Singapore (Puzzle 4).

Singapore's leaders argue that it is vital to maintaining their image and
reputation. Not only is it essential to maintain domestic peace and confidence
but also to assure world investors of the stability and reliability of the state, its
leaders, and institutions. Thus, any attack on their integrity, on their reputation,
any aspersions cast on their rectitude, and suggestions of corruption or abuse
of power are an attack on the government as well as on the individuals who
lead that government. The traditional response to unflattering foreign press
coverage from authoritarian states is to arrest and imprison the offenders or, at
the least, to expel them and ban their publications. But Singapore is different.
Banning a publication typically only adds to its luster, and provides grist
for attacks on the government for blocking information and impeding free
speech. In Singapore, the government has been willing to tolerate critical
foreign press coverage, but responds instantly and with enormous litigation
efforts. Lee argues that it does so because the "voters have come to expect any
allegation of impropriety or dishonesty to be challenged in the courts" and
that they must be litigated because allegations of corruption or dishonesty are
potentially crippling "in a region where corruption, cronyism, and nepotism
are still a plague" (Lee 2000: 130–131).

The Newspapers Act has been amended a number of times, and the government has used statutory authority, actions for contempt of court, and civil
suits for defamation as powerful tools to bring the foreign media to heel. Suits
have produced sizable damages and abject, published apologies from some of

the Western media's most august institutions, including Dow Jones & Company, which apologized for articles in its *Asian Wall Street Journal* in 1985 and again in 1986 and 1989; it also apologized and withdrew articles in 1987 in the *Far Eastern Economic Review* (a Dow-Jones-owned publication). Dow Jones was not alone. In 1994, the *International Herald Tribune* – owned jointly by the *New York Times* and *Washington Post* – also apologized for published articles. Suits also produced withdrawals, apologies, and significant damages from the *Economist* magazine in 1993, 2004, and 2005; from Time Incorporated's *AsiaWeek* magazine in 1987 and 1995; from Time magazine itself, for an article in 1986; and from Bloomberg LP in 2002.

The 2002 Bloomberg case suggests that Lee well understood the advantages of using a transparent legal process and the effective combination of statutory rules and an aggressive use of classic British defamation law. The Bloomberg settlement demonstrated an effective learning curve. Unlike many of the other media outlets, Bloomberg never waited for the case to make it to court – but expunged the offending article concerning the appointment of Lee's daughter-in-law (the wife of Lee's son, Lee Hsien Loong, then Deputy Prime Minister, now Prime Minister of Singapore) to head up one of the most important government-linked corporations, the behemoth Temasek investments company.[20] "We admit and acknowledge that these allegations are false and completely without foundation." Bloomberg said, and we "unreservedly apologize . . . for the distress and embarrassment caused" and offered to pay an undisclosed amount of compensation for damages to head off a libel suit (Arnold 2002; Safire 2002).

Libel suits and statutory controls (gazetteing and ownership rules) are two of the three prongs by which law and the courts have played an important role in Singapore's relationship with the press. The other more directly involves the courts, and turns on contempt of court proceedings that have swiftly followed articles suggesting that Singapore's courts might lack independence or autonomy from the ruling party.

Singapore insists that its sensitivity is justified since it is a nation with no natural resources, surrounded by less stable regimes, and sitting on its own potential powder keg of religious and racial tension (Singapore has significant minority populations of Muslims, Tamil Hindus, and Sikhs, as well as a large population of ethnic Malays, Indians, and expatriates from Britain and

---

[20] Temasek, established in the 1970s, manages the Singapore government's substantial corporate investments, with holdings that include about 20% of Singapore's total market capitalization, including controlling interests in Singapore Airlines and Singapore Telecommunications (Arnold 2002).

the United States, among others). As Singapore's Ambassador to the United States, S.R. Nathan, insisted in an op-ed essay in the *Washington Post* in 1995, "an honest, independent judiciary is a pillar of our political system." Singapore, he wrote, is "a wide-open society. Four thousand five hundred foreign publications, including 150 newspapers, circulate there. BBC World Service and CNN are available 'round the clock. Anyone can log on to the Internet and cruise the information superhighway. This is why Singapore is a key communications and financial center in the Asia-Pacific" (Nathan 1995).

Nathan's op-ed article was titled "Singapore: The System Works." And indeed, it does. These rules, and rulings, these court actions, may well have had the effect of getting the international media to think twice about publishing articles critical of the Singapore government and its judiciary. And though it is hard to prove a negative, the Bloomberg story is not the only anecdotal evidence that this has been at least a somewhat successful strategy. William Safire, who had long been a ferocious and public critic of Lee, Singapore's government, and its judiciary, wrote a scathing column on July 10, 1995, titled "Honoring Repression." The column ran in its usual spot on the op-ed page of the New York Times. But it did not run in its usual place in the *International Herald Tribune (IHT)*, the then-joint publication of the *Times* and the *Washington Post*. The *IHT*, with a worldwide circulation at the time of about 190,000, had by then "stopped printing articles critical of Singapore" (Wallace 1995). Singapore may be small, but its laws and rules and rulings have a wide impact. An exiled critic, former Solicitor General of Singapore Francis Seow notes that "there are no two ways about it, the news media have been intimidated through their pocketbook" and are "now more wary about the sensitivities of the Singapore Government" (Wallace 1995).

The use of properly promulgated, publicly known statutes, libel and defamation law derived from British law, and strict contempt of court proceedings have proven effective in shaping Singapore's international image. The rule of law has proven an effective tool in shaping Singapore's international press coverage. There are powerful incentives to avoid covering politics, which only amplifies the stories that do get published about Singapore's economic success and dependability, its safety and stability, all of which undoubtedly serve to bolster Singapore's standing in the world's global-business community.

Puzzle 4 ... Law, Courts, and Domestic Political Opposition

The courts and civil process have proven to play an even more dramatic role in the standoff between the People's Action Party and the very few opposition politicians who have come close to cracking the PAP's domination of elected office in Singapore. Where once Singapore made wide use of strict detention provisions in its Internal Security Act (another British leftover), that statute has lapsed in importance. "[S]uing an opponent for libel, or pursuing him for tax evasion, gets far less ink than throwing him in prison, and it is every bit as effective. In Singapore, only those who are willing to risk financial ruin dare to challenge the government openly. There are only so many Joshua Jeyaretnams" (Gee 1997).

Joshua Benjamin Jeyaretnam was not Singapore's first opposition leader, nor its last. But he has been something of a poster child for the evolving ways in which Singapore, hewing to formal rules, statutes, and civil process in open court, has developed both significant barriers to the development of opposition leadership and, at the same time, employed the carrots of innovative campaign finance law, minority representation, and the creation of appointed Members of Parliament (with limited voting power) to bring opposition voices into government – and, yet, perhaps undercut the ability of opposition parties to develop the capacity to run credible campaigns against the governing party. These innovations combined with strict rules, and stringent defamation laws, all overseen by the well-regarded Singapore judiciary, demonstrate the power and effectiveness of courts not as the price of globalization, as has been the case for a number of authoritarian governments in this study, but quite to the contrary, as an integral part of the development, and entrenchment of the ruling party. And though Jeyaretnam was not the only opposition leader to face these limits and constraints, he experienced all of them.

Though the PAP controlled every seat in Parliament from 1968 to 1981 – and since 1981 has never lost more than three seats in a Parliament that varied in size from fifty-eight Members in 1968 to eighty-four Members today – it has battled hard to win those seats and defeat the efforts of various opposition parties to gain a toehold. The Workers' Party probably has the longest history of opposition in Singapore, having once been led by David Marshall, the only non-PAP member to serve as Singapore's chief executive. Born in Singapore in 1908 to an Orthodox Jewish family of Iraqi descent, Marshall was imprisoned by the Japanese during World War II, and in 1955 led a left-wing Labor coalition, ultimately forming a minority government in which he served as Chief Minister prior to independence. After failing to negotiate complete self-rule for Singapore in talks with Great Britain, Marshall resigned, later founding the Workers' Party – which eventually was taken over by Jeyaretnam in 1972 (Sim 1995).[21]

---

[21] Marshall was widely acknowledged to be a master defense attorney, who lost but one murder trial in 100 cases that went before a jury. Marshall's legendary success with juries was, in

The long run of PAP dominance unquestionably reflects the party's (and Lee's) broad popularity in the nation. But as the years passed, the younger generation no longer could recall the deprivations (or security threats) of the war years that propelled the PAP to power, and convinced the population to return the party to power election after election. Lee himself worried that younger party members were becoming soft and complacent without an opposition to test them and push them. And yet, when Jeyaretnam finally won a seat in Parliament in 1981, Lee and the PAP quickly lost patience with his attacks, questions, and demands. But the government did not order him jailed, or 'disappeared.' Instead, they pursued him in the courts – both criminal and civil. On the criminal side, the government applied a very strict and narrow reading of campaign laws. On the civil side, over the years, Jeyaretnam was brought to court repeatedly (and lost regularly), with damage awards that eventually drove him into bankruptcy. These court cases were about more than just finding fault and collecting damages, however. They were very much designed to push Jeyaretnam out of Parliament itself. And this was possible because of a combination of statutes, constitutional provisions, and parliamentary rules.

In Singapore, any criminal fine of S$2000 or more means immediate expulsion from Parliament, along with a five-year ban on running for office again. On the civil side, Singapore disqualifies from parliamentary office (and bans from running for five years) anyone who has been legally declared bankrupt. And while it seems perfectly reasonable to exclude from public office those convicted of serious criminal offenses and those whose personal finances might make them unreliable, distracted, or more easily subject to bribes, these rules have also served to push out of office four of the very few opposition candidates to have made inroads in parliamentary elections – Jeyaretnam (convicted and fined more than S$2000, later sued repeatedly for defamation, and eventually bankrupted), Wong Hong Toy (convicted on campaign irregularities, fined more than S$2000), Tang Liang Hong (sued for defamation, fled Singapore before being declared bankrupt), and Chee Soon Juan (sued for defamation and convicted of public speaking without a permit).

Jeyaretnam won his first seat in Parliament in a 1981 by-election. In the next general election, in December 1984, not only was Jeyaretnam reelected, but

---

fact, cited by Lee Kuan Yew as one reason why the country eventually eliminated jury trials altogether in 1970 – having eliminated juries in all but capital cases in 1960. Lee noted in his memoirs that in 1969, "during a parliamentary select committee meeting, David Marshall, then our most successful criminal lawyer, claimed he had 99 acquittals out of the 100 cases he defended for murder. When I asked if he believed the 99 acquitted had been wrongly charged, Marshall replied his duty was to defend them, not judge them." After the bill passed, Lee added, and juries were eliminated, "there were fewer miscarriages of justice arising from the vagaries of jury sentiments" (Lee 2000: 213).

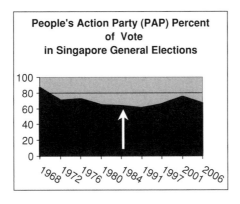

FIGURE 3.1a.

the PAP suffered its most dramatic drop in support since 1963, winning just 64.8 percent of the popular vote. This certainly would seem unlikely to cause any ruling party discomfort – after all, 64.8 percent is a dramatic victory in any democratic system (see Figure 3.1a).

But if we look at the election through the eyes of the PAP, it becomes clear that there was reason for real concern. Given that the PAP rarely faced opposition in more than a minority of the available seats, we, like the PAP, might see the same figures from a different perspective (see Figure 3.1b).

Rather than a pleasing 65 percent approval, one might see a dramatic drop in support. Little wonder, then, that the ruling party and its dominant figure – who was expected to retire after the next election – might be determined to undercut any gains by the opposition. But instead of canceling elections, or tossing opponents in jail, Singapore relied on strict election laws, strictly enforced, combined with strict interpretation and application of even stricter defamation laws.

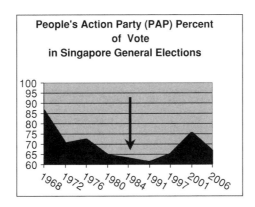

FIGURE 3.1b.

Could the judges have turned to Singapore's due process clause and other rights provisions in the Singapore Constitution to try to ameliorate the reach and impact of these laws? It's plausible, but there is no reason to expect they would have. Given the structure of the courts, and the small size of the island nation, the sorts of influences and forces one might see lending the courts sufficient autonomy and independence to develop in defiance of the central authority were not and are not present in Singapore.

Singapore has also developed, promulgated, debated, approved, and enforced a number of other laws and rules that make it difficult for the opposition – and therefore the courts, again, to play a role in this process. Not by skewing or ignoring the law, but by enforcing it. Among others, Singapore has created two alternative ways to bring opposition voices into Parliament and, at the same time, reducing any demand for a genuine opposition. Singapore launched two programs to bring controlled opposition into the government – the Nominated Member of Parliament (NMP) and the Non-Constituency Member of Parliament (NCMP) plans. The NMP plan was seen as a way to tap "the expertise of persons unwilling to enter politics." Often these are people drawn from the academy and other professions, and while they probably do enhance parliamentary discussions, it is critical to know that these Members are not allowed to vote on revenue and spending bills, nor on constitutional amendments. One Singaporean scholar argues that this is an odd throwback to the "paternalistic colonial practice of appointing nominated legislative assembly members, drawn from among the better natives" (Thio 2002a: 46). The NMP plan also provides an avenue of participation short of joining an opposition party, and running for office independently. Similarly, the NCMP plan is designed to bring the opposition in from the cold, and provides for the appointment to a seat in Parliament for up to three opposition candidates – those who, though they did not win a seat outright, came closest to doing so. One can see this plan as a innovative way to provide for some genuine representation of opposition views – or one can see it as a "cosmetic lure to distract voters from voting in genuine opposition MPs through the placatory effect of a guaranteed token presence of opposition NCMPs who do not have full voting rights" (Thio 2002b: 46). But once again, the rules, the laws, are being followed. And these laws are known and widely publicized, they are not retroactive, they are clear and consistent, plausible, and lasting, and are to be abided by both rulers and ruled alike.

These institutional innovations are supplemented by a set of strict campaign laws that powerfully favor incumbency – though, as the PAP would surely remind us, what ruling party in what democracy in the world has not done everything it could along similar lines? In Singapore, elections are regularly held on a five-year cycle, though as with all Westminster systems left behind by the British, the majority party can call early elections at any point. In Singapore, campaigning is strictly limited, often to a period of ten to seventeen days before the general election is held. Singapore also has strict campaign finance laws, requiring the full disclosure of the identity of any contributor making political donations over S$5000. This is the sort of law many in the United States and Britain have demanded for years – but for a shaky opposition facing a government not shy about suggesting that there are consequences for supporting the opposition, being willing to finance opposition politicians without anonymity is a very difficult sell.[22] But these rules are known, widely publicized, they are not retroactive, they are clear and consistent, plausible, and lasting, and apply to the PAP as well as the opposition – though obviously the burden is not identical.

On top of strict campaign rules and finance limits, Singapore's controlled version of free speech is a daunting barrier to political campaigns. The Singapore Constitution protects free expression, but oddly "begins by focusing on *restrictions* of freedom of expression," making clear that free expression is not an absolute value (Gomez 2005). Article 14 of the Singapore Constitution states that Parliament "may by law impose on the rights" to freedom of speech and expression "such restrictions as it considers necessary or expedient in the interest of the security of Singapore or any part thereof, friendly relations with other countries, public order or morality and restrictions designed to protect the privileges of Parliament or to provide against contempt of court, defamation or incitement to any offense" (Singapore Constitution, Article 14). And though Singapore's limits on speech are tight, these laws are known and widely publicized, they are not retroactive, they are clear and consistent, plausible, and lasting. and are to be abided by both rulers and ruled alike.

SINGAPORE: A MODEL OR AN EXCEPTION?

As is the case with our assumptions about the rule of law, many of our assumptions about the meaning, requirements, preconditions, and challenges of democracy and a republican form of government are "integrally related to the rise of *liberal* democracy in the West." As Randall Peerenboom notes

---

[22] In the general election campaign in 1997, Prime Minister Goh Chok Tong grabbed the third rail of Singapore politics – public housing – when he made it explicitly clear that precincts where support for the government was strong would get a priority for housing upgrades: "When the PAP wins, it still has to decide on priority. The MPs will know which precincts support them and their programme more.... The stronger the support, the further ahead you are in the front" (Chua 1997; see Rodan 2005, 2006).

(2004b: 4) for many *the* rule of law "means some form of a liberal democratic version of rule of law." The same might be said of the republican form of government. After securing all but two of his Parliament's eighty-three seats in the 1997 recent general election, Singapore's Prime Minister Goh Chok Tong proudly declared that voters had "rejected Western-style liberal democracy and freedoms" and rejected "putting individual rights over that of society" (Suh and Oorjitham 1997).

Obviously, we must be cautious about looking at Singapore as a test case for authoritarian governments, the role of courts, and the rule of law. At the same time, Singapore does have important lessons for emerging democracies, particularly those that are interested in emulating Singapore's emphasis on economic development and full integration with the global business world, and yet reluctant to fully embrace the culture and political development that many in the West like to assume are inextricably linked to these.

China has (as have others no doubt) studied the ways in which Singapore has come to understand that the basic requirements of the rule of law can be embedded in a "non-liberal thick conception" (Peerenboom 2004b: 5), just as it can be embedded in a liberal, thick conception as in the United States and Europe. And, perhaps more importantly in an age of globalization, Singapore teaches that global finance and capital care less about the cultural and institutional system in which the thin rule of law functions – provided the law meets the essential criteria of the thin rule of law.

Many of Singapore's lessons will be hard to apply in large, poor, and under-developed authoritarian regimes. Nevertheless, there is much to study here, particularly for those who admire Singapore's security, prosperity, and relative social stability, and particularly its ability to create and maintain an electoral system that, as Singapore's leaders are fond of saying in one form or another allows their country to "take the best of the west and leave the rest" (Goh 1991).[23] Can the Singapore miracle be sustained? Can it be replicated? And if so – at what cost?

---

[23] Singapore's Minister for Information and the Arts – George Yeo – noted in a 1991 speech that while "Orientalism" selectively absorbed the best of Eastern science, art, and ideas, Singaporeans were now living in an era of "Occidentalism" as Asians need to take the best of the West without losing their essential Asian character; Kishore Mahbubani, the top civil servant in Singapore's Foreign Ministry and later Singapore's UN ambassador, in 1995 insisted that while Asia is absorbing the best of the West, the West clings blindly to outmoded ideas. Americans, he said, "worship the notion of freedom as religiously as Hindus worship their sacred cows. Both must be kept absolutely unfettered, even when they cause great social discomfort" (*Economist* 1995).

APPENDIX: SINGAPORE BY THE NUMBERS

Current account balance in billions (US$)	2003	Rank	2004	Rank	2005	Rank	2006	Rank
Japan	136.238	1	172.07	1	163.891	1	140.175	1
Singapore	**22.319**	2	**26.3**	2	**33.584**	2	**34.494**	2
France	7.937	3	− 8.396	3	−27.628	4	−40.647	4
Italy	−19.406	4	−15.137	4	−26.645	3	−18.524	3
United Kingdom	−26.065	5	−43.17	5	−58.053	5	−61.298	5
United States	−519.678	6	−668.082	6	−804.951	6	−864.189	6

Source: International Monetary Fund, World Economic Outlook Database, April 2006.

GNP per capita in US$	1998	Rank
Japan	32,350	1
Singapore	30,170	2
United States	29,240	3
France	24,210	4
United Kingdom	21,410	5
Italy	20,090	6

Infant mortality per 1,000 live births	2000	Rank	2001	Rank	2002	Rank
Singapore	**2.9**	1	**2.2**	1	**2.5**	1
Japan	3.2	2	3.1	2	3.1	2
France	4.4	3	4.5	3	4.4	3
Italy	4.6	4	4.7	4	4.5	4
United Kingdom	5.6	5	5.5	5	5.2	5
United States	6.9	6	6.8	6	7	6

Source: http://www.worldbank.org.

GDP growth annual %	2000	Rank	2001	Rank	2002	Rank	2003	Rank	2004	Rank
Singapore	**9.41**	1	−2.1	6	**3**	1	**2.46**	2	**8.41**	1
France	4.07	2	2.05	2	1.22	4	0.8	5	2.32	5
United Kingdom	3.86	3	2.3	1	1.77	3	2.19	3	3.14	3
United States	3.69	4	0.76	4	1.88	2	3.06	1	4.2	2
Italy	3.03	5	1.76	3	0.38	5	0.25	6	1.22	6
Japan	2.39	6	0.2	5	−0.3	6	1.31	4	2.7	4

Source: World Bank; http://devdata.worldbank.org.

Gross capital formation (% of GDP)	2000	Rank	2001	Rank	2002	Rank	2003	Rank	2004	Rank
Singapore	**32.85**	1	**26.31**	1	22.80	3	**14.84**	6	18.3	3
Japan	26.27	2	25.76	2	23.97	1	23.89	1		
United States	20.49	3	18.85	5	18.05	5	18.04	4		
France	20.47	4	20.07	3	18.97	4	18.93	3	19.75	2
Italy	20.20	5	19.71	4	19.97	3	19.46	2	19.81	1
United Kingdom	17.51	6	17.31	6	16.68	6	16.53	5	16.96	4

Source: World Bank http://devdata.worldbank.org.

Unemployment rate (%)	2003	Rank	2004	Rank	2005	Rank	2006	Rank
Singapore	4	1	3.4	1	**3**	1	2.9	1
United Kingdom	5	2	4.8	3	4.8	3	4.9	3
Japan	5.3	3	4.7	2	4.4	2	4.1	2
United States	6	4	5.5	4	5.1	4	4.9	4
Italy	8.2	5	8.3	5	8.1	5	7.8	5
France	9.5	6	9.5	6	9.6	6	9.6	6

Source: International Monetary Fund, World Economic Outlook Database, April 2006.

Life expectancy at birth (years)	2000	Rank	2001	Rank	2002	Rank	2003	Rank	2004	Rank
Japan	81.08	1	81.42	1	81.56	1	81.68	1	81.8	1
Italy	79.52	2	79.68	2	79.78	2	79.83	2	79.98	3
France	78.91	3	79.11	3	79.31	3	79.26	3	80.16	2
Singapore	78.05	4	78.35	4	78.67	4	78.99	4	79.30	4
United Kingdom	77.53	5			77.59	5	78.40	5	78.52	5
United States	77.03	6	77.03	6	77.24	6	77.14	6	77.43	6

Source: World Bank http://devdata.worldbank.org.

4

Agents of Anti-Politics: Courts in Pinochet's Chile

Lisa Hilbink

INTRODUCTION

On September 11, 1973, General Augusto Pinochet helped lead the over-throw of one of Latin America's most democratic regimes. As part of the coup, Chile's military leaders bombed the presidential palace, shut down the Congress, banned political parties, and purged the state bureaucracy. They left the courts, however, completely untouched. Pledging their commitment to judicial independence, the generals kept intact the long-standing system of judicial appointment, evaluation, discipline, and promotion, which placed primary control in the hands of the Supreme Court, and refrained from dic-tating or otherwise manipulating judicial decisions. The 1925 constitution, which provided a host of liberal and democratic guarantees, remained for-mally in effect, though the junta gradually (and sometimes retroactively or secretly) supplanted many of these with their own decree-laws, and later, their own constitution. Throughout, the military government insisted it was acting in the name of the rule of law, though its approach violated the most basic principles of that concept.

Despite the formal independence they enjoyed, however, and the resources that the country's legal texts and traditions provided them, Chilean courts never sought to challenge the undemocratic, illiberal, and antilegal policies of the military government. Indeed, they cooperated fully with the authoritarian regime, granting it a mantle of legitimacy not only during the seventeen years of dictatorship, but well beyond the transition back to formal democracy in 1990 (see Hilbink 2007: ch. 5). Ignoring the constitutional text that they had sworn to uphold and dismissing the legal arguments advanced by national and international human rights advocates, the courts overwhelmingly supported the military government's arrogation, concentration, and abuse of power. They unquestioningly accepted the explanations offered by the government regarding the fate of the disappeared, and readily implemented vague, retroactive, and even secret decrees that violated the country's legal codes. Moreover, the Supreme Court voluntarily abdicated both its review power over decisions of military tribunals and its constitutional review power.[1] Even after the government declared an end to the official state of war and leaders of other legal institutions began pushing (along with other social forces) for more liberal interpretation of the country's new constitution, the judiciary remained at the service of the regime. Judges continued to justify the expansive police powers of the military government, to abdicate constitutional control of legislation, and to offer little protection to the many victims of repression.

In this chapter, I seek to explain why Chilean courts never sought to use their formal autonomy to challenge or cabin the regime in any way. As Osiel (1995: 486) notes,

> A distinguishing feature of authoritarian regimes, when contrasted with totalitarian ones, is that it is often possible for judges to engage in genuine dialogue with executive rulers through critical examination of the regime's most repressive policies.... (C)ourts in authoritarian regimes are not the blunt and perfectly pliable instruments of executive power.... Judges are allowed to express their criticism publicly, from the bench (and) their views are accorded serious consideration because their participation is regarded as indispensable to the regime's effective operation and to its continued acceptance among an influential sector of the public.[2]

In the bureaucratic-authoritarian regimes of Brazil and Argentina, judges took advantage, where they could, of this unique status to assert limits on the use of power and demand respect for basic rights (Helmke 2002; Osiel 1995; Nadorff 1982). Why is it, then, that in Chile, whose history of democratic practice and respect for legality was much longer and more continuous than those of Brazil and Argentina, and whose human rights movement was one of the strongest on the continent, judges proved to be such faithful agents of the military regime?

The argument I offer here is that the institutional structure and ideology of the Chilean judiciary, grounded in the ideal of judicial apoliticism, furnished judges with understandings and incentives that discouraged assertive behavior in defense of rights and rule-of-law principles. While rival propositions capture some aspects of the story, only the institutional explanation can account for behavior that cut across individual, attitudinal, and objective

---

[1] For the official critique of the conduct of the judiciary under the military regime, see Ministerio Secretaría General (1991: vol. 1 ch. 4).

[2] On this, see also Toharia (1975) and Tate (1993).

class lines; went far beyond a simple "plain fact" application of Chilean law; and remained quite consistent before, during, and after the authoritarian interlude.[3] The *institutional structure* of the judiciary, in which the Supreme Court controlled discipline and promotion, gave incentives for judges to follow closely the examples set by their superiors. Given that most judges depended on the security of their posts and the promise of promotion to guarantee their livelihood and perhaps improve their social status, they had every reason to play along with those who controlled their careers, and even to absorb or adopt their perspectives. This structure served to reproduce a very conservative understanding of the judicial role, or what I label the *institutional ideology*. The core of this ideology was a belief that adjudication was and should remain strictly apolitical. Judges who desired to increase their chances of promotion or simply to maintain their professional integrity (the two were not unrelated) had to take care to demonstrate their commitment to "apoliticism." At best, then, the institutional setting encouraged judges to avoid taking any stands at all against the government, to be quietist and deferential. At worst, it permitted and amplified the defense of conservative values and interests, which were deemed timeless, natural, and hence not "political."

THE JUDICIAL ROLE IN THE PINOCHET REGIME: CONTEXT AND CONTENT

Before proceeding with a discussion of the judicial role under the Pinochet regime, it is important to establish just how law-focused the Chilean military government was. While the junta clearly didn't desire any limits on what it could do with its power, the generals did take great pains to give their policies a patina of legal formality. Having seized power in the name of the rule of law, which they claimed had been trampled by the government they overthrew,[4] they were eager to cultivate an image of respect for and commitment to law and courts. They thus opted to leave existing judicial personnel in place and sought, from the earliest weeks of their rule, to codify their policies into positive law. Much like their counterparts in Brazil, they seemed to "desire to have a

---

[3] For a much more detailed version of this argument, analyzing judicial behavior under both democratic and authoritarian regimes in Chile, see Hilbink (2007).

[4] In its first official statement justifying the coup, Edict No. 5 (*Bando No. 5*), the governing junta declared that the Allende government had "placed itself outside the law on multiple occasions, resorting to arbitrary, dubious, ill-intentioned, and even flagrantly erroneous [legal] interpretations," and had "repeatedly failed to observe the mutual respect which one power of the state owes to another." For more on the period preceding the coup, see Hilbink (2007, ch. 3).

legal rationale for their assertion of arbitrary authority" (Skidmore 1988, cited in Osiel 1995: 530). But if in Brazil, this approach reflected a concern for how the military regime would appear internationally (Osiel 1995: 530), in the Chilean case, the audience was more domestic. As one prominent Chilean social scientist argued in 1974, "One of the most characteristic political realities of Chile is the importance of legality as a superior standard [*instancia*] to which all behaviors and the resolution of conflicts between people and institutions are referred.... Legality is the foundation of the government's legitimacy" (Arriagada 1974: 122).[5]

Given the centrality of legal forms to political legitimacy in Chile in general, and the fact that the military seized power in the name of the rule of law in particular, judges were actually quite well placed to put the generals in a "rule of law dilemma" (Dyzenhaus 1998). One might thus have expected them to act more like their counterparts in Brazil and force the junta to do their own dirty work (Osiel 1995: 533) or, as in Argentina, to seize on opportunities before and after the transition to democracy to assert themselves in the defense of rights and rule-of-law principles (Brysk 1994a; Helmke 2005). Instead, Chilean courts "tied their own hands and submitted themselves to the sad 'rule of law show'" (Velasco 1986: 159).

To offer a sense of just how servile the courts were to the authoritarian regime, the following sections summarize judicial performance in four areas central to the rule of law and rights protection: habeas corpus or, as it is known in Chile, *amparo*; Supreme Court review of military court decisions; constitutional review of laws (*inaplicabilidad por inconstitucionalidad*); and the constitutional review mechanism introduced by the military government in 1976 with the explicit goal of protecting liberal rights, the *recurso de protección*.

Habeas Corpus (Amparo)

Perhaps the most notorious category of judicial decisions under Pinochet is that of habeas corpus or, as it is known in Chile, *amparo*. As Barros (2002: 141) notes, "Personal liberty was sacrosanct in the many texts that form Chile's constitutional and legal tradition – under no circumstance could an individual be deprived of his or her freedom without legal justification." Upon coming to power, the junta did nothing formally to alter such norms. Yet, according to

---

5 Similarly, Cea (1978: 6) notes that at the conclusion of the 1960s, "the Chilean population, by and large, had been educated in respect for the principle of legality, which it had internalized as its own. In accordance with said principle, the rulers as well as the ruled could act only to the extent that an explicit legal precept, technically generated, had previously ordered, permitted, or prohibited that action."

a 1985 report of the Inter-American Commission of Human Rights, Chilean courts accepted only 10 of the 5,400 *recursos de amparo* filed by human rights lawyers between 1973 and 1983 (Constable and Valenzuela 1991: 122). In the remaining seven years of the military regime, only 20 more such *recursos* prospered, leaving the total at 30 out of almost 9,000 (Rigby 2001: 92, fn 34). This means that the courts only challenged the legality of the military regime's detentions in *two or three tenths of a percent* of cases.[6]

Not only were the decisions themselves negative, but the courts took extraordinarily long to process *amparo* petitions, in many cases a month or more, despite the fact that they were legally obligated to rule on them within twenty-four hours. In some cases, the Supreme Court added formalistic impediments to filing such writs, although the law designed the writ to be totally informal and easy to file. In most cases the courts didn't challenge the legality of detention orders issued under the state of exception, nor did judges use their powers to check that detainees were being treated lawfully, either by visiting detention centers or demanding that individual detainees be brought before the court. Complaints of torture thus went ignored or uninvestigated, and confessions offered under torture were accepted. Moreover, if no decree ordering an individual's arrest could be proven to have been issued, judges ruled that the person must not have been detained, and denied *amparo* on the grounds that the writ had been filed on insufficient evidence or with the intention of causing concern or alarm (Amnesty International 1986).

Review of Military Court Decisions

The willingness of the Supreme Court to abandon established legal principles and procedures and, thereby, extend carte blanche to the military's "war on terror," was also evident in its abdication of review power over the decisions of military tribunals. Its first major decision in this regard was issued soon after the coup, in a petition brought against the life sentence that a Valparaíso war tribunal had issued for an alleged leftist spy. The Supreme Court not only refused the appeal, but renounced altogether its power to review the decisions of wartime military courts. The decision argued that because Decree-Laws 3 and 5 had declared the country to be in a state of war, the Military Code of Justice was in effect and war tribunals were in operation. It was the general in charge of the territory in question who had the exclusive power to approve, revoke, or modify the decisions of the wartime tribunals and discipline its members. The Court claimed that, "for obvious reasons," it could not exercise

---

[6] See Hilbink (2007) for an independent, but smaller, data set, with similar characteristics.

jurisdictional power over the military line of command, and thus could not intervene to alter the decision.[7]

Although both article 86 of the 1925 Constitution and article 53 and article 98, no. 5 of the Judicial Code stipulated that the Supreme Court had supervisory power over all of the nation's tribunals, including military tribunals, and despite the fact that the Court had used the power in previous wars (Tavolari 1995: 79), the Court stuck firmly to its position, reiterating it in the months and years that followed. The result was that several thousand Chileans were subjected to trial by tribunals whose judges "often had no legal training and who were mid-level officials, filled with hatred and with the desire to demonstrate their 'toughness' in order to earn merit in the eyes of the junta" (Velasco 1986: 156).[8] Between 1973 and 1976, approximately 200 individuals were sentenced to death and executed, and thousands of others received harsh, disproportionate prison sentences (Luque 1984: 26–29; see also Ministerio Secretaría General de Gobierno de Chile 1991: vol. I, ch. 3; Pereira 2005). Long after the state of war was formally declared to have ended, the concepts of "potential states of war" and of the "internal enemy" persisted in the doctrine of national security, which was incorporated into the 1980 Constitution. Claiming what was among the broadest jurisdiction in the world, Chile's military justice system tried approximately four civilians for every one member of the military, without basic due process (Verdugo 1990; see also López Dawson 1995; Pereira 2005). Moreover, the military courts shielded members of the armed forces and their civilian collaborators from prosecution. As Barros notes, "Montesquieu's description of justice in despotic regimes – 'the prince himself can judge' – applies to the war tribunals, since justice was being dispensed by officers hierarchically subordinate to the commanders in chief, who were creating the law" (2002: 138). The Supreme Court's abdication of its jurisdiction over cases in the military justice system, and its willingness to hand cases over to the armed forces on demand, thus permitted, under a patina of formal legality, a practice that was fundamentally at odds with even the most basic definition of the rule of law.

Constitutional Review (Inaplicabilidad por Inconstitucionalidad)

As noted above, upon coming to power, the junta left the 1925 Constitution in place, leaving it theoretically possible for citizens to challenge in court the

---

[7] See *Fallos del Mes* No. 180 (1973): 222–225.

[8] Pereira reports that the average acquittal rate in Chile's military courts was only 12.42% (2005: 267).

constitutionality of military government policies. In some areas of the law, the Supreme Court did stand by the 1925 Constitution, at least early on. While the junta had established, in Decree-Law (DL) 128, that it had both legislative and constituent powers, the government did not always make clear when it was exercising which of these powers. In several rent and labor law cases, the Supreme Court thus asserted both its continued acceptance of the 1925 Constitution as a controlling document, and its own power to declare part or all of a decree-law unconstitutional (Precht Pizarro 1987).[9]

The Court never came close to using this power in more politically sensitive cases, however. In my sample of published decisions from the 1973–1980 period, the justices rejected the petition for *inconstitucionalidad* in twenty-nine of thirty-two instances, and the three accepted were not particularly sensitive cases. Despite the fact that human rights lawyers constantly appealed to the Constitution in their defense of regime victims, the justices never embraced these ready examples of more liberal reasoning. Indeed, in December of 1974, when the junta issued Decree-Law 788, stating that all previous decree-laws in contradiction with the Constitution should be considered modifications thereof, the Court quickly accepted the proposition.[10] In subsequent *recursos de inaplicabilidad* and in other cases in which arguments were presented regarding the unconstitutionality of early decree laws, the Court stated simply that any decree-law issued between September 11, 1973, and the day that DL 788 was issued could not conflict with the 1925 Constitution, since "it must be necessarily accepted that [these laws] have had and have the quality of tacit and partial modifications" to the Constitution.[11] That DL 788 itself made a mockery of the Constitution, judicial review, and the rule of law seemed either to elude or simply not to bother the justices.

Later, after the regime's new constitution went into effect (1981), the Supreme Court offered interpretations that placed almost no limit on the power of the government to restrict or eliminate individual rights. In my sample of the sixteen published *inaplicabilidad* decisions from this period, the Court found constitutional violations in only two cases, both involving a law, passed by the junta, that sought to resolve, in favor of the state, disputes dating

---

[9] See for example the decision of July 24, 1974, in the case of *Federico Dunker Biggs*, *Fallos del Mes* No. 188: 118–121.

[10] DL 788 was issued while a *recurso de inaplicabilidad* filed by former Senator Renán Fuentealba was pending before the Supreme Court. Fuentealba's lawyers were arguing that his expulsion, based on DL 81, was unconstitutional.

[11] *Luis Corvalán Lepe (amparo)*, *Fallos del Mes* No. 203: 202–205.

to the pre-authoritarian agrarian reform.[12] In these cases, the Court argued that the law violated article 73, paragraph 1 of the 1980 Constitution, which states that the power to resolve civil and criminal disputes belongs exclusively to the judiciary, and that neither the president nor the Congress can, in any circumstances, revise the content of judicial decisions or revive cases that have closed. Thus, the Court jealously guarded its authority over civil law matters and the traditional strict separation of powers; when matters of public law were in question, however, the Court refused to challenge the executive.[13]

The New Constitutional Review Mechanism: Recurso de Protección

In one of its Constitutional Acts of 1976, the military regime introduced a new mechanism for the judicial defense of civil and political rights: the writ of protection (*recurso de protección*). A petition for a writ of protection could be filed in an appellate court by any individual or group that believed that a third party, public or private, had violated one or more of their civil or political rights. It required that the court issue a ruling within 48 hours, and allowed for an appeal to the Supreme Court. This new petition was given greater permanence by the 1980 Constitution, and after 1981 Chileans increasingly employed this mechanism to claim their rights before the courts (appellate and Supreme). Of the 118 published decisions in *protección* cases involving civil and political rights cases (excluding property) for the 1981–1990 period,[14] the courts voted to grant the writ in 30 instances, or in approximately 25 percent of the cases. However, in ten of these cases the ruling actually favored the state or community over the individual, and those that did favor the individual did so only to the extent that the regime's own legal text provided explicitly for this.

In general, decisions on *recursos de protección* tended not to challenge the administrative acts of the regime. For example, judges ruled that university rectors had the right to expel students from their institutions for participating in illegal demonstrations, and that wartime tribunals were legally empowered to judge specified acts committed by civilians. In other words, individuals judged

---

[12] *Sociedad Agrícola y Maderera Neltume Limitada (inaplicabilidad)*, April 19, 1985, *RDJ* 82 (1985) 2.5: 86–104; and *Jaime Bunster Iñíguez y otros (inaplicabilidad)*, January 29, 1987, *RDJ* 84 (1987) 2.5:23–30. Note that in these same cases, the Court rejected the challenges based on formal/procedural unconstitutionality.

[13] For details on these cases, see Hilbink (2007, ch. 4).

[14] These include physical and psychological integrity, freedom of expression, freedom of assembly, freedom of conscience, freedom of association, equality before the law, freedom of labor, and the right to work and education.

by such entities could not claim that their rights to equality before the law and/or due process were infringed.[15] Courts also ruled that the government's cancellation of the "legal personality" (*personalidad jurídica*) of the Hare Krishna – making it impossible for the group to conduct legal transactions as an entity – was not a violation of the freedom of religion, and that the armed forces did not violate the individual's right to association by prohibiting their members from belonging to the Free Masons.[16]

In cases involving the right to assembly, the courts held both the government and the public to the rules of the regime; that is, they upheld the rule that all meetings held in public places had to have previous government authorization, but declared that the government could not require authorization for nonpolitical gatherings held in private locales.[17] Freedom of expression and the press was another area in which the courts did not allow the government to stretch its own (limited) boundaries. For example, judges reminded the government that the Constitution prohibited prior censorship under a state of emergency (though it allowed it under a state of siege), and ruled that the retraction of previous authorization for publication, as well as the indefinite postponement of a decision on such authorization, was also unconstitutional.[18] However, they also ruled that police harassment of journalists, in the form of covert infiltration of a reporting site, forced removal of journalists from a news scene, or seizure of journalistic equipment, did not constitute a violation of freedom of the press.[19] In addition, they endorsed the argument that hunger

---

[15] See *Raúl Acevedo Molina con Vicerrector Académico de la Universidad de Santiago* (*protección*), December 27, 1984, *RDJ* 81 (1984) 2.5:40–50; *Colón con Vice-rector Universidad de Santiago* (*protección*), March 20, 1985, *Gaceta Jurídica* 57:68–74; and *Jorge Donoso Quevedo y otro* (*protección*), May 8, 1984, *Fallos del Mes* No. 306:193–199.

[16] *Círculo Védico* (*protección*), March 12, 1984, *Fallos del Mes* No. 304:9–11; *Renato Verdugo Haz y otros* (*protección*), July 29, 1989, *Fallos del Mes* No. 368:366–371.

[17] See *Presidente del Consejo Regional del Colegio de Matronas y otros* (*protección*), March 17, 1986, *Fallos del Mes* No. 328:35–37, and *Luis Ibacache Silva y otros* (*protección*), March 20, 1986, *Fallos del Mes* No. 328:51–54.

[18] See *Sociedad Publicitaría y de Servicios Informativos Ltda. con Ministro del Interior* (*protección*), January 5, 1983, *RDJ* 80 (1983) 2.5:3–7; *Jorge Lavandero Illanes y otro* (*protección*), April 19, 1984, *Fallos del Mes* No. 305:107–115; *Sociedad Editora La República Limitada, Editora de la Revista Cauce contra Director de DINACOS* (*protección*), May 2, 1984, *RDJ* 81 (1984) 2.5:124–129 (which cites another case decided on the same grounds nine days later); *Sociedad Impresiones y Comunicaciones Ltda. con Ministro del Interior* (*protección*), March 31, 1986, *Gaceta Jurídica* 70:27–31

[19] See *Consejo Regional de Concepción del Colegio de Periodistas de Chile A.G.* (*protección*), March 25, 1985, *RDJ* 82 (1985) 2.5:6–10; *Mario Aravena Méndez* (*protección*), October 10, 1985, *Fallos del Mes* No. 323:667–671.

strikes were illegitimate forms of protest on the grounds that they violated the strikers' own right to life.[20]

In sum, in *recurso de protección* cases, judges were sometimes willing to check specific administrative acts via adherence to the letter of the law, but proved unwilling to challenge the regime's illiberal policies by seeking out a democratic spirit in the 1980 Constitution. Their approach to interpretation in *recursos de protección* was thus far from the "active, dynamic, creative and imaginative" role that one prominent (and conservative) legal scholar proclaimed it should be (Soto Kloss 1986).

CONTRASTING PERFORMANCE OF THE CONSTITUTIONAL TRIBUNAL

In stark and surprising contrast to the performance of the ordinary judiciary under Pinochet is that of the Constitutional Tribunal, an organ (re-)created by the 1980 Constitution as a body separate from the ordinary judiciary.[21] The Tribunal was charged uniquely with abstract review of legislation; that is, at the official request of the president or one-fourth of the members of either house of Congress (or under the military regime, the junta), the Tribunal was to review the constitutionality of draft laws, decrees with the force of law, ordinary decrees referred by the Comptroller General, constitutional reforms, and international treaties. The Tribunal was staffed by three acting Supreme Court justices, selected by the Court itself, and four lawyers, one appointed by the President of the Republic, one by an absolute majority of the Senate (before 1990, the junta), and two by the National Security Council (again, before 1990, the junta). The Constitution stipulated that the members appointed by the president and the junta/Senate must have served as substitute judges in the Supreme Court for at least three consecutive years. Members would serve eight-year, staggered terms. In sum, the majority of the Tribunal's members were appointed directly by the government, and did not enjoy the secure and lengthy tenure of ordinary judges. While one might thus expect the Tribunal to be even more subservient to the government than was the Supreme Court, the reverse proved true.

[20] *Fernando Rozas Vial y otros con Párroco de San Roque y otros (protección)*, August 9, 1984, *RDJ* 81 (1984) 2.5:161–165; Intendente de la Región de Atacama con Párroco de El Salvador, July 3, 1986, *RDJ* 83 (1986) 2.5:108–111.

[21] A Constitutional Tribunal was first established in 1970 by President Frei Montalva. It reviewed seventeen cases in the two years it operated, most of which were decided unanimously in favor of the executive. It was abolished shortly after the military coup. Its brief and largely unremarkable history is well captured in Silva Cimma (1977).

In 1985, for example, the Constitutional Tribunal issued the first of a series of crucial decisions that set basic standards for free and fair elections in the 1988 plebiscite and beyond.[22] Appealing to the overall structure and spirit of the fundamental law, which both guaranteed political rights and outlined a return to democracy, the Tribunal insisted on the establishment of an independent electoral commission – the *Tribunal Calificador de Elecciones* or TRICEL – for the 1988 plebiscite. According to transitory article 11 of the Constitution, the TRICEL was to begin operating "on the appropriate date" for "the first election of senators and deputies." The bill that the junta presented to the Constitutional Tribunal for review thus established that the TRICEL would begin to function in December of 1989. However, Tribunal member Eugenio Valenzuela – who was, it should be noted, one of the four members directly appointed by the junta – appealed to the spirit rather than letter of the law, arguing that if the Constitution itself recognized the existence of a "public electoral system," then there was no reason to exempt the 1988 plebiscite, which would inaugurate the transition process, from the rules of such a system. Valenzuela was able to persuade three other Tribunal members, including two members from the Supreme Court, to vote with him. The Tribunal thus issued a 4–3 ruling, and the government was forced to revise the legislation.[23]

POSSIBLE EXPLANATIONS FOR THE BEHAVIOR OF THE ORDINARY COURTS

If the Constitutional Tribunal was able to stand up to the military government, insist that it respect basic principles of legality, and hold it to its pledge to return the country to democracy, then why did ordinary courts remain so obsequious toward the regime?

Regime-Related Factors

In any analysis of judicial behavior under authoritarianism, the first and most obvious hypothesis is that regime-related factors – that is, direct or indirect interference with and manipulation of the courts by the government – explain

---

[22] Subsequent decisions included that of October 1, 1986, which revised the law on electoral registers; that of March 7, 1987, which reduced the constraints on political party organization; and that of April 1988, which set campaign standards and required clear dates for the 1988 plebiscite and for subsequent presidential and parliamentary elections. See *Fallos del Tribunal Constitucional Pronunciados entre el 23 de diciembre de 1985 y el 23 de junio de 1992* (Santiago: Editorial Jurídica, 1993).

[23] For an in-depth discussion of the significance of the Constitutional Tribunal in limiting the authoritarian government, see Barros (2002).

the outcomes. While Chile's military government did use a variety of tactics to make its will known to judges, and changed some rules along the way to strengthen its influence in the judiciary, an explanation that attributed judicial behavior in Chile from 1973–1990 solely or primarily to fear of and manipulation by the government would overlook crucial elements of the picture.

To begin, I must emphasize that judicial independence was, on the whole, respected under the authoritarian regime. In the interviews I conducted for this study, not only acting judges themselves but also retired judges, lawyers, and law professors from across the political spectrum maintained that the courts had not been subjected to threats or other types of interference from the military government, insisting upon the continuity of judicial autonomy across time.[24] Indeed, this is why criticisms of the judges' behavior under Pinochet are so strong in Chile: people believed in the independence of the judiciary and therefore had high expectations of it.

This is not to deny the clear evidence of more subtle forms of pressure brought to bear by the military government on the judiciary. While my review of the records of the plenary sessions of the Supreme Court revealed no instance in which judicial promotions were dictated by the government, nor even any cases where the Ministry of Justice rejected a list of nominees proposed by the Court, it did indicate that some of the early investigations into judicial behavior, as well as some transfers during the authoritarian regime, were made at the recommendation of the Ministry of Justice (see esp. Volumes 18 and 22).[25] Furthermore, while the new military leaders did not themselves conduct a purge of the judiciary, they did pass some laws making it easier for

[24] On three different research trips (one in 1996 and two in 2001), I conducted a total of 115 interviews with legal scholars and practitioners, former ministers of justice, and, most importantly, judges. In 1996, I interviewed thirty-six acting highcourt judges (fifteen of seventeen Supreme Court members and twenty-one members of the appellate courts of Santiago and San Miguel, which was two-thirds of the total in the Metropolitan Region) plus ten lower-court and/or former judges. In 2001, I interviewed fifteen highcourt judges, ten of whom I had interviewed in 1996. All interviews were semi-structured and lasted forty-five minutes to four hours. Through the interviews, I probed the judges' role conception, their political leanings, and their understandings of the institutional and/or political constraints that they were subjected to under different regimes and administrations. I sought to ask questions in the most open-ended way possible, so as not to lead the subjects or to put them on the defensive. Since interview responses cannot necessarily be taken at face value, I sought to triangulate and contextualize the responses through interviews with a variety of actors, and, where possible, through archival material.

[25] The case could easily be made, however, that such indirect steering of the judiciary was nothing new. The executive is, for obvious reasons, always going to attempt to exert whatever influence possible on judicial selection and tenure. Moreover, Chilean law had long authorized the president to oversee the conduct of judges, though the power to evaluate and remove judges

the Supreme Court to dismiss potential troublemakers. Decree-Laws 169 and 170, published on December 6, 1973, modified both article 323 of the Judicial Code and article 85 of the 1925 Constitution, allowing judicial employees to be removed from service for an annual evaluation of "poor performance" by a simple majority (rather than the previous requirement of two-thirds) vote of the Supreme Court. The vote was to be secret, and the justices were under no obligation to give reasons for the negative evaluation. These decrees facilitated the internal purge conducted by the Supreme Court in January of 1974 (discussed later).[26]

In the 1980s, rather less subtle pressure was brought to bear by Pinochet's ideological ally, Hugo Rosende, who was sworn in as the new Minister of Justice in January of 1984. Rosende was reportedly obsessed with judges' ideological leanings, and made it clear to the Court that he wanted appointees who "will never meddle in politics," with "politics defined, of course, as the politics of dissidence" (Matus Acuña 1999: 180). In 1984, he oversaw the expansion of the Supreme Court from thirteen to seventeen members, which allowed at least one hard-line regime supporter, Hernán Cereceda, to rise to the High Court. Cereceda allegedly became the main informant for the government on the opinions and activities of judicial personnel (Matus Acuña 1999: 158). In 1989, in the wake of Pinochet's loss in the (October 5, 1988) plebiscite, Rosende succeeded in getting the junta to approve what became known as the "candy law" (*ley de caramelo*).[27] The legislation was so called because it allowed justices over age seventy-five to retire within ninety days with a sweet financial deal. Seven justices took advantage of the offer, allowing the military regime to make seven new appointments to the Court, albeit drawn (as always) from nomination lists proposed by the Court itself.

There is thus, not surprisingly, some evidence that the military government tried to exert some control over the judiciary, although the means it used were mostly indirect. While certainly the government brought direct pressure to bear in specific cases,[28] Chile's judicial system did not become a system

---

was given exclusively to the Supreme Court (see esp. article 72, no. 4 and article 85 of the 1925 Constitution).

[26] Note that these changes were later reversed, first by a modification of the content of DL169 and then with the 1980 Constitution.

[27] This was DL 18,805 of June 17, 1989. In addition, just before the transition, the military government added a line to the Judicial Code to prevent those who had been fired from the judiciary from serving as substitute judges, and to prohibit the future impeachment of government officials for behavior under the military regime.

[28] One famous example is the *Apsi* case of 1983, in which one chamber of the Supreme Court initially accepted, but then, in an unprecedented "clarifying decision," reversed and rejected a *recurso de protección* on behalf of the editors of the magazine. See *Sociedad Publicitaria y de Servicios Informativos Ltda. con Ministro del Interior (protección)*, RDJ 80 (1983) 2.5:3–9.

of "telephone justice." Indeed, as explained above, the military government wanted to preserve its image of respect for law and courts, and thus, rather than interfere in the judicial process, its leaders preferred simply to restrict the scope of jurisdiction of the ordinary courts and expand that of tribunals over which they (thought they) had more direct control, namely the military courts and (later) the Constitutional Tribunal. Like governments before and after theirs, they did their best to influence judicial selection and tenure, but they did so within the limits of the established system, in which the Supreme Court continued to play the dominant role.

Moreover, it bears noting that it was the judges themselves who tended to interpret their own role very narrowly, abdicating early on the authority they had to rein in the state's police powers or protect constitutional rights, and later refusing to take advantage of opportunities to join with even moderate regime critics and push for liberalization. My analysis of judicial decisions in published civil and political rights cases for the period 1964–2000 revealed that this general pattern was evident long before the 1973 military coup, persisted through even the weakest moments of Pinochet's seventeen-year rule, and continued well after the transition to civilian rule in 1990 (see Hilbink 2007).

The Attitudinal Explanation

With regime-related variables thus thrown into question, many scholars of judicial behavior would immediately suspect that it was the judges' personal policy preferences that explain their support, implicit or explicit, for the Pinochet regime (e.g., Segal and Spaeth 1993). In this view, little resistance from the judiciary reflects little personal opposition to the government (whatever its stripe) on the part of judges. This has certainly been the popular interpretation of judicial behavior among Chileans. Many press articles, both during and after military rule, implied that judicial complicity was a function of ideological sympathy and/or a lack of individual moral integrity (e.g., Luque and Collyer 1986: 23–7; Pozo 1983: 9–10), and a number of the lawyers and judges I interviewed pointed to the right-wing attitudes of certain judges, particularly on the Supreme Court (see Hilbink 2007, ch. 4).

Nevertheless, there is evidence that the judiciary was not, at the individual level, monolithic in its enthusiasm for the authoritarian regime. To begin, the fact that the military government deemed it necessary to issue Decree-Laws 169 and 170 (see the earlier discussion) reveals that the generals were not convinced that they could count on unified and unfailing judicial support, even from the Supreme Court itself. That they sought to restrict the jurisdiction of the ordinary courts, preferring to have politically sensitive cases tried in military courts, or later, the Constitutional Tribunal, also indicates a general lack of confidence that ordinary judges were and would remain solidly behind them. Moreover, my indirect probing of judges' political views in 1996 interviews revealed *Pinochetistas* to be in the distinct minority.[29] In fact, only six of the thirty-six acting High Court judges I interviewed demonstrated themselves to be clearly approving of Pinochet's rule, or ideologically aligned with the military regime.[30] By contrast, fourteen judges made it clear that they were ideologically at odds with the military regime and well aware of the historical and international standards of democracy.[31] Finally, there were sixteen judges "in between," who asserted differing levels of disagreement with and distance from the Pinochet regime, but didn't articulate a clear democratic ideology in the course of the interview (see Hilbink 2007, ch. 4).

What the interviews and other data (Hilbink 2007, ch. 3) suggest is not that political preferences had nothing to do with judicial performance under the authoritarian regime, but rather that any real romance between judges and military leaders was restricted to a powerful bloc on the Supreme Court, as well as some zealots in the inferior ranks, whom the former were able to reward through promotion. Most judges, I contend, were not personally enamored of or committed to the military regime, particularly as time wore on, but because the Supreme Court controlled discipline and promotions within the judiciary, any judge who aspired to rise in the judicial ranks had to curry favor with – or at least not invite scrutiny by – his or her superiors. A right-wing bias at the top of the judiciary thus meant a likely right-wing bias (even if only strategic) all the way down. In other words, the political bias of the Chilean judiciary cannot be understood as a simple function of individual-level attitudes; rather, institutional dynamics were also at play.

Moreover, the fact that a number of members of the 1973 Supreme Court sympathized with the Pinochet regime can itself be attributed, in part, to institutional factors. At the time of the coup, a majority of the justices had been

[29] All of these judges had served under the authoritarian regime, and many of them under Frei and/or Allende, as well. Most of them spoke quite freely about how the regime changes of the past thirty years had affected their work. In addition, they were open about their views on such issues as whether the Allende regime had destroyed the rule of law, or whether the critique made of the judiciary by the Truth Commission was fair or unfair. Only a few (four) acting High Court judges refused to answer these questions on the grounds that they were "political."

[30] In general, clearly pro-military regime judges were very forthcoming with their political views. Contrary to what I expected, it was they who generally raised political issues in the interview, before I got to the explicitly political questions. It is interesting that they, like most of the Right in Chile, were proud of and totally unrepentant about military rule. It was, rather, the democrats who walked on eggshells and felt the need to apologize for or whisper their beliefs.

[31] I use the term "historical and international standards of democracy," because the *Pinochetistas* often attempt to apply the term "democracy" to the regime they created.

appointed by the progressive presidents Eduardo Frei and Salvador Allende. Without understanding how the appointment process works in Chile, one might assume, then, that these justices would sympathize with and defend the mainly working-class and/or left-wing victims of the regime, and certainly not lend continuous support to the military regime. However, as I detail later, because the Supreme Court itself selects the nominees for appointments to its own ranks, the Court actually has more control over its ideological composition than the executive does, and the influence it exerts was and is conservatizing. While there were also conjunctural factors at work, and while some members of the Court would have certainly been right-wingers regardless, even the aspect of the explanation that appears most attitudinal, then, is itself partially institutional.

The Class-Based Explanation

Another possible (and related) explanation for judicial capitulation to authoritarianism, particularly in the Chilean case, where the military staged a coup against the socialist government of Salvador Allende, is that the judges were defending their class interests. This would be the obvious response from many critical legal theorists, who argue that courts *always* serve the interests of the powerful, whether under democratic or authoritarian regimes. Since, in many countries, judges do tend to come from elite backgrounds, and are thus socialized in similar family, community, and educational institutions, their approach to interpreting law and administering justice may well be a function, conscious or not, of class interests (Hirschl 2004; Kairys 1982; Unger 1986).

The first point against this argument as it applies to Chile is that many lawyers and politicians who proved to be ardent defenders of human rights, or at least critics of military rule, came from elite social backgrounds. Moreover, some lawyers and politicians who initially supported the coup later became fervent public critics of the military regime, whereas judges' behavior remained quite consistent over time.

Second, by the middle of the twentieth century, the Chilean judicial ranks were no longer filled with elites (as they had been in the nineteenth century). Because entry-level judicial posts were very low paying and not very prestigious, the judicial career attracted those who desired a stable income and career, rather than those who had the social connections or financial cushion to pursue a (potentially less secure) future in private legal practice. This was evident not only in secondary sources (Couso 2002: 177; de Ramón 1999; Dezalay and Garth 2002: 226) but also in the social background information that I gathered in my interviews with judges. This data, which included high school attended; father's, mother's, or maternal grandfather's occupation; and prior or present land holdings, showed that a full three-quarters of respondents came from lower-middle to middle-class backgrounds, while only about one-quarter were of upper-middle to upper-class extraction. Few judges came from landed families; most had fathers who were merchants or public employees; and all but a handful attended lower-middle to middle-class high schools, many of these public (see Hilbink 2007: ch. 3).

Clearly, then, the bias of the Chilean judiciary cannot be attributed to class, at least not understood in objective terms. Some judges may have identified with the traditional elite, but my claim is that this identification was constructed *within* the institution. Seeking to please their superiors and move up in the judicial ranks, middle-class judges learned to "mimic the conduct and aristocratic demeanor of some of the elite judges who were still there when they began their careers" (Dezalay and Garth 2002: 226). Indeed, precisely because they tended to be individuals without significant financial cushions or well-heeled social networks, they came to identify their own interests – in job security and social dignity – with those of the institution and its elite.

The Legal Theory Explanation

A final possible explanation, then, and the one that has attracted the most attention from those troubled by judicial complicity in authoritarian regimes, is that the judges' professional understandings of the nature of law and adjudication rendered them unwilling or unable to hold regime leaders legally accountable for repressive acts and policies. The most common culprit is legal positivism, which analysts blame for leading judges to believe that their role is passive and mechanical; that is, that their function is to apply the letter of the law without concern for the outcomes of their decisions or for the preservation of general principles of the legal system (Cover 1975; Dyzenhaus 1991; Dubber 1993; Fuller 1958; Ott and Buob 1993). Judges who work under legal positivist assumptions, or what David Dyzenhaus (1991) calls "the plain fact approach," believe they have a professional duty to execute the will of the legislator(s), regardless of the law's content. This conviction incapacitates them in the face of "wicked law," and thereby renders them easy servants of authoritarianism. Defenders of legal positivism counter that the major alternative, natural law philosophy, offers no more security against tyranny and repression than does positivism, and in fact, may offer less. The "absolute values" shared by judges and used to interpret or even bypass the positive law may not be the ideal values that liberal humanist proponents envision, particularly in authoritarian contexts (Hart 1958; MacCormick 1993; Raz 1979). In other words, judicial reasoning in accordance with "higher law" will not meet liberal standards of justice where the "higher law" itself is not politically liberal.

Chile's legal tradition since independence is strongly legal positivist, and many Chilean analysts have laid the blame for judicial complicity during the Pinochet years at the doorstep of legal positivism (Cea 1978; Cúneo Machiavello 1980; Squella 1994). However, while Chilean judges did take shelter behind positivist defenses, washing their hands of any responsibility for the brutality and longevity of the authoritarian regime, both case analysis and interviews revealed that judges were often willing and able to ignore or look beyond the letter of law, so long as the resultant rulings favored or restored the status quo, and could thus bear a mantle of "apoliticism."

As indicated earlier, from 1973–1980, judges ignored long-standing legal norms on habeas corpus and review of military tribunal decisions, granting unchecked discretion to the military in the "anti-subversive war." Furthermore, judges put up no protest as the junta proceeded to gut the 1925 Constitution, issuing blanket decrees to amend or supersede any provision that might stand in its way. After 1981, when the regime's new constitution went into effect, judges adhered to the letter of the law, but in a manner that maximized the government's discretion to determine when public order was threatened and, therefore, when constitutional rights could be suspended. In other words, rather than emphasizing those parts of the 1980 Constitution that set limits on the exercise of power, the courts perpetually ignored or denied them in favor of the vague clauses that extended executive discretion. It thus seems inappropriate – even generous – to attribute judicial behavior in Pinochet's Chile to a professional commitment to legal positivism.

Moreover, in interviews, a significant number of acting high court judges (twenty-three of thirty-six) openly recognized that the judicial decision-making process is not simply "mechanical," as a plain fact positivist would have it. Indeed, they admitted being guided by the grand principles of the Chilean system, the national conscience, or the general understanding of the community (see Hilbink 2007, ch. 4). This view cut across the political lines discussed above, although it was nearly always couched in a broader discourse of apoliticism.

Thus, it is not legal positivism *per se* that accounts for judicial behavior in Chile, though part of the explanation does appear to rest in the related, and broader, professional ideology of apoliticism, which was transmitted and enforced within the judiciary. The premium on "apoliticism" within the institution meant not that judges ignored altogether the choices they faced in adjudication, or felt some absolute fidelity to the letter of legal text; rather, it

meant that, when it came to public law, judges were expected to lend unques-
tioning support to the executive. The support could be passive or active, but
the key was to refrain from second-guessing "political" decisions or from taking
principled stands in defense of those who challenged the established order. In
the case of the military government, this was even more pronounced, since
the military presented its rule as a (superior) *alternative to* politics (Loveman
and Davies 1989).

THE INSTITUTIONAL ARGUMENT

As is clear from the preceding discussion, each of the conventional explanations for judicial capitulation to authoritarian rule applies partially to the
Chilean case, but none provides a completely satisfying account. I thus present
as an alternative an institutional argument, which integrates some of the
insights from the competing hypotheses and more accurately explains the
phenomenon in Chile. Specifically, I argue that the institutional structure
and ideology of the Chilean judiciary together rendered it highly unlikely that
judges would be willing and/or able to take stands in defense of liberal and
democratic principles.

The argument has two main elements: one structural, one ideological.
When I refer to the institutional *structure*, I mean the formal rules that determine the relationship of judges to each other and to the other branches of the
state, and that thereby offer incentives and disincentives for different kinds of
behavior. Particularly important are the rules governing the judicial career;
that is, rules regarding appointment, promotion, remuneration, and discipline.
When I refer to the institutional *ideology*, I mean the understanding of the
social role of the institution into which judges are socialized, the content of
which is maintained through formal sanctions and informal norms within the
institution.

The institutional structure of the Chilean judiciary can be described as that
of a highly autonomous bureaucracy. While there have been some changes
to the structure in recent years, the following describes it accurately from the
late 1920s until 1997. Judges entered the career at the bottom rung, wherever
there was a vacancy, and sought to work their way up the hierarchy. Salaries
for district-level judges were very low, particularly compared to what lawyers
could expect to earn in private practice. Yet tenure was generally secure,
and a judge with a good record could hope to move up in rank (and hence
pay) through appointment to a higher court. To do so, however, the judge
had to curry favor with his or her superiors, who controlled the disciplinary
process within the judiciary and played a dominant role in the appointment

and promotion process. Indeed, to enter the judiciary, an individual had first to approach the appellate court with jurisdiction over the district where a post was available. The appellate court composed a list of three candidates from which the Ministry of Justice (MJ) selected the appointee. To advance to the appellate level, the judge had to be nominated by the Supreme Court to appear on a similar list of three nominees from which the MJ made its appointment. Finally, to get to the Supreme Court itself, an appellate judge had to be nominated by the Court. The Court composed a list of five nominees, two of whom appeared by right of seniority,[32] but the other three whom the Court chose by plenary vote. The MJ made its appointment from this list.[33]

In choosing the nominees, the higher courts always referenced the judge's disciplinary record and the formal evaluations that the judges had received. The Judicial Code (which dates to 1943) defines internally punishable (i.e., noncriminal) judicial "faults and abuses" to include any expressions of disrespect for hierarchical superiors, or, in the case of appellate judges, any "abuse of the discretionary faculties that the law confers on them." The respective superiors have the duty to respond to all such "faults and abuses" and to choose the appropriate disciplinary measures, ranging from a private reprimand to suspension for months at half-pay.[34] The Supreme Court has the ultimate responsibility of overseeing the conduct of all the judges in the nation. To this end, the Court conducts regular performance evaluations for all judicial employees. These evaluations were triannual until 1971, when they became annual. The Supreme Court meets in January of each year to discuss the performance of every employee of the institution, from the most menial worker (e.g., the elevator operator) to the most senior appellate court judge.[35] Prior to 1971, judges were evaluated every three years on the "efficiency, zeal and morality" of their performance. In 1971, a four-list system was instituted: a List One rating meant good performance, a List Two signaled some dissatisfaction

---

[32] The 1925 Constitution specified that two individuals on the lists of five and one on the lists of three had to be chosen on the basis of seniority. The others were to be chosen on "merit," the meaning of which was left to the discretion of the superior court justices. This system remained in force until 1981. The 1980 Constitution established that only one of the nominees on any list be reserved for the individual with most seniority and added the requirement that said individual have an impeccable evaluation record.

[33] I reviewed all the minutes of the plenary sessions from 1964 through the late 1990s, and there was never an instance of the MJ rejecting the list of nominees and requesting that another be drafted. Moreover, when I interviewed former ministers of justice, they all grumbled about the fact that they frequently had to choose "the lesser of the evils" from the list; that is, it was clear that they felt constrained by the process.

[34] See *Código Orgánico de Tribunales*, articles 530–545.

[35] Evaluations of district-level employees are supposed to be based on reports provided by the respective appellate courts, but the Supreme Court still votes on them.

above, a List Three rating served as a stark warning (since two consecutive years on List Three meant dismissal), and a List Four rating meant immediate removal.[36] The formal criteria of evaluation were still the same ("efficiency, zeal, and morality"), but since the justices (as before) didn't have to justify the evaluations in any way (indeed, the votes were anonymous), subordinates had to be sure not to anger their superiors or, indeed, give them any reason to scrutinize or question their work.

This autonomous bureaucratic institutional structure provided strong incentives for judges to play, primarily if not exclusively, to the Supreme Court. Professional success was clearly linked to pleasing, or at least never upsetting, the institutional elders. From their earliest days in their careers, then, judges had to worry about how their superiors would perceive and assess their work. The likelihood that they would so worry was heightened by the fact that entry-level posts were very poorly compensated. Those who accepted them generally had low levels of financial independence, and thus relied on the security of the job and the promise of upward mobility within the judicial hierarchy. The incentives operating on judges thus encouraged conformity and reproduced conservatism within the institution.

Evidence of the effects of this institutional structure on judges is overwhelming. It came up again and again in my interviews – cited by nineteen of thirty-six acting High Court judges, as well as by all the retired and lower court judges I interviewed – and was clear in the discipline and promotion record as well. As one judge noted, under the military regime, "there were different conceptions of what was happening, but the Supreme Court was very powerful over the hierarchy and controlled the responses" (Interview SCJ96–7, June 5, 1996, 18:00).[37]

The first and most obvious way in which the Court acted to bring the judicial ranks in line after the coup was through an internal purge of avowed and suspected Allende sympathizers in January of 1974. With the legal path prepared by Decree- Laws 169 and 170, discussed earlier, the Supreme Court used its power to dismiss or force the retirement of an estimated 12 percent of

---

[36] See *Código Orgánico de Tribunales*, articles 270–277.

[37] Because interviewees were promised anonymity, I use a coding system that identifies subjects only by category and assigns them each a number that corresponds to the year and the (random) order in which I interviewed them. For example, the appellate court judge that I interviewed first in 2001 is identified as "ACJ01-1;" the seventh Supreme Court justice interviewed in 1996 as "SCJ96-7," and so on. The key to the categories is as follows: SCJ-Supreme Court Justice; ACJ-Appellate Court Judge; LCJ-Lower Court Judge; FJ-Former Judge; AI-Abogado Integrante; HRL-Human Rights Lawyer; and OL-Other Lawyer and/or Law Professor (includes Ministers of Justice).

judicial employees, among them approximately forty judges.[38] For the most part, this was done via poor evaluations for their performance in 1973, although some "early retirements" were achieved via a transfer of "troublemakers" to undesirable (geographically isolated) posts (Interview FJ96-5, June 18, 1996 12:00).[39]

Having observed the internal purge, judges "became afraid to do anything, even if they weren't in agreement with what was taking place" (Interview HRL96-1, July 4, 1996, 11:00). As one retired judge explained, "Because of the hierarchy, there exists a sort of reverential fear of the Supreme Court, such that even when they have a determined opinion on some issue, judges normally wind up resolving it in accordance with what the Supreme Court has ruled. There are very few cases, even under democracy, in which a subordinate judge has maintained his way of thinking on a given matter when the Court has ruled in a different way" (Interview FJ96-2, June 13, 1996, 13:00). Under the military regime, this pressure intensified. Recalling the mood set for the judiciary by the High Court before and around the plebiscite on the 1980 Constitution, one judge stated the following:

> I remember as the plebiscite approached, people were talking about it, and naturally within a logic of the "yes" vote, as if it were impossible to think that someone there would consider voting "no." And I was afraid, I *broke out in a sweat* worrying that someone would ask me which way I was going to vote. Nobody asked me, because nobody thought I was for the "no," but if they had asked me, I probably would've been booted from the judiciary – and that is no exaggeration – for my answer (Interview ACJ96-2, May 6, 1996, 8:30).

This fear was not unfounded. In 1983, after Santiago Appeals Court judge and long-time president of the National Association of Magistrates, Sergio Dunlop, made some mild criticisms of the judicial retirement system, the Supreme Court responded first by giving him a warning and then putting him on List Two (of four) in the annual evaluations.[40] Dunlop, who had been a fierce opponent of Allende, thus resigned from the judiciary in 1983 and

---

[38] The exact numbers here are difficult to come by. I tabulated these figures using a list of names and posts from a support group for judges expelled for political reasons, checked against the official evaluations ledger at the Supreme Court. However, because of all the possible extenuating circumstances, it is difficult to confirm the exact number. It is interesting to note, however, that out of 260 judges evaluated for their performance during 1973, 82 were put on the "satisfactory" list, or List Two (out of four), which is basically a slap on the wrist, or a "tomato," as one judge called it. This figure is more than twice the average for List Two in other years.

[39] These are documented in the records of the plenary of the Supreme Court, Volume 18.

[40] A List Two rating was a slap on the wrist, designed to put subordinate judges on alert that their behavior was displeasing to the Supreme Court.

became a loud critic of the institution. In public statements over the following years, Dunlop contended that the institutional structure of the judiciary was such that only those willing to "remain prudently silent" could find their way to the top (Constable and Valenzuela 1991: 131). "Although judges have tenure," he argued, "in reality their careers depend on the members of the Supreme Court," and those judges who take stands at odds with that of the Supreme Court become "marked." As regards the role of the judiciary under the military regime he stated, "Those who lead [the institution] are those who must signal the standards and the direction to take. . . . The Supreme Court justices could have acted peacefully defending a different interpretation without having anything happen to them" (Interview in *La Epoca*, May 9, 1989, 12–13).

This last statement began to appear increasingly valid as the 1980s progressed. Not only did the opposition begin organizing and dissenting ever more openly in the wider society, but elements within the regime began to suggest a need for democratic transition. As discussed earlier, the Constitutional Tribunal played an important role in pressing the government to reconstruct and respect certain democratic legal norms. The Supreme Court, however, did little to nothing in this regard. On the contrary, the Court as a whole actively discouraged judges from challenging or criticizing the military government. The justices even went so far as to censure the Court's own president, Rafael Retamal, when he expressed his disapproval of the regime's policies in 1984.

Lower court judges observed and took note of Retamal's actions and their consequences. When conferences on human rights began in the mid-eighties, some lower court judges attended, but as one related, "you couldn't let your superiors know you were participating in such acts" (Interview LCJ96-1, April 25, 1996, 11:00). During this period "lower court judges were paranoid about being poorly evaluated or expelled from the judiciary if they let slip some commentary or did something which their superiors in the Supreme Court or the government wouldn't like" (Matus 1999: 148). And, indeed, a group of judges who met privately to discuss rights issues in their work were subsequently informed in their yearly evaluations that they "had received votes in favor of putting them on List Two." This served as "a signal that their names would not figure on the nomination lists for future promotion" (Matus 1999: 159–160).

More open critics of the regime, meanwhile, suffered more serious repercussions. For example, when Santiago Appeals Court judge, Carlos Cerda Fernández, announced that he would not apply the amnesty law to a case of disappeared Communist leaders, nor turn over the case to the military courts, on grounds that to do so would be "evidently contrary to law (*derecho*)," the Supreme Court suspended him from the judiciary for two months with only half-pay.[41] Approximately a year and a half later, in May of 1988, the Supreme Court censured another judge, René García Villegas, for refusing to renounce jurisdiction over crimes committed by the regime's security forces and including a statement "disrespectful of military justice" in an official resolution. Within months, the Court sanctioned García again, this time suspending him for fifteen days at half-salary, for having "gotten involved in politics." García's alleged impropriety consisted of a statement offered in a radio interview with Radio Exterior de España that "torture is practiced in Chile." The excerpt had been used, allegedly without García's authorization, in the public campaign for the "no" vote in the plebiscite on Pinochet's tenure as president. In annual evaluations for both 1988 and 1989, the Court thus ranked García in List Three for "incompetent performance," forcing his resignation from the bench on January 25, 1990.[42] The Court also sanctioned several appellate court judges, including the head of the National Judicial Association, Germán Hermosilla, for having expressed their solidarity with García during his suspension. The punishment was "duly reflected in their annual assessment" (Brett 1992: 232).

Institutional structure thus goes a long way to explaining why even democratic-minded judges refused to take public stands, personal or professional, against the authoritarian regime. As previously noted, most judges came from very modest social backgrounds, and had chosen the judicial career because it was respectable and secure. They were thus largely predisposed to be risk-averse when it came to professional matters. Once on the judicial career ladder, this tendency was reinforced by the "reverential fear" of the Supreme Court. Judges learned quickly that the best way to get ahead was to avoid making waves, and thereby "avoid getting burnt" by their superiors (Interview FJ96-4, June 17, 1996, 12:30).

Of course, fear of punishment and career sabotage by superiors cannot explain the behavior of the Supreme Court judges themselves, who, having reached the pinnacle of the hierarchy, were untouchable within the system. As noted above, personal attitudes and preferences were clearly at work in some cases, and the military government did its best to create opportunities for its most devoted supporters to rise in the ranks. But it would be a mistake to treat judicial attitudes and preferences as entirely exogenous to the institution. Supreme Court justices reached their posts after having spent forty or more years in an institutional setting that discouraged creative, innovative, and

---

[41] Monthly report of the Vicaría de la Solidaridad for October 1986, on file at the FDAVS, 55–59.
[42] "Supremazo Final contra Juez García," *ANALISIS* (January 15–21, 1990): 22–24. See also García's autobiography, *Soy Testigo* (1990).

independent decision making. Those who succeeded in rising in the ranks
were not those with bold or fresh perspectives, but rather those who best emulated and pleased their superiors; that is, those who demonstrated conservatism
and conformity.

The parallels between this pattern of professional socialization and that of
the Chilean military are pronounced. According to Constable and Valenzuela
(1991), the typical military officer is characterized by loyalty, discipline, and
circumspection, and the "desired military mold" is "competent and plodding,
rather than brilliant." Those seeking to reach the rank of general should (as
did Pinochet) do "just well enough to advance, but not so well as to arouse
suspicion"(1991: 48). Indeed, one of my interviewees claimed, "What happens
to judges is something like what happens to Chilean military men. They
are brainwashed. And he who is independent, intelligent, [and] brave *won't be*
promoted. They will bother him and will most likely brand him a 'communist'
so that he will be marginalized from the judiciary" (Interview FJ96-2, 13 June,
1996, 13:00). Thus, it could hardly be expected that Chile's Supreme Court
justices would, in general, possess the skills and initiative necessary to stand
up to the authoritarian leaders.

Moreover, the Supreme Court judges, like all members of the judiciary,
were socialized from day one to believe that, to be professional, judges must
remain "apolitical." This understanding is what I refer to as the institutional
ideology of the judiciary, and it was evident in judicial discourse throughout the authoritarian era. As I elaborate elsewhere (Hilbink 2007, ch. 2), the
definitions of the "political" and the "judicial" were established in the nineteenth century, when Chilean state-builders sought to achieve political stability
through the "rule of law." To this end, they imposed a strict understanding
of the separation of powers doctrine: judges handled private law (property
and contract); politicians handled public law (public order and morality).[43]
Judicial adherence to this division of authority was secured through partisan
manipulation of the courts. In the constitutional overhaul of the 1920s, judicial independence was secured by eliminating the power of the executive to
discipline and appoint judges, and transferring that power to the Supreme
Court. In addition, the Court was given the power of judicial review for the
first time. However, there was no purge of the judicial ranks, and legal and
judicial training remained the same. Thus, nineteenth-century views regarding the legitimate scope of judicial (and political) authority were, effectively,
frozen in the judiciary, as those at the top of the hierarchy (the Supreme Court
justices) were newly empowered to promote to their own ranks those who best

---

[43] This interpretation is supported by Barros (2002: 112–114) and Couso (2002: 152).

emulated their own professional, if not also personal, attitudes and practices. At the same time, they had, through the evaluations system, an effective means of deterring dissent (see Hilbink 2007, ch. 2). In the decades that followed, the judiciary thus remained quietist in the face of abuses of public power, except when that power was used to alter private law matters (as under the progressive governments of Eduardo Frei and Salvador Allende; see Hilbink 2007, ch. 3).

What made this institutional ideology particularly relevant in the authoritarian period, I argue, is the fact that the military government itself claimed to be above politics. On the view that it was politicians, with support from democratic civil society, who had caused the socioeconomic debacle of the Allende years, the generals had seized power with the explicit mission of depoliticizing the country (Loveman and Davies 1989; Nef 1974; Valenzuela 1995). Thus, questioning the policies of the military regime was, by the regime's own definition, political and dangerous, while supporting the military was apolitical, patriotic, and noble. My claim is that the judiciary's traditional commitment to apoliticism fed perfectly into this "anti-politics" project. To prove their commitment to law (and order) over politics (and disorder), judges either refrained from challenging the military's policies or outright endorsed them.

It is difficult to document the independent effect of this ideology on judicial behavior, particularly under the authoritarian regime when Supreme Court justices invoked it to threaten their subordinates or to justify punishing them. Nonetheless, taken together with the evidence from before and after the authoritarian interlude (see Hilbink 2007, chs. 3 and 5), the examples that follow suggest that for many judges, deferring to the (self-proclaimed "apolitical") military government need not have been a conscious strategic choice, but was simply a matter of abiding by professional expectations.

In early 1974, in his speech inaugurating the judicial term, Supreme Court president Enrique Urrutia Manzano explicitly reminded judges of their professional duty to eschew politics. He explained that two months earlier the Supreme Court had transferred or removed from office a number of employees who had participated openly in politics under Allende. He argued that this was necessary to guard "the full independence of the judiciary, and that, in consequence, any participation whatsoever of employees in partisan proselytizing impaired the administration of justice and deserved condemnation." Later in the address, he boasted of the active role taken by the Supreme Court against the Allende government, and of its official endorsement of the coup on September 12, 1973, which he clearly viewed as something other than political behavior. In contrast to the Allende government, he argued, the military government had fully respected the judiciary as the symbol of Chilean law and justice. He closed by calling upon his audience to aid in the "reconstruction of the Republic . . . with the objective of making a better Chile, to which, with a healthy, prudent, opportune, and disinterested administration of justice, the judiciary could contribute so much."[44]

Urrutia thus contrasted the prejudicial, illegitimate politicking of the Allende government and its judicial sympathizers with the impartial, professional, and patriotic action of the Supreme Court. Because the military, too, acted out of "impartiality, professionalism, and patriotism" (Munizaga 1988; Nef 1974),[45] it was both logical and completely legitimate for the judiciary to cooperate with the military government in the "construction of a better Chile." It was thus clear that "the courts should be at the service of the new legality that the military power was creating and at the service of the entire process that began with the coup" (Interview with HRL96-5, August 2, 1996) and that those who would critique or disregard that position might throw into question their professional integrity and fitness for judicial service.

This understanding was also articulated in the 1984 plenary censure of Supreme Court president Rafael Retamal, in which the justices reminded their colleague that judges were prohibited by law from engaging in politics. Likewise, the basis for the suspension and, ultimately, the dismissal, of Judge René García in 1988 was his having "gotten involved in politics." Both cases not only served to perpetuate the "reverential fear" of the Supreme Court discussed above but also to reinforce the notion that the good judge, the true professional, is one who goes along and plays along, who sides with tradition, unity, and order. By contrast, he who dares to challenge the forces of tradition, unity, and order, to speak up in defense of liberal or democratic principles, is playing "politics" and thereby betraying his lack of professionalism. In such an ideological environment, it is unsurprising that most judges would remain quietest and deferential.

In sum, the structural and ideological features of the Chilean judiciary, in combination, effectively served to mobilize bias (Thelen and Steinmo 1992: 10) – specifically, a conservative bias – among judges. These features allowed and supported the expression of traditional, conservative juridico-political views by actors in the institution, while discouraging and sanctioning the expression of alternative views. Because of the institutional structure, the primary, and in some ways, exclusive "audience" or "reference group" for judges was the Supreme Court, whose members were not representative of

---

44 *RDJ* 71 (1974) 1: 18–21.
45 Urrutia's position clearly acccepts this perspective.

the diversity in the wider polity.[46] They were clearly more conservative than the majority of society, in part because of the way the same institutional features had shaped their views. Given the power they bore over their subordinates' careers, it is clear that the expression of alternative juridico-political views was severely constrained. The institutional ideology also helped preclude the expression of alternative views because it equated professionalism with apoliticism. To behave professionally, so as to merit respect from peers and secure success in the career, meant to remain above "politics," or at least to appear to do so. This meant that passivity was prized, in general, and activism was only deemed acceptable when it was aimed at preserving or restoring the sociopolitical status quo. With this prevailing understanding of professionalism in the institution, and with the conservative Supreme Court monitoring adherence to this understanding, it is no wonder that Chile's judges offered little resistance to the abusive policies of the Pinochet regime.[47]

CONCLUSIONS AND IMPLICATIONS

In his recent book on courts in contemporary Egypt, Moustafa notes that, although judges are agents of the state, they never administer the will of the regime "in an automatic fashion" (2007). This is an important point. Just as we should not expect judges in democratic regimes to assert themselves automatically in defense of rights and the rule of law, so in authoritarian contexts, we should not assume that judges will always be hopeless tools of the government. But if this is the case, why were judges in Chile judges such faithful agents of the authoritarian regime? Why in a country whose legalist and democratic traditions were much stronger than those of many countries that *have* produced significant judicial resistance (e.g., Brazil, Franco Spain, Egypt), did judges display "a willingness to collaborate that bordered on the abject" (Constable and Valenzuela 1991: 134)?

This chapter has contended that while regime-related factors, social class, and individual attitudes were all part of the equation, judicial capitulation in Chile was, above all, facilitated and maintained by the institutional structure and ideology of the judiciary. The Supreme Court held tremendous power over

---

[46] I borrow the idea of "audience" from Schattschneider (1960) and the notion of judicial "reference groups" from Guarnieri and Pederzoli (2002). The claim fits nicely within the framework of Baum (2006).

[47] This argument bears some resemblance to that of Müller (1991), which explores how and why judges and lawyers cooperated so fully with the Hitler regime. The major difference, of course, is that in Germany, it was the Ministry of Justice (i.e., the government) that controlled judges' careers, not the judicial elite itself, as in Chile and other cases (see Hilbink 2007, ch. 6).

the judicial hierarchy, through which it induced conservatism and conformity among appellate and district court judges. It was able to do so by dismissing or taking disciplinary action against the few judges who refused to fall in line with its servile stance vis-à-vis the military government. These efforts were facilitated by the long-standing ideology of the judiciary, according to which judges were to remain "apolitical." Any judge desiring to preserve professional integrity and standing needed to take care to demonstrate his or her fidelity to "law" alone, and "law" was to remain distinct from and superior to "politics." Challenging the decisions of the military junta, the self-proclaimed apolitical guardians of the national interest, would both violate a judge's professional duty to remain apolitical and imperil his or her chances of professional advancement. Thus, even democratic-minded judges were, with few exceptions, unwilling to take public principled stands in cases brought against authoritarian laws and practices.

These findings have two main implications for theorizing on judicial behavior. First, the Chilean case demonstrates that institutional context matters to judicial behavior. Judicial decision making in authoritarian Chile was not a simple response to the political context; namely, the absence of political competition under Pinochet (Chavez 2004; Ginsburg 2003; Ramseyer and Rasmusen 2003). Indeed, as I show elsewhere (Hilbink 2007), judicial behavior in Chile did not change radically with the onset of authoritarianism in 1973, nor with the return to democracy in 1990. Rather, the performance of the courts remained quite constant, despite radical changes in the surrounding level of political competition. At the same time, as this chapter shows, judicial comportment was not a simple reflection of individual policy preferences that judges brought with them to the bench, nor of judges' objective class loyalties or sensibilities. And it was clearly not a function of legal positivist or formalist commitments, since judges cannot be said to have merely applied the laws on the books. Instead, the comportment of Chilean judges was the product of interests and understandings forged *within* the institutional setting in which they worked. Hence, whether inclined to view judicial behavior as sincere or strategic, theorists should devote greater attention to the institutional contexts in which different judges work and to the impact these have on what judges want, can, and think they ought to do (Gibson 1986: 150).[48]

Second, the Chilean case suggests that where judicial institutions are designed to keep judges maximally apolitical, it is unlikely that judges will seize on the formal autonomy they enjoy to challenge actions or decisions of regime leaders. An "apolitical" institutional structure works against the cultivation

---

[48] For an excellent recent argument that supports this view, see Baum (2006).

of the professional understandings and capacities that allow judges to assert themselves against abuses of power. Rather than promoting independent- and critical-mindedness, such a structure fosters servile and mechanical mentalities and practices. Rather than cultivating a sense of connection and responsibility to the citizenry, it encourages an inward orientation and a refusal to engage with "nonexperts." And rather than breeding openness to difference, debate, and interpretive innovation, an "apolitical" judicial structure serves to enforce unity and repress dissent (Damaska 1986; Shapiro 1981; Solomon 1996). Likewise, where the institutional ideology of the judiciary is anchored by an imperative to remain apolitical, judges are generally discouraged from taking principled stands against members of a sitting government, from engaging deliberately and responsibly in polity-wide debates, and from taking seriously unconventional or unpopular perspectives (Cover 1975; Peretti 1999; Shklar 1986). In sum, while judicial capitulation to authoritarian regimes is never automatic (Moustafa 2007), judges who function in a system "cut off from wider [political] influences and assessments" (Solomon 1996: 469) are unlikely to act as anything but faithful agents of established power.

5

Law and Resistance in Authoritarian States: The Judicialization of Politics in Egypt

Tamir Moustafa

Scholars generally regard courts in authoritarian states as the pawns of their regimes, upholding the interests of governing elites and frustrating the efforts of their opponents. Yet in Egypt, a country with one of the most durable authoritarian regimes in the world, courts enjoy a surprising degree of independence and they provide a vital arena of political contention. From the standpoint of mainstream comparative law and politics literature, the Egyptian case presents a surprising anomaly. This chapter sets out to explain why Egyptian leaders chose to empower judicial institutions in the late 1970s when only twenty-five years earlier the same regime had stripped the courts of their power.

I find that state leaders deployed judicial institutions in an attempt to ameliorate a series of economic and administrative pathologies that are endemic to many authoritarian states. First, the consolidation of unbridled power resulted in a severe case of capital flight, depriving the economy of a tremendous amount of Egyptian and foreign private investment. Additionally, the concentration of political power paradoxically exacerbated principal-agent problems and impaired the ability of the regime to police its own bureaucracy, resulting in administrative abuse and corruption. These substantive failures damaged the ability of the regime to fulfill its populist agenda, and they undermined the revolutionary legitimacy that the regime had enjoyed for its first fifteen years. Faced with these compounding crises, Sadat eventually turned to judicial institutions to ameliorate the dysfunctions that lay at the heart of his authoritarian state. Judicial institutions were rehabilitated in an effort to attract investment, to provide the regime with new tools to monitor and discipline the state's own bureaucratic machinery, and to shape a new legitimizing ideology around the "rule of law." But while judicial institutions helped ameliorate some state functions, they simultaneously opened avenues through which activists could challenge state policy. The result was a new field of political contention within the authoritarian state.

JUDICIAL INSTITUTIONS AND ECONOMIC DEVELOPMENT

After the 1952 Free Officers' coup that brought Gamal 'Abd al-Nasser to power, Egypt's new rulers made a decided shift away from the established political system and showed no intention of restoring liberal-democratic political institutions. The constitution was annulled by executive decree in December 1952, and the following month all political parties were disbanded. Egyptian legal institutions were also weakened significantly. 'Abd al-Raziq al-Sanhuri, one of Egypt's greatest legal scholars and the architect of the Egyptian civil code, was physically beaten by pro-regime thugs and forced to resign in 1954. Another twenty prominent members of the *Maglis al-Dawla* (Egypt's supreme administrative court) were forcibly retired or transferred to nonjudicial positions. The regime further consolidated its control by circumventing the regular court system and establishing a series of exceptional courts throughout the early 1950s, including *Mahkmat al-Thawra* (The Court of the Revolution) in 1953 and *Mahakim al-Sha'ab* (The People's Courts) in 1954. These courts had sweeping mandates, few procedural guidelines, and no appeals process, and they were staffed by loyal supporters of the regime, typically from the military (Brown 1997; Ubayd 1991). Simultaneously, Nasser began to steer the country in a new economic direction, unilaterally seizing 460,000 feddan of land for redistribution and nationalizing hundreds of British and French companies in the wake of the 1956 Suez War.

With no check on the political power of the new regime, either through political parties or through credible legal institutions, private investors understandably hesitated to make major new investments in the economy. Instead, foreign and Egyptian capitalists actively divested their assets, depriving the Egyptian economy of large sums of capital. According to Fuad Sultan, one of the chief architects of the economic liberalization program, an estimated $20 billion (£E 8 billion) was held abroad by Egyptian citizens in the 1960s, and another $20 billion was transferred abroad in the 1970s (Beattie 2000: 150).[1] When the regime found that private sector industrialists were unwilling to invest in the economy, it seized what assets remained to mobilize capital for investment. Between 1960 and 1964 the regime initiated one of the most extensive nationalization programs in the non-Communist world.

---

[1] By comparison, in the ten-year period between 1965 and 1974, domestic sources of investment in the economy totaled £E 2,319,400,000 ($5,800,000,000). In other words, the private savings of Egyptian citizens that were transferred abroad amounted to nearly three and a half times the total amount of domestic sources of investment in the Egyptian economy during the same period.

Nasser's preference for an expansion of executive powers at the expense of autonomous rule-of-law institutions continued into the late 1960s, despite its crippling effect on the economy. The final and most significant blow to Egyptian judicial institutions came in the 1969 "massacre of the judiciary." In an executive decree, Nasser dismissed more than 200 judicial officials, including the board of the Judges' Association, a number of judges on the Court of Cassation, and other key judges and prosecutors in various parts of the judicial system. To ensure that resistance to executive power would not easily reemerge, Nasser then created the Supreme Council of Judicial Organizations, which gave the regime greater control over judicial appointments, promotions, and disciplinary action. This marked the pinnacle of Nasser-era domination of the judicial system and the nadir of formal institutional protections on property rights. By the time of Nasser's death in September 1970, the Egyptian economy was in a state of extreme disrepair. The public sector was acutely inefficient and required constant infusions of capital, the physical infrastructure of the country was crumbling, and massive capital flight deprived the economy of billions of dollars each year. Nasser's successor, Vice-President Anwar Sadat, turned almost immediately to foreign sources of capital to make up for the domestic shortfall. However, it proved extremely difficult to convince investors that their assets would be safe in Egypt given the fact that this was the same regime that had seized foreign assets only a decade earlier.

The possibility that the Egyptian regime might renege on its renewed commitment to private property rights proved to be a major disincentive for both foreign and Egyptian investors. Worldwide, foreign investors were obsessed with the risk that investment in the developing world entailed after a string of expropriation movements in the 1950s and 1960s. A partial list of foreign countries that seized foreign assets through the 1960s included Algeria (1967), Argentina (1959), Brazil (1959–1963), Burma (1963–1965), Ceylon (1962–1964), Cuba (1960–1962), Egypt (1956, 1961, 1963–1964), India (1956), Indonesia (1963–1965), Iraq (1964), Syria (1965), and Tanzania (1966–1967). In the wake of national independence movements and economic nationalization campaigns worldwide, a virtual industry focusing on "political risk assessment" emerged in the 1960s and 1970s. Economists and business faculty produced a prodigious volume of studies aspiring to create a framework for the measurement of political risk (Aliber 1975; Baglini 1976; Delupis 1973; Knight 1971; Nehrt 1970; Robock 1971; Truitt 1974; Zink 1973), business consultants attempted to assess the degree of political risk in individual countries, and trade magazines obsessed about the perils of expropriation.[2] The overriding sentiment in much of this literature was that "a common cause of hesitancy

---

[2] For examples, see Kelly (1974), Van Agtmael (1976), and Hershbarger and Noerager (1976).

in committing funds is fear of expropriation or nationalization of the investment. . . . Companies are still reluctant to take all the risks of establishing a new business abroad, and fostering and developing it, only to have it taken over. . . . According to investors, the danger [of expropriation] lurks throughout much of the world" (Truitt 1974: 13).

In many of these studies, investors were urged to examine the host country's legal system to assess the general investment climate and the extent of concrete protections on property rights. For example, one study from the period suggested the following:

> The quality of a legal system in a host nation is a major element of the investment climate. The investor is forced to make at least implicit judgments about certain elementary concepts of justice, continuity, and predictability as dispensed by the legal system.
>
> The presence of a strong, independent, and competent judiciary can be interpreted as an indicator of a low propensity to expropriate. . . . If this judicial system is strong, independent, and competent, it will be less likely to "rubber stamp" the legality of an expropriation and more likely to accede to a standard of fair compensation. The effect of this would be to lower the propensity of the host nation government to expropriate (Truitt 1974: 44–45).

It was in this context of elevated concern about the risks of expropriation and the insecurity of property rights that Sadat attempted to attract foreign investment and Egyptian private investment. Sadat's first attempt to assure investors that Egypt was turning a new corner came with law 34/1971, which repealed the government's ability to seize property.[3] Law 65/1971 extended anti-sequestration guarantees to Arab capital in addition to providing tax incentives for investments.[4] Sadat also approved the International Bank for Reconstruction and Development (IBRD) framework for the settlement of foreign investment disputes through international arbitration by way of presidential decree 90/1971. But the most important assurance of the early 1970s that the regime was committed to respecting private property rights was contained in the new Egyptian Constitution of 1971. While still reserving a central role for the public sector in the development process, it sought to reestablish the sanctity of private property:

> Article 34
> Private property shall be protected and may not be put under sequestration except in the cases specified in the law and with a judicial decision. It may not be expropriated except for a public purpose and against a fair compensation

[3] *al-Jarida al-Rasmiyya*, no. 124, 17 June 1971.
[4] *al-Jarida al-Rasmiyya*, no. 40, 30 September, 1971.

in accordance with the law. The right of inheritance is guaranteed in it.

Article 35
Nationalization shall not be allowed except for considerations of public interest, by means of law and with compensation.

Article 36
General confiscation of property shall be prohibited. Special and limited confiscation shall not be allowed except with a judicial decision.

The proposed constitution was put to a national referendum and approved by a supposed 99.98 percent of voters. The irony of the situation was surely not lost on potential private investors. The regime was intent on attracting private investment, and it was employing the language of "property rights" to do so. But what kind of real guarantees were being extended, particularly in light of the fact that the national referendum, like every referendum since the Free Officers' coup in 1952, was rigged by the government? The "99.98 percent voter approval" was an absurd illustration of the power of the regime to unilaterally expand and contract legal rights to suit its needs at the time.

Moreover, even the assurances provided both in law 34/1971 and in the constitution were not absolute. Rather, they were to be interpreted by other laws on the books. For example, in the case of law 34 of 1971, property could still be seized by court order in the event that "criminal offenses" were involved. But with a whole array of loosely worded criminal offenses on the books, including financial crimes damaging the "public interest," real guarantees to private property were questionable at best. Similarly, the constitution stated that private property would be protected, *"except in the cases specified in the law"* and *"in accordance with the law."* Not only did this language open the door to the interpretation of constitutional guarantees based upon illiberal laws already on the books but it also failed to resolve the issue of the regime's ability to unilaterally issue new legislation to suit its current needs. Nor did law 34/1971 or the new constitution address the lack of independent legal institutions with the power to protect private property. In short, repeated assurances by the regime that it would respect property rights fell far short of providing concrete safeguards against state expropriation on the ground.

The disappointing response from private investors from 1971–1974 prompted the regime to make a more forceful and comprehensive statement about its commitment to its new open door policy. The regime created an "October Paper" outlining the state's new development strategy and put it to a national referendum on May 15, 1974. Like the referendum on the 1971 constitution, the new economic policy received nearly 100 percent voter approval thanks to electoral fraud orchestrated by the Ministry of Interior. The October Paper laid the groundwork for law 43/1974, which provided a new, more detailed framework in which foreign capital could operate in Egypt. Law 43 provided a number of guarantees and incentives to foreign investors, including tax exemptions, the ability to import new technology and machinery for production, partial exemptions from currency regulations, exemptions from Egypt's stringent labor laws, exemptions on limits to annual salaries, and, once again, guarantees against nationalization and sequestration. In this last regard, article 7 repeated the government's commitment that "[t]he assets of such projects cannot be seized, blocked, confiscated or sequestrated except by judicial procedures."

Egyptian newspapers and government officials anticipated a flurry of economic activity and the prompt injection of much-needed foreign capital into the economy after the passage of law 43/1974. They were sorely disappointed. By the late 1970s, it became increasingly clear that investors were not willing to simply take the word of the government when the same regime and the same personalities had only fifteen years earlier engaged in one of the most sweeping nationalization programs in the developing world. Studies conducted in the late 1970s by consulting firms and by the Egyptian government itself confirmed that investors "remained reluctant to invest in long-term projects due to uncertainty about the future of the Egyptian economy" (Nathan Associates 1979: 216). Investor concerns about expropriation were also reflected more concretely in the volume of foreign operations, which amounted to only $442,144,000 over the decade.

Even more revealing than the low volume of investment were the sectors of the economy where investments were made. Only 19 percent of total investments were made to the industrial sector, which entailed high initial outlays of capital, a long-term return on investment, and therefore the necessity of long-term security in the economy. Eighty-one percent of total investments were directed to nonindustrial sectors such as services and tourism. These sectors of the economy conversely required low initial outlays of capital, provided a short-term return on investment, and risked less in the event of nationalization. Egypt was attracting neither the volume nor the type of capital that it needed to sustain long-term economic development.

The reluctance of foreign investors to enter the Egyptian market for fear of expropriation was also reflected in the fact that most American businesses in Egypt undertook capital-intensive operations only when they received medium- and long-term financing for projects from the U.S. Agency for International Development under its "Private Investment Encouragement Fund." These long-term, capital-intensive investments in the Egyptian economy were publicly rather than privately financed because private investors were unwilling to risk expropriation. Moreover, nearly every American firm investing in Egypt during this period did so only after securing costly insurance from the Overseas Private Investment Corporation, substantially reducing profit margins (U.S. Department of Commerce 1981).[5]

The low volume of total investments and the emphasis on low-risk investments with promises of quick returns did little to help the ailing economy. More than seven years after the passage of law 43/1974 and a full decade after the first moves to attract foreign capital through law 65/1971, these projects provided a total of only 74,946 jobs (Arab Republic of Egypt 1982: 54, 68). Compared with the total Egyptian workforce of nearly 11 million, law 43 projects accounted for only 0.7 percent of total employment in the country. With the Egyptian population growing at a rate of approximately one million per year by the end of the 1970s, law 43 projects were not generating nearly enough new employment to address Egypt's population explosion. By 1979, total external debt had reached $15.4 billion, and debt servicing consumed a full 51 percent of all export earnings. It was in this context that Sadat finally decided to strengthen institutional guarantees on private property rights through the establishment of an independent constitutional court with powers of judicial review. Former Prime Minister Mustafa Khalil recalled,

> There were efforts to encourage foreign investment in Egypt at the time because we were dealing with a fiscal crisis. One major factor that was impeding investment was the lack of political stability – both foreign and domestic. We issued a number of laws aimed at guaranteeing private investment such as law 43. But a major problem was that the NDP, having the majority in the People's Assembly, could push through any legislation it wanted and change the previous laws. This was at the forefront of Sadat's thinking when he created the Supreme Constitutional Court. He primarily wanted to make guarantees [to investors] that laws would be procedurally and substantively sound (personal interview, June 14, 2000).[6]

The new Supreme Constitutional Court (SCC) enjoyed considerable independence from regime interference. The Chief Justice of the SCC was formally appointed by the President of the Republic, but for the first two decades

---

[5] This insurance was specifically arranged to cover for three types of risk: inconvertibility of profits, expropriation, and war loss.

[6] In a separate interview with Kirk Beattie, Khalil provided a similar assessment of Sadat's general understanding of the tie between political and economic reform. According to Khalil, "he [Sadat] was anxious to have the open door policy work, and in his mind the political *infitah* was directly related to and a necessary adjunct of getting the open door policy to 'take off'" (Beattie 2000).

following its establishment, the president always selected the most senior justice serving on the SCC to the position of Chief Justice. A strong norm developed around this procedure, although the president always retained the formal legal ability to appoint anyone to the position of Chief Justice who met the minimum qualifications as defined by the law establishing the court.[7] New justices on the court are appointed by the president from among two candidates, one nominated by the General Assembly of the court and the other by the Chief Justice, but in practice the nominations of the Chief Justice and the General Assembly of the SCC have been the same. Extensive protections were also provided to SCC justices to guard against government interference. Justices cannot be removed by the government, and the General Assembly of the SCC is the only body empowered to discipline members of the court, insulating SCC justices from the threat of government pressure and reprisals. Finally, provisions in law 48/1979 also give the SCC full control of its own financial and administrative matters.

With protections against government interference, the Supreme Constitutional Court set to work establishing a new property rights framework. SCC rulings enabled thousands of citizens to receive compensation for property seized by the state. In fact, the SCC went much farther than even Sadat envisioned when it struck down laws limiting the extent to which compensation claims could be made against the government (Moustafa 2007). The impressive activism of the new Supreme Constitutional Court helped the regime assure both Egyptian and foreign private investors that property rights were now secure in Egypt and that formal institutional protections existed above and beyond mere promises by the regime. However, as we see later in this chapter, the SCC also opened an institutional channel through which political activists could challenge the government.

JUDICIAL INSTITUTIONS AND BUREAUCRATIC DISCIPLINE

Political scientists make the common and recurring error of imagining "the state" as an organization that is far more unified than it is in reality. Reification of the state, or the process of imagining state organizations as a unified set of institutions working in lock-step with one another, is particularly seductive when considering state functions in authoritarian regimes for two reasons. First, we commonly assume that authoritarian rulers maintain absolute authority over their subordinates; second, low levels of transparency often obscure

---

[7] This informal norm ensuring SCC autonomy broke down in 2001, as documented in Moustafa (2007).

our ability to observe the considerable discord and breakdowns in hierarchy
that regularly occur in authoritarian settings.[8] But the Weberian ideal of a
rational bureaucracy does not adequately capture the dynamics of how state
institutions operate in real-world contexts (Migdal 1997). Far from acting in
unison, each bureaucrat has his or her own set of personal interests and ideological preferences that are often at odds with those of the central regime.
A variety of studies from the state-in-society approach also demonstrate that
state institutions are transformed from the moment they begin to interact with
social forces championing various competing agendas (Migdal 1989; Migdal,
Kohli, and Shue 1994).

Counteracting these centripetal forces is one of the primary challenges
for the central leadership of any state, but it is a particular challenge for
authoritarian leaders for precisely the same reason that we, as observers of the
state, tend to reify it: authoritarian rulers suffer from a lack of transparency
in their own state institutions. Part of the difficulty of collecting accurate
information on bureaucratic functions is due to the hierarchical structure of
modern states more generally, as articulated by Martin Shapiro:

> Certain pathologies arise in the hierarchical lines designed to transmit infor-
> mation up and commands down the rational-legal pyramid. Such "family
> circles" – conspiracies among the lower-level workers to block or distort the
> flow of information upward – are successful in large part because of the sum-
> marizing that is essential to such a hierarchy.... The process of successive
> summarization gives lower levels ample opportunity to suppress and distort
> information, particularly that bearing on their own insubordination and poor
> performance (Shapiro 1980: 641–642).

Accurate information on bureaucratic misdeeds is even more difficult for
authoritarian regimes to collect because the typical mechanisms for discovery, such as a free press or interest group monitoring of government agencies,
are suppressed to varying degrees. Moreover, since administrators are unaccountable to the public in the same ways that they are in democracies, and
because fear of retribution typically pervades political life, authoritarian rulers
at the top of the administrative hierarchy receive little or no feedback from
the public, making it particularly difficult to assess the day-to-day functions of
state agencies. The classic principal-agent problem, which has been examined
extensively in democratic settings, is therefore aggravated in authoritarian political systems. With low levels of transparency and exacerbated principal-agent

---

[8] To some considerable degree, reification of state power works to the advantage of authoritarian
    rulers because those living under authoritarian rule, like political scientists, often overestimate
    the power, presence, and coordination of state institutions.

problems, local administrative officers regularly circumvent, undermine, or subvert central government policies to promote their own competing policy agendas or simply to translate their administrative power into supplementary income streams. These dynamics are so commonplace that a completely alternate set of norms often emerges around how much one is expected to line a bureaucrat's pocket with every interaction with agents of the state, whether to renew a driver's permit, process paperwork for a court case, or secure a business license.[9] At a minimum, low levels of transparency and principal-agent problems can undermine the central regime's developmental goals. At their worst, low levels of transparency within state agencies can mask the emergence of power centers aspiring to challenge the central regime.

We have grown accustomed to various coping strategies that authoritarian regimes use to maintain their control of state institutions, including the retention of particularly sensitive posts in the military and the central security agencies for trusted relatives, or, alternately, constantly rotating officials whose loyalty cannot be trusted based on blood relations.[10] However, ad hoc shuffling of state functionaries and reliance on familial, tribal, clan, and personal solidarities are tremendously inefficient, and they have distinct limitations in modern states with complex bureaucracies. More institutionalized methods of monitoring are necessary for authoritarian states with expansive bureaucracies.

In his seminal study, *Courts*, Martin Shapiro (1981) observes that judicial institutions are used as one of several strategies to promote discipline within the state's administrative hierarchy because they generate an independent stream of information on bureaucratic misdeeds that is driven by citizens themselves. Shapiro explains that "a 'right' of appeal is a mechanism providing an independent flow of information to the top on the field performance of administrative subordinates." This observation helps explain why even authoritarian regimes with little regard for civil liberties often preserve the right of citizens to have their day in court (Shapiro 1981: 49). Courts play "fundamental political functions" by acting as avenues "for the upward flow of information [and] for the downward flow of command" (Shapiro 1980: 643).

---

[9] Ironically, the more a regime seeks to extend its political and administrative capacities, the more opportunities for corruption develop in tandem. Perhaps the best example of this was the global expansion of public sector enterprises in the developing world in the post-independence period, a move that was intended to extend the state's political patronage networks as much as it was intended to build the state's economic capacity. This rapid expansion of state functions produced countless opportunities for bureaucrats to translate official power into individual gain (Waterbury 1993).

[10] For numerous examples in the Middle Eastern context, see Herb (1999).

Two models of administrative supervision, "police-patrol oversight" and "fire-alarm oversight" developed by McCubbins and Schwartz are also particularly instructive (1984; McCubbins et al. 1989). In the police-patrol model of supervision, administrative oversight is centralized, active, and direct. The legislator (principal) continuously monitors his or her administrators (agents) by observing as many administrative actions as possible. The disadvantage of this form of monitoring is that it is costly and the legislator lacks the capacity to comprehensively monitor all the actions of the agents.[11] By using a model of police-patrol oversight, the legislator can only evaluate a small sample of administrative activities, and most problems are likely to go undetected.[12] The alternative, fire-alarm model of oversight is a more passive, indirect, and decentralized system of rules and procedures through which citizens can appeal to courts or special agencies when they experience problems with administrators. These formal channels for citizens to call attention to administrative abuses enable legislators to focus on the root causes of administrative deviance and to punish administrators who have diverged from their legislated mandates. Although McCubbins and Schwartz are concerned with strategies for administrative supervision in democratic contexts, their models are equally useful for understanding how judicial institutions are used by authoritarian regimes as a means to collect accurate information and instill discipline within the state's own institutions.[13]

Sadat (1970–1981) and Mubarak (1981–present) facilitated the reemergence of the administrative courts in the 1970s and 1980s in an effort to rein in the state bureaucracy (Rosberg 1995). The public sector had mushroomed with the vast waves of nationalizations, and the state bureaucracy continued to swell as

---

[11] The delegation of state activities to particular agencies is, in the first place, due to the inability of the legislator to implement policies directly due to constraints on time and expertise.

[12] The police-patrol model of administrative monitoring is even more costly and ineffective in authoritarian contexts. Not only do authoritarian rulers typically have multiple agencies devoted to supervising, auditing, checking, and cross-checking the actions of administrators throughout the state hierarchy. In addition, monitoring agencies are known to devote as much or more energy to spying on one another as they do monitoring threats coming from society, as authoritarian rulers guard against the emergence of power centers even within the regime's monitoring agencies themselves.

[13] The framework developed by McCubbins and Schwartz is inspired from an American context, but it appears that the utility of the fire-alarm model of administrative oversight is not tied exclusively to administrative oversight in democracies. Rather, it applies more broadly to the degree of complexity of state institutions, regardless of whether a state is democratic or authoritarian. "Although our model refers only to Congress, we hazard to hypothesize that as most organizations grow and mature, their top policy makers adopt methods of control that are comparatively decentralized and incentive based. Such methods, we believe, will work more efficiently... than direct, centralized surveillance" (McCubbins and Schwartz 1984: 172).

TABLE 5.1 *Growth of the Egyptian Bureaucracy,*
1952–1987

Year	Number of state employees
1952	350,000
1957	454,000
1963	770,000
1966	1,035,000
1970	1,200,000
1978	1,900,000
1980	2,876,000
1987	3,400,000

Sources: Ministry of Finance, Arab Republic of Egypt, *Statistical Statement for the 1979 Budget*; Nazih Ayubi, *Overstating the Arab State*, p. 299.

a result of the government's provision of jobs to new graduates to stave off social unrest (see Table 5.1). One of the most pressing problems that Nasser and his successors faced under these circumstances was the inability to adequately monitor and discipline bureaucrats throughout the state's administrative hierarchy. With political parties dissolved, judicial independence impaired, the free press suppressed, and citizens stripped of access to institutions through which they could effectively protect their interests, there was little transparency in the political and economic systems. Corruption began to fester as administrators and bureaucrats abused their power and position to prey on citizens, and public sector managers siphoned off resources from the state (Ayubi 1980; Baker 1978; Rosberg 1995: 76–82; Zaki 1999). Not only did this affect the state's institutional performance, but corruption and abuse of power began to undermine the revolutionary legitimacy that the regime enjoyed when it came to power in the 1950s (Rosberg 1995: 83–91). Nasser also feared that the lack of transparency within the state's own administrative hierarchy masked the emergence of "power centers" within the military, the police, and the intelligence services that could challenge his authority.

Nasser attempted to bolster administrative monitoring and discipline through a series of centralized mechanisms. The first was to create a "complaints office" to which citizens could lodge their grievances. This office morphed over time into a vast array of complaints offices attached to various ministries, public sector companies, governorates, and the office of the president itself. Nasser also attempted to carry out administrative reform and monitoring through the establishment of the Central Agency for Organization and Administration; Sadat would later create his own National Council for

Administrative Development. Both strategies were deemed failures (Ayubi 1980: 305–310).

The monitoring agencies suffered from the same principal-agent problems and information asymmetries that had led to administrative abuses in the first place. Complaints offices were better able to overcome principal-agent problems, because they generated an independent stream of information from citizens filing petitions. However, the volume of petitions reaching the central government presented an equally damning problem. The presidential complaints office alone received 4,000 petitions per day, or nearly 1.5 million per year (Ayubi 1980: 285–287). With such an overwhelming volume of petitions, the office could not effectively process even a fraction of the petitions, nor could it identify *a priori* which complaints pointed to the most egregious abuses and which ones were frivolous. Ad hoc arrangements for the discipline of civil servants also proved to be inefficient and prone to abuse.

Administrative problems took on increased urgency with the initiation of Sadat's open door economic policy. The sudden transition from a socialist economy to a mixed public/private sector economy increased the opportunities for corruption and graft exponentially, and by all accounts the problem was severe (Ayubi 1980; Baker 1978: 175–195, 258–265; Hinnebusch 1985: 138–142). Reports from within the state's own National Center for Social and Criminal Research observed that corruption had "become the rule rather than the exception" (Hinnebusch 1985, cited in Ayubi 1979). Lack of bureaucratic discipline furthermore resulted in the inconsistent application of the law and an uncertain investment environment. A major business consulting group operating in Egypt in the 1970s reported that "while new legislation prompted many international companies to examine the possibilities of Egypt as an investment site, most of them found that the Law 43 guidelines were too broad and their application too inconsistent by an Egyptian bureaucracy which was not uniformly committed to the new policy. Largely for this reason, substantial foreign investment was slow to materialize" (Sullivan 1976; see also Carr 1979: 40–53). In some cases, low-level bureaucrats created needless obstructions in order to extract bribes. At other times, bureaucrats interfered with firms because they were ideologically opposed to the new open door economic program.[14] In still other cases, squabbles erupted within various branches of

---

[14] According to the report, "Said a senior official of one of the key ministries recently: 'I have just come out of a meeting with my key coordinating people in the ministry, and they are behind execution of the policy to liberalize the economy and bring in more foreign investment. But the difficulty comes in getting the people further down to go along. The very last man on the totem pole can get things snarled since he is involved in the daily application of decisions. Until you get the little people to go along, you have problems'" (Sullivan 1976: 4).

the bureaucracy, with severe negative consequences for the foreign business community.[15] The *Business International* report recounts numerous examples of foreign companies that lost large sums of money due to the inconsistent application of laws on the books (Sullivan 1976: 75–78, 122–129).[16] The lack of discipline throughout the bureaucratic hierarchy and its adverse impact on the investment environment are summed up in the report's finding that "top people in President Sadat's government sympathize with the difficulties foreign investors will face in Egypt, because they face the same problems themselves" (Sullivan 1976: 4) The *Investment Climate Statement*, compiled by the U.S. Department of Commerce, and the *Economic Trends Report* published by the American embassy found similar problems.

As it became clear that centralized monitoring strategies were failing to produce reliable information on the activities of the state's own institutions, Sadat enhanced the independence and capacity of the administrative court system to serve as a neutral forum in which citizens could voice their grievances and to expose corruption in the state bureaucracy. The regime facilitated the strength and autonomy of the administrative courts in 1972 by returning to them substantial control over appointments, promotions, and other internal functions, all of which were weakened or completely stripped from the administrative courts by presidential decree in 1959.[17] The regime also expanded the institutional capacity of the administrative courts through the 1970s by establishing courts of first instance and appeals courts throughout the country.[18] That the expanded administrative court system provided new avenues for litigants is clear from the increased volume of cases that went to court throughout this period.[19]

The administrative courts helped the regime overcome the design failures inherent to both centralized monitoring agencies and the complaints offices. Administrative courts did not suffer from principal-agent problems as did

---

[15] "Businessmen may get caught in the crossfire between warring factions of the Egyptian bureaucracy, which may disagree on the interpretation of regulations vitally affecting a company's operating efficiency, such as customs duties or taxes" (Sullivan 1976: 4). For an academic analysis of these dynamics, see Baker (1981).

[16] Other business consultants reported the same problems. See, for example, Reckford International, *U.S. Business Experience in Egypt*.

[17] Law 136/1984. For more on these amendments see 'Ubayd, *Istiqlal al-Qada'*, pp. 290–305.

[18] The expansion of the administrative courts is documented in *Waqa'ai Misriyya* and *Majalat Majlis al-Dawla*. A concise list of the expansion of the administrative court system is reproduced in Rosberg (1995: 191).

[19] Moreover, the rate of increase in the number of administrative cases is greater than the rate of increase in other types of cases in the civil courts. This indicates that the increase was not simply due to population growth and other similar factors, but was rather a consequence of the government's new method of monitoring and enforcing bureaucratic discipline.

independent monitoring agencies because they produced a stream of information from aggrieved citizens themselves. At the same time, the hierarchical
structure of the administrative courts enabled the regime to identify the most
significant cases of administrative dysfunction through a coherent system of
procedural rules, standing criteria, and the like.[20] Frivolous petitions were win-
nowed out in the primary courts, but more significant cases made their way up
the judicial ladder, all the while leaving a paper trail for the regime to survey.
Finally, administrative courts provided a built-in mechanism to discipline the
bureaucracy, illustrating Shapiro's observation that judicial institutions play
"fundamental political functions" by acting as avenues "for the upward flow of
information [and] for the downward flow of command" (Shapiro 1980: 643).
To say that the administrative courts could solve all of the dysfunctions of the
Egyptian bureaucracy would surely be an overstatement. But, undoubtedly,
the administrative courts proved more effective than the aborted strategies of
centralized monitoring agencies and complaints offices.

MARKETING JUDICIAL REFORM AT HOME AND ABROAD

Egyptian government officials were keen to bring judicial reforms to the attention of the international business community whenever possible. The General
Authority for Investment and Free Zones published investment guides high-
lighting legal reforms (Arab Republic of Egypt 1977: 9–10), the Minister of
State for Economic Cooperation elaborated on the security of the investment
environment (El-Nazer 1979: 613–622), and the Speaker of Parliament was dis-
patched to talk with American lawyers (Sayed 1980: 167–170). President Sadat
himself talked countless times about the sanctity of the rule of law (*sayadat
al-qanun*), explaining that "the transition from the state of revolution to that
of continuity, a permanent constitution, and state institutions" was underway:

> The time has come for us now to change this stage of revolutionary legitimacy
> to the stage of constitutional legitimacy, particularly since the principles of
> the 23 July Revolution have become deeply entrenched in our land and
> in the conscience of the wide masses so that now they are capable of protecting
> themselves by ordinary means, laws and institutions.
>   We raised the slogan of the sovereignty of the law, and by so doing, we
> restituted the respect and independence of the judicial authority. That is how
> the sovereignty of the law, the establishment of constitutional institutions
> and the independence of the judicial authority enable us to close down

---

[20] These are further examined in Massadeh (1991).

all detention camps for the first time in forty years. All sequestrations were liquidated, and the few particularly cases which needed to be studied were examined, allowing us to turn this page over. No citizen was ever again to be deprived of his political rights and no privileges were to be allowed to one citizen over another in the practice of these rights.[21]

This rule-of-law rhetoric had more than one audience. For foreign investors, it was used to attract capital. For foreign governments, and the United States in particular, it helped signal Egypt's political realignment from the Soviet Union to the West. For Egyptian capitalists, rule-of-law talk was intended to bring back the $40 billion held abroad. And for all Egyptians, rule-of-law rhetoric was used to build a new legitimating ideology after the policy failures and political excesses of the Nasser regime.

There was, of course, a significant gap between the government's rule-of-law rhetoric and the operation of judicial institutions on the ground. As I have noted throughout this chapter, the disparity between rhetoric and reality was particularly significant through the 1970s when the regime sought to attract private investment without placing any practical constraints on its power. It is no wonder that private investors did not risk their assets throughout the 1970s. But institutional constraints on the state became more credible with the establishment of the Supreme Constitutional Court in 1979 and the rehabilitation of the administrative courts. The SCC began to rebuild a property rights regime through dozens of rulings in the economic sphere. The administrative courts also opened new avenues to challenge the decisions of bureaucrats, increasing accountability and giving citizens some measure of satisfaction that the political system had mechanisms for ensuring justice – at least against low-level civil servants in areas that were less politically sensitive.

Business consultancy reports in the 1980s noted these judicial reforms as crucial steps in providing concrete mechanisms for the protection of property rights, and political risk indices also registered positive change (Carr 1979, 40–42). For example, the "bureaucratic quality" index and the "law and order" index compiled by Political Risk Services both recorded positive movement beginning in 1985.[22] These indices provide only a crude approximation of the variables that they purport to track, and they are perhaps better understood as

---

[21] Speech by Anwar Sadat, July 22, 1977. Arab Republic of Egypt, State Information Service, *Speeches and Interviews of President Anwar El Sadat*, p. 108; July 22, 1976, pp. 28, 38.

[22] The Political Risk Services "bureaucratic quality" index measuring the "institutional strength of and quality of the bureaucracy" moved from zero to two on a scale of four. Similarly, their "law and order" index, measuring the "strength and impartiality of the legal system" advanced from two to four on a scale of six.

measures of investor perceptions than the reality on the ground. Still, the new institutional environment was one of the primary reasons for the increase in private investment starting in the 1980s after a full decade of failed attempts to attract capital without institutional reforms.[23]

The success of these institutional reforms should not be overstated. The Egyptian judiciary continued to face overwhelming problems, particularly in terms of limited capacity (Arab Republic of Egypt 1998; Bentley 1994), which to this day has an adverse impact on the country's investment climate (Zaki 1999). What is intriguing is that an authoritarian regime was first compelled to use rule-of-law rhetoric, eventually going well beyond mere statements to carry out concrete and meaningful institutional reforms. The pressures facing the regime were not idiosyncratic, nor were the motives for initiating judicial reform. In fact, the government was grappling with many of the same dysfunctions that plague other authoritarian regimes. With unchecked power, the government was unable to attract private investment. With low levels of transparency and accountability, the government faced difficulties maintaining order and discipline throughout the state's administrative hierarchy. With the failure of pan-Arabism and the deterioration of the economy, the substantive basis of the regime's legitimacy suffered.

The new Supreme Constitutional Court and the reformed administrative courts helped the regime ameliorate these pathologies by attracting investment capital, strengthening discipline within its own administrative bureaucracy, forging a new legitimizing ideology around "the rule of law" and a "state of institutions," and doing away with populist, Nasser-era legislation in a politically innocuous way (Moustafa 2007).[24] However, judicial reforms provided institutional openings for political activists to challenge the executive in ways that fundamentally transformed patterns of interaction between the state and society. For the first time since the 1952 military coup, political activists could credibly challenge regime legislation by simply initiating constitutional litigation, a process that required few financial resources and enabled activists to circumvent the regime's highly restrictive, corporatist political framework.

---

[23] It must also be noted that 1979 was the year that Anwar Sadat signed the peace treaty with Israel, thus putting to rest one of the most important foreign policy concerns of foreign investors.

[24] Elsewhere (Moustafa 2007), I examine how dozens of rulings in the areas of privatization, housing reform, and labor law reform enabled the regime to overturn socialist-oriented policies without having to face direct opposition from social groups that were threatened by economic reform. Liberal rulings enabled the executive leadership to explain that they were simply respecting an autonomous rule-of-law system rather than implementing controversial reforms through more overt political channels.

MOBILIZING THROUGH THE COURTS

From the beginning of its operations in 1979, the Supreme Constitutional Court did not shy away from challenging the government on a number of politically charged issues. In one of its earliest rulings, the SCC enabled hundreds of prominent opposition activists to return to political life, including Wafd Party leader Fuad Serag al-Din and the Nasserist Party founder Dia' al-Din Dawud.[25] Another ruling in 1988 forced the legalization of the opposition Nasserist Party against government objections.[26] The SCC even ruled national election laws unconstitutional in 1987 and 1990, forcing the dissolution of the People's Assembly, the creation of a new electoral system, and early elections.[27] Two similar rulings forced comparable reforms to the system of elections for both the Upper House (*Majlis al-Shura*) and local council elections nationwide.[28] Although the rulings on election laws hardly undermined the government's grip on power, they did significantly undermine the corporatist system of opposition control by opening the political field to independent candidates and enabling the Muslim Brotherhood to run independent candidates in the 2000 and 2005 People's Assembly elections.

The SCC also issued a number of important rulings in the area of press liberties.[29] In February 1993, the SCC struck down a provision in the code of criminal procedures dealing with libel cases. The provision required defendants charged in libel cases to present proof validating their published statements within a five-day period of notification by the prosecutor. The SCC ruled that the time limit was too strict and that it interfered with the ability of the press to monitor the government, to uncover corruption and inefficiencies, and to encourage good governance. The ruling asserted that freedom of expression is an essential feature of a proper functioning democracy and that the five-day provision was a flagrant and unnecessary violation of article 47 of the constitution.[30] Following on the heels of this legal victory, the Labor Party successfully defeated a law that had made heads of political parties responsible for all publications in party newspapers, along with the reporter and the

[25] SCC, 26 June 1986, *al-Mahkama al-Dusturiyya al-'Ulya* [hereafter *al-Mahkama*], vol. 3, 353.
[26] SCC, May 7, 1988, *al-Mahkama*, vol. 4, 98.
[27] SCC, May 16, 1987, *al-Mahkama*, vol. 4, 31; SCC, 19 May 1990, *al-Mahkama*, vol. 4, 256.
[28] SCC, April 15, 1989, *al-Mahkama*, vol. 4, 205; SCC, April 15, 1989, *al-Mahkama*, vol. 4, 191.
[29] The SCC also issued a number of rulings protecting other important civil liberties throughout this period, but due to space constraints I discuss only those pertaining to press liberties. Other notable rulings overturned laws presuming the guilt of the accused and those empowering the executive to punish suspects without trial. See SCC, Jan 2, 1993, *al-Mahkama* vol. 5.2, 103 and SCC, June 15, 1996, *al-Mahkama* vol. 7, 739.
[30] SCC, Feb. 6, 1993, *al-Mahkama*, vol. 5(2), 183.

editor-in-chief of the newspaper in cases of libel claims against public officials. Two years later, the SCC extended its ruling to ban the application of vicarious criminal liability to libel cases involving the editors-in-chief of newspapers.[31]

This ruling represented an important precedent, as it was the first time that a human rights nongovernmental organization (NGO), the Center for Human Rights Legal Aid (CHRLA), successfully challenged legislation in front of the Supreme Constitutional Court. The CHRLA represented a new breed of human rights organization that went beyond simply documenting human rights abuses to confronting the government in the courtroom. It quickly became the most dynamic human rights organization, initiating 500 cases in its first full year of operation, 1,323 cases in 1996, and 1,616 by 1997. In hopes of emulating the model provided by CHRLA, human rights activists launched additional legal aid organizations with different missions. The Center for Women's Legal Aid was established in 1995 to provide free legal aid to women dealing with a range of issues including divorce, child custody, and various forms of discrimination.[32] The Land Center for Human Rights joined the ranks of legal aid organizations in 1996 and dedicated its energies to providing free legal aid to peasants.[33] The Human Rights Center for the Assistance of Prisoners (HRCAP) similarly provided legal aid to prisoners and the families of detained individuals by investigating allegations of torture, monitoring prison conditions, and fighting the phenomenon of recurrent detention and torture through litigation.[34] Opposition parties began to offer free legal aid as well, with the Wafd Party's Committee for Legal Aid providing free representation in more than 400 cases per year beginning in 1997.[35]

Legal mobilization became the dominant strategy for human rights defenders not only because of the opportunities that public interest litigation afforded

---

[31] SCC, Feb. 1, 1997, *al-Mahkama*, vol. 8, 286.

[32] The Center initiated 71 cases in its first year, 142 in 1996, and 146 in 1997, in addition to providing legal advice to 1,400 women in its first three years of activity.

[33] With the land reform law 96 of 1992 coming into full effect in October 1997, hundreds of thousands of peasants faced potential eviction in the late 1990s. Lawsuits between landlords and tenants began to enter into the courts by the thousands. Between 1996 and 2000 the Land Center for Human Rights represented peasants in more than 4,000 cases and provided legal advice to thousands more (Interview with Mahmoud Gabr, Director of Legal Unit, Land Center for Human Rights, November 18, 2000).

[34] In each of its first five years of operation, the Human Rights Center for the Assistance of Prisoners launched more than 200 court cases and gave free assistance (legal and otherwise) to between 7,000–8,000 victims per year (Correspondence with Muhammad Zar'ei, Director of the Human Rights Center for the Assistance of Prisoners, January 24, 2002).

[35] Interview with Muhammad Gom'a, vice-chairman of the Wafd Committee for Legal Aid, February 17, 2001.

but also because of the myriad obstacles to mobilizing a broad social movement. Gasser 'Abd al-Raziq, director of CHRLA for much of the 1990s, explained that "in Egypt, where you have a relatively independent judiciary, the only way to promote reform is to have legal battles all the time. It's the only way that we can act as a force for change."

This brief review of opposition and human rights activism through the 1990s illustrates how the new Supreme Constitutional Court and the administrative courts provided institutional openings for political activists to challenge the state. For the first time since the 1952 military coup, political activists could credibly challenge the government by simply initiating litigation, a process that required few financial resources and allowed activists to circumvent the highly restrictive, corporatist political framework. Most importantly, litigation enabled activists to challenge the government without having to initiate a broad social movement, a task that is all but impossible in Egypt's highly restrictive political environment.

THE LIMITS OF LEGAL MOBILIZATION: STATE SECURITY COURTS AND "INSULATED LIBERALISM"

Although the Supreme Constitutional Court took surprisingly bold stands on most political issues, there were important limits to SCC activism. At odds with its strong record of rights activism, the SCC ruled Egypt's Emergency State Security Courts constitutional, and it has conspicuously delayed issuing a ruling on the constitutionality of civilian transfers to military courts. Given that Egypt has remained in a perpetual state of emergency for all but six months since 1967, the Emergency State Security Courts and, more recently, the military courts have effectively formed a parallel legal system with fewer procedural safeguards, serving as the ultimate regime check on challenges to its power (Brown 1997; Center for Human Legal Rights Aid 1995; Ubayd 1991).[36]

By 1983, dozens of cases had already been transferred to the Supreme Constitutional Court contesting a legal provision denying defendants the right to appeal rulings of Emergency State Security Courts in the regular judiciary. Plaintiffs contended that the provision violated the right of due process and the competency of the administrative courts, as defined in articles 68 and 172 of

---

[36] For more on the structure, composition, and procedures of the Emergency State Security Courts and the Military Courts see Brown (1997), Ubayd (1991), and The Center for Human Rights Legal Aid (1995).

the constitution.[37] But the following year the Supreme Constitutional Court ruled the Security Courts constitutional (Arab Republic of Egypt, *al-Mahkama* 1984: 80). The SCC reasoned that since article 171 of the constitution provided for the establishment of the State Security Courts, they must be considered a legitimate and regular component of the judicial authority.[38] Based upon this reasoning, the SCC rejected the plaintiff's claim concerning article 68 protections guaranteeing the right to litigation and the right of every citizen to refer to his competent judge. The SCC also reasoned that the provision of law 50/1982, giving the State Security Courts the sole competency to adjudicate their own appeals and complaints, was not in conflict with article 172 of the constitution. Finally, the SCC contended that the procedures governing State Security Court cases were in conformity with the due process standards available in other Egyptian judicial bodies, such as the right of suspects to be informed of the reasons for their detention and their right to legal representation.

Although this ruling was based on legal reasoning that many constitutional scholars and human rights activists found questionable at best, the Supreme Constitutional Court never looked back and refused to revisit the question of State Security Court competency. Six months after this landmark decision, the SCC summarily dismissed forty-one additional cases contesting the jurisdiction of the State Security Courts (*al-Mahkama* 1984: 90–95). The SCC dismissed another thirty cases petitioning the same provision over the course of the following year (*al-Mahkama* 1984: 108–113, 152–157, 189–194). The flood of cases contesting the competency of the State Security Courts in such a short period of time reveals the extent to which the regime depends upon this parallel legal track as a tool to sideline political opponents. The large volume of cases transferred to the SCC from the administrative courts also underlines the determination of administrative court judges to assert their institutional interests and to fend off encroachment from the State Security Courts. Finally, the Supreme Constitutional Court's reluctance to strike down provisions denying citizens the right of appeal to regular judicial institutions, despite the dozens

---

[37] Article 68 reads, "The right to litigation is inalienable for all. Every citizen has the right to refer to his competent judge. The state shall guarantee the accessibility of the judicial organs to litigants, and the rapidity of rendering decisions on cases. Any provision in the law stipulating the immunity of any act or administrative decision from the control of the judiciary shall be prohibited." Article 172 of the Constitution reads that "[t]he State Council shall be an independent judicial organ competent to take decisions in administrative disputes and disciplinary cases. The law shall determine its other competences."

[38] Article 171 of the Constitution reads, "The law shall regulate the organization of the State Security Courts and shall prescribe their competences and the conditions to be fulfilled by those who occupy the office of judge in them."

of opportunities to do so, illustrates the SCC's reluctance to challenge the core interests of the regime.

In the 1990s, the SCC faced a similar dilemma with even more profound implications when it received petitions requesting judicial review of the regime's increasing use of military courts to try civilians. Despite the extensive controls that the president holds over the Emergency State Security Courts, there were isolated cases in which the emergency courts handed down rulings that were quite embarrassing for the regime in the late 1980s and early 1990s.[39] These occasional inconveniences in the Emergency State Security Courts prompted the regime to begin using the military courts (*mahakim al-askariyya*) to try terrorism cases throughout the 1990s.[40] Military courts provide an airtight avenue for the regime to try its opponents; all judges are military officers appointed directly by the Minister of Defense and the president for two-year renewable terms, and there are almost no procedural safeguards, with trials held in secret and no right to appeal.

The first cases transferred to the military courts concerned defendants accused of specific acts of terrorism. However, within just a few years the regime began to try civilians for mere affiliation with moderate Islamist groups, such as the Muslim Brotherhood.[41] The regime's use of military courts to try civilians was hotly contested, and opponents of the regime attempted to wage a legal battle over the procedure in the early 1990s. Both liberal reformers and Islamist activists argued that, at best, military law 25/1966 gave the president the authority to transfer whole categories of crimes to the military judiciary, but it did not permit the president to hand-pick individual cases for transfer

---

[39] For example, in 1990 an emergency court acquitted Sheikh Omar Abdel Rahman and forty-eight of his followers when it was revealed in court that confessions were extracted through torture. The government was able to overturn the verdict on "procedural grounds" and retry the defendants, but only after an uncomfortable exposition of the regime's disregard for human rights. In another trial of twenty-four Islamists charged with assassinating parliamentary speaker Rifa't al-Mahgoub in the early 1990s, the panel of judges again dismissed the case when they found that confessions were extracted through torture. Judge Wahid Mahmud Ibrahim did not spare any details, announcing that medical reports proved the defendants had been severely beaten, hung upside down, and subjected to electric shocks to their genitals (Farahang 1997). Additional acquittals based upon allegations of torture are provided in Brown (1997: 98–99).

[40] The first such case was transferred to a military court by Mubarak by Presidential Decree 375/1992. From December 1992 through April 1995 alone a total of 483 civilians were transferred to military courts for trial. Sixty-four were sentenced to death. According to the 1998 annual report of the Arab Center for the Independence of the Judiciary and the Legal Profession, civilian transfers to military courts reached as high as 317 in 1997 alone.

[41] Presidential Decree No. 297/1995 transferred the cases of forty-nine members of the Muslim Brotherhood from Lawsuit 8 Military No. 136/1995 in the Higher State Security court to the military judiciary (Center for Human Rights Legal Aid 1995). In 1996 the government again transferred twelve members of the emerging Wasat Party to the military court.

(Brown 1997: 115). Despite an extensive legal battle, activists were unable to prevail.

SCC justices must look after their long-term interests vis-à-vis the regime and pick their battles appropriately.[42] Although the Supreme Constitutional Court had ample opportunities to strike down the provisions denying citizens the right of appeal to regular judicial institutions, the SCC almost certainly exercised constraint because impeding the function of the exceptional courts would likely have resulted in a futile confrontation with the regime.

Even outside of the military courts the regime effectively detains its political opponents for long periods of time through a procedure known as "recurrent detention." Under article three of the emergency law, prosecutors can detain any citizen for up to thirty days without charges. Once a subject of administrative detention is released within the required thirty-day period, he is sometimes simply transferred to another prison or holding facility and then registered once again for another thirty-day period, essentially allowing state security forces to lock up anyone it wishes for months or even years at a time. Human rights organizations first brought the phenomenon of recurrent detention to light through extensive documentation in the 1990s. The Egyptian Organization for Human Rights (EOHR) noted that the problem became particularly prevalent after 1992 when the regime began to wage a protracted campaign against militant Islamists.[43] Between 1991 and 1996 the EOHR documented 7,891 cases of recurrent detention, and the number of actual cases was almost certainly much higher (EOHR 1996). Ninety percent of EOHR investigations revealed that detained subjects suffered from torture, and most were denied the right to legal representation or family visits.

Article three of the emergency law permits the President of the Republic, or anyone representing him, to "detain persons posing a threat to security and public order." However, the emergency law does not define the terms "threat," "security," and "public order," leaving it to prosecutors to apply the provision with its broadest possible interpretation. Administrative courts issued a number of rulings attempting to define and limit the application of article three, but their rulings landed on deaf ears.

Ironically, the regime's ability to transfer select cases to exceptional courts and even to detain political opponents indefinitely through the practice of

---

[42] In an interview, former Chief Justice Awad al-Morr described the Egyptian political system as a "red-line system," where there are implicit understandings between the regime and the opposition over how far political activism will be tolerated (personal interview, June 11, 2000).

[43] The problem of recurrent detention was further aggravated by the "antiterrorism" law 97/1992, which expanded the authority of the public prosecutor's office and weakened the oversight of the administrative courts.

recurrent detention facilitated the independence of the regular judiciary. The Supreme Constitutional Court and the administrative courts were able to push a liberal agenda in less significant areas of political life and to maintain their autonomy from the executive largely because the regime was confident that it ultimately retained full control over its political opponents. Supreme Constitutional Court activism may therefore be characterized as "insulated liberalism." Court rulings had an impact upon state policy, but judicial institutions were ultimately bounded by a profoundly illiberal political system.

6

Courts Out of Context: Authoritarian Sources of Judicial Failure in Chile (1973–1990) and Argentina (1976–1983)

Robert Barros

INTRODUCTION

The purpose of this chapter is to investigate how military dictatorships that concentrate formerly separated and shared powers affect the activity of regular courts that survive from a prior, formally constitutional regime. Specifically, I explore two dictatorships, the Argentine (1976–1983) and the Chilean (1973–1990), to examine whether courts can conceivably uphold rights and liberties, as warranted by the constitutional definition of their powers, out of context; that is, once dictatorship has displaced the regular constitutional-institutional framework. This study thus points to the limits on courts in authoritarian regimes and to the limits of what might be called "partial constitutionalism" – the idea that a judiciary, as structured by a given constitution, ought to uphold and defend another part of the constitution, its guarantees of rights, even after the core institutions of that constitution – elected legislative and executive institutions – have been suppressed and displaced by an autocratic centralization of power.

This formulation may appear peculiar, but it is noteworthy that such expectations regarding the potentialities of courts in authoritarian regimes are implicit in many critical accounts of the judiciary under dictatorship. Such expectations are even to be found in the final official reports issued by the truth commissions formed in the aftermath of military rule to clarify the worst violations of rights in Argentina and Chile, the *Comisión Nacional sobre la Desaparición de Personas* (hereafter CONADEP) and the *Comisión Nacional*

This chapter benefited from discussions with Paola Bergallo, Martín Böhmer, María Angélica Gelli, Lucas Grosman, and the participants at the Philadelphia conference on courts in authoritarian regimes.

de Verdad y Reconciliación's (hereafter *Comisión Rettig* [1]), respectively. Each of these reports squarely identified the national armed forces, intelligence, and police agencies as responsible for the massive rights violations that each state for the first time thus officially recognized, quantified, and began to seek to repair (CONADEP 1984 and *Comisión Rettig* 1991); however, each report also included a chapter on the judiciary that maintained that the courts were partially responsible for the massive rights violations that had occurred.

The arguments of both reports are strikingly similar: in the face of unprecedented, systematic, arbitrary repressive acts by organs of the state, the power charged with upholding rights, the judiciary, had absolutely failed to protect the thousands of individuals who were victims of this onslaught of illegal force. More specifically, in both countries the courts had allowed the state free rein in its use of powers applicable under states of siege, stood aloof from supervising military courts, and abandoned the disappeared to their fate by making complacent, formalistic decisions on the writ of habeas corpus. Both commissions found that the judiciary had failed in its constitutional mission to uphold rights and had thereby been complicit in the deaths of thousands of victims of state violence. The tone of these charges is clear from the following excerpts. According to the CONADEP (1984: 392), "The Judicial Power, which should have set itself as a brake on the prevailing absolutism, became in fact a simulacra of the jurisdictional function to protect its external image.... The reticence, and even the complacency of a good part of the judiciary, completed the picture of abandonment of human rights." In Chile, the *Comisión Rettig* maintained that the stance adopted by the judiciary during the military regime "produced, in some important and involuntary measure, an aggravation of the process of systematic human rights violations, both in regards to immediate violations, by not providing protection to the persons detained in the cases denounced, as well as by giving repressive agents growing certainty of impunity for their criminal actions" (*Comisión Rettig* 1991: 97).

The objective of this chapter is not to criticize these reports, defend the actions of the Argentine or the Chilean judiciary, or evaluate the ethical dilemmas before judges in authoritarian situations. Rather I seek to contribute to an understanding of judicial institutions in autocratic polities by exploring the counterfactual implicit in each truth commission's finding that the judiciary had failed: that even in authoritarian contexts, if there had been

---

[1] This unofficial name was coined after the commission's president, the former Senator Raúl Rettig.

the appropriate volition among judges, courts could have effectively exercised
their powers and upheld the liberties and legal procedures whose defense
was ascribed to each judiciary under their respective national constitutions.[2] I
address this question by examining how the broader political context created
by dictatorship impinged upon the operation of courts as institutions setting
limits upon arbitrary repressive practices in the two cases.

One might argue that to concentrate on judicial failure in the face of
state terrorism is to focus on an extreme situation that cannot possibly elucidate the operation of courts in authoritarian regimes. However, I suggest that
the mutations in the political-institutional setting of the courts not only explain
the judiciary's inability to uphold rights of due process, liberty, and integrity but
also illustrate general dynamics that constrain courts in authoritarian regimes;
these dynamics in turn reflect and intensify restrictions upon judicial activity
that are common in regular constitutional systems.

The shifts effected by dictatorship that transformed the political-institutional
setting of courts, with variations in each case, involved the following: (a) a turn
toward the mass utilization of discretional forms of coercive political control by
state agents situated outside of the judiciary, such as administrative detention
under state-of-siege powers and absolutely unlawful abduction and extrajudicial murder; (b) the activation of special courts also external to the judiciary
that employed procedures and standards of proof far less demanding and rule-
bound than regular judicial procedures and that were staffed by officials tied to
the same military hierarchies that wielded legislative and executive power; and
(c) most fundamentally, the suppression of representation and the separation
of powers, as executive and legislative functions were concentrated at the apex
of the same military forces whose subordinate officers or units were effecting
the repression (a) and exceptional forms of justice (b).

In both Chile and Argentina these institutional mutations were sufficiently
consequential as to give rise to the type of judicial failure identified by each
country's truth commission. Dictatorships do not have to interfere with judges
(although they did in Argentina), nor involve the courts in political repression,
to render courts ineffectual before extralegal and/or extraordinary repression.
In the face of the formidable shifts in the setting of judicial activity just mentioned, judges had only to apply the law and decide cases following standard
procedures to be rendered (1) ineffective before extralegal repression since the

---

[2] Strikingly, apologists for military rule shared this assumption with critics of military rule when
the former insisted that the independence of the courts after military intervention provided for
the protection of rights and the rule of law. For a Chilean example, see Navarrete (1974). On
the status of the constitutions nominally in force in both countries, see footnote 13.

state agencies that courts regularly turned to for investigatory assistance were now in the hands of agents *directly or indirectly associated with or subordinate* to the forces wielding prerogative repressive force; (2) incompetent before administrative detentions ordered under states of siege because both court systems, under the guise of the separation of powers, had traditionally refrained from qualifying the executive's use of these prerogative powers; and (3) generally secondary and dependent, given each regime's facile capacity to make laws that the courts had to apply and that could be made to circumvent the courts when and if necessary. In this regard, existing features of courts under democracy (2 and 3 just mentioned) facilitated each dictatorship's ability to apply massive coercive force against political enemies unconstrained by the judiciary. These effects were primarily the consequence of transformations in the context external to the judiciary. The courts were devitalized by the authoritarian context, yet it was perhaps inevitable also that the Argentine and Chilean judiciaries would bear part of the blame for rights violations, if only because courts were associated with expectations about rights that had their origins in nonauthoritarian contexts.

THE CONTEXT OF JUDICIAL FAILURE: MILITARY DICTATORSHIP AND CONSTITUTIONAL EXCEPTION

Notably, "judicial failure" arose in countries that, otherwise, were very different along significant dimensions, such as their prior political-institutional history, traditions of judicial independence, and nature of the crises that gave rise to military rule, as well as each dictatorship's organization of authority, composition of its security apparatus, and patterns of repression. The significance of many of these variables, particularly those that concern the organizational format of each authoritarian regime, for the operation of courts is unclear: we lack the fine-grained knowledge of the inner workings of these dictatorships that would allow us to analyze how the characteristics mentioned impinged upon the situation, strategies, and decisions of military and judicial actors. Nevertheless, these dimensions are worth sketching as they provide context for the analysis that follows, are a source of hypotheses for further research, and, given judicial failure in both polities, suggest that the common institutional mutations associated with military rule were more significant than differences in prior political-institutional history, particularly in regard to the judiciary, or in the structure of each authoritarian regime.

Within the post-World War II Latin American context, the Chilean and Argentine polities stood at opposite extremes on a continuum of regime stability and instability. Chile, along with Uruguay, was the exception to the Latin

American pattern of recurrent military intervention, typified and taken to an extreme by Argentina. Prior to the 1973 coup, Chile was renowned for its highly legalistic, competitive politics and the solidity of its representative and judicial institutions – the operation of Congress, for example, had only been interrupted briefly on two occasions during the twentieth century (in 1924 and 1932). This institutional stability was associated with the emergence of professional armed forces, as well as a functionally independent judiciary that never experienced the political dismissal of justices that accompanied regime crises in Argentina. A further consequence of this history – one that weighed heavily on the military government – was that the breakdown of democracy in Chile emerged from within the constitutional system, after a democratically elected left-wing government – the *Unidad Popular* – attempted to implement a program of socialist transformation through legality. These events precipitated sharp social conflict, polarization, an insoluble constitutional crisis, and eventually military intervention. Prior to the coup the clash between government and opposition increasingly took the form of a conflict over the legality and constitutionality of the Allende government's measures; over time the Supreme Court fell in with the opposition after repeatedly lodging complaints that government officials were not implementing judicial resolutions.[3] Against this backdrop, within a day of the military coup the president of the Supreme Court publicly declared his satisfaction with the new government's intention to uphold judicial rulings without interference.

After the first *coup de etat* in 1930, the Argentine political history leading up to the 1976 military coup, as is also well known, was one of repeated military intervention following brief interludes of civilian government and a failure – particularly after the emergence of Peronism in the mid-1940s – to find a political-institutional formula that could protect dominant class interests without involving military rule or the proscription of Argentina's single largest political party, the Peronist *Partido Justicialista*. With military coups in 1943, 1955, 1962, 1966, and 1976, this "impossible game" entangled the military and the judiciary in the "Peronist" versus "anti-Peronist" struggle, generating

---

[3] On at least eleven occasions the president of the Supreme Court notified President Allende or his Minister of the Interior of situations when judicial resolutions were not being implemented. The rulings in question usually ordered the eviction of illegally occupied farms or factories. These notes are reproduced in Orden de Abogados (1980: 69–129). The Supreme Court was not involved in the central constitutional controversy that divided the government and the opposition Congress, which concerned the super-majority required to override a presidential veto of a constitutional reform. This task fell to the newly created Constitutional Tribunal, which declared itself incompetent to decide. On Chile's first Constitutional Tribunal, see Silva Cimma (1977).

factionalism within the armed forces and unstable tenure among Supreme Court justices, notwithstanding the 1853 Constitution's provision for office during "good behavior."

After the first Peronist government impeached three of five justices in 1946, the military responded upon taking power in 1955 with a purge of the court. This purge proved to be the first act in what would become a cycle of judicial turnovers whereby the Supreme Court was reappointed with each transition to and from military rule.[4] A related byproduct of this pattern of regime instability was the development by the Supreme Court of a peculiarly Argentine branch of jurisprudence, the *"doctrina de facto,"* regarding the continuous force of the legal enactments of *"de facto"* governments.[5]

This ongoing history also shaped the events that culminated in the 1976 coup. Shut out by proscription and military rule, factions within Peronism and the Left turned to armed activity in 1970 as a tactic to push for a return to civilian rule. These operations, however, continued after the military withdrew in 1973 and Peron himself returned to Argentina and the presidency. In contrast to Chile, the threat to order in Argentina emerged outside of constitutional channels. Particularly after Peron's death in 1974, it took the form of internecine warfare between right-wing and left-wing factions of Peronism, as government-organized death squads responded to the left guerrillas, as well as clashes between the guerillas and the military.

Argentina and Chile prior to the onset of military rule, therefore, were societies with very different patterns of political organization and conflict, had undergone very different crises, and bore very different traditions of judicial independence, understood as independence from the executive. These contrasts in political, institutional, judicial, and military history were associated

---

4 Following coups in 1955, 1966, and 1976, the entering military governments sacked the Supreme Court. In turn, succeeding civilian presidents maintained the cycle by appointing new justices after the resignation of the military appointees. Except for the first coup in 1930, the 1962 coup, which ousted President Arturo Frondizi after Peronist-backed candidates won gubernatorial and legislative elections, was the only coup that did not involve military reappointment of the Supreme Court. Following Peron's presidency the change in the turnover rates of Supreme Court justices is striking: prior to his government 82% of all justices' terms ended because of death or retirement; subsequently, 91% of all justices left the court prematurely because of irregular removal, resignation, or impeachment (Iaryczower, Spiller, and Tommasi 2002: 702). On the relations between the Supreme Court and prior military governments, see Ancarola (2001), Carrió (1996), Gelli 2000, Pellet Lastra 2000, and Snow (1975).

5 On the *"doctrina de facto"* and its evolution since 1930, see Bidart Campos (1989: II:505–537); Cayuso and Gelli (1988), and Groismann (1989). This jurisprudence did not impugn the illegitimacy of authoritarian power. Rather on the grounds of a *"de facto"* government's factual control of power, it sought to define the scope of the powers possessed by military regimes and, in particular, the validity over time and transitions of their administrative and legislative acts.

with important differences in the specifics of how each military dictatorship organized its rule[6]; some of these differences were also influenced by lessons that military officials and advisors in one country drew from events in the other.[7] Nevertheless, these many differences also were set within broadly similar political-ideological universes that defined some variant of liberal constitutional democracy as the "normal" political order, even as important sectors of the upper and middle classes, the political class, and the military in both countries came to advocate military rule as an "exception" that was preferable to continued political conflict and social disorder.

[6] The interservice negotiations within the Argentine military in 1976, for example, are said to have been overshadowed by prior experiences of military rule, particularly the preceding dictatorship of General Juan Carlos Ongania, in which Ongania exercised executive and legislative powers without a military junta. To avoid such personalization of power, the armed forces in 1976 formed a military junta that, as "supreme organ of the Nation," designated the president and granted him executive and legislative powers, but retained powers associated with the armed forces as well as the declaration of the state of siege. Provision was also made for junta participation in the legislative process through a legislative advisory commission whenever this commission resolved that a bill submitted by the executive was of "significant transcendence." The legislative advisory commission was staffed by three representatives from each of the three branches of the armed forces. Both the military junta, except when considering the removal of the president, and the legislative advisory commission were to decide by absolute majority. At least on paper, these were the terms of the dictatorship's internal organization as stipulated in the "Statute for the Process of National Reorganization" and Law 21.256, respectively published in the *Boletín Oficial*, March 31, 1976 and March 26, 1976. Whether and how these institutions operated in practice is only hazily known. The chief source (Fontana 1987) is based on scant documentation of the internal workings of the dictatorship.

Similarly, it has been suggested that the reversals of repressive legislation and policy upon each pendular shift in regime in Argentina, particularly the 1974 amnesty of political prisoners, convinced high-ranking military officers of the futility of administrative (state of siege) and repressive penal responses to subversion and contributed to the turn to a strategy of physical annihilation of opponents (Acuña and Smulovitz 1995; 29; Pereira 2005; 130).

In Chile, on the other hand, despite the concentration of executive power in General Pinochet and the widespread interpretation of the Chilean regime as a personalistic dictatorship, Pinochet's hold on the executive, important sectors of the political class, and the military was counterbalanced by a military junta that wielded legislative and constituent powers. Until the 1980 Constitution went into force in March 1981, General Pinochet was one of four members of the junta; subsequently an army general represented him. However, unanimity was the effective decision rule, which allowed Pinochet and his later delegate to veto legislation, but it also denied him of the power to legislate without the agreement of the other commanders. The adoption of these institutions and their effect upon the military regime are reconstructed in Barros (2002).

[7] Thus, Acuña and Smulovitz (1995: 29) conjecture that a clandestine strategy of repression was adopted in Argentina to avoid the international protests and pressures that the Chilean military faced after an initial period of open repression. In Chile, Pinochet's chief constitutional advisor, Jaime Guzmán, on the other hand, explicitly referred to Argentina to argue that prolonged military rule was futile and that a new constitution was imperative (Barros 2002: 206).

Military Dictatorship as Constitutional Exception

This liberal-constitutional political-ideological backdrop to the Argentine and Chilean political crises of the 1970s shaped the range of alternatives to civilian rule that were acceptable internationally and internally, and indirectly contributed to defining the character of each military dictatorship.[8] In particular, this liberal-constitutional tradition, however qualified in practice by the reality of dictatorship, set constraints on how law and the courts could be utilized publicly by each authoritarian regime.[9] As a result, in Chile and Argentina the military presented their intervention and rule as an exception impelled by the force of circumstances and stipulated that their government would last only until the normalization of conditions allowed democracy to be restored. In both cases, the military made clear that temporary rule could be protracted and that it was the regime's prerogative to decide when normalcy prevailed. Nevertheless, the range of conceivable regimes tended to be restricted to two forms: either some variant of constitutional democracy, which in the short term appeared untenable, or military rule that could be more or less prolonged, but could not easily be established as an acceptable form of regular rule. Accordingly, unlike their totalitarian or revolutionary counterparts, neither military dictatorship set out to organize a "new regime" on a permanent basis.[10]

In their form and objectives, both regimes then portrayed themselves as variants on the classical model of dictatorship: in response to severe threats to state continuity, a body or individual assumed extraordinary powers of rule, unconstrained by ordinary constitutional limits, precisely to restore order and

---

[8] As Juan Linz noted in reference to the post-1964 Brazilian military dictatorship, the international political-ideological climate after World War II left little room for nonliberal, authoritarian experiments. Given these constraints, he characterized the Brazilian military government as an "authoritarian situation," rather than an authoritarian regime because it enjoyed little space to institutionalize itself as a regime. On similar terms, recent Latin American dictatorships were distinguished from interwar European mobilizing totalitarian regimes during the theoretical discussion of the late 1970s (Cardoso 1979).

[9] In many situations the consequences of these constraints were perverse because their acknowledgment by military rulers tended to result in the opposite of freedom and worse, as what could not be done legally in public was done without judicial oversight in secret by each dictatorship's security forces. Elsewhere (Barros 2002: 152–158) I have shown that the turn to clandestine repression in Chile occurred after members of the junta recognized that they could not lawfully try prominent figures from the Allende regime. Similarly, Osiel (1995: 521, 524) suggests that the Argentine military's perception that Supreme Court judges were not sufficiently cooperative drove political repression underground.

[10] This claim may appear controversial in regard to the 1980 Chilean Constitution. However, despite the constitution's objectionable features and associations with prolonging military rule, it was conceived as a variant of constitutional democracy. On this point, see Barros (2002).

conditions under which the constitution could again function. Despite this characterization, the distance from the classical model was always in evidence: in neither military dictatorship were exceptional absolute powers conferred by civilians according to prior constitutional procedures, nor were dictatorial powers authorized subject to a temporal limit.[11] Still, in both Argentina and Chile, notwithstanding the fact of usurpation, the military regimes that took power in the 1970s bore some affinity, although qualified, to the model of dictatorship: in both cases an exceptional institute had been constituted that obtained – in fact, arrogated – supreme power to confront a situation perceived to be beyond the capacity of regular constitutional institutions. Fundamentally, this meant that neither military regime could easily move beyond the dichotomy that opposed constitutional and exceptional regimes.[12]

Exception, Dictatorship, and the Courts

This type of exceptional military dictatorship involved at least two types of departure from the rule of law that impinged upon the operation of the pre-existing judicial system in each country. The first concerned the constitution as a higher law. In both cases, the military's arrogation and centralization of legislative and executive power shattered the constitutional organization and separation of powers. This had the effect of "deconstitutionalizing" the constitutional text nominally in force, as the constitution became endogenous to the authoritarian ruling body that could at its prerogative enact or amend nominally constitutional norms.[13] The second departure concerned the rule

---

[11] For the same reason, neither case can be subsumed under Schmitt's (1923/1985) category of "commissary dictatorship." On the classical model of dictatorship, see Nicolet (2004) and Rossiter (1948). As discussed later, both military regimes drew upon each country's constitutional provisions for exceptional powers to frame and justify some emergency measures, particularly administrative detentions and restrictions on rights. However, in neither case were the extraordinary measures taken limited to those permissible by pre-coup constitutional emergency powers. Similarly, in neither case was the use of emergency powers conferred by the constitutionally defined authorizing power, as the Congress had been suppressed in both countries.

[12] In both cases, factions advocated permanent military rule and presented projects to mobilize civilians. However, proponents of a military-civic movement made no headway in Chile, whereas the best-known project of civil-military convergence in Argentina, Admiral Massera's scheme to co-opt Montonero prisoners, was intended to build a personal power base in anticipation of eventual competitive elections.

[13] Regarding the status of the constitution under each dictatorship, there are some interesting differences. The Chilean junta, after specifying that it had assumed Supreme Command of the Nation (*Mando Supremo de la Nación*), declared in its "Act of Constitution of the Junta of Government" that it would guarantee the full powers of the Judiciary and respect the Constitution and the laws, but conditioned upon "the extent that the present situation

of law as a procedural guarantee of rights. Under the imperative of the emergency situation, constitutionally anticipated emergency powers allowed the abeyance of regular legal forms. The chief instrument that effected and typified this type of displacement of law was the provision for administrative arrest and detention without legal cause or due process under powers given by a state of siege.

Both types of departure from the rule of law – the collapse of higher law constitutionalism and the suspension of due process – involved a shift from legalistic to discretionary forms of articulating political power. This shift was intensified in both Chile and Argentina by the parallel activation of military courts that, particularly when operating under provisions for time of war, followed less than standard burdens of proof and evidence.

In this regard, in contexts of severe political and social crises, the immediate tasks of social control faced by each dictatorship were conceived as essentially extrajuridical. In both Chile and Argentina, political repression largely sidestepped the regular system of justice and was situated within the ruling military-administrative apparatus; it produced an awesome, unpredictable area of discretionary power, which generally overstepped the extraordinary powers associated with constitutional states of exception. These discretionary mechanisms of social control – extrajudicial repression, administrative emergency powers, and military courts – were centered in the military and were not legalistically rule-bound. To the extent that these control mechanisms were

---

of the country allows" (Decree-Law No. 1, [hereafter, DL], *Diario Oficial*, [hereafter, DO], September 18, 1973)." Subsequent decree laws clarified that the junta held constituent powers, and in late 1974 at the instigation of the Supreme Court the junta established that only decree laws enacted in express exercise of constituent powers would modify the 1925 Constitution.

A similar concern with the formalities of the 1853 Constitution was apparently absent from the 1976 Argentine dictatorship. The already mentioned "Statute for the Process of National Reorganization" invoked the constitution only as a source for the specific powers that were divided between the president and the junta. Otherwise, this founding document asserted the sovereignty of the junta, describing it as "supreme organ of the Nation" that would "ensure the normal functioning of the rest of the powers of the State and the basic objectives to be reached (art. 1)." Articles 9 and 10 regulated new appointments to the Supreme Court, even guaranteeing justices tenure in good behavior. Strikingly, despite the absence of any reference to the 1853 Constitution, the junta decreed the statute in express "exercise of the constituent power," thus suggesting that the junta had arrogated constituent powers. The absence in 1976 of any explicit acknowledgment of the continued force of the constitution, albeit qualified, was a departure from the founding acts of the 1955 and 1966 dictatorships, each of which stated that the constitution and the law would remain in force but only as long as they did not thwart each revolution's objectives. It should be noted that the 1955 regime's acknowledgment of the constitution did not inhibit it from suppressing the constitution in force – Peron's 1949 Constitution – and restoring the 1853 Constitution as it stood when it had been replaced in 1949.

recognized, they were generally portrayed by the ruling militaries as exceptional political measures or command functions, not acts of adjudication, and therefore were held to be beyond the supervision of the ordinary judiciary.

This separation of political repression from the judiciary permitted the courts to operate with legal standards of justice in areas subject to their jurisdiction and gave shape to a dual state of prerogative and law, as well as some semblance of judicial independence.[14] However, the sidestepping of the judiciary did not leave the courts untouched, as in both cases the judiciary ended up being tainted by their failure to provide redress to the thousands and thousands of families and individuals who turned to the courts to protect rights in the face of administrative and extralegal dictatorial force.

Before turning to examine why judicial remedies designed for democratic contexts were unlikely to limit authoritarian power, it should be noted that in both Argentina and Chile the turn to administrative-political forms of political control under dictatorship was parasitic upon norms and jurisprudence drawn from the prior legal and constitutional order.[15] Rather than being a response to noncompliant courts, as has been suggested in some theories of courts in authoritarian regimes, the shift away from law and the courts was effected by activating exceptional instruments that were already at hand in the constitution and statutes. This was the case with state-of-siege powers, which were inscribed in both the Chilean 1925 Constitution and the Argentine 1853 Constitution, as well as with the military courts that were regulated in each country's code of military justice.[16] Both military dictatorships immediately built on these

---

[14] The concept of the dual state is drawn from Fraenkel (1969). His concept is compatible with the dependence of courts upon the legislative enactments of an authoritarian regime – the distinctive feature of Fraenkel's "normative state" is that controversies in this sphere are resolved according to law rather than the arbitrary discretion of the authoritarian ruling body as occurs in the parallel realm of the "prerogative state." Authoritarian law as a limitation on authoritarian judicial independence appears to have been overlooked by Toharia (1975). The fact that even prototypically independent courts, such as the English, are rendered subordinate by legislative sovereignty is a central theme in Shapiro (1981).

[15] More generally, both military regimes enacted decree-laws and statutes to link their rule to already established faculties and legal orders. In part, this was done to assure legal and administrative continuity within the state apparatus. Such references to prior norms also provided a means to establish specific balances among the forces composing each military regime, as the constitution could be drawn upon to specify and distribute particular powers.

[16] Under the Chilean Constitution of 1925 (Art. 72, no. 17) the declaration of a state of siege empowered the president only to restrict personal liberty, "to transfer persons from one department to another and to confine them in their own houses, or in places other than jails or intended for the confinement or imprisonment of ordinary criminals." The Argentine provisions were broader and allowed for the suspension of individual liberties and allowed the executive to detain individuals and transfer them to other parts of the country. By article 23 of the constitution individuals so affected were allowed the option of leaving the country, although the military government immediately and repeatedly suspended this option.

frameworks by enacting through decree-law new penal offenses subject to military jurisdiction, and each, at different points, modified the powers associated with the state of siege. Yet by being framed against prior institutions, these innovations could be tied to an ongoing jurisprudence regarding the state of siege and military justice that tended to favor executive prerogative and noninvolvement of the regular judiciary in both areas.

MODALITIES OF REPRESSION AND THE RULE OF LAW

To make sense of how these authoritarian transformations in the political-institutional context of the courts affected the Chilean and Argentine judiciary's capacity to guarantee individual rights of liberty and personal integrity, it is helpful to distinguish different modes of repression and their relationship to law. The following list orders various modalities by which a state may pursue the repression of political enemies according to the manner that each conforms with or departs from the rule of law.[17] Proceeding from unlawful to legal forms we can distinguish the following four modalities of repression:

(1) Extrajuridical repression (state terror), which consists of all punitive acts inflicted by state agents without any prior authority that affect individual rights and lives without any legal cause, exceptional authorization, or adherence to judicial or administrative formalities. Given their illegality, such arbitrary measures tend to be taken covertly and are rarely acknowledged by state authorities that execute them.[18]

(2) Administrative repression, which includes detentions authorized by a state of siege, as noted above, departs from the rule of law because it involves restrictions on individual liberty without any prior trial and conviction for a

---

A state of siege had been in force since November 1974 when the Argentine military took power in March 1976 and remained standing until October 28, 1983, only days before the elections that inaugurated the return to democracy. The Chilean military upon taking power immediately declared a state of siege. In effect until March 11, 1978, the state of siege was reinstated on two occasions during the mid-1980s: first in response to mass opposition protests in late 1984 and after the September 1986 assassination attempt on Pinochet. Throughout the period the lower ranking "state of emergency" was also in effect.

[17] Elsewhere (Barros 2003), drawing on Raz (1979), I have explained how the rule of law can be compatible with autocracy. The two intermediate modalities of repression presented here should not be interpreted as points on a continuum toward the rule of law as it is unclear which of the two should be seen as closer to the rule of law. My final category, legal repression, conforms to Raz's conception of the rule of law.

[18] Many times, these acts – abduction, unauthorized detention, torture, disappearance, and execution – are unlawful even by the inflicting regime's own legality. Such measures constitute terror because individuals have no security when a state power arbitrarily disavows legal protections and remedies.

legal violation. In contrast to wholly arbitrary extrajuridical measures, these discretionary administrative acts have some legal foundation when they are anticipated in constitutional and statutory norms governing emergency situations and are effected by competent authorities.[19]

(3) Summary (quasi-) judicial repression, which as a form of punitive action differs from the administrative measures in that it involves some form of trial proceeding. However, such trials depart from rule-of-law standards because they apply laws that are either retroactive, secret, or unclear; limit the defendant's right to a defense; and/or employ doubtful standards of evidence. In these cases, a veneer of legality is given to the discretionary repression of political enemies and opponents.

(4) Legal repression, which is a form of political control that involves the repression of individuals for political offenses but that proceeds via regular judicial mechanisms that afford the accused full protection from arbitrary applications of the law. In other words, individuals may be convicted of political crimes but only after their guilt has been established in a fair and legal trial. Repressive law in this context may be draconian, but it allows individuals to form reasonable expectations about the consequences of different courses of action since it is prospective, public, clear, relatively stable, and fairly applied – individuals can have some certainty that if they submit to the law's constraints they will not be punished.

At different times, one or more, or all of these modalities of political repression may be used by a regime, and the use of one or another may wax or wane as a function of the nature of the specific political targets at which they are directed, levels of perceived threat and insecurity, and the relative costs associated at the moment with the use of each mode.

This classification of extralegal, administrative, summary, and legal modalities of repression leaves open the identity of the agents or institutions that engage in each. This gap is intentional because these different forms of punitive action can be effected by numerous, heterogeneous agencies and organs, which may be specialized or competing, more or less subordinate to or autonomous of superior hierarchies, as well as more or less proximate to

---

[19] When employed properly, administrative measures can afford individuals some minimal protection insofar as their correct use requires adherence to formalities that can be subject to review. In fact, the legalization of an initially secret illegal detention via its acknowledgment and subsumption under state-of-siege authority often meant that an individual was no longer subject to torture and would not disappear. Whether this actually constituted protection attributable to the institution, however, is unclear, since being in the legal system may only have signaled that someone had decided that the prisoner in question would live. In both countries, individuals under officially authorized administrative detention subsequently disappeared, and tragically thousands of persons disappeared without any protection from emergency powers.

the executive, the regular judiciary, or the armed forces and its branches. Since authoritarian regimes are likely to combine various modalities of political control, rather than identify a single repressive legal strategy for each case as Pereira does (2005; see also Chapter 1), I think that research should try to identify and reconstruct punitive spaces and networks, as well as trace stages in their evolution, notwithstanding the informational problems that hamper empirical research on authoritarian repression.[20]

To fully comprehend the political-institutional context in which courts operate, we need to be able to make sense of these authoritarian punitive spaces in their institutional and practical complexity, as this varied field shapes the pressures facing courts, something that this chapter only sketches. In this regard, it is important to note not only that multiple competing organizations may be engaged simultaneously in repressive activities but also that different components of a single institution may engage in multiple modes of repression; for example, simultaneous army engagement in clandestine repression and military justice. Similarly, the distinction between summary judicial repression and legal repression does not have to imply a set division between special and regular courts. Special courts may apply regular legal procedures or far less stringent standards depending on states of events anticipated by law and so successively organize legal or summary repression. This pattern was characteristic of military justice systems in both countries, as procedures and burdens of proof varied enormously depending on whether courts were operating under juridical time of war or peace.[21] In a similar fashion, a regime can define trial procedures for specific categories of crimes and through such legislation compel regular courts to use summary procedures and thereby implicate them in a regime's quasi-judicial shams. The same effect can also be achieved when the administrators of justice disregard standing rules and convert in practice what might formally have been a legal trial form into a mechanism for

[20] Brysk (1994b) discusses the obstacles faced by any assessment of the full extent of extrajudicial repression. It should additionally be noted that our images of patterns of repression in different cases have been greatly influenced by the work of national truth commissions, which have produced necessarily partial accounts given that their mandates are usually delimited to specific types of rights violations. Another complication is the limited availability of documentation of military justice systems in most cases. In Latin America, the slimmest public documentary record probably concerns administrative forms of repression.

[21] In time of peace, military justice provided considerable guarantees to defendants. The Chilean code, for example, assimilated ordinary judicial rules and procedures from the organic code regulating the civilian courts. Military justice in time of war, on the other hand, was summary and afforded defendants few guarantees. This was also the case in Argentina. The Argentine procedures in force during the 1970s, for example, allowed a defendant facing a *Consejo de Guerra* only three hours to prepare his defense and only one hour to appeal a conviction. See arts. 497 and 501, respectively (Igounet h. and Igounet 1985: 149, 150).

summary punishment or exacerbate the arbitrary character of an already summary procedure.

This array of possible modes of punitive action and the multiplicity of
potential enforcers suggest that types of regimes, subtypes, and specific cases
are likely to differ in their matrices of political control. Clearly, competitive
democratic regimes are subject to greater legal, political, and ideological
constraints on the modalities of repression that can be publically employed
because under normal political conditions only legal forms of repression are
permissible. Different types of nondemocratic regimes, on the other hand,
may draw on a broader range of modes and agents of control as a function
of the institutional or political basis of their ruling bodies, the format of their
internal organization of power, their capacity for institutionalizing their rule
by absorbing social demands, and, most centrally, the extent to which ruling
elites consider themselves to be threatened and insecure. As I am suggesting
here, how a regime carries out political control fundamentally shapes the
judiciary's ability to protect rights, particularly those of individuals targeted by
state coercive activity.

JUDICIAL FAILURE IN CONTEXT

As already described, the Argentine and Chilean military regimes were dictatorships that emerged as exceptions within liberal-democratic political, constitutional, and ideological frameworks, following severe social, political, and
institutional crises that had arisen from processes of intense popular political
mobilization and elite counter-reaction. In this broad context, as I have noted,
the ruling military juntas sought to procure their supremacy by suppressing perceived threats to state security and restoring order on their terms. The urgency
and severity of this situation as experienced by the military led to setting aside
ordinary legal constraints, as was evidenced in the swell of repressive force
that was unleashed; the modalities of repression ranged over the extralegal,
administrative, and quasi-judicial forms just described, with a preponderance,
at least during the worst years of repression, of arbitrary state terror, in a context
of censorship, restrictions on rights, and a general prohibition upon political
party and union activity.

In both Argentina and Chile this turn toward repressive military dictatorship
took place against the backdrop of standing judicial systems whose courts were
left largely on the margins of this punitive process. However, this dictatorial
dejuridicalization of political control, despite the separation and autonomy
of political repression from the judiciary, necessarily implicated the courts,

given the expectations that each populace had of the legal and judicial system. Following liberal notions of the separation of powers and constitutionalism in Argentina and Chile the judiciary held exclusive power to try civil and criminal cases, subject to constitutional guarantees designed to protect individual liberty from unlawful restriction, and to review the constitutionality of legislation when questioned in cases before the courts.[22] Thus, although each dictatorship's repressive activities generally bypassed the courts, it was inevitable that individuals and families affected would seek remedy before the courts, since it was the judiciary's task to apply the law and to guarantee freedom from arbitrary abuses of power.

The tragedy, which perhaps was also inevitable, was that the standard writs and remedies available within the legal system, out of context, could at best effect marginal, generally insignificant, correctives, while the court's jurisprudence developed during democratic periods regarding political questions, out of context, only validated the space of dictatorial prerogative. The resulting judicial failures illustrate the structural weaknesses of carryover judiciaries in contexts of dictatorship, particularly in areas concerning individual rights.

From a standpoint of rights, the task before each judiciary was to guarantee that each dictatorship contained its acts of political control within the limits of what I have above called legal repression and, if a less stringent view is allowed, the strict confines of preestablished constitutional emergency powers. In other words, the judiciary ought to have assured that political control proceeded through courts that followed reasonable procedures of justice, under the supervision of the Supreme Court or, if one concedes that exceptional situations may warrant administrative detention, through administrative measures that conformed to law.

In both countries, the reality on the ground far exceeded these limits and, as the CONADEP and the *Comisión Rettig* reports insisted, the judiciary was incapable of checking arbitrary dictatorial repressive force. With intensities and mixes that varied at different conjunctures, in both countries state agents engaged in acts of repression that involved summary military courts, administrative detentions and exile, and absolutely extrajudicial abduction,

---

[22] The judiciary's exclusive power to exercise judicial functions, as well as express prohibitions on judging by the executive (Argentina) and by both the executive and Congress (Chile), was established in articles 94–95 of the Argentine Constitution and article 80 of the Chilean Constitution. Guarantees conforming to rule-of-law standards for detention and trial were given in articles 18 and 11–20 of the respective constitutions, whereas the constitutional review powers of the respective Supreme Courts were established in article 86 of the Chilean Constitution and in Argentina by the Court's own jurisprudence in 1887.

torture, and execution.[23] Generally, extrajudicial acts of repression were executed in secret, with victims abducted by unidentified teams and sequestered in clandestine detention centers where their fate was decided.[24] Thus, as I have been suggesting, not only did lethal political repression sidestep the courts during the most intense periods of state violence; it also was deliberately shrouded from judicial oversight and further shielded by restrictions on press freedoms that prohibited reporting on political acts of violence (Knudson 1997). These forms of clandestine repression could not be restrained with standard judicial remedies, as these remedies were disabled by each regime's obstinate denial that it was effecting the acts that each was in fact executing in secret.

The principal shortcoming of regular judicial remedies was that they were designed to be effective within a system of rule of law, not an autocracy intent on crushing its political enemies. Out of context, these instruments, especially the writ of habeas corpus, became inane. In both legal systems, habeas corpus or the *recurso de amparo*, as it is called in Chile, was the traditional instrument with which a person who was arbitrarily detained, or a party on his behalf, could file to have a court remedy an unlawful detention. In both Chile and Argentina the writ was absolutely ineffectual before disappearances, as the petition presumes that illegal detentions are unlawful on the margins of an otherwise lawful system of justice, not wholly unlawful, clandestine acts that completely circumvent the legal system.[25] As the Second Chamber of the

---

[23] The number of deaths resulting from state repression is evaluated in each truth commission's reports and, particularly in Argentina, remains a subject of debate. The CONADEP concluded that 9,000 people were murdered in Argentina, whereas other estimates of the number of disappeared reach 30,000.

  A careful comparative analysis of the specific organization of repression within each dictatorship is needed to evaluate how internal tensions may or may not have arisen in each case over the "costs of repression" and led some officers to seek to rein in extrajudicial and quasi-judicial modes of coercion. In both countries, military justice in time of war was closely integrated within the chain of command and applied by ad hoc war councils formed on the order of regional zone and subzone commanders. In broad strokes, after an initial period of open mass repression, extrajudicial repression in Chile was primarily, though not exclusively, centralized within a specialized security apparatus, the DINA, which was subordinate to President Pinochet. In Argentina, on the other hand, special units within the army and the navy operated within each military zone. These military units, which operated covertly, were organized outside of the regular chain of command and operated with considerable autonomy from superior officers.

[24] According to Calveiro (1995: 38–39) in Argentina the stages in the disappearance of an individual – abduction, interrogation, confinement, and execution – were compartmentalized into discrete tasks discharged by different groups of officers and soldiers, which limited knowledge of the overall process even among many of those directly implicated.

[25] This point becomes apparent if one examines the contemporary statutory and constitutional regulation of habeas corpus. Articles 11–16 of the Chilean Constitution and articles 306–17 of the Chilean penal code, as well as articles 617–645 of the Argentine penal code, regulated the

Chilean Supreme Court noted in an April 1978 decision, to put an end to an arbitrary deprivation of freedom, "the precise place where the *amparado* is must be known."[26] In such circumstances, when the whereabouts of a person presumably detained was unknown, the courts had little alternative but to follow the standard procedure of requesting, by official letter, information from the Minister of the Interior, local military authorities, or intelligence agencies as to whether they had in detention the person in question. In these instances, when the official response, whether out of duplicity or ignorance, informed the judge that no registry could be found indicating that the person in question was being held by the executive under state-of-siege authority or under indictment before the military courts, the courts had little further recourse. Neither judiciary possessed its own independent investigative police. Each could investigate allegations of illegal detention only by eliciting the cooperation of executive and military agencies that were either directly associated with clandestine repression, complicit in protecting these perpetrators, or being kept in the dark about these acts by knowing officials.

Given the scope of repression in each country, the repetition of this pattern on thousands of occasions, and the attendant breakdown of *habeas corpus* as an effective remedy placed considerable strain upon the courts. In both cases there is evidence that these situations created tensions between the judiciary and each dictatorship, which indicates that justices were cognizant that the intelligence agencies' refusal to provide accurate information to the courts was impeding the judiciary's ability to defend individual liberty and life. These tensions between the Appellate Court of Santiago and the National Directorate of Intelligence (DINA) in 1975 were particularly deep (Barros 2002: 147–149), whereas in Argentina the stone wall before the Supreme Court during 1978 was so firm that the Court exhorted the military executive to create conditions in which the courts could effect justice in the many cases where parties were seeking the protection of individual liberty in the face of disappearances.[27]

---

writ in reference to the order of arrest or imprisonment; the legal irregularities that habeas corpus was to correct related to the competence of the authority ordering an arrest, its legal merit, and the adherence to procedural formalities.

[26] "*Hernán Santos Pérez*," May 8, 1978. This decision confirmed an appellate court resolution. The Rettig Commission resolved that Santos Pérez, on leaving his workplace in October 1977, had been abducted by DINA agents and, henceforth, his whereabouts are unknown.

[27] The decision "*Pérez de Smith, Ana María y otros s/pedido*" was handed down on April 18, 1978, and reiterated on virtually identical terms on December 21, 1978 (*Fallos de la Corte Suprema*, vol. 297, p. 338 and vol. 300, p. 1282, respectively). The principal condition that the Court demanded as requisite for the judiciary to effect justice was that the executive be forthcoming with information regarding the whereabouts and situation of the individuals reported as disappeared. The case is discussed in Carrió (1996: 102–105). In Chile the military

As to administrative and quasi-judicial forms of authoritarian political control, the courts in both countries, on the grounds of the separation of powers, largely forsook any judicial oversight of the military executives and the military justice systems. In neither country were courts, particularly the High Courts, willing to challenge the executive's use of state-of-siege powers. Legal challenges to these measures were consistently rejected as being political questions beyond the courts' authority: long-standing jurisprudence in both countries defined state-of-siege powers as exceptional administrative powers whose merit and use were solely the prerogative of the executive authorized to employ them. On this basis, it was held that to review the merit of these acts would be to invade the legitimate domain of executive authority and encroach upon the separation of powers.

Strikingly, these references to the separation of powers ignored the momentous fact that in contexts of dictatorship the executive was no longer exercising exceptional powers that had been conferred by another regular and separate constitutional power (i.e. Congress); this incongruity was rendered innocuous by each court's countenance of the concentration of executive, legislative, and constituent powers in the military. Subject to these limitations, then, courts in Argentina and Chile did on rare occasion accept habeas corpus petitions that challenged the executive's failure to observe the formalities legally prescribed during the use of state-of-siege powers. These, however, were constraints on the margins that had little or no impact upon the overall situation, but that in these rare instances held the executive to the legal bounds of emergency powers.[28] Generally, however, in cases where an administrative detention was officially acknowledged, once the courts received notification that an individual was being held by order of the executive in application of the state of siege, they would reject the appeal for habeas corpus.

The courts took a similar tack in response to complaints filed to challenge the constitutionality of military war councils or to petition the Supreme Court to correct legal errors committed by military courts. Just two months after the coup of September 11, 1973, the Chilean Supreme Court sidestepped this

---

repeatedly pressured the courts to limit the number of *recursos de amparo* or else to allow them to be processed by the military courts.

[28] In Chile the few rulings that I am aware of that ordered the Minister of the Interior to rectify procedural irregularities concerned the holding of a minor among common criminals – a violation of the constitution's requirement that administrative detainees be held apart from criminals – and a 1978 petition involving prominent members of the Christian Democratic Party who had been transferred to a province other than that indicated on the executive's order. In Argentina the principal case associated with the use of state-of-siege powers was the internationally high-profile case of Jacobo Timerman. Timerman, the publisher of the daily *La Opinión*, was expelled from the country after the Supreme Court ordered his release.

potential confrontation with the military by ruling that military tribunals in time of war fell outside the Supreme Court's constitutional authority to oversee and discipline all courts of justice. The reason, which though controversial may not have been without foundation from a rule-of-law standpoint given the summary character of the war councils, was that military tribunals in time of war were not courts of law but a part of the military command function. This finding was reiterated in a 1976 decision that again declared the Supreme Court's incompetence, explicitly stating, "The military tribunals of time of war configure a hierarchical organization autonomous and independent of all other authority of the ordinary or special jurisdiction, which culminates in the General in Chief to whom is granted the plenitude of this jurisdiction."[29] In effect, the Chilean High Court was disavowing competence to correct the injustices of summary proceedings on the grounds that that they were summary and hence non-judicial![30] When faced with challenges to the constitutionality of military war councils, the Argentine Supreme Court did not elaborate separation of power arguments, but following prior jurisprudence merely asserted that summary military trials of civilians in emergency situations were not incompatible with the constitution's guarantee of a fair trial.[31]

In these three domains of dictatorial punitive activity – extra-juridical repression, administrative repression, and summary quasi-judicial repression – judicial interference with executive measures was avoided by bypassing ordinary courts and trial procedures. Clandestine detention centers, official camps for holding individuals detained under states of siege, and military tribunals were the sites where political control was effected beyond the superintendence

---

[29] *"Jorge Garrido y otro. Recurso de queja,"* Rol 10.397, September 21, 1976.

[30] This reasoning suggests that the Court conceived its superintendency over all tribunals to be internal to courts whose organizations and procedures could be assimilated to minimal standards of the rule of law. This hypothesis also suggests that the Supreme Court justices were implicitly acknowledging that to correct and contain quasi-judicial practices external to the regular court system implied a confrontation with the military regarding the rationality and merit of summary procedures. I suspect that the juridical-ideological worldview of these jurists, as well as strategic considerations, limited contemplation of this alternative.

[31] *"Saravogi, Horacio Oscar s/alteración del orden público,"* November 9, 1978, *Fallos de la Corte Suprema,* vol. 300, p. 1173. Another constitutional issue that generated considerable controversy in Argentina was the regime's repeated suspension of the constitutional *"opción de salida"* whereby individuals subject to administrative arrest during a state of siege could opt to leave the country. The Supreme Court accepted these restrictions on the grounds that the *Actas Institucionales* that suspended the right to option, like the *Estatuto para el Proceso de Reorganización Nacional,* were norms that integrated the constitution as long as the conditions that gave them legitimacy persisted – as long as there was, in the words of the Court, "a real state of necessity that forced the adoption of measures of exception." For the November 1, 1977, ruling, see *"Lokman, Jaime,"* *Fallos de la Corte Suprema,* vol. 299, p. 142.

of the courts. As I have noted, on the grounds that they involved "political questions" or stood outside the regular judicial system, both the Argentine and the Chilean Supreme Courts stood aloof from directly confronting each dictatorship's use of emergency powers and administration of military justice.

While in the three areas of political control just examined the military dictatorships acted without restriction by sidestepping the courts, in both countries the military also subordinated the courts to their purposes by means of their capacity to legislate new law or modify standing provisions. Thus, despite the apparent independence of the judiciary from the ruling military executives, courts were immediately subject to the dictatorships insofar as they were bound by the law enacted by each dictatorship. Not only were the courts compelled to apply each regime's law when applicable in litigation but dictatorial law was also used to directly keep the courts in line. By enacting new legislation or modifying constitutional norms, the military ruling bodies asserted their supremacy over the judiciary. Unfavorable rulings were overturned through such modifications, and any progress that judges made in investigating crimes committed by agents of each dictatorship was hindered by altering jurisdictions or through amnesties.[32] And, particularly once military justice became politically costly, law could be used to attempt to drag the courts into political disciplinary activity by placing repressive legislation under their jurisdiction.

This dependence of courts on legislation that structures not only the organization, jurisdiction, and procedures of the court system but also the substantive law that the courts must apply is hardly exclusive to authoritarian regimes; as Martin Shapiro (1981) insisted in his now-classic volume on courts, judiciaries, such as the English that are generally seen as independent, are in fact subject

---

[32] Thus in Chile after the worst years of repression the discovery of evidence of heinous crimes often gave rise to the following sequence: semi-tolerated institutions, such as the Catholic Church, would express outrage; the Supreme Court would appoint a special investigatory judge (*Ministro en Visita*); the judge would discover evidence of military involvement; the judge would declare his incompetence given the involvement of persons subject to military jurisdiction; once in the hands of the military courts, the case would be dismissed if it fell under the 1978 amnesty law. This cycle occurred for the first time after the discovery of the remains of fifteen persons in a clay pit in Lonquen in November 1978. The investigation of notorious crimes committed by state agents after the 1978 amnesty usually languished or was dismissed after being transferred into the military justice system. On one occasion, however, the diligent work of the special investigating judge, José Cánovas Robles, produced solid evidence that members of the national police, *Carabineros*, were behind the March 1985 assassination of three members of the Communist Party, leading to the arraignment of high-level officers of the national police force and the resignation of its director, who was also a member of the military junta. For the case, which was eventually dismissed after repeated obstructions, see Cavallo, Salazar, and Sepulveda (1989: 468–478).

to legislation. However, under dictatorships this subordination is taken to an extreme that usually leaves very little space for "judicializing" authoritarian politics. If, as contemporary strategic theories of judicial behavior suggest, courts can diverge from the legal status quo only when the fragmentation of political forces within a legislature allows judges to anticipate that their rulings will not be overturned, then these conditions were generally absent under the Argentine and Chilean dictatorships.[33] In both cases, legislative and constituent powers were concentrated in the hands of an extremely limited number of actors. Despite our generally limited knowledge regarding the internal workings of both military regimes, there is evidence that differences emerged in each authoritarian legislative process. However, to what extent these differences were known to the courts is unknown, particularly as the legislative function was exercised in secret in each regime. Still, a central implication of strategic approaches to judicial politics is that divergent judicial interpretations in contexts of dictatorship could not emerge on issues around which the ruling military actors remained united.[34]

PRELIMINARY CONCLUSION

In this chapter, I have avoided attributing "judicial failure" in Argentina and Chile to irresolute or complicit judges and instead have tried to sketch the larger political and institutional context in which courts operated under the two dictatorships. It is indeed the case that many judges in both countries celebrated military intervention. Still, further comparative research on courts under military rule in Argentina and Chile would also reveal that there were judges who were resolute in their pursuit of justice even when deference appeared to be the only rational strategy for judges interested in their careers. In a number of cases, this independence cost judges their jobs, suggesting in fact that the explanation for "judicial failure" during recent military dictatorships in Latin America should go beyond charges about reprehensible judges and analyze judicial activity in the broader political and institutional context created by authoritarianism.

---

[33] For the argument that fragmentation among political forces is a condition for judges to pursue preferred modes of judicial interpretation or policies, see Ferejohn and Weingast (1992) and Ferejohn (2002).

[34] It is on this point that differences in the internal organization of regimes become relevant. As I have documented (Barros 2002), institutionalized intraservice differences within the military junta provided the ballast that allowed the 1980 Constitution to take on a life of its own through constitutional court decisions.

This type of research is all the more necessary because criticisms of judicial behavior under military rule rest upon a striking theoretical assumption: that courts, as structured by a given constitution, ought to able to uphold and defend another part of the constitution, its guarantees of rights, even after the core institutions of the constitution have been destroyed by a military usurpation of legislative and executive powers. As I have tried to show in this chapter, this assumption is probably untenable: military authoritarianism in Argentina and Chile destroyed the ordinary context of judicial activity in the realm of protecting individual liberties. Out of context, available judicial procedures were of little avail before state agencies that had ceased to accept legality as a binding constraint.

This question of the existence of constitutional and, in particular, judicial devices to check an authoritarian state brings to mind John Locke's argument that there is no legal remedy in the face of a state turned tyrant, only the remedy of an "appeal to heaven" – Locke's euphemism for violent resistance. Leaving aside the strategic and ethical dilemmas associated with the use of force, it might first be objected that Locke's theory is pre-constitutional and that modern constitutional systems contain internal mechanisms that guarantee rights and ward against abuses of power. However, it must be underscored that these mechanisms are designed and intended to function within the context of an ongoing constitutional regime, not a dictatorship. As I have argued here, out of context the parts of a constitution are likely to be woefully inadequate in service of their original purposes. In this regard, Locke was right. Any move by the Chilean or the Argentine judiciary to step beyond their regular jurisdiction would have placed either judiciary at loggerheads with the military over essentially political questions for which there were no shared legal criteria nor acknowledged mechanism of resolution. This never happened, but the point holds that only political decision, not judicial action, could contain, if not always eliminate, nonjudicial state punitive action under these dictatorships.

Perhaps inevitably, what I have been calling "judicial failure" has cast a long shadow over research on judicial behavior in Latin American authoritarian regimes. Nevertheless, the judiciary is one institution for which we have available considerable documentary sources even for the military periods. In this regard, my sketch of the broad context of judicial activity needs to be complemented by further research, particularly on lower courts, which have usually not been studied. Furthermore, research on the ordinary aspects of judging might also reveal points of tension between the courts and the military. Though its possibility has been overshadowed by the fact of judicial failure, we should not scoff at the idea that the judiciary's defense of legality within its ordinary jurisdiction may have prevented a spillover of arbitrary power beyond the realm of emergency punitive control. This possibility will never repair the crimes of the military dictatorships, but it may open up questions that allow us to begin to explore less diametric understandings of judicial activity under military autocratic regimes.

7

Enforcing the Autocratic Political Order and the Role of Courts: The Case of Mexico

Beatriz Magaloni

INTRODUCTION

Autocrats have a hard time enforcing political order. They are unable to rely solely on coercion to enforce rules against their subordinates in the state apparatus, the citizenry, and powerful members of the ruling clique. This chapter explores the various strategies the Mexican autocratic regime employed to enforce political order and how courts were transformed from weak to more powerful institutions.

In democratic political systems, courts are employed to arbitrate all sorts of conflicts, ranging from commercial disputes, labor disagreements, and criminal cases to major constitutional conflicts arising between citizens and the state and between different branches and levels of government. Autocrats employ courts to enforce their commands directed to bureaucratic subordinates and the citizenry, but they normally do not resort to these institutions to arbitrate conflicts among members of the ruling elite. These types of conflicts are more likely to erupt into violence. What alternative instruments do autocracies use to enforce political order and arbitrate conflicts among members of the ruling elite? When are autocracies likely to empower courts to settle political conflicts? What other roles do courts play in autocratic regimes? This chapter answers these questions in the context of Mexico.

A previous version of this paper was presented at the 2001 Annual Meeting of the American Political Science Association. I thank for their comments Alberto Diaz-Cayeros, Federico Estévez, Barbara Geddes, Tom Heller, Erik Jensen, Tom Ginsburg, and participants at the conference, "THE POLITICS OF COURTS IN AUTHORITARIAN REGIMES," August 30–31, 2006, at the University of Pennsylvania Law School. I also thank the Rule of Law Program, Center for Democracy, Development and Rule of Law, Stanford University, for financial support. The chapter was revised while I was a W. Glenn Campbell and Rita Ricardo-Campbell National Fellow and the Susan Louis Dyer Peace Fellow at the Hoover Institution.

The literature stresses that autocracies often turn to courts as mechanisms for inducing bureaucratic discipline within the administrative apparatus (Moustafa 2006; Shapiro 1981). Akin to "fire-alarm" oversight mechanisms (McCubbins and Schwartz 1984), this form of oversight is driven by the citizenry, who can generate an independent stream of information about bureaucratic abuses that other forms of vertical oversight cannot. This chapter emphasizes that in designing courts to oversee their subordinates, autocrats face a dilemma – creating a system of courts strong enough to allow top-level state officials to monitor lower level officials and judges, but weak enough to prevent citizens from enforcing their rights vis-à-vis the regime.

The chapter discusses how the Mexican autocratic regime solved this dilemma by establishing a procedure for citizens to challenge state abuses before federal courts (the *amparo* trial) and at the same time giving to these courts very limited "constitutional space" to keep them weak. In important issues involving expropriation of property, harsh economic regulation, and the violation of due process, citizens were subject to government abuses but could not challenge these abuses through the courts. Key to the maintaining the judicial system for the benefit of the autocracy was the politicization of the federal courts – nominations and promotions were decided by the Supreme Court, which in practice behaved entirely as an office of the presidency. With these institutions, the Mexican autocracy managed to create a highly responsive and subservient judiciary, whose main role was to ensure that subordinates applied the laws according to the top leadership's commands.

Courts were purposely given no jurisdiction over so-called political conflicts, the numerous fights arising among the members of the ruling elite; such conflicts were more likely to erupt into violence than those arising between individual citizens and the state. How then did the Mexican autocracy enforce political order vis-à-vis members of the ruling clique? To answer this question, I develop a theoretical framework making use of a simple game. The Mexican PRI (Institutional Revolutionary Party) created an ingenious system to enforce political order among members of the ruling elite that was based on three mechanisms: (1) the president was the arbiter of political conflicts among members of the ruling clique; (2) the president was leader of the official party, which had the monopoly of office and the spoils derived from it; and (3) the party sanctioned noncompliance with the president's decisions with expulsion. The game shows that the ruling elite submitted to the autocratic political order based on presidential arbitration instead of fighting because the system was self-enforcing *as long as the PRI retained a monopoly on political office* and could guarantee members of the ruling elite a share of power over the long run. With multiparty competition emerging in the 1990s, the political order began to unravel because the president's leadership was challenged, first by opposition politicians and then by his co-partisans. The president was forced either to side with the opposition and offend the PRI or to side with the PRI and repress the opposition. To solve this dilemma and enforce political order, I argue that the president opted to empower the Supreme Court as the new arbiter of political conflicts. In acquiescing to empower the Supreme Court, the former ruling party faced the dilemma of creating an institution that would protect its interests but would not turn against this party in the event it lost power.

My account is consistent with Ginsburg (2003) in stressing that a powerful Supreme Court in Mexico could only come about when power became diffused and the ruling party could no longer anticipate with certainty that it would hold on to power in the future. However, my account stresses that the empowerment of the Supreme Court resulted more from the president's need to find alternative ways to enforce political order among subnational politicians than from his anticipation that the ruling party might lose office.

The chapter unfolds as follows. The next section discusses the nature of autocratic rule in Mexico and the role courts played. It discusses the nature of the *amparo* trial and how courts were given limited jurisdiction to solve small conflicts, while important political disputes remained in the president's sphere. The third section focuses on autocratic abuse and citizens' rights. The fourth section discusses how the Mexican autocracy solved the dilemma of enforcing political order among members of the ruling elite. Through the use of a simple game, I show that the president could serve as ultimate arbiter only because he was the leader of the official party, which had a monopoly on political office. After a large number of politicians from different political parties acceded to office at the subnational level in the 1990s, the president's authority was challenged, generating the need to empower the Supreme Court. The fifth section discusses the 1994 constitutional reform that created a powerful Supreme Court. The sixth section presents a discussion of empirical findings concerning the functioning of the new Supreme Court in the last years of authoritarian rule in Mexico and after 2000, when the official party finally lost power. The seventh section contrasts my approach with the existing literature on judicial review in systems in transition. I end the chapter with a conclusion.

AUTOCRATIC RULE AND THE COURTS

The PRI governed for seventy-one years, from 1929, when the precursor to the party was created,[1] until 2000, when it lost the presidency to the long-standing

---

[1] The PNR (National Revolutionary Party) was created in 1929, was renamed the PRM (Party of the Mexican Revolution) in 1938, and subsequently was renamed the PRI in 1946.

opposition party, the PAN (National Action Party). During this period parties other than the PRI were allowed to compete.

The autocratic regime in Mexico was not characterized as particularly repressive. As I explain elsewhere (Magaloni 2006), hegemonic party autocracies do not conform to the model of what we normally regard as dictatorships. Communist regimes, for example, aspired to total domination "of each single individual in each and every sphere of life" (Arendt 1968). In part, this goal was achieved by the atomization of human relationships – the destruction of classes, interests groups, and even the family unit – a process in which terror played a key role. Many military dictators were also very repressive (O'Donnell 1973; Stepan 1971; Wood 2000). Most theories of autocracy are implicitly or explicitly based on the notion of repression. The "existence of a political police force and of extremely severe sanctions for expressing and especially organizing opposition to the government (such as imprisonment, internment in mental hospitals, torture, and execution) is the hallmark of dictatorships of all stripes" (Wintrobe 1998: 34).[2]

The Mexican autocracy was a more benign form of dictatorship. This is not to say that there was no repression at all.[3] Since its creation, the PRI permitted the opposition to compete in multiparty elections – although it banned the Communist Party, a decision that pushed radical left-wing movements into insurgency and was largely responsible for the guerilla activity in the 1960s and 1970s. The 1978 electoral reform legalized the Communist Party and managed to co-opt most of the violent opposition to the regime by significantly reducing their entry costs to the legislature. Through the 1980s and 1990s, the PRI maintained its power through a combination of strategies, including vote buying and electoral fraud, against an increasingly stronger opposition. After a sequence of important institutional reforms in the late 1990s, this party finally lost power in 2000.

The Mexican constitution formally establishes numerous checks and balances, such as division of powers, bicameralism, and federalism. However, the authoritarian political system during the era of hegemonic party rule by the PRI was characterized by a strong *presidencialismo*, a strong dominance of the president over other branches of government, which derived from sources beyond the constitution (Carpizo 1978; Weldon 1997). The conditions driving *presidencialismo*, in particular the executive's domination over Congress, are well understood. Formally the Mexican president was not a

---

[2] Linz (2000) challenges the view that repression is an essential characteristic of autocracies.
[3] Repression in Mexico was selective, although in some regions and municipalities in the states of Chiapas, Oaxaca, Guerrero and Veracruz, political killings on a per capita basis rivaled levels of per capita repression in military dictatorships. I thank Guillermo Trejo for pointing this out to me.

very powerful player. In practice, however, the president dominated the other branches of government for the following reasons: first, the president was the leader of the hegemonic party; second, the hegemonic party controlled the majority of seats in the Lower Chamber and the Senate; and third, the hegemonic party was extremely disciplined (Casar 2002; Weldon 1997).

Presidencialismo also implied a lack of judicial checks on the executive. Three conditions explained presidential domination over the Supreme Court and the federal judicial branch (Magaloni 2003).

1. The constitution was endogenous to partisan interests. The constitution is formally rigid: amendments require the approval of two-thirds of both federal assemblies plus the majority of state legislatures. During the years of party hegemony, however, the constitution was in practice flexible because the PRI enjoyed the necessary super-majorities to unilaterally amend it without the need to forge coalitions with the opposition parties. Since it was originally drafted in 1917, the constitution has been amended more than 400 times. Many of these changes were substantial, resulting in changes in electoral institutions to the PRI's advantage; the centralization of political power and fiscal resources in the hands of the federal government; the systematic weakening of the judicial power and the Supreme Court; and the restructuring of the system of property rights to the PRI's advantage. During the autocratic era, almost every single president began his six-year term with a long list of constitutional reforms. The practice was to imprint in the constitution the president's policy agenda.

The following example illustrates the importance of the *endogeneity* of constitutional rules. To consolidate his power, President Lázaro Cárdenas (1934–1940) began his term by implementing land reform to which the 1917 Constitution had entitled peasants. The existing Supreme Court, representing the interests of conservative forces and property owners, attempted to block the president's agrarian redistribution. Cárdenas responded by dissolving the Supreme Court and reappointing a new, significantly enlarged body with amicable justices; these new justices would serve six-year terms, instead of appointments for life. The crackdown on the Supreme Court required a con-stitutional change, which President Cárdenas could accomplish only because the PRI had the necessary super-majority in the federal Congress and control of the state assemblies. The implementation of land reform would prove cru-cial for the consolidation of the PRI's hegemony because it gave this party a key instrument to buy peasants' support. The crackdown on the Court created a powerful precedent that convinced justices never to cross the line where their decisions would offend the president.

2. The president exercised strong control over judicial nominations and dismissals, despite formal rules or so-called judicial guarantees. Table 7.1

TABLE 7.1. *Change of constitutional rules regarding size, appointments, terms, and dismissal of Supreme Court*

	No. of justices	Subunits	Appointments of justices	Terms of justices	Dismissal of justices	Appointments of magistrates and judges (federal judicial power)	Terms of magistrate and judges (federal judicial power)
1917	11	None	States with a two-thirds vote of Chamber of Deputies and Senate	Life (from 1923)	Impeachment	Supreme Court	4 years(law establishes life tenures for appointments after 1923, not constitution)
1928	16	3	President with approval by majority in Senate	Life	Impeachment "or" misconduct	Supreme Court	Life (law establishes, however, life tenures only for appointments after 1928)
1934	21	4	President with approval by majority in Senate	Six years	Impeachment "or" misconduct	Supreme Court	Six years
1944	26	4	President with approval by majority in Senate	Life	Impeachment "or" misconduct	Supreme Court	Life

(continued)

TABLE 7.1 (continued)

	No. of justices	Subunits	Appointments of justices	Terms of justices	Dismissal of justices	Appointments of magistrates and judges (federal judicial power)	Terms of magistrate and judges (federal judicial power)
1951	26	5	President with approval by majority in Senate	Life	Misconduct with prior impeachment	Supreme Court	4 years and after tenure revision, life
1967	26	5	President with approval by majority in Senate	Life	Impeachment "or" misconduct	Supreme Court	4 years and after tenure revision, life
1982	26	5	President with approval by majority in Senate	Life	Impeachment, according to Title IV of Constitution	Supreme Court	4 years and after tenure revision, life
1987	26	5	President with approval by majority in Senate	Life	Impeachment, according to Title IV of Constitution	Supreme Court	6 years and after tenure revision, life
1994	11	2	President with approval by 2/3rd vote of Senate	15 years	Impeachment, according to Title IV of Constitution	Federal Judicial Board	6 years and after tenure revision, life

Source: Magaloni 2003.

TABLE 7.2. *Number of justices appointed by the president*

President	Number of justices	% of a court appointed by sitting president
Venustiano Carranza (1916–1920)	19	172%
Álvaro Obregón (1920–1924)	10	90%
Plutarco Elías Calles (1924–1928)	3	27%
Portes Gil (1928–1930)	12	75%
Ortiz Rubio (1930–1932)	5	31%
Abelardo Rodríguez (1932–1934)	5	31%
Lázaro Cárdenas (1934–1940)	24	114%
Manuel Ávila Camacho (1940–1946)	24	96%
Miguel Alemán (1946–1952)	12	48%
Adolfo Ruiz Cortínez (1952–1958)	18	72%
Adolfo López Mateos (1958–1964)	9	36%
Gustavo Díaz Ordaz (1964–1970)	14	56%
Luis Echeverría Álvarez (1970–1976)	13	52%
José López Portillo (1976–1982)	16	64%
Miguel de la Madrid Hurtado (1982–1988)	20	80%
Carlos Salinas de Gortari (1988–1994)	8	30%
Ernesto Zedillo (1994–2000)	11	100%

Source: Magaloni 2003.

provides a list of the numerous constitutional modifications to the Supreme Court's appointment and dismissal rules (Magaloni 2003), which had the effect of systematically diminishing the Court's power through the years. After 1988, the Court began to be gradually strengthened, although, as I argue later, it was never to become a fully independent political player until the PRI lost power in 2000.

Notwithstanding life appointments during most of the autocratic era, justices' tenures were extremely short, and every single president from 1934 to 1994 was able to shape the composition of at least 50 percent of the Court (see Table 7.2). Most justices tended to follow *partisan careers* before or after leaving the Court, creating strong incentives to please the leader of the party, namely the president, as a means of furthering their political ambitions (Domingo, 2000). Table 7.3 shows the turnover of justices. Although the average tenure was ten years, close to 40 percent of justices left the Court in less than six years, which is the length of the presidential term. These data reveal that although there were a few very stable tenures (some even lasting for thirty years), the majority of the Court's justices came and went with the presidential term.

TABLE 7.3. *Turnover rates of justices of the Supreme Court*

Range of term (years)	Percentage
1 to 5	39%
6 to 10	27%
11 to 15	25%
16 to 20	7%
21 to 25	2%
Average term	10
Average age of incoming justices	56
Average age of outgoing justices	63

Source: Magaloni 2003.

The standing president could thus employ a combination of inducements, sanctions, and threats to entice Supreme Court justices to behave as loyal agents. He could appoint amicable justices who would guard the implementation of his policy agenda; he could threaten to remove rebellious justices despite life appointments; and he could change constitutional rules to either expand the size of the Court or change its constitutional prerogatives. All of these measures turned the Court into a highly political body that responded to the president.

3. Until 1994, Mexican politicians purposely chose *not to delegate enough power* to interpret the constitution to the Supreme Court and the federal judicial power, excluding from judicial review virtually all cases with so-called political content: cases related to the organization, monitoring, and implementation of elections and electoral laws; "constitutional controversies" or conflicts among different branches or levels of government with respect to their constitutionality of their acts; and expropriation and distribution of property rights in the countryside. This meant that an impressive variety of cases were out of the reach of the courts.

If courts were prevented from ruling on so many types of conflicts, what then was their role in the autocracy? The Supreme Court and federal tribunals decided on *amparo* trials. Through the *amparo*, individuals can sue the state for violating their rights or issuing and applying laws that go against the constitution. However, the federal courts seldom questioned the substantive content of the regime's laws, and even when courts did question those laws, decisions on constitutionality on *amparo* trials did not have general effects, but only affected the parties in the specific dispute. If a law was declared unconstitutional five times, this had the effect of creating a general legal precedent (*jurisprudencia*) that obliged lower level courts. However, since the *amparo* trial had very strict procedural rules and could only be initiated within a short period of time following the application of the challenged law or state act, the precedent only protected those who were able to sue the government within the required time. In practice this meant that the autocracy was able to legally continue to apply laws even when the federal courts had declared these laws unconstitutional. Since there was virtually no publicity given to these decisions, their political consequences were minor.

The *inter partes* clause had the effect of reducing courts to institutions fully devoted to controlling the application of the laws. On a case-by-case basis – a forum where individuals could confront government officials, mostly for minor violations, and challenge the decisions of lower level courts. Federal courts were thus in charge of monitoring that lower-level bureaucrats and state officials acted in accordance with the directives of top-level government officials. The system for monitoring and sanctioning played a similar func- tion to the "fire-alarm" versus "police patrol" regime in the United States in which administrative procedures are established so that Congress can control the bureaucracies indirectly and in a decentralized fashion, through citizens' claims, rather than setting direct controls on federal agencies (Shapiro 1981). In Mexico the president as top leader of the party and chief executive played the role of the principal, low-level government officials and judges were its agents, and the federal courts served to monitor and sanction behavior but only if citizens enticed courts to act through an *amparo* suit.

To make sure that courts acted as agents of the regime and its central leadership, several institutional controls were devised. As mentioned above, the president shaped the composition of the Supreme Court, nominating individuals who were loyal to the autocracy and had similar ideological pre- dispositions. The president also retained powerful informal mechanisms to sanction independent justices who refused to interpret the laws according to his commands, ensuring that the Supreme Court *shifted its interpretations according to the changing policy agenda of incoming administrations*. These controls guaranteed a very responsive and politicized Supreme Court rather than a body insulated from politics.

Furthermore, the autocracy delegated to Supreme Court justices all the authority to discipline, promote, and sanction lower level federal courts. This meant that federal judges who were interested in keeping their jobs and ascend- ing the ladder of promotions were obliged to closely follow the Court's legal interpretations, which were highly responsive to the regime's top leadership.

The system worked in such a way that it imprinted a strong pro-regime ideological bias in the entire federal judiciary.

Finally, the *amparo* trial was designed to ensure that the president and the party's central leadership could exert strong controls over the states' courts. The states' courts were highly responsive to the governors, who controlled appointments and promotions. However, the rulings of every single trial in the country – criminal, civil, commercial – could be appealed first before the states' Supreme Tribunals (*Tribunales Superiores de Justicia*), second before the federal courts, and lastly before the Supreme Court. This meant that the Supreme Court was the last court of appeals in charge of controlling and reviewing the application of the laws by judges in the entire country. Since the Court was an agent of the president's office, through the appeals process the president was able to set the criteria for the interpretation of the laws in the entire country.

CITIZENS' RIGHTS AND AUTOCRATIC ABUSE

The official discourse was that the *amparo* trial established the necessary constraints for the creation of a limited government and the rule of law. This discourse was to a large extent also promoted by the legal profession and the law schools. In practice, however, the overwhelming majority of *amparo* cases were dismissed, and citizens found little effective redress for their grievances through the courts.

The Mexican Constitution established a series of fundamental rights, including the right to own property, to due process of law, to associate politically and to protest peacefully, to vote, and to free speech, among others. To any autocratic regime, this list of rights would sound threatening, but in practice they were extremely limited. Those who confronted the regime or who had to deal with the police and state bureaucracies found themselves at the mercy of government officials and courts that served the interests of those officials. The autocratic regime was carefully designed such that courts were powerful enough to allow the president to supervise and control its agents in the bureaucracy and lower level courts, but weak enough to prevent citizens from effectively enforcing their rights vis-à-vis the regime.

First of all, despite the constitutional discourse there was no due process in the autocratic regime. The Mexican criminal justice system was purposely designed to give the executive leeway to apply the law with ample discretion, ensuring punishment for the dissident while guaranteeing impunity to the ally. The criminal justice system was designed such that law enforcement agencies (public prosecutors and their agents in the *ministerio público*, MP) and the police, had the monopoly over investigative and prosecutorial actions," which meant that no other authority could compel the MP to initiate an investigation and to prosecute a crime before a court of law.[4] In addition, courts lacked jurisdiction over the broader investigative and prosecutorial process. Finally, in practice all detainees were regarded as guilty until proven innocent.

The criminal justice system allowed the ruling class to prey with impunity – corruption and rent-seeking was rampant, the state coffers were systematically abused, and numerous crimes were committed – and politicians would never be punished because the regime used its monopoly over the investigatory and prosecutorial apparatus to protect members of the ruling class. The enormous legal discretion promoted state arbitrariness in the application of the laws *even in cases that had no political significance*. Torture was frequent and systematic. Methods included beatings, electric shocks, simulated executions, suffocation with plastic bags, and deprivation of food and water. Torture was used (and continues to be used) as an investigative tool for obtaining information or confessions. Coerced confessions were used as evidence – often the main evidence against the accused. Members of the police and military who committed torture were generally not punished. Despite the fact that detainees had to be judged by a tribunal, criminal cases were decided on the basis of what transpired *before* the suspect was brought to a judge (Magaloni and Zepeda 2004).

Given formal restrictions on the *amparo* trial and the Supreme Court's own jurisprudence, these human rights abuses could not be sanctioned and controlled through the judiciary. For example, acts of state brutality could not be redressed through the *amparo* trial because the Court regarded those acts as "consumed acts not subject of appeal." Despite evidence that the police systematically employed torture and illegal detention to obtain confessions, the Supreme Court's jurisprudence established that confession should be regarded as the "queen of a trial's evidence." These permissive laws and legal precedent allowed judges to condemn victims on the basis of these confessions while ignoring abuses. The autocratic regime was pressed by the international community and civic society organizations to put in place human rights commissions in the 1990s. However, the autocracy purposely designed powerless institutions, whose recommendations were "nonbinding" and of a non-compulsory nature for the authorities to which they are addressed. Furthermore, human rights commissions possessed no legal authority to institute

---

[4] In 1995 President Zedillo introduced a reform that allows citizens to seek a court injunction against the MP's decision not to prosecute (*ejercer la acción penal*).

legal proceedings to conduct criminal investigations, severely limiting their ability to protect human rights.

Second, Mexican courts were also prohibited from enforcing political rights – the right to vote, the right to form political parties, the right to free speech, etc. In 1946 the PRI modified the constitution to centralize the organization, monitoring, and adjudication of elections in the hands of the federal government and the PRI's central bureaucracies (Molinar 1991). Through this constitutional reform, the PRI acquired impressive institutional power over the whole electoral process, including voter registration, monitoring of the ballots, and the so-called self-certification of the elections. Opposition political parties could not resort to the courts to contest electoral fraud and other electoral misdeeds, including the manipulation of voter registration, the government's refusal to grant legal registry to its candidates, the partisan abuse of state finance, and the exclusion of opposition candidates from the mass media, among many others. Furthermore, the "self-certification of the electoral process" implied that the majority of the incoming elected congressional politicians from the PRI were in charge of officially sanctioning the elections. The *amparo* trial was not permitted to contest electoral laws, which meant that these were not subject to judicial review. All of these implied an absolute absence of political rights.

These electoral institutions began to change in the 1990s, when Electoral Courts were first established (Eisenstadt 2004). The most fundamental institutional reform, however, was the granting of true independence to the Federal Electoral Institute (IFE), the body charged with organizing the elections, with the 1994 electoral reform (Magaloni 1996). As I discuss later, the Supreme Court was given jurisdiction over electoral matters in 1996, when the Electoral Courts were brought into the judiciary and judicial review over electoral laws was finally permitted (Magaloni 2003).

Third, property rights were also subject to state arbitrariness. The autocracy flourished under a system of mixed property rights in which a private economy coexisted with a highly activist state. The Mexican Constitution gave incredible economic powers to the state. Article 27 established that all land and natural resources originally belonged to the state, which could expropriate private property if it could be justified in light of the "common good." The article also established that the state would be in charge of redistributing land and defining the property right structure of the countryside, where strict limits to the size of property were established. Articles 25 and 28 of the constitution also gave the state ample leeway to regulate the economy, intervene in key sectors, direct industrialization, and restrict commerce and international trade.

Expropriations were fairly common during the 1930s and 1940s, when land reform began to be implemented on a massive scale, and when many important industries, including oil, were nationalized. Many of these conflicts ended in the Supreme Court, as discussed above, triggering Lazaro Cardenas' (1934–1940) decision to crack down on the liberal Court and to appoint a new, enlarged body of more amicable justices. After numerous conflicts that entailed the government's refusal to adequately compensate property owners whose lands were expropriated, the Court established the criterion that it was legal to expropriate with a mere promise to compensate, leaving citizens at the mercy of government abuse. The original wording of article 27 was that expropriation should be carried out *previa indemnizacion* (through compensation that should be given prior to the expropriation). The Court established, however, that expropriations could be carried out *mediante indemnizacion* (through compensation). The constitutional article was later changed to adjust this subtle wording difference, which would allow ample leeway to expropriate by promising a noncredible and unenforceable future compensation. The numerous land expropriations carried out during the autocratic era left property owners with no effective legal recourse against the regime. The tremendously insecure property rights in the countryside destroyed incentives to invest and to a large extent are responsible for the tremendous decline in agricultural productivity that made Mexico a net importer of foodstuff by the late 1960s.

The insecurity of property permeated beyond the countryside, to the banking and industrial sectors as well. The methods employed to prey on citizens varied, however. For example, when President Lopez Portillo (1976–1982) nationalized the banking system and expropriated savings through the infamous Mexdollar fraud where dollar-denominated bank deposits were returned at their pre-devaluation rate, numerous individuals resorted to the Supreme Court to challenge the president. This time the administration responded by changing the constitution to legalize the nationalization of the banks. In the autocratic regime, the president was the ultimate authority and his powers were not limited by the courts in any fundamental way.

ENFORCING POLITICAL ORDER

During the era of PRI hegemony, the constitution did not constrain power holders, because the ruling party could easily reverse any rule, including constitutional ones. The Supreme Court did not possess jurisdiction to adjudicate political conflicts arising among different levels and branches of government and among politicians competing for political office in elections. The president, as chief executive and leader of the autocratic ruling party, was the ultimate arbiter. This section shows the how the system generated incentives for politicians to obey the president's decisions, rather than turning to violence to settle their disputes.

After the Mexican revolution ended, power was extremely fractionalized among warlords, and conflicts were often settled through violence. The consolidation of the PRI as a hegemonic party took place during the 1930s and early 1940s (Garrido 1982). The federal government had first to disarm the warlords, consolidate military power in the center, and put the army under civilian control (Camp 1992). The revolution was fought under the banners "sufragio efectivo, no reelección"[5] and "la tierra es de quien la trabaja"[6] against the dictator, Porfirio Diaz, who had ruled Mexico for more than thirty years. The political pact that symbolized the end of the revolution – the 1917 Constitution – forbade presidential reelection and reestablished multiparty elections. After having modified the constitution to allow for his reelection, President Alvaro Obregón was murdered in 1928. After the assassination of Obregón, politicians created the predecessor of the PRI with the explicit intent to make the transition from a system of "caudillos" to one of "institutions." The goal of the PRI was to prevent personal dictatorship – any individual from grabbing all the pie for himself – while allowing members of the "revolutionary family" to share the spoils of office among themselves (Magaloni 2006).

The system granted immense powers to the president during his six-year term. The balance of power between the president and the numerous states' warlords shifted in favor of the former with the 1933 constitutional reform, which established the rule of nonconsecutive reelection for all elective offices – governors, local and federal legislators, and municipal presidents. After this reform, local bosses could no longer count on enduring power and had to channel their ambition in search of attractive positions in the federal government. The president, as leader of the official party, thus became an extremely powerful political player, because he was in charge of distributing offices among the ruling elite.

A simple game-theoretic framework reveals the factors that allowed the president to enforce political order. There are three political players, the president, P, and two other elected political actors, G and L (e.g., a governor and a local legislative assembly or two politicians competing for nomination). The president must decide how to adjudicate a conflict between the two political

---

[5] The English translation is "No reelection and the right to have votes effectively counted."
[6] The English translation is "land for the tiller."

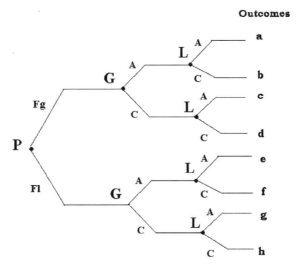

Outcomes

FIGURE 7.1. Game of presidential arbitration of authoritarian political order.

actors; for example, whether a governor can dissolve the local assembly or the local assembly can impeach the governor. The president has two available strategies: decide in favor of G (Fg) or decide in favor of L (Fl). These two actors, in turn, have two available strategies: abide by the president's decision (A) or contest it (C) by openly disobeying and resorting to violence. The game is depicted in its extensive form in Figure 7.1.

Each actor's preferences are derived from the following assumptions. The president prefers to "get his way," deciding in favor of whichever actor he sincerely prefers. I assume that he prefers to decide in favor of G. However, the president also seeks to protect the existing political order so he would rather have both actors not challenge his decision than decide in favor of his preferred actor. Thus, the president's most preferred alternative is *a*, to get his way: decide in favor of G, his preferred player, and have both actors comply. His second most preferred outcome is *e*: decide in favor of L and have both actors comply. The third most preferred alternative is to decide in favor of G and that only one actor, L, contests. He then prefers to decide in favor of L and that only one actor, G, contests. Obviously, the worst possible outcome, *h*, is to decide against his most preferred player, G, and that both actors contest.

The payoffs of the game for players G and L depend on the prevailing "state of the world" of partisan politics, which is derived from three sets of issues: the distribution of military power among the players, the probability that both actors belong to the same party or a different one, and the degree of party discipline within the PRI. For the sake of simplicity, I assume that the PRI has already consolidated military power in the center, local bosses have been disarmed and no single local political actor can mount a successful violent insurrection to unseat the president.

To solve the game, I distinguish three eras of partisan politics during this period. The first is the hegemonic era of the PRI, when this party has the monopoly of office. In this era, players G and L belong to the same party, and the PRI strongly sanctions lack of discipline with expulsion from the party. The sub-game perfect equilibrium in the game of presidential arbitration of authoritarian political order is outcome *a*, the president gets his way, deciding in favor of the actor he prefers, and both actors comply with the decision.

To see why both actors comply, suppose that the president solves a conflict between G and L by asking the governor to resign. The payoff for the governor of this sanction is o. Why would a PRI politician choose to give up his post instead of rebelling? The answer to this question lies in the continuation value (the payoff from the next period forward) and the costs of disobeying. If the politician obeys the president, he gets o in this period but he has a probability, p, that he will be rewarded by the party with office in the future, O_t. Assume that the party guarantees some form of progressive ambition so that the next office is more valuable than the previous ones according to a constant parameter π such that $O_{t+1} = O_t(1 + \pi)$ This means that the politician who obeys the president gets $\frac{\delta}{1-\delta} dO(\frac{1+\pi}{\pi})$ which is the expected value of getting o in this period and getting a career in office with probability d (for the practice called *dedazo or* finger pointing) after that. The payoffs are discounted at a rate $\delta \in (o, 1)$.

The politician who chooses to rebel knows that he will be expelled from the party. He has a probability *f* of keeping control of office after fighting for it. Fighting imposes a cost of *c*. However, once expelled from the party, the politician would need to challenge it through elections to attain office in the next period. The probability of winning the elections is *e*. Thus, the politician who disobeys the president gets $Of - c + \frac{\delta}{1-\delta}Oe$. The politician will not rebel against the president as long as

$$\frac{\delta}{1 - \delta} dO \left(\frac{1 + \pi}{\pi} \right) > Of - c + \frac{\delta}{1 - \delta} Oe \qquad (7.1)$$

This says that the politician will abide by the autocratic political order as long as the continuation value of remaining loyal to the ruling party is larger than what the politician would obtain by fighting to retain his current post and the expected value of contesting for office outside the party through elections in the next period. This condition is likely to be true as long as

(1) the expected value of being rewarded with office and spoils in the future is large, (2) the expected chance of winning an election *against* the PRI is low, (3) the costs of fighting are large, and (4) the politician does not discount the future too heavily. Note that the value of fighting for office is relatively low during the era of hegemony because, given the rule of nonconsecutive reelection, the politician unavoidably needs to step down from office at time t + 1. If reelection were possible, the incentives to grab power by force increase because, after a successful rebellion, the politician could presumably impose a "local dictatorship" and hold on to office thereafter.

Thus, in this account the rule of nonconsecutive reelection not only makes politicians dependent upon the party's nomination for access to political office but also lessens the desire to employ violence by reducing the value of office. This form of political order is autocratic in the sense that the president "gets his way" and political conflicts are not decided according to the constitution.[7] Federalism exists only in the constitution, and power in practice is extremely centralized.

The Crumbling of the Autocratic Political Order

The game of presidential arbitration of authoritarian political order unravels when the PRI loses its monopoly of office and it unravels for two reasons. First, once multiparty politics emerges, the president must adjudicate conflicts among politicians belonging to different parties, and the opposition possesses no incentives to abide by what the president decides unless the decision favors it. Second, once multiparty politics emerges, disgruntled PRI politicians possess more incentives to rebel against the president because the difference between d and e in equation 1 decreases. Now the expected chance of attaining office by challenging the PRI electorally increases.

The game with multiple parties has two possible equilibria depending on the extent to which the players can credibly threaten to rebel – I assume that G belongs to the PRI and L to the opposition. Consider the following possibility: the opposition politician threatens that if the president does not decide in his favor, he will paralyze the state, call for a boycott of commercial activity, and mobilize the population to engage in civil resistance. Assuming that the president refuses to employ brute force to repress the opposition, he will side with L if he anticipates that the PRI politician will abide by his decision. Thus,

---

[7] I assume that politicians within the PRI will not coordinate their actions to overthrow the president – in this game there are no incentives to coordinate because at least one of the players obtains a reward from compliance.

a sub-game perfect equilibrium of the game in the era of multipartyism and high discipline within the PRI is *e*: the president decides in favor of L and both actors comply. This derives from three assumptions: first, the president seeks to maintain political order and refuses to brutally repress the opposition; second, an opposition politician can respond with a costly civil mobilization to an adverse decision by the president; and third, the PRI politician abides by the president's decision because he fears the future costs of expulsion from the party.

During the Salinas presidency (1988–1994), these forms of bargains appear to have been fairly common. The *concertacesiones* were postelectoral bargains through which the president transferred elective office from the PRI to the opposition after the latter protested the official results through postelectoral mobilization. The most infamous *concertacesión* took place in the 1991 gubernatorial elections of Guanajuato, where the postelectoral bargain transferred the gubernatorial seat to Carlos Medina Placencia, of the PAN. Salinas also asked the PRI governor-elect of the 1991 elections in San Luis Potosí and the governor-elect of the 1992 elections in Michoacán to resign for similar causes. In these cases, however, interim PRI governors more agreeable to the opposition were appointed as substitutes.

However, outcome *e* is not sustainable as an equilibrium over the medium run because the president can't abuse the leadership conferred by the PRI without facing consequences. The third era I distinguish is that of competitive multiparty politics with lack of discipline within the PRI. The sub-game perfect equilibrium here is *b*, which entails that the president decides in favor of G and L responds by challenging the president's decision. In this third game, the president's leadership over the party is implicitly challenged by his own co-partisans, because outcome *b* derives from the fact that off the equilibrium path, the PRI (G) credibly threatens to contest a decision by the president that favors the opposition. Note that for this threat to be credible, PRI politicians must be ready to employ violence.

The Madrazo rebellion against President Ernesto Zedillo illustrates this argument. President Zedillo attempted to solve an electoral conflict in the 1994 elections of the state of Tabasco between the PRD (Party of the Democratic Revolution) and the PRI through a *concertacesión*. The PRI was no longer willing to swallow these bitter deals. The candidate of the PRI, Roberto Madrazo, threatened to use all the power at his disposal, including asking for support from other governors in the Southern states of Mexico, to defend his victory in the gubernatorial elections of Tabasco (Eisenstadt 2004). The official results of the election gave him 56 percent of the vote against 37 percent to Andrés Manuel López Obrador, of the PRD. The PRD protested

Madrazo's victory by blocking the oil refineries of the state and taking the *Plaza de Armas* by force, which impeded Madrazo to take control of the Gubernatorial Palace. After rumors began to spread that the president would ask Madrazo for his resignation, PRI politicians in the state blocked several roads, and the state's private sector, which was supporting Madrazo, responded with a boycott. Ernesto Zedillo ended up having to swallow Madrazo's refusal to step down from office. In an attempt to appease PRI politicians, Zedillo promised Madrazo that they would "govern together until 2000." Instead of hurting Madrazo, the rebellion ended up boosting his prominence within the PRI.

The Madrazo rebellion against the president marks a turning point in Mexican politics. It signals that something major in the system had changed such that the president could no longer serve as the central arbiter of the autocratic political order. To settle their disputes without resorting to violence, politicians needed to turn elsewhere and they turned to the Supreme Court.

EMPOWERING THE SUPREME COURT AND THE 1994 CONSTITUTIONAL REFORM

The 1994 constitutional reform transformed the Supreme Court into a true constitutional tribunal (see also Cossío 2000, 2001 and González Compeán and Bauer 2002). The reform reduced the number of justices from twenty-five to eleven. Life appointments were changed to fifteen-year appointments. By establishing the "constitutional controversies" and the "constitutional actions," the reform significantly expanded the power of the Supreme Court, which could now adjudicate on all sorts of issues that the president had previously arbitrated. The Court could now hear conflicts among the executive and the legislative branches; the federal government and the states; and the municipalities and the governors.

The constitutional actions are a form of judicial review. Constitutional actions against federal laws or international treaties can be filed by any group of 33 percent of the members of the Chamber of Deputies or the Senate, and against state laws by 33 percent of the members of the local assemblies. The Solicitor General (*Procurador General*) can promote constitutional actions against federal and state laws or international treaties, and the leadership of any political party registered before the Federal Electoral Institute can challenge federal electoral laws. Local parties can also file an action of unconstitutionality against local electoral laws.

To support the constitutional reform, the PRI imposed several limitations to the power of the Supreme Court so as to protect itself. First, the PRI originally refused to delegate jurisdiction to the Court on electoral issues. The Court did not acquire the right to review the decisions of the Federal Electoral Tribunal and to rule on the constitutionality of electoral laws until 1996.

The second way in which the PRI attempted to limit the power of the Court was to make it harder to undo legislation previously approved by this party. The reform established that the Court's decisions would not have the effect of annulling legislation unless eight of the eleven justices ruled that a law was unconstitutional. The reform also established that the constitutionality of laws must be appealed within thirty days of enactment of the law or the first act of application. In practice, the rule of thirty days significantly reduced the opportunity to challenge many laws.

Third, the reform also reduced the stakes of constitutional controversies by establishing that the decisions of the Supreme Court on constitutional controversies would only have effects *inter partes* (suspending the action only among the parties) when a lower level of government acted as plaintiff against a higher level; for example, when a municipality challenged a state or the federation, a state challenged the federation, in controversies between two states, and in controversies between two municipalities from different states.

The PRI and the president attempted to legitimize the new Supreme Court by giving the opposition a chance to influence its composition. When the constitutional reform was approved, Zedillo was in a position to choose all the Court's justices, because the PRI controlled the two-thirds super-majority in the Senate necessary to ratify nominations single-handedly. However, Zedillo opted to negotiate the nomination of the new justices with the opposition. The PRD and the PT (Labor Party) explicitly denied their support to the constitutional reform and refused to participate in the negotiations for the nomination of the justices. The PAN, however, chose to participate in the process.

My approach underscores that President Zedillo's reform of the Supreme Court responded primarily to the need to enforce political order among the politicians. Political order began to unravel with the emergence of multiparty politics. There are 31 states in Mexico plus the Federal District and more than 2,400 municipalities. By 1994, the PAN controlled the governorships of Baja California, Guanajuato, and Chihuahua, and it also controlled numerous municipalities, including some of the most important cities in the country. The opposition's victories at the local level significantly accelerated after the 1994 peso crisis, just when the Supreme Court reform was enacted. The opposition won fourteen gubernatorial races between 1994 and 2000, and non-PRI municipalities increased from 12 percent in 1994 to 33 percent in 2000, representing close to 45 percent of the population. The Supreme Court became the new arbiter of political conflicts once the president could no longer serve this role.

THE DEMOCRATIC COURT

A clear implication of the reform is that the Supreme Court became the new arbiter of federalism, a task that the president used to perform in the era of party hegemony. Table 7.4 presents the constitutional controversies brought to the Supreme Court from its creation until 2005. The overwhelming majority are between the municipalities and the federal government, and between the municipalities and the states' assemblies and the governors. The vast majority of these controversies involve institutions controlled by different political parties. In Magaloni and Sanchez (2006), we code each case by the partisan identity of the public office involved in the dispute. Without considering the 329 controversies over indigenous rights, the defendant was a public organization controlled by the PRI in 72 percent of the constitutional controversies, the PAN in 16 percent, and the PRD in percent. A public organization controlled by the PAN was the plaintiff in 42 percent of the cases, by the PRD in 23 percent, and by the PRI in 17 percent. Hence, constitutional controversies have become the most important vehicle through which the lower levels of government controlled by the PAN and the PRD could fight against the higher levels of government, mainly the states, controlled by the PRI.

We also coded the partisan identity of the parties to the constitutional actions. The PRI was the defendant in 68 percent of the cases, the PAN in 23 percent, and the PRD in 3 percent. One of the smaller opposition parties (e.g., the Mexican Green Party, Social Alliance, or Convergence for Democracy) was the plaintiff in 37 percent of these cases, the PAN in 22 percent, the PRD in 12 percent, and the PRI in 7 percent. Thus, constitutional actions are the most common vehicle of access to the Supreme Court by the smallest parties.

In Magaloni and Sanchez (2006) we explore whether the Court rules disproportionately in favor of the former ruling party. Our results reveal a strong partisan bias in the Court's decisions, in which it disproportionately ruled to strike down legislation or challenge state acts by "opposition-affiliated" institutions and to uphold laws or acts by the former ruling party. Our results also reveal that the Court tended to rule more often in favor of the former ruling party in "important cases." The Court favored the opposition over the former ruling party predominantly in lower salience local-level conflicts.

Our results also indicate that the Court responded strategically to the PRI's lost of power. When the PRI lost the majority of seats in the Lower Chamber

TABLE 7.4. *Constitutional controversies by institution in conflict, 1994–2004* (% in parentheses)*

Plaintiff	Defendant						
	Municipality	Local Assembly	Governor	State S. Court	President	Federal Congress	Total
Municipality	1 (0.14)	155 (22.21)	67 (9.6)	5 (0.72)	16 (2.29)	368 (52.72)	612 (87.68)
Local Assembly	1 (0.14)	0 (0)	7 (1)	1 (0.14)	0 (0)	2 (0.29)	11 (1.58)
Governor	7 (1)	18 (2.58)	0 (0)	0	11 (1.58)	9 (1.29)	45 (6.45)
State S. Court	0 (0)	16 (2.29)	2 (0.29)	0	1 (0.14)	0 (0)	19 (2.72)
President	1 (0.14)	2 (0.29)	2 (0.29)	0	0 (0)	3 (0.43)	8 (1.15)
Federal Congress	0 (0)	0 (0)	0 (0)	0	3 (0.43)	0 (0)	3 (0.43)
TOTAL	10 (1.43)	191 (27.36)	78 (11.17)	6 (0.86)	31 (4.44)	382 (54.73)	698 (100)

Source: Magaloni and Sanchez 2006.

of Deputies in 1997, the Court began to rule in favor of the opposition more often so as to build up credibility. As the Court became more credible and its legitimacy increased, however, the propensity to rule in favor of the PRI began to increase again. Most cases have been decided overwhelmingly in favor of the former ruling party even after it lost power in 2000. Our results do not necessarily imply, however, that the Supreme Court decided cases based solely on the partisan affiliation of the parties to a dispute. There are many cases in which ideology clearly matched with party affiliation.

The famous electricity decision illustrates this point. As we discuss in Maga-loni and Sanchez (2006), the Mexican Constitution places the electricity sector in the exclusive domain of the state. However, the Electricity Law allows the Federal Electoral Commission (CFE) to buy electricity from private genera-tors. President Vicente Fox from the PAN, in power since 2000, reformed the regulatory framework of the sector to permit a higher percentage of privately generated electricity to be sold to the CFE. The reform did not establish any limits on the amounts of excess energy that private investors could sell to the CFE. Rather, it provided that the executive, through regulations, would set such limits. The PRI and PRD factions in both chambers of Congress brought a constitutional controversy against Fox's electricity reform. For the first time, the Supreme Court had to judge on a dispute between the executive and both chambers of Congress.

Congress claimed that Fox's plan to increase the limits of existing regulation on buying excess power from private generators was an encroachment of its legislative power. The Court sided with the congressional factions, arguing that Fox's reform was "a genuine falsification of the law." The majority opinion was divided into two groups. The first considered that the reform contradicted the Electricity Law because its legislative intent had not been to authorize the indirect privatization of the electricity sector. The second group declared that the reform violated article 27 of the constitution, which places the sector exclusively in the hands of the state. The Court's decision resulted in the defeat of President Fox's attempt to promote private investment in the electricity sector and revived the economic nationalism embedded in the constitution that was drafted during the autocratic era of the PRI.

ALTERNATIVE THEORIES OF JUDICIAL EMPOWERMENT

One alternative theory accounting for the creation of powerful courts stresses the need of the autocratic regime to create a credible commitment to property rights to increase investment (Moustafa 2007). The argument would be that President Zedillo wanted to signal to the international financial community his commitment to the market-oriented reforms, the rule of law, and private property. Judicial review was necessary, according to this account, to credibly limit government predation and the risks of expropriation.

The problem with this approach is that foreign and national investors had more to fear from a powerful court than from the executive's discretion. As the electricity case cited above suggests, the creation of a powerful court entailed serious risks to investors because it made the constitution binding. The Mexican constitution is an extremely obsolete document, combining strong nationalism and statism with a few liberal principles. When the existing constitutional framework is not liberal, judicial review does not provide stronger limits on government predation. Furthermore, the Mexican case also suggests that investors have more to fear from justices whose legal ideologies are nationalistic and old-fashioned than from the uncertainty stemming from a democratically elected government.

Another view stresses Ernesto Zedillo's personality and his desire to bring democracy and the rule of law to Mexico. My approach sees Zedillo as the key proponent of the constitutional reform but emphasizes his desire to solve the critical dilemma of enforcing political order among the politicians rather than his desire to bring about the rule of law for Mexican citizens. The 1994 constitutional reform was fundamentally designed for the politicians, not for the citizens. Emphasis was placed, above all, in establishing a procedure to resolve conflicts among different levels of government because in the new era of multipartyism, these conflicts could only be solved through costly political bargaining and often violence. The new procedures established by the reform (the constitutional actions and the constitutional controversies) can be utilized) exclusively by the politicians, not the citizens. Furthermore, the constitutional reform did nothing to improve the *amparo* trial, which remains one of the key impediments for limiting governmental abuse, suggesting that Zedillo's motivation for carrying out the constitutional reform lay elsewhere.

An alternative account to the empowerment of constitutional courts is provided by Ginsburg (2003). He argues that autocrats will create powerful judicial review institutions as a form of "political insurance" when they calculate that they might lose power in the future. "A constitutional design allowing unlimited flexibility for electoral winners, as in the model of parliamentary sovereignty, is much less attractive in a politically diffused setting that in a setting wherein a single party holds sway. While prospective governing parties would like flexibility, prospective opposition parties value limited government" (25). By contrast, "self-interested politicians will not set up an arbiter to solve disputes about constitutional meaning when they believe they are likely to hold on to political power" (24). This theory is related to various works on judicial independence, including Ramseyer (1994) and Landes and Posner (1975), as well as works on bureaucratic insulation (McCubbins, Noll, and Weingast 1987 and 1989; Moe 1990) and civil service reform (Geddes 1994).

My account is consistent with these works in stressing that a powerful Supreme Court in Mexico could only come about when power became diffused and the ruling party could no longer anticipate with certainty that it would hold on to power in the future. However, my account stresses that the empowerment of the Supreme Court resulted more from the president's need to find alternative ways to enforce political order among subnational politicians than from his anticipation that the ruling party might lose office. Ernesto Zedillo proposed to Congress the constitutional reform in December of 1994, just one month after assuming office and much before it was clear that the PRI might lose the coming presidential elections of 2000. It is true that the constitutional reform was negotiated during the following months, once the peso crisis had exploded and the PRI began to lose more and more local elections (Magaloni 2006).

Thus, consistent with Ginsburg's (2003) account, the PRI might have reasoned that it was in its interest to support Zedillo's proposal to reform the Court as a form of insurance in the event the party were to lose power. However, it appears that Zedillo's motivation to propose the reform was to solve a more urgent problem, that of enforcing political order among lower level politicians. In the end, the constitutional reform that empowered the Supreme Court resulted from a combination of these two factors – a president interested in finding mechanisms to enforce political order, and a ruling party interested in establishing an institutional insurance in the event it lost power.

CONCLUSION

This chapter explored the strategies the Mexican autocracy employed to enforce political order. The autocracy employed courts to monitor low-level government officials by granting citizens the right to challenge them through the *amparo* trial. The procedure, however, had very limited effectiveness in restraining state abuse. Courts were purposely designed to be weak and subservient. In establishing this "fire-alarm" monitoring device, the Mexican autocracy carefully designed the judicial apparatus to prevent citizens from challenging the regime through these courts.

This chapter distinguished three areas in which citizens were left at the mercy of state abuse. First, the regime gave itself a monopoly over the investigatory and prosecutorial criminal apparatus, which was used to guarantee the impunity of the ruling class. The *amparo* trial could not be used to challenge state brutality, or to challenge the state's decision *not to prosecute a crime* when powerful political players were involved. By contrast, the system was merciless against the enemy, with suspects being guilty until proven innocent. Second, political rights only existed in the constitution because the PRI's electoral monopoly and its numerous electoral malpractices could not be challenged before the courts, nor could electoral laws be questioned through the *amparo* trial. Third, a private economy coexisted in the shadow of an overpowering state, and property rights were extremely insecure.

Furthermore, courts were not given jurisdiction to solve critical political conflicts among members of the ruling elite. Instead, the autocratic political order was arbitrated by the president, whose power was respected because (1) he was the leader of the official party, (2) the party sanctioned non-compliance with expulsion, and (3) the party possessed the monopoly of political office.

When the PRI lost its monopoly of office and politicians could aspire to office by joining other political parties, this institutional equilibrium began to fall apart. After a significant number of opposition politicians acceded to office at the subnational level, political conflicts needed to be resolved through costly political bargaining or violence. The chapter stresses that the need to create a new arbiter to enforce political order played a prominent role in the 1994 constitutional reform, through which the Supreme Court was empowered to solve "constitutional controversies" among different levels and branches of government and to undertake "constitutional actions," a form of judicial review. After this reform, the Mexican Court gained new prominence in the political system.

8

The Institutional Diffusion of Courts in China: Evidence from Survey Data

Pierre Landry

It should not be surprising that authoritarian regimes seek to establish courts. The victims of the Moscow trials of the 1930s; political opponents in fascist Italy, Argentina, and Brazil in the 1970s, and in China the famous "gang of four" were all tried in formal courts, with the explicit support of their respective regimes. Authoritarian systems rely on courts because formal legal institutions are expected to bring legitimacy to decisions that may not be fair or equitable. These courts' jurisdiction is not limited to criminal or political cases. Courts handling civil, economic, and administrative cases exist in many authoritarian regimes as well.

What is surprising is the development of genuinely active and popular courts within an otherwise authoritarian system. Tate and Haynie (1993) are rather pessimistic about courts in authoritarian regimes, but others show that view is not always warranted. Argentinean judges tended to sympathize with the dictatorship, but their Brazilian counterparts did not, and used their position to undermine military rule (Osiel 1995). Spanish courts played an active role in the transformation of Francoist dictatorship and the eventual democratization of the regime (Giles and Lancaster 1989; Pinkele 1992; Toharia 1975). Without claiming that an authoritarian regime can establish a genuine "rule of law" as the term is widely understood in democratic societies, legal scholars and social scientists are compelled by the diffusion of formal legal institutions within authoritarian regimes to explain how (and preferably why) these courts do – in some instances – develop into credible institutions.[1]

Few cross-national studies on the impact of legal innovations in authoritarian regimes exist, but it appears that the degree to which such courts approach

---

[1] For a detailed discussion of the underlying theories of institutional diffusion and its application to China, see Tang and Holzner (2006).

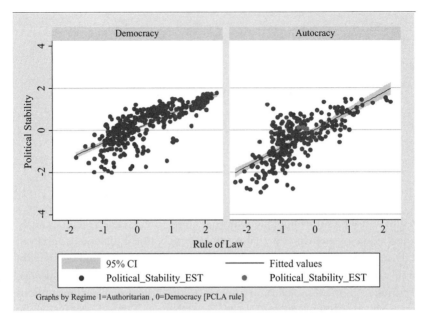

FIGURE 8.1. Rule of law vs. political stability indicators among democracies and autocracies (1994–2002). *Sources:* Global Governance Indicators (2005) and Cheibub and Gandhi (2005). Due to data constraints on regimes, these plots show the results from 1994 to 2002, in two-year increments. The lighter dots represent China.

a meaningful rule of law affects their prospect for survival. Using the global governance indicators (GGI) compiled by Kaufmann, Kraa, and Mastruzzi (2005) and the updated data set on regimes by Cheibub (2004), we find that autocracies that rate highly on the rule-of-law dimension also appear more stable politically (Figure 8.1). It is less clear *how* autocracies successfully introduce reforms that strengthen the rule of law.

The case of the People's Republic of China since 1978 presents us with a remarkable case in which to unpack the process by which legal innovations are diffused in an authoritarian regime. It is a truism among comparativists that China has never been a democracy, regardless of the specific coding rules that are used to categorize regimes in political science. Therefore, the persistence of authoritarianism in China allows us to rule out any possibility of institutional contamination as occurs when new authoritarian regimes "inherit" legal institutions from the democracy that they overthrow. Historical Chinese regimes may have developed distinctive legal systems (Bernhardt, Huang, and Mark 1994; Huang 2001), but one cannot reasonably claim that Qing, Republican

(Xu 1997), or PRC courts under Mao operated in a manner consistent with modern principles of the rule of law.

The regime's self-proclaimed goal of building the "rule of law" in China (以法治国) is a large-scale social experiment in a "hard" case: formal institutions have been introduced by the state on a social terrain that seems highly unfavorable to the development of the rule of law. The contradiction inherent in the Chinese legal reforms has been widely noted. There is no pretense of judicial independence: judges – who are almost always members of the Communist Party – are appointed by the state and vetted by Party Organization Departments set up within the judiciary that must in practice answer to bureaucratic superiors within local governments (Cohen 1997; Zhao 2003). Rule of law "with Chinese characteristics" requires party control over the judiciary (Lubman 1996; Peerenboom 2002). Though appeals are possible, there is no proper judicial review, and the execution of civil judgments is uncertain (Clarke 1995). Furthermore, information flows are heavily controlled, and social activists and lawyers who engage judicial institutions are routinely harassed, or worse. Going to court – particularly if one challenges state actors or seeks to sue the state – remains a highly charged political affair (Gallagher 2005; O'Brien and Li 2005).

If the Chinese experiment were to succeed under these adverse conditions, we would stand on less precarious ground arguing that authoritarian regimes *can* build something approaching a meaningful rule of law. Indeed, despite the vast shortcomings of the Chinese legal system, the progressive trend is unmistakable: the party is publicly committed to modernizing the legal system and building more autonomous judicial and legal institutions than is typically the case in Leninist regimes (Diamant, Lubman, and O'Brien 2005; Peerenboom 2002; Potter 2003; U.S. Congressional-Executive Commission on China 2002).

This chapter does not seek to argue whether China is or is not a rule-of-law society. A process that has taken centuries to mature in many countries cannot possibly be compressed over a few years, even by elites that are prone to social and institutional engineering. More modestly, my goal is to take Chinese legal institutions as they are perceived and utilized by ordinary Chinese citizens and to specify how and why these seemingly incongruous institutional innovations in an authoritarian regime are taking root, or not. I argue that understanding the initial phase of the diffusion of institutions (here, courts) is a necessary but not a sufficient step to establishing the basic conditions for the development of the rule of law in the long run. The long march toward *fazhi* requires at least courts that are reasonably trustworthy and render meaningful judgments that increase the appeal of the institution among potential adopters.

Quantitative evidence on Chinese legal reforms is scarce. Pioneering empirical work has taken place (Michelson 2002, 2006), but to our knowledge, the national survey on the Institutionalization of Legal Reforms in China (ILRC) is the first national sample of its kind. We collected data on the types and extent of civil, economic, and administrative disputes on a national scale to examine in detail the multiple mechanisms by which grievances evolve.

The survey is based on a multistage stratified sample in which each province, municipality, or autonomous region is taken as a stratum. Within each stratum, counties (or urban districts) were selected at random by PPS. Within each county, two townships (or their street committee counterparts in urban areas) were also selected at random. We used 2000 census data to develop measures of size at the township level. Below townships, a spatial sampling design was used to avoid the problem of coverage errors caused by imprecise household registration lists that exclude internal migrants and temporary residents (Landry and Shen 2005). Thus, the survey provides a solid foundation for testing the validity of prior case study findings and also allows making point predictions and generalizable propositions about the behavior of ordinary citizens. In summary, the sample is conveniently large enough that it captures rare events (such as disputes), conforms to the principle of equal probability selection, and is representative of China's varied geographic, demographic, social, and economic environment. The sampling points (at the township level) are mapped in Figure 8.2.

INSTITUTIONAL DIFFUSION IN AN AUTHORITARIAN SETTING

Trust

A great deal of the literature on institutional innovation stresses trustworthiness as a key determinant of the success of institutional innovations, or their failure when it is lacking. If, under conditions that need to be specified, people trust a given institution, they are likely to rely on it should the need arise. If they do not, they will instead turn to reasonable alternatives. Trust is also a condition of these institutions' endurance in the long run (Hetherington 1998; Levi 1999; Levi and Stoker 2000; Ulbig 2002).

In the case of China, many scholars have demonstrated empirically that both interpersonal trust and system-based trust are comparatively high (Inglehart 1997; Shi 2001; Tang and Parish 2000). However, generalized trust may not

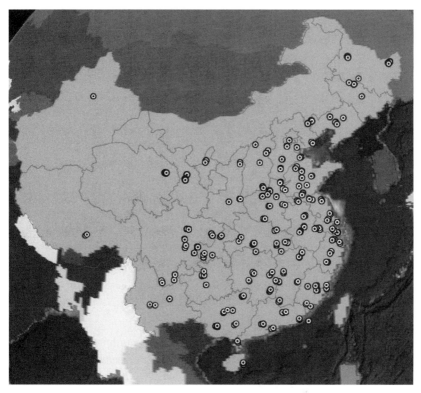

FIGURE 8.2. The ILRC Survey of China (2003–2004). *Note:* Dots represent townships.

be as reliable a predictor of success or failure of a specific institution. Just as trust between individuals can be generalized or particularistic (Uslaner 2002), Jennings (1998) has shown that individual trust in government institutions can be highly differentiated (Levi 1998). Li Lianjiang(2004) has found that rural Chinese exhibit highly differentiated levels of trust regarding central and local institutions.

The ILRC survey results demonstrate that these broad findings also hold with respect to legal institutions. Political correctness probably accounts for the high score of the Communist Party (CCP) in absolute terms, but the CCP provides at least a useful benchmark against which to gauge relevant legal institutions. We find that trust is institution-specific: whereas organizations that are frequently involved in dispute mediation (such as village committees) fared especially poorly, the courts and the procuracy are held in relatively high regard. Furthermore, most respondents trust institutions that are closely

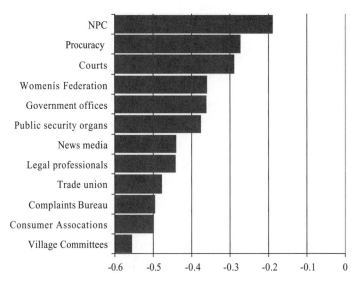

FIGURE 8.3. Relative measures of trust in public and legal institutions. Scores are first-differences from average trust scores for the CCP.

associated with the state to a far greater extent than nonbureaucratic actors: legal professionals are less trusted than public security organs, whereas village committees fare the worst of all institutions listed on the survey instrument (see Figure 8.3).

Popular trust is overwhelmingly tilted in favor of central political and judicial institutions. As a follow-up question to a general measure of trust (for instance, in courts), we asked respondents to reveal whether they trust the Supreme People's Court, the local court, or neither. We also asked them to make similar central/local comparisons of People's Congresses, the Communist Party, and general government agencies. Although party members tend to be more trusting than nonparty members, central institutions enjoy a considerable degree of support in both groups (see Table 8.1).

These high levels of trust in legal institutions bode well for the capacity of Chinese citizens to adopt institutional innovations. If Margaret Levi is correct that "trust is, in fact, a holding word for the phenomenon that enables individuals to take risks" (Levi 1998: 1), the large segment of trusting Chinese citizens must be eager to test legal institutions, especially the courts, even if they have little personal experience in them.

Courts are an institutional novelty in China. Although they have existed throughout the history of the People's Republic, they did not play a significant role in dispute resolution during the Mao era. Their functions expanded in

TABLE 8.1. *Relative trust in central political and judicial institutions, contrasted with local equivalents*

	Non-CCP members	CCP members
Supreme People's Court (vs. local courts or neither)	90.5%	94.9%
National People's Congress (vs. local People's Congress or neither)	90.9%	95.3%
Central CCP organizations (vs. local or neither)	90.7%	95.0%
Central government institutions (vs. local or neither)	90.8%	93.0%

All measures are estimates that account for the design effect.

the 1980s and 1990s with a breathtaking series of reforms, the promulgation of numerous laws and regulations, as well as sheer physical institutional construction. In contrast with the situation in 1978, virtually every Chinese county (or district) now has a functioning court.

The aggregate statistical evidence strongly suggests the diffusion of this institutional innovation: while the act of going to court was virtually unheard of in 1978, the ratio of court users has now reached approximately four per thousand (Figure 8.4). If we make the assumption that citizens use an institution because they trust it, trust in Chinese courts is decidedly on the rise. The changing mechanisms of dispute resolution provide further evidence of the rising popularity of the courts. A much larger proportion of disputes are settled in court rather than being "mediated" in quasi-governmental organizations (*tiaojie weiyuanhui*/调解委员会), as was the norm during the Mao era. Since 2001, the number of civil and administrative cases settled in court has reached about 4.6 million per annum, on par with the number of mediated disputes (Figure 8.5).

Surely, the popularity of the courts cannot be explained by a long record of openness and fairness of Chinese judicial institutions. Nor can we invoke institutional developments that predate the Communist regime to argue that popular trust in courts was acquired before the reform era, and that citizens are eager to use them now that they have the opportunity to do so. Introducing (or reforming) courts may be a necessary component of legal reforms, but the supply side is not a convincing explanation of sustained innovation. State propaganda may persuade citizens to become first-time users of the court system, but if they encounter abuse, corruption, or unfair treatment, disappointed litigants are unlikely to maintain their trust in the institution and adopt it in the

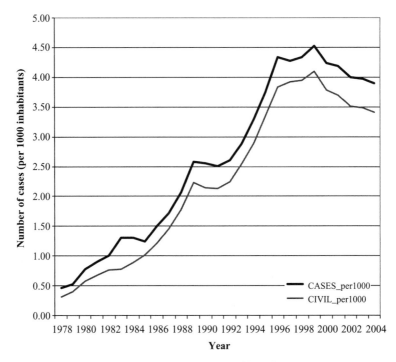

FIGURE 8.4. Number of cases per capita accepted by Chinese courts. *Note:* Computed from *Zhongguo Tongji Nianjian* (multiple years).

long run. Without the trust and tangible benefits of end-users, we would expect the introduction of courts in authoritarian systems to be short-lived. After an initial fad, disillusioned first-time users would not only personally turn to more efficient alternatives but they would also probably discourage relatives, friends, and acquaintances from following their path. Under such conditions, courts should see a steady stream of users only among citizens with small social networks or those who are poorly informed about the practical realities of legal institutions. Over time, the number of court cases would dwindle, leading to the gradual failure of the innovation.

Explaining Institutional Diffusion: Networks

Social networks are central to theories of diffusion, and the problem of the adoption of institutions like courts in authoritarian regimes can be better understood by examining in detail the social structure of the regimes that innovate. The number of actors, the structure and the density of their networks,

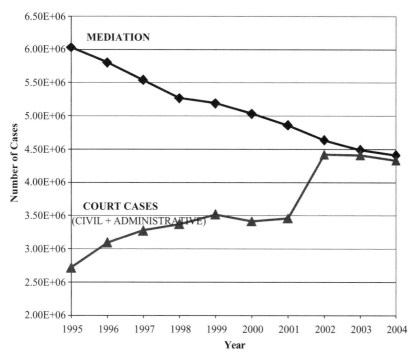

FIGURE 8.5. Evolution of court cases and cases handled by mediation committees. *Source: China Statistical Yearbook* (multiple years).

as well as the distribution of adopter and nonadopters within a network have been used in formal modeling and computer simulations to explain not only the rate of diffusion of innovations but also patterns of partial diffusion within networks (Hägerstrand 1967; Hall 2004; Mahajan and Peterson 1985). Bandwagoning is more likely to occur when potential adopters learn from actual adopters with whom they are networked that an innovation is worthwhile, or not. Computer simulations have uncovered counterintuitive results: even among networks that were seemingly small, the idiosyncrasies of their structure sometimes allow for their rapid diffusion (Abrahamson and Rosenkopf 1997).

Court users in transitional regimes fit this description quite well. In societies where the rule of law is not well developed, the proportion of court users is likely to be very low. Furthermore, in authoritarian regimes that control information flows, rapid diffusion is likely to be concentrated among small clusters of individuals who enjoy privileged access to information. The patterns of diffusion should closely match the ways in which citizens are tied to the regime, both in terms of individual attributes (for instance, membership in the ruling party) and their social networks (having friends in high places never hurts). Furthermore, when the performance of the courts is uncertain, the ways in which satisfied and dissatisfied users are clustered in the population may have a considerable impact on the behavior of potential adopters.

The role of social networks is especially intriguing given the nature of Chinese society and the structure of the post-Maoist state. Considerable research in anthropology (Kipnis 1997; Ku 2003; Yang 1994), sociology (Bian 1999; Gold, Guthrie, and Wank 2002; Guthrie 1999), economics (Krug 2004; Luo 2000; So and Walker 2006; Wong and Leung 2001), and political science and law (Lee 1997; Oi 1986) has been devoted to the study of *guanxi*, its extent and its impact on individual behavior. If the importance of *guanxi* has indeed endured in the contemporary period, Chinese society should therefore be more prone to the quick adoption (or rejection) of an innovation once it becomes known to members of a tightly knit social network. Dense ties facilitate information flows and the rapid diffusion of the benefits and shortcomings of innovations among connected individuals. In the past few years, we have indeed witnessed extraordinary rates of diffusion of several innovations among Chinese consumers, such as electric appliances, cellular phones, and Internet usage. The same logic applies to institutional diffusion.

When we are concerned with the innovation and the diffusion of an institution, it is more difficult to specify when saturation occurs. Unlike cheap consumer products, courts are not devised for persistent use by most citizens, most of the time. Principles of fairness and the ideas that underpin a rule-of-law society suggest that access to courts ought to be universal, but making the decision to actually go to court is, for most individuals, a rare event. A dispute resolution mechanism is only relevant when a dispute actually occurs, and only a subset of disputes ever reaches the judicial stage. We should not be overly surprised that the process of institutional diffusion is a slow one.

The aggregate statistical data on court cases for China seem to match the S-shaped pattern that theorists of diffusion have identified in other disciplines. During the 1980s and 1990s, the use of judicial institutions grew very rapidly, a reflection not only of rising demand for such institutions within society but also and more prosaically because judicial institutions were a novelty. After the chaos of the Cultural Revolution, existing courts were reopened and new ones were built down at the county level, while a host of innovations (such as the creation of a professional corps of lawyers) and specific laws and regulations facilitated access to the courts. However, the picture seems to have changed since 2000. While "rule-of-law reforms" have continued, the number of judicial cases – both civil and criminal – has reached a plateau of about four cases per thousand inhabitants.

Supply constraints may explain this plateau to some extent: the time-series data presented in Figure 8.4 only reflect cases *accepted* by the courts. Over-burdened courts may simply not be able to cope with the demand for the institutions. The state may also limit access to the courts for fear that unbridled access to legal institutions may become politically destabilizing. A third explanation is that social heterogeneity produces idiosyncratic networks that are only conducive to partial diffusion. If access to the courts and initial successes are clustered within a narrow social elite (or specific geographical regions), the lack of connectivity between the beneficiaries of the courts and the general population may have slowed or even interrupted the diffusion process. It is possible that even ordinary citizens with close ties to somebody who was victorious in court will not emulate him or her if they infer that it is the particular characteristics of the winner – and not the choice of institutional venue – that explain the outcome. For instance, nonparty members may believe that only party members can win court cases. If the sole winner of a court case in a given community happens to be a party member, nonmembers do not have enough information to sort out whether party membership or the decision to go to court is the decisive factor in that success. Diffusion would then occur only among party members.

The ILRC sample is uniquely suited to test the impact of small community networks because of its special design. Below the township level, respondents were selected from micro-spatial communities in which all households were interviewed to ensure an equal probability of inclusion (Landry and Shen 2005). Though I aggregate the results by township in this chapter, a sampled township is in fact composed of two "half-square minutes" (equivalent to a natural village) in which clusters of about 90 × 90 meters were drawn. Thus, the probability that respondents know each other is very high.

I hypothesize that two parameters are jointly conducive to rapid institutional diffusion: the trustworthiness of the court and the presence of individuals within small communities who have engaged courts successfully are conducive to the acceptance of the court as the proper dispute resolution venue (see Table 8.2). We cannot directly observe social networks, but it is reasonable to make the assumption that if the community is small enough, its members interact with each other frequently and learn quickly about unusual events. Given its rarity, victory in court certainly qualifies as the kind of news that is likely to spread fast in small communities. Rapid diffusion is likely to occur when a high proportion of satisfied and trusting end-users propagate their behavior through dense social networks.

If only one of these factors in present, the process will be more gradual. If neither is present, we should see little or no diffusion. Note that the absence of diffusion does not imply that the number of court users will not rise: it

TABLE 8.2. *Conditions for institutional diffusion*

		Trustworthiness of the institution	
		Low	High
Density of adopters	High	Gradual diffusion	Rapid diffusion
	Low	No/very slow diffusion	Gradual diffusion

simply means that individuals who use the courts will not be emulated in their communities. However, if individual-level variables that predict this behavior change over time, a greater proportion of the population will still adopt the institution.

Community Experiences and Institutional Diffusion

The ILCR survey allows us to identify respondents in their specific communities who were directly involved in legal disputes, went to court, and are therefore in the position to influence their network based on their experiences with the courts. For each dispute category covered by the instrument – civil, economic, and administrative – we inquired whether the choice to go to court was decisive in the resolution of their dispute. If so, we further asked whether they would be willing to use the same method should a similar dispute occur in the future. We can thus identify the specific communities in which adopters (defined here as past disputants who would use the courts in the future) are present.

Although diffusion theory assumes that "adopters" are local opinion makers, it must be emphasized that these experienced individuals constitute only a small fraction of a community. Using the township as the level of analysis, we encountered very few localities where more than one respondent has actually experienced a dispute that was decisively resolved in court. Furthermore, in the majority of the communities we could not identify any experienced users: we only found 69 townships (out of 200 surveyed) in which civil disputes were resolved in court, 47 for economic disputes, and only 16 for administrative ones (see Table 8.3). As small as these numbers may be, diffusion research suggests that they may have a large impact on the behavior of the community.

The aggregate data suggest that adopters outnumber nonadopters. We estimate that 90 percent of the citizens who have settled an economic dispute in court would do so again, as would 78 percent in the case of civil disputes

TABLE 8.3. *Distribution of actual court users who claim that the court was decisive in the disposition of their dispute*

Dispute category	Would you use the same method again?			Design-based estimated probability of using courts in the future
	Yes	No	No answer	
Civil	72	17	7	.78
Economic	56	6	1	.90
Administrative	9	7	0	.54

(see Table 8.3). The odds are more even among administrative disputants, most likely because the scope and the chances of success in administrative litigation remain limited. Overall, these proportions are consistent with the diffusion hypothesis: very few people ever go to court, but since those who did use the court express the desire to use the institution in the future, they are likely to diffuse their behavior within their social network. This would explain the rising proportion of court users among citizens who are engaged in a legal dispute for the first time.

We can gauge the potential impact of these adopters by comparing the propensity of inexperienced respondents to go to court across communities with varying densities of actual adopters. Specifically, we asked respondents who had not experienced a dispute whether they would be inclined to go to court based on a hypothetical situation presented in a vignette for each dispute category. If the diffusion hypothesis is correct, we should observe a greater propensity to go to court among respondents who happen to live in communities where one (or more) of their neighbors has "adopted" the institution.

The preliminary evidence is again encouraging for the diffusion hypothesis: using townships as the unit of analysis, two of the three simple bivariate regressions show that in townships where residents who have been to court in civil and administrative disputes and are willing to use the institution again, their neighbors who were never engaged in a dispute are more prone to go to court than residents of communities where no one has any experience with courts (see Table 8.4). However, this does not seem to be the case for economic disputants. To be certain of the net impact of these "adopters" on institutional diffusion, we require a fully specified model that captures both the impact of individual characteristics of the respondents and the impact of institution adopters in their community. Such models allow measure proper measures of the magnitude of these diffusion effects.

TABLE 8.4. *Impact on court adopters on the mean propensity to go to court*

	Civil	Economic	Administrative
N	200	200	200
$F_{(1, 198)}$	5.86	0.08	3.85
Model Prob > F	0.02	0.78	0.05
	Coef.	**Coef.**	**Coef.**
Share of court adopters in township	1.662**	0.345	4.43**
Constant	0.419***	0.492***	0.30***

INDIVIDUAL CHARACTERISTICS

Social Networks

The kind of diffusion that we have considered so far does not account for the more direct and personal ties that citizens may have with legal institutions. The diffusion theory assumes that people learn from the direct experiences of their peers, but social networks can affect behavior in other ways. This is particularly true in authoritarian systems where information flows are controlled and where connections with political and legal institutions of the regime can confer a decisive advantage over those who lack the requisite connections to "work" the system, particularly if a well-connected citizen is engaged in a dispute with a less-connected one. In a society like contemporary China where social relations (*guanxi*) are highly valued (Bian 1997, 1999), these ties are likely to have powerful cognitive and behavioral consequences.

We attempted to capture the density of ties to key political and legal institutions by asking ILRC respondents whether they have regular contact with persons holding jobs in organizations that require (or are likely to result in) specialized legal knowledge (see Table 8.5). Such ties with "experts" may have differentiated impacts depending on the specific problem that respondents encounter: an acquaintance in the official trade union may be helpful in resolving economic disputes, whereas contact with a party cadre may be particularly useful in case of administrative disputes. The point is that well-connected citizens can gain specific knowledge and engage legal institutions more effectively thanks to their social interactions with the political and legal elite in their community. These include party and government cadres, members of People's Congresses (at any level), employees of the courts or the procuracy, as well as lawyers, legal aid bureau personnel, and trade union officials. Most – but not all – of these professionals are likely to be CCP members.

TABLE 8.5. *Density of social ties with political and legal professionals*

	All respondents	Nongovernment employees	Government employees	CCP members
Party & government leaders	24.7	23.9	71.1	50.1
Court & procuracy cadres	13.9	13.2	53.1	33.5
People's Congress representative	9.5	9.0	41.4	25.0
Labor union cadre	11.6	10.9	48.4	30.3
Legal Aid Bureau officials	4.5	4.0	29.7	12.9
Lawyers	6.9	6.6	29.7	17.2
Any of the above	36.8	36.0	85.9	64.5

All estimates account for the design effect.

Not surprisingly, party members have a considerable networking advantage over ordinary citizens. These ties have even stronger effects among government employees, but even ordinary CCP membership confers a clear advantage. The empirical question is whether 36 percent of ordinary citizens who interact regularly with the political, legal, and administrative elite do in fact capitalize on these ties by gaining greater access to the courts.

Political Institutions and the Acquisition of Legal Knowledge

A successful rule-of-law program requires at minimum a basic understanding of the institutions and norms that help sustain it. Ordinary social actors need not be legal experts, but they must at least have sufficient practical knowledge of the system to know where to turn and what basic choices are available to them when legal issues arise. Superior knowledge and information can also help end-users reduce the transaction costs of using an institution. In the Chinese context, these costs are high because many legal institutions – such as administrative litigation or private law firms – are still a novelty. Learning how to use them effectively while they evolve so rapidly is particularly challenging.

Membership in political institutions like the Youth League and, more important, the Communist Party can help reduce these costs. CCP membership has direct benefits (Bian, Shu, and Logan 2001; Dickson and Rublee 2000; Walder 1995; Walder and Treiman 2000). It confers a competitive edge and offers various shortcuts that facilitate access to valuable information. For example, the policy diffusion process favors party activists because all important

TABLE 8.6. *Items used to test basic legal knowledge*

Item	Estimated % of correct answers
It is illegal to cohabit prior to marriage.	26.04
Our laws explicitly prohibit extramarital affairs.	24.07
Citizens can have permanent land ownership.	42.02
Firms can employ 15-year-old workers.	12.11
All financial contracts signed by both parties are legal.	30.56
A married woman does not have the duty to support her parents.	71.70
Criminal suspects have a right to not answer when questioned by law enforcement agencies.	27.44
Married daughters don't have inheritance rights.	59.08
Courts have a legislative function.	36.80
The procuracy cannot file a civil lawsuit.	25.72
Local governments can put forward suggestions about court decisions.	6.01

Percentages account for the design effect (N = 7714).

policy changes are announced through the CCP document system ahead of their dissemination to the general public. Information that is transmitted through party channels is also less likely to be distorted than what is available through the general media. Party members have access to specific media that discuss issues that are otherwise censored and are theoretically reserved to members. Some of these materials have higher levels of classification and are reserved to cadres. Thus, both the timing and the quality of information confer a substantial advantage on CCP members. If they are in conflict with non-members, they can use such information strategically as they seek to resolve their disputes.

To test the proposition that party members are more knowledgeable about the law than ordinary citizens, I relied on an additive knowledge score that is designed to capture the underlying variation in basic legal cognition within the population (Table 8.6). The ILRC survey asked each respondent eleven questions with varying levels of difficulty. This methodology is similar to efforts in public opinion research to measure the political knowledge of mass publics (Zaller 1991).

The indicators are aggregated into a simple additive index that ranges from zero (no correct answers) to eleven (all correct answers). We obtained an index that is very close to a normally distributed variable, with a slight tilt to the left: 262 respondents scored 0, whereas only 2 persons had a perfect score. Design-based estimates clearly show that this score is tied to membership in

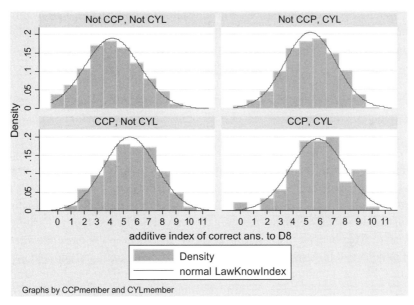

FIGURE 8.6. Distribution of the Basic Legal Knowledge Score, by membership in the CCP and the CYL (0–11 scale).

political institutions (Figure 8.6). Non-CCP members who never joined the Communist Youth League (who represent 80.9 percent of the population) had a mean score of 4.2, in contrast to the elite of CYL members who later joined the CCP (1.1 percent of the population) whose average score was 6.0. Current or past CYL members who never joined the party (11.8 percent of the sample) and party members who never joined the CYL (6.2 percent of the population) had identical knowledge scores of 5.2. To some extent, the diffusion of legal knowledge among CCP members reflects the increasing importance of educational attainment as a criterion for membership. In this sense, membership may not result in additional knowledge after entry. Since legal knowledge and educational attainment are positively correlated, the party's recruitment policy in the 1980s and 1990s that favored the well-educated may have indirectly selected out people with poor working knowledge of the law.[2]

Since many party members are cadres, the command of administrative and political resources gives them a first-hand understanding of the concrete

---

[2] See Gerber (2000) and Rona-Tas and Gudeva (2001) for the debate about the inherent benefits of membership versus selection effects among members of the Communist Party of the Soviet Union.

operations and shortcomings of the legal system. The CCP is also actively promoting legal awareness to the cadre corps. Most officials must attend training courses in party schools at various levels, where law is becoming an explicit part of the curriculum.[3] These courses target cadres who are either being groomed for future promotion (Zhong 2003) or, having been promoted, are sent for training before actually taking up a new assignment. Cadres who receive legal training in party schools as part of their professional development can easily convert this knowledge for private gains.

Beyond the Communist Party, other political institutions can also help diffuse legal cognition. The CYL is less exclusive than the CCP, but a filtering mechanism similar to the CCP's is also in place in the League (Bian et al. 2001). Education is also a very important criterion for membership: it is now virtually impossible for somebody with a mere primary school education to join the League. Membership in the league exceeds 70 percent in the current cohort of middle- and high-school graduates, a major increase from past generations. The CYL has traditionally been a vehicle of policy diffusion (Ngai 1997), and has been very active in recent efforts to publicize legal reforms in rural areas. CYL members who are mobilized for such campaigns are likely to learn about these reforms, probably better than the public they are supposed to reach.

Media Consumption

Even without access to or connection with political and legal institutions, ordinary citizens can indirectly improve their legal knowledge. In recent years, the government has deployed considerable efforts to spread legal education and information through the media. Television stations carry numerous shows and mini-series depicting all kinds of legal disputes and their resolution. The publishing industry has seen an explosion of handbooks and guides designed to assist ordinary citizens in navigating China's evolving legal system. We observed considerable variation in the level of media consumption, which is now dominated by television. Only 5 percent of the sample claims to never watch it. In contrast, printed media reach a narrower group of wealthier, better educated, and usually urban residents (see Table 8.7).

We anticipate that much of knowledge of the law is acquired through the consumption of media, particularly among the subset of older adults who were not exposed to formal legal education in the school system.

---

[3] We estimate that 65% of government employees are CCP members, in contrast to 5.9% of the rest of the adult population aged 18–65.

TABLE 8.7. *Frequency of media consumption*

	Newspapers	Magazines	TV	Radio
Often	1,223	615	5,076	874
Sometimes	1,245	1,045	1,394	1,150
Very rarely	1,652	1,587	808	1,637
Never	3,463	4,272	386	3,889

Education

Education is another obvious channel through which legal knowledge is acquired. In today's middle and high schools, compulsory politics and civics classes weave new legal concepts into traditional political teaching. The lessons taught (and presumably learned) naturally reflect the priorities of the regime, yet standard politics textbooks are now much more sophisticated than the materials to which older generations were exposed during their youth. Furthermore, the young have a strong incentive to internalize new legal norms, because politics is a required subject on the college entrance examination. Entire generations of Chinese teenagers are now being exposed to a body of knowledge to which their parents simply never had access. In a context where general educational attainment is also rising rapidly, we expect a large generation gap in substantive command of basic legal issues. Our instrument captures this effect well: younger age groups clearly have higher mean scores than older ones (see Table 8.8).

TABLE 8.8. *Legal knowledge score, by age group*

Age group	Estimated mean	SD
18–24	5.2	2.0
25–29	4.9	2.1
30–34	4.5	2.0
35–39	4.4	2.1
40–44	4.5	2.0
45–49	4.2	2.1
50–54	4.1	2.1
55–59	3.9	2.2
60–66	3.9	2.2

All measures are estimates that account for the design effect.

MULTIVARIATE ANALYSIS

Modeling the Propensity to Go to Court

The propensity to go to court is modeled as a probit equation that takes into account the multistage stratified nature of the sample design, and uses probability weights. Separate estimates were computed for each class of disputes that was covered in ILRC project. We asked all respondents whether they had been involved in civil, economic, or governmental disputes in the past twenty years, and whether they chose to go to court to resolve those disputes. The dependent variable is coded 1 if the respondent went to court, and zero otherwise. Those who did not experience disputes were asked to react to a simple vignette and describe the actions they would likely take under such circumstances. This technique is more reliable than asking unstructured questions, particularly since we do not have the problem of cross-cultural comparisons in a single country study (King, Murray, Salomon, and Tandon 2003). The translation of each vignette is provided in Table 8.9. If respondents never encountered a civil (respectively, economic or administrative) dispute, the dependent variable is also coded 1 if they asserted that they would use the courts in their evaluations of the hypothetical civil, economic, and administrative cases presented as vignettes.

The model accounts for the disparity between respondents who actually experienced disputes and those who responded to these hypothetical situations on the left-hand side.

$$prob(Court)_{|d=0} = \Phi(X\beta) + \varepsilon$$

for individuals who did not experience a dispute of type d and,

$$prob(Court)_{|d=1} = \Phi(X\beta + d) + \varepsilon$$

for individuals who did.

The respondents who answered the "costless" hypothetical questions after a vignette were more likely to state that they would go to court: their expressed preferences were costless. However, disputants who actually chose to go to court face tangible transaction costs. It is not too surprising that all else being equal, their propensity to go to court under such circumstances would be lower. I interpret the magnitude of the coefficients associated with these dispute-specific dummy variables as markers of the transaction costs of going to court.

TABLE 8.9. *Vignettes for hypothetical disputes*

Civil Dispute

C2. *Since you have not had such experiences, let's use a hypothetical case to understand your views. The labor contractor of a construction site has been embezzling the workers' wages, and the workers were denied their demands for payment numerous times. If you were one of the workers, what would you do? Would you take action to settle the dispute, or would you not do anything?*

Economic Dispute

C20. *Since you have not had such experiences, let's use a hypothetical case to understand your views. To help a township business through some financial difficulties, a township government borrows 100,000 Yuan from villager Wang Lin. The agreement specifies that this amount should be repaid in two years. But two years go by, and the amount has still not been repaid. If you were Wang Lin, what would you do? Would you take action to settle the dispute, or would you not do anything?*

Administrative Dispute

C38. *Since you have not had such experiences, let's use a hypothetical case to understand your views. Zhang Jie is an individual industrial household with a license to set up his stall. But the City Management Department found his stall detrimental to the aesthetics of the city, and thus confiscated his goods and fined him. If you were Zhang Jie, what would you do? Would you take action to settle the dispute, or would you not do anything?*

Institutional Diffusion

Since the diffusion hypothesis rests on the impact of two variables (the trustworthiness of courts and the density of adopters in the community), we need to test whether adding these variables to a baseline model actually improves its predictive power and statistical significance. The standard likelihood-ratio (LR) test cannot be performed on probit regressions for complex survey design. We must rely instead on a more indirect approach based on unweighted probits with the same set of independent variables. Furthermore, because of missing data when these two variables "trust in court" are added to the baseline model, we need to further restrict the LR test to the subset of observations that are observed in both the saturated model and the nested model.

Whether we consider civil, economic, or administrative disputes, these LR tests are all consistent with the diffusion hypothesis. The saturated models are always superior to the nested ones. However, the specific significance of the variable that captures the presence of adopters in the community varies by dispute category: it is considerable in the case of civil disputes, less so for economic disputes, and not significant for administrative disputes. Since the coefficients are always positive (in the expected direction) for both variables,

TABLE 8.10. *Probit estimates of going to court in civil, economic, and administrative cases*

	Civil	Economic	Administrative
Number of strata (24)	24	24	24
Number of PSUs (counties)	100	100	100
Number of observations	7160	7160	7160
Estimated population size (millions)	850	850	850
Prob > c	0.0000	0.0000	0.0000
Control for Actual Disputes			
Civil dispute	−0.841 ***	—	— Civil
Economic dispute	—	−0.862 ***	—
Administrative dispute	—	—	−1.062 ***
Human Capital & Information			
Formal education (years)	0.023 **	0.030 ***	0.020 ***
Legal knowledge score	0.061 ***	0.044 ***	0.056 ***
Television	0.119 ***	0.052 **	0.076 **
Political & Social Capital			
CYL member	0.172 ***	0.130	0.005
CCP member	0.229 ***	0.189 **	0.102
Contact w/ party or gov. cadre	0.055	0.091 *	0.063
Contact w/ legal or public security official	0.225 ***	0.174 ***	0.162 ***
Contact w/ People's Congress	0.084	0.050	−0.001
Contact w/ lawyer	0.131	0.191 **	0.017
Contact w/ Legal Aid Bureau	0.038	−0.181 *	−0.176
Contact w/ labor union	0.030	0.129 *	0.047

Diffusion Variables			
Trustworthiness of courts	0.177 ***	0.252 ***	0.208 ***
Share of court adopters in township			
Civil cases	5.903 **	—	—
Economic cases	—	5.845 !	—
Administrative cases	—	3.717	—
Demographic Variables			
Age	0.006	0.008	−0.024 **
Age-squared	0.000	0.000	0.000 *
Female	−0.019	−0.026	0.105 **
Han nationality	−0.016	0.008	−0.102
Urban registration	0.334 ***	0.123	0.148 *
Full-time farmer	−0.040	−0.098	−0.041
Constant	−1.548 ***	−1.356 ***	−1.133 ***
LR test of full vs. nested model without diffusion variables (unweighted probit with 7160 observations)			
LR c	102.61	131.33	112.15
Prob c	.000	.000	.000

Notes: Because only one PSU was draw in small provinces, the original strata are grouped in 24 postestimation strata. ! = significant at the 0.108 level. Insignificant coefficients are shaded in gray. Linearized variance estimates account for complex multistage survey design effects, with stratification, first; stage selection of PSUs (counties), and second-stage selection of SSUs (townships). These calculations ignore design effects at and below the third stage. Coefficients and standard errors shaded in gray are not significant at the 0.1 level.

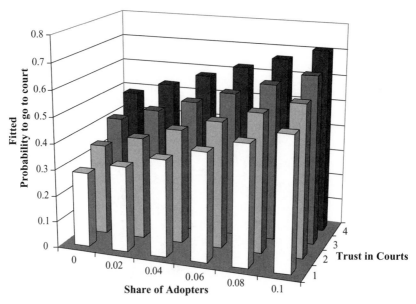

FIGURE 8.7. Fitted probability of adopting the court in future civil disputes. *Note:* All other variables are held at their mean values.

the dynamics of diffusion presented in Table 8.2 seem to hold very well for civil disputes. The propensity to go to court varies across individuals and communities as a function of these parameters. Varying these parameters and holding all other variables at their sample mean yield a more intuitive picture of the substantive impact of these variables (see Figure 8.7). The findings in diffusion research obtained through simulations that small idiosyncrasies in a network can have large behavioral consequences apply here as well: even a small share of adopters of the courts in a community greatly increases the likelihood that other members of the same community will in turn adopt the same behavior.

It is also obvious that the rate of diffusion (measured as the fitted probability of going to court in a civil dispute) varies across communities systematically. Since the ILRC is a national sample stratified by province, it is legitimate to compare findings across provinces where the number of primary sampling units is not too small, though of course variance estimates within provinces are larger than the sampling variance of indicators measured at the national level: we forecast more rapid diffusion in Beijing in the case of civil disputes than anywhere else in the country, but this finding should be interpreted with caution because Beijing's contribution to the national sample is small, as it should be, given the size of the municipality.

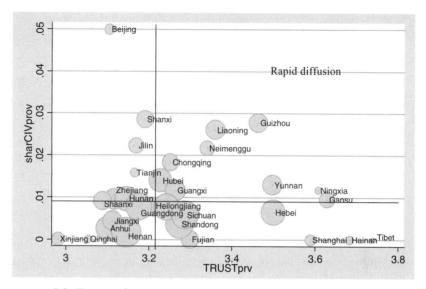

FIGURE 8.8. Trustworthiness of courts and share of adopters, by province. *Note:* Gray circles are proportional to provincial population in 2004. Quadrant boundaries are drawn at the mean of each variable.

If we separate the points on the scatterplot of average levels of trust and shares of court adopters in civil cases into four quadrants, the upper-right corner of the figure represents the set of provinces where we expect rapid diffusion, since both the level of trust and the share of court adopters are higher than the national average (see Figure 8.8). With the exception of Liaoning, all of the cases in the quadrant represent relatively poor, hinterland provinces. Most coastal provinces that have benefited the most from economic reforms since 1978 belong instead to the intermediate quadrants, where one of the two factors conducive to diffusion takes a low value. Three large interior provinces (Henan, Anhui, and Jiangxi) are especially noteworthy for their low values on both scores. Overall, there seems to be no systematic relationship between the level of economic development and the likelihood of diffusion of judicial institutions.

The rarity of court adopters in economic and administrative cases relative to civil ones also suggests that the institutionalization of the courts is likely to occur only through the process of civil dispute resolution. The novelty of administrative litigation, which only began in earnest in the 1990s (the Administrative Litigation Law [ALL] was passed in 1989), and the low rate of success of citizens who sue government agencies will defer the diffusion of the habit of "suing the state" in court in the more distant future. Currently, the odds of finding satisfied ALL litigants in a given community are simply too remote to have any detectable impact on community behavior.

The Impact of Individual-Level Variables

Two variables alone cannot explain the popularity of the courts in China. The individual characteristics of the respondents also play an important role in the decision to adopt or reject an institutional innovation. Some of these factors are not specific to authoritarian regimes: education and legal knowledge are often cited as important conditions of access to the legal system in democracies as well. Other individual characteristics are more regime-specific, such as membership in the Communist Youth League or the Communist Party.

Social Ties
The diffusion process that we examined so far focuses on networks linking actual adopters of an innovation to potential adopters. However, other types of social ties can also affect the propensity to adopt an innovation, such as *guanxi* ties. Citizens with privileged access to the political and administrative elite can gain valuable information and perhaps even mobilize these ties to manipulate the institution to their advantage. There is indeed evidence that the value of ties with employees of the judiciary varies systematically with the nature of the disputes. As is true with the effect of adopters in the community, the substantive impact of these ties is larger when the disputes are less likely to involve state institutions (i.e., civil disputes), but one's social network is less decisive in administrative cases than in civil disputes where state interests are not threatened.

Party and Youth League Membership
Political connections magnify the impact of these ties: CCP membership systematically increases individual propensities to go to court. In addition, the effects of party seniority are stronger when the issue is less politically charged. Both Youth League and party members are more likely to go to court in civil disputes than nonmembers, but only party members – whose political credentials are stronger than mere CYL members – are willing to go to court in economic and governmental disputes to a lesser extent than for civil disputes. Party members may be reluctant to bring their disputes to court, because such a drastic action may be construed as a breach of party discipline if it involves a conflict with CCP or government officials. However, in economic and – even more so – in civil disputes, the political costs of going to court are likely to be lower and the benefits large: in conflicts with nonparty members, it is to the

party member's advantage to rely on courts that are institutionally dependent on the CCP.

Media Exposure, Education, and Legal Knowledge

Unlike Chen and Shi (2001) who found no evidence of a relationship between media usage and general political trust in China, television viewers in the ILRC sample are more prone to use the court than nonviewers, regardless of the nature of the dispute. This difference may be due to the specificity of the institution considered: contemporary Chinese media broadcast very pointed educational or fictional programs that convey clear messages that propaganda departments are eager to disseminate during legal education campaigns (*pufa jiaoyu/* 普法教育). Judges and lawyers embody a stylized modern society that citizens are encouraged to join, and a host of soap operas include characters who see their disputes adjudicated in invariably well-organized and corruption-free courts staffed by righteous judges. Post-Leninist regimes are better equipped than other authoritarian regimes to use the media to their advantage. Once the state has decided to innovate, as the Chinese state has in the area of judicial institutions, its propaganda apparatus can be a highly effective agent of institutional change. Propaganda alone may not be sufficient to convince litigants to return to the courts if they are disappointed after a first experience, but it can at least prime the population of potential first-time users to be favorably predisposed toward judicial institutions. Furthermore, many media organizations test the boundaries of political correctness and do report on legal affairs in a far less stereotypical fashion than in the past, which may further increase the popularity of lawyers, judges, and the courts.

Television programs are particularly important because broadcasts originally intended for provincial audiences are watched nationwide. Satellite dishes usually carry a large bundle (if not all) of provincial stations, in addition to closed-circuit television channels. A farmer from Yunnan can seamlessly learn from documentaries on Shanghai Television, and apply what he has learned on TV in his local community. Of course, formal education and legal knowledge strongly complement the impact of the media in the promotion of the courts. The impact of these factors is large and highly statistically significant across all dispute categories.

CONCLUSION

China's effort to build the rule of law seems paradoxical given the nature of party control over judicial institutions in a post-Leninist state. Stanley Lubman's (1999) metaphor of the "bird in a cage" is a powerful reminder of the limits of this enterprise. Indeed, the skeptics could point at several empirical findings of this chapter and forecast doom, because key individual-level factors that explain the propensity to use the courts are closely related to the nature of Chinese authoritarianism: exposure to state-owned media, ties to the judicial elite, as well as membership in the Youth League and in the Communist Party all explain why citizens would (and in some cases did) solve their disputes in court. If access to the legal system is restricted to the regime's elite, the legitimacy of Chinese courts could be seriously eroded.

On the other hand, the party facilitates the diffusion of legal knowledge among its members, as well as access to the courts. Party membership and to a lesser extent Youth League membership have a direct and positive impact on the likelihood of going to court in civil and economic cases. To the extent that one of the key goals of Chinese legal reformers is to shift the traditional burden of dispute adjudication away from the party and government agencies to more autonomous courts, party and CYL members seem to be a positive force for change. A reform sequence in which nonparty members would be incited to use the courts while party members would rely on other institutions to solve their disputes would almost certainly weaken the legitimacy of legal institutions among nonparty members. We find no evidence that this is the case. Instead, the CCP enhances access to legal institutions among its members. This is good politics, and is likely to strengthen China's reform effort: if party members receive selective benefits from these institutions, they are more likely to support them in the long run.

The diffusion effects that are noticeable in the ILRC sample are a cause for further optimism. The transaction costs of going to court are high, and a fair amount of social, political, and human capital is required to overcome these costs at this early stage of Chinese legal reforms. If ordinary citizens – who are often deprived of these forms of capital – were to suddenly engage the courts in large numbers, most would lose or give up, and probably turn into cynical and embittered opponents of legal innovations. We are instead witnessing a gradual diffusion process in which rare but satisfied users who probably owe a great deal of their success to their social and political capital help diffuse their experience in the communities in which they live. Local elites may well be one step ahead of the general population, but the benefits that they derive from their close ties to the regime and, with that, their increased odds of success in court, allow the public to learn from positive rather than negative experience, and ensure the gradual but steady diffusion of the institution.

9

Building Judicial Independence in Semi-Democracies: Uganda and Zimbabwe

Jennifer Widner with Daniel Scher

This chapter draws upon African cases to consider the circumstances under which a court can build and maintain a high degree of independence in an authoritarian setting. Trials that uncover corruption in high places, affect electoral fortunes, or cause a political supporter to pay large sums of money often test the willingness to delegate power to a court. In any context, including democracies, executive branches and legislatures may occasionally attempt to infringe judicial independence when there are strong incentives to do so. The issue is, first, whether they succeed in influencing the outcomes of these particular cases, and, second, whether their efforts undermine the ideal of neutral third-party dispute resolution for future controversies. We may be able to learn something about the development of institutional autonomy by comparing country experiences. In highly charged disputes, why do executive branch efforts to influence outcomes end with the judiciary substantially intact in some instances, whereas in others the autonomy of the court from the other branches of government diminishes?

In the context of this discussion, judicial independence means freedom from partisan influence in particular cases. There are many ways in which a determined executive faction may secure the outcomes it wishes short of threatening or firing judges, packing the court, or ousting jurisdiction – the three most spectacular ways to abrogate the independence of the judiciary. Making litigation prohibitively dangerous or expensive is one tactic that does not undermine judicial independence *per se*, though it may erode the integrity of the legal system writ large. Manipulating members of the bar is another common tactic that again brings ill repute upon the legal sector and represents a hidden attack on the judiciary, but does not necessarily trigger concern about the impartiality of the judges themselves. Nonenforcement of judgments and noncompliance are tantamount to attacks upon the court as well.

This chapter treats judicial independence as a deal among key political actors to delegate power to a nonpartisan body. It identifies several points at which such autonomous units in Africa's common law systems are vulnerable. Then it asks why some authoritarian governments decide to dispense with independent courts entirely, whereas others seek to influence a few sensitive cases and leave the rest of the system substantially intact. It compares and contrasts the cases of Zimbabwe and Uganda in this regard and suggests that, while underlying social and economic conditions may increase the probability that independent courts will persist over time, whether initial acts of delegation endure in the short run is highly contingent on the skills of judges and configurations of support and opposition inside executive branches. Although it is therefore difficult to spin general theories about "institutional origins," because of the highly parameter-specific character of the bargains struck and the importance of feedback effects, it may nonetheless prove possible to draw useful adages.

JUDICIAL INDEPENDENCE AS AN EQUILIBRIUM

A variety of motives may inspire a leader to support the delegation of power to a nonpartisan body in the short run. Semi-democratic and authoritarian governments sometimes recognize the advantages of having an independent and effective court system for internal control purposes. For example, when corruption in the lower levels of administration incites popular anger and impedes investment, courts potentially provide a cheaper means to control such transgression than does better supervision. Regular administrative review, a form of "police patrol," is costly in both monetary and political terms. Especially when a state is relatively weak, it may be more sensible to let aggrieved individuals and firms bring their complaints to courts and sound a "fire alarm" (McCubbins and Schwartz 1984) than to try to curtail corruption by other means. Rosberg (1995), Moustafa (2007), and Ginsburg (Chapter 2) have made this point.

There are other reasons why having a court popularly perceived as independent, fair, and effective may make sense. Independent courts may help resolve local disputes that might otherwise end up in the street. If lower ranks of the ruling party are on the take or locked in conflict, then the judgment of a neutral third party may do less political damage to the head of state than intervention by the party leadership. Second, in a period when international norms vest great significance in "rule of law," allowing courts greater institutional autonomy may also signal "good international citizenship," which facilitates candidacy for accession into regional arrangements or eligibility for foreign assistance. On occasion an authoritarian government also might invest in independent courts to distinguish itself from its predecessors, who themselves abused the rule of law.

Willingness to delegate power to an independent court tends to be fairly ephemeral, however. "Political will" rarely takes the form of a fixed commitment. An independent court may prove extremely inconvenient when a corruption case involves a major political ally or someone who can command armed gangs or militias. An independent court may also prove threatening when there is a serious contender in a presidential election, and both the head of state and his entourage face the prospect that they might lose control of office and patronage resources. Multiparty elections may create a constituency for an independent court (the opposition politicians), but they also create a period of high challenge and increase the temptations to intervene. Under these pressures, some rulers will try to dispense with the whole institution. Threats, attacks against judges, court packing, nonrandom transfers, salary reductions, refusal to produce people who have been jailed, changing outcomes after the fact through manipulation of registries, and ouster of jurisdiction are all part of the response repertoire.

How does a temporary delegation of power become a long-term commitment? The courts have neither the power of the purse nor the power of the sword. They cannot easily defend themselves. Thus, one circumstance in which independent courts are more likely to endure is when there are clear constituencies, not only among the members of the bar but also within important parts of the society – business groups and opposition politicians, for example. A second is where actions attract considerable international attention and where a departure from international norms may result in criticism or a reduction in aid. A third is where the complex of norms supportive of the rule of law generally has shaped the attitudes of the political class or of a significant and active segment of public opinion. Public outrage may be a significant deterrent in countries sufficiently stable that the medium-range and longer term matter in the politician's calculus. A fourth circumstance, more quixotic and idiosyncratic, is one in which the members of the court are simultaneously able to appease and draw some lines, as in *Marbury*. This strategy may well be short term, but the successive negotiation of crises may give public opinion and solid constituencies time to form.

A TALE OF TWO COURTS

A comparison of Uganda and Zimbabwe may help elucidate the conditions under which a court in an authoritarian system can begin to anchor a temporary delegation of independent decision-making power and foster the growth of institutional independence. Uganda and Zimbabwe are both nominally multiparty systems, but neither is a liberal democratic polity. In both instances, the sitting president took power in a rebel struggle and later stood for election in an imperfectly managed contest. The president's entourage grew to include people who personally benefited from access to the public treasury and sought to preserve their positions. Both countries had independent upper-tier courts as their stories open, and both governments tried to intervene when a relatively serious presidential contender appeared. The passages in their constitutions regarding the judiciary are almost identical for the two cases.

As in most accounts of strategic interaction, the details matter; hence the stories are complex. In both instances, politically sensitive issues and judgments provoked a crisis in the relationship between an independent court and the executive. In both cases, there were efforts to infringe the independence of the judiciary. Thus each country's story begins with a crisis. The Uganda story, though not closed, ends perhaps more happily, if ambiguously, than the Zimbabwe story . . . for now. The question is what distinguishes the two. What can we learn from the differences?

Uganda: Persistent Ambiguity

Uganda's recent debacle illustrates the partial (perhaps short-lived) repulsion of an effort to dismantle judicial independence. The country's president, Yoweri Museveni, took power through an armed struggle that resulted in the capture of the capital by the National Resistance Movement in 1985. Museveni sought to dislodge a series of notorious autocrats and promised security, roads, respect for human rights, and economic recovery, roughly in that order, in an effort to distinguish himself from his predecessors and appeal to potential investors. By the early 1990s, he had reinstated judges who had fled into exile after harassment under Idi Amin and Milton Obote, or had landed in jail or faced dismissal. He had further sought the help of the international community to build the rule of law by overhauling the constitution, revising statutes, building a more competent and independent public prosecutor's office, and enhancing the effective operation of the courts. The court had demonstrated independence in several ways, including enforcement of norms about reasonable time to trial in criminal cases, thereby eliminating the government's ability to hold people it didn't like indefinitely.

The president had championed a "unity government" or "movement system" instead of political parties, and when multiparty competition became a reality, forced upon the government by international pressure and a referendum, the enthusiasm of the incumbents for an independent judiciary suddenly came under stress. An effective and fair court system remained important for many purposes, particularly for investment, and as a result many of the classic stratagems of an earlier era –firebombing judges' houses, threatening their children, replacing judges with yes-men – appeared off limits to some in the executive branch, though not to all. Instead, the government turned to several devices historically common in other parts of the world too: abuse of process to harass opponents and ouster of the courts' jurisdiction. Although eventually rebuffed, or at least partly so, the government's actions served as a reminder that, where independent courts endure, they do so only because of a constant quiet struggle.

The story unfolded in several stages. In 2001, Yoweri Museveni's main opposition in the presidential elections came from Kizza Besigye, a man whom he had long known. Besigye had attended Makerere University and obtained a medical degree in 1980. He had joined with Museveni to help found the Uganda Patriotic Movement, which contested the country's 1980 elections. When the party lost, allegedly because of vote rigging by the incumbent, Museveni launched a rebel struggle, while Besigye went to Nairobi to continue his medical training. Two years later Besigye returned to Uganda and joined Museveni, serving as medical officer in the struggle and acquiring the rank of colonel. When the National Resistance Army forced Milton Obote to flee and took power in Kampala, Besigye became Minister of State for Internal Affairs for two years and then Minister of State in the Office of the President and National Political Commissar. He married a woman Museveni had long known, from a family that had hosted him earlier in his life. An engineer, she ran for political office and became a member of Parliament. Besigye was replaced as National Political Commissar and became Commanding Officer of the Mechanised Regiment in Masaka, then Chief of Logistics and Engineering, and finally Senior Military Adviser to the Ministry of Defence until his retirement in October 2000. He also served as a representative of the army in the country's constituent assembly in 1994, an experience that may have shaped his political education. A rift of some sort began to develop between the two men in the mid- to late 1990s, possibly because Besigye believed the nonparty "movement" system should indeed be temporary, as promised, and considered it time to make changes. He was also critical of procurement procedures within the military.

The relationship between the two men grew tenser as a result of the 2001 nonparty elections and became still more difficult as a result of the multiparty competition of 2005–2006. Besigye competed in the nonparty presidential contest in 2001 and lost to Museveni by a substantial margin, capturing just over a quarter of the vote. Some of his supporters allegedly discussed forming a new rebel opposition. It is not at all clear that Besigye was a party to these conversations, or even that the discussions took place. After the 2001 elections, Museveni sought to eliminate the term limit provisions and pushed a constitutional amendment through the legislature, allowing him to run again. Under international pressure, he also grudgingly sent the decision to move to a multiparty system to a national referendum, as required under the constitution. Thus in the multiparty contest that took place in February 2006, Museveni was again a candidate. Besigye returned from self-imposed exile only a few months before the race, on October 26, 2005, as leader of the Forum for Democratic Change (FDC), which he had helped organize while abroad. He was clearly aware that danger might attend this decision to return. Although he did not immediately declare himself a contestant, one might reasonably have anticipated he would do so.

The political elites surrounding Museveni, especially some of the top military officers, quickly perceived Besigye as a serious threat. They clearly harbored concerns that Besigye could command a significant share of the vote, although it is not evident he could have won. Some may have worried that Besigye, once a military man, might reveal damaging information on the campaign trail about corruption or abuse of power within the army. It is also likely that, for several, democratic politics ran against deeply engrained norms that were intolerant of criticism. Whatever the genesis, the problem for those who felt insecure was to try to limit the threat in ways that would not provoke the ire of donors, who were already alarmed by the political turn in the country. The first volley was launched by Amama Mbabazi, Minister of Defence, who once had simultaneously held the ministerial positions of Defence, Attorney General, and Foreign Affairs.

The government's behavior suggests division about the best strategy to follow to limit opposition. The strategy of one faction within the ruling cabal was to try to initiate a series of court proceedings that would keep Besigye in jail and tie down his campaign. Rumors of impending accusations began to leak out in October, although the Director of Public Prosecutions, Richard Buteera, said he was unaware of any criminal charges against Besigye emanating from his office.[1] On November 14, the Attorney General issued a warrant for Besigye's arrest on grounds of treason, concealment of treason, and rape. Twenty-two others were arrested as well. The government charged that Besigye and others

---

[1] Reported in *Daily Monitor* and carried by BBC Worldwide Monitoring, October 23, 2005. Accessed through LexisNexis.

had plotted a coup after the 2001 election loss.[2] It also accused Besigye and his supporters of having contact with rebel groups within the country, forming their own People's Redemption Army, and possessing a number of weapons. Finally, it claimed that Besigye had raped a young woman for whom he served as guardian, based on an incident that occurred in 1997, nearly ten years earlier, though it was later revealed that the Director of Public Prosecutions had objected to filing the case. Besigye's arrest sparked riots in Kampala, the capital.

Two days after the arrests, fourteen of Besigye's co-defendants were to appear in court to be considered for a bail hearing. At this point, the new military heavies within the government intervened and broke with the slightly more subtle strategies of the Ministry of Justice. Just before the hearing was due to begin, thirty armed commandos dressed in black jumped out of taxis, entered the court, and tried to force their way to the holding cell. The court security resisted and quickly evacuated the judges from the building. The commandos, later dubbed the "Black Mambas," permitted a group of foreign envoys through the main gates, but blocked the delegation when it tried to reach the holding cell.[3] The defendants refused to accept bail, although so granted, on the belief that if they left the court on their own recognizance they would be rearrested and seized by the military.[4] Civilian prison seemed preferable. The commandos, possibly members of a Joint Antiterrorism Task Force,[5] eventually departed. Justice Edmund Ssempa Lugayizi, who was scheduled to hear the case, withdrew from both the rape and treason cases after the siege.

In the press and the street, the news of the "Black Mambas" became the focus of attention. In an effort to dampen criticism, the government pretended to seize the legal high ground, claimed that the *sub judice* rule meant that no one could speak about a case currently before the court, and banned media discussion of the treason charges. Principal Judge James Ogoola granted temporary bail, but the government continued to hold Besigye and his confederates, and police blocked press access to the bail hearing.

The military faction within the cabal then again broke with the faintly more subtle, if nonetheless egregious strategy pursued by the Attorney General. On November 24, the Military General Court Martial stepped in and charged

[2] "Judge quits Ugandan Opposition Leader's Treason Trial," *Agence France Press*, February 3, 2006. Accessed through LexisNexis.
[3] "Armed Men Disrupt Opposition Leader's Court Case," *Financial Times Information/Uganda Monitor*, November 17, 2005, accessed through LexisNexis.
[4] Human Rights Watch, November 23, 2005 as reported by AllAfrica, Inc. Accessed through LexisNexis, July 2006.
[5] Human Rights Watch, November 29, 2005, accessed through LexisNexis.

Besigye with terrorism. Taking a cue from one of the great powers, Uganda's Parliament had earlier enacted an Antiterrorism Act that permitted suspects to be held indefinitely without charge. The court martial said Besigye and some of his followers planned terrorists acts and had accumulated a variety of weapons to carry out their ambitions. Besigye thus remained behind bars despite the fact that the courts of general jurisdiction had extended him bail. He would be tried in the General Court Martial, according to the government.

The military's ouster of the court's jurisdiction, coupled with the breach of judicial independence committed by the Black Mambas, triggered demonstrations. A number of opposition FDC activists were arrested for planning some of the protests, but were released by a Kampala court two weeks later. The country's lawyers organized their own manifestation of support for the courts. On November 28, four days after the military's action, some of the Uganda Law Society's 800 members showed up outside the High Court to express concern about the deterioration of the rule of law in the country. The Law Society resolved to sue the government over the actions it had taken, and the demonstrators said they would make the court a "no go area" for security forces.[6] On December 2, the High Court ordered a stay of the military trial until the Constitutional Court could rule on the constitutionality of the government's action. Meanwhile, the Constitutional Court issued a 4-1 decision concurring with the Law Society's position.

Members of the court confronted a terrible dilemma about how best to uphold the standards of judicial independence and the rule of law under a severe threat. Chief Justice Benjamin Odoki, who, ten years earlier, had led the constitution-writing process, expressed his concern twice in the immediate aftermath of the events. Principal Judge Ogoola later expressed sharp criticism at a law forum in which he delivered a paper entitled, "Black Mamba Invasion and the Independence of the Judiciary." Acting Chief Registrar Lawrence Gidudu commented that there had been many related incidents since 2001.

Through the months of December and January, a tug of war took place between the judiciary and the Law Society, on the one hand, and the army faction within the executive. The Constitutional Court ruled that the General Court Martial had no jurisdiction. A new judge, John Katutsi, was assigned to hear the cases, and the defense lawyers immediately asked the justice to quash the proceedings on the grounds that the charges did not indicate who plotted with whom and were therefore defective. On December 11, at roughly the same time that a poll put Besigye ahead of Museveni in several key towns around

---

[6] "Lawyers Strike Over Army Siege," *The Monitor*, November 28, 2005, accessed through Lexis-Nexis.

the country, the president issued a statement defending a military trial. The government accused the courts of playing partisan politics, supporting Besigye by agreeing to take Law Society petitions seriously. The court countered by issuing an order to the Commissioner General of Prisons to produce Besigye in court and to offer an explanation of why he was still being held when he should have been released. It also asked the government to respect the independence of the court, saying, "The judges considered circumstances and the impact of the November 16 siege of the high court by military personnel deployed within the precincts of the court, to re-arrest suspects that the high court had lawfully released on bail, apparently in order to re-charge the same suspects in the General Court Martial."[7]

Still the army failed to release Besigye. On January 17, General Elly Tumwine announced that the court martial would start on the last day of the month. Precisely on the 30th, the Constitutional Court ruled 4-1 on the Law Society petition, which claimed that the army was not the right forum to try the offenses of terrorism and the illegal possession of firearms. On the basis of this ruling, the High Court then issued an order to suspend the actions in the military tribunal and directed that the case be heard in a civilian court beginning March 15. Disregarding the decision, however, the army continued the standoff, claiming that it would not be ordered around by judges and accusing the judiciary of favoring defendants, though it nonetheless postponed proceedings in the military tribunal.[8] The government sought to find a way to get the Constitutional Court to reconsider.

As events unfolded, the Attorney General asked the electoral commission to halt Besigye's nomination as a candidate for president. The commission had earlier granted its permission to proceed with the candidacy, and the Minister of State had concurred, as had some in the Attorney General's office. The Attorney General argued that a conviction on any of the charges brought against him would disqualify the FDC candidate. Two lawyers also allegedly filed a petition to nullify Besigye's nomination on the grounds that he was wrongly nominated as candidate in absentia, but the law firm named in the petition said that in fact it never had filed such and was unaware of the matter. A senior partner said, "This morning, I read in the papers that I have filed a petition against Besigye. I didn't know about it. My [team] went to the Court of Appeal and discovered that there was indeed a petition, but we are not party

---

7 *Financial Times*, BBC Monitoring International Reports, December 24, 2005, accessed through LexisNexis.

8 "Has Army Court Martial Overthrown Constitution," *AllAfrica, Inc/ Uganda Monitor*, February 16, 2006, accessed through LexisNexis. The head of security forces, General David Tinyefuza, allegedly claimed that "the army would not be 'ordered around' by judges."

to it."[9] The court appointed judges to hear the petition as the election date neared. The Law Society denounced the Attorney General for his actions, claiming its members would no longer respect his opinions.

The elections took place on February 23, with one candidate commuting to court for hearings on multiple charges. Besigye lost the race, but by a smaller margin than he had in 2001. He immediately filed charges in the courts against the electoral commission, charging that it had failed to carry out its responsibilities and caused the election to be unfair. Other opposition candidates chose not to protest the handling of the election in the interests of peace. A week after the election took place, with the pressure off, the government announced that it would comply with the Constitutional Court ruling that only the civilian courts could hear the criminal charges against Besigye and others, a decision that coincided with a meeting between the president and ambassadors from the EU and the United States. The court martial continued to hold the twenty-two co-accused defendants, however.

The court hearings on the cases brought by the government and by Besigye proceeded, even as the election results came in. Justice John Katutsi had heard the rape case against Besigye. The rape was alleged to have taken place around October or November 1997. As the proceedings unfolded, however, six government witnesses failed to appear and others appeared only after long delays, the police logbook was found to have been forged, the alleged victim was discovered to be living at State House at the time the charges were made and proved inconsistent on the stand, and one of the witnesses was living in a house provided by a general. At the end of the hearings, Katutsi summed up the case for the assessors and pointed out lies and inconsistencies. The assessors advised acquittal. In his judgment, Katutsi criticized the government for abuse of process. The government filed an appeal, while Besigye sued for wrongful prosecution.

The matter of the treason charges proved more complex. The basis for the accusations were vague and appeared to relate to letters in the possession of a slain Lord's Resistance Army commando that allegedly expressed favorable opinions of Besigye.[10] Besigye's defense lawyers faced off against a team of private lawyers paid by the government and rumored to include assistance from the British law firm of Denton Wilde Sapte. Justice Katutsi, who had heard the rape case, was assigned to hear the treason and arms charges as

---

[9] "Besigye Case Hits Snag, Court Petition a Forgery," AllAfrica, Inc. *The Monitor*, January 21, 2006, accessed through LexisNexis.

[10] *Financial Times Information*, BBC Monitoring Service. July 8, 2006, accessed through LexisNexis.

well, but as the date approached, in the highly political atmosphere of early February, Katutsi asked to step down. He cited both health reasons and the fact that he hailed from Rukungiri, Besigye's home area, and thought that, to be perceived to be fair, the court should appoint someone else in his stead.[11]

While donor country representatives and even some of the government's ministers pushed the Attorney General to agree not to prosecute, on the grounds that the charges were politically motivated, Besigye's lawyers asked the new justice to throw out the indictment on the grounds it was defective because it failed to disclose sufficient information about the allegations to permit the defendants to prepare their cases. The new judge, Vincent Kagaba, walked a thin line. He ruled that the indictment did disclose sufficient information, though he expressed concern about the underlying statutes, saying, "Unfortunately the court will apply the law as it exists on the statute books now. What the law was or what it should be may be mere wishes, opinion and advice for future improvement."[12] A month later, the judge stayed the court proceedings to give the defense time to challenge the constitutionality of some aspects of the trial. Eventually the judge required the lawyers on both sides to meet with each other and decide on what basis the case could go forward. Although the proceedings continue, it is likely they will end when the government no longer feels it will lose face by backing off. The court returned Besigye's passport, enabling him to travel abroad.

In the matter of Besigye's charges against the election commission, the country's Supreme Court took a decidedly cautious approach, slightly reminiscent of *Marbury*. Besigye claimed a variety of election irregularities: violence against party members and supporters, pre-ticked ballots, and the striking off of supporters from vote registers. He also claimed that the National Resistance Movement was not a registered political party and could not sponsor candidates.[13] In early April, the Supreme Court, sitting en banc, declined 4-3 to annul the election. Instead, it ruled that, yes, the electoral commission had failed to observe the electoral law and there was evidence of malpractice, but, no, the results would not have been substantially different, so no action could be forthcoming. The Court noted that the act of Parliament in question says that the judges must be convinced that the noncompliance with the law affected the result of the election in a substantial manner, and the judges did not so conclude. A disappointed Besigye subsequently hinted that frustrated

---

[11] "Besigye Judge Quits," AllAfrica, Inc. *The Monitor*, accessed February 4, 2000 through Lexis-Nexis.

[12] AllAfrica, Inc., accessed March 16, 2006, through LexisNexis.

[13] BBC Worldwide Monitoring, accessed March 8, 2006, through LexisNexus.

candidates in future elections might resort to a bush struggle instead.[14] Some members of the court were accused of corruption by Besigye's political party, but the charges were later withdrawn publicly when the accusations were found to be without merit.

By August 2006, lines of fracture within the government had started to appear. Some of those who had objected to the attacks on Besigye received promotions. The Minister of Defence who had lobbed the first attacks lost his portfolio, although he received another, in security. The Attorney General criticized those in his office who had disagreed with him, suggesting that there had indeed been lines of division. The twenty-two co-defendants in the treason case remained in prison despite a court order granting bail, however, implying that the military-AG faction remained at least partly intact. The trial unfolded slowly over succeeding months, during which time the court allowed the government to call witnesses who were self-confessed criminals, an act that elicited the ire of Besigye and the twenty-two co-defendants. Further high-profile attacks on the court were not forthcoming, however, and the court granted Besigye a passport to travel abroad. Although the story continues to unfold and "justice," in the purest sense of the term, was not always done, the courts remained intact, and the main opposition politician remained free to call for sweeping reform of the government and to launch a suit over the management of the central bank.

In this instance, members of the court had used court rules and the rules of criminal and civil procedure to try to negotiate for the independence of the judiciary from the executive branch – giving each side a bit of what it wanted, extending the debate about what constitutes fairness, and ultimately, on key issues, taking a strong stand on the proper relationship among government officers, the court, and the law. They also had taken on more public roles. Several judges had spoken at public meetings about the role of the judiciary and the importance of an independent judiciary. They openly spoke about their willingness to organize a review of their own operations. Supreme Court Judge George Kanyeihamba, whose relationship to Museveni dated to the years before the president's bush struggle, publicly applauded the successes of the government at the same time he criticized those who sought to manipulate situations for their own benefit and pinpointed where he thought the government had erred. He did not mince words when speaking with newly elected members of the National Resistance Movement, Museveni's "party," and the government did not push back hard.

Throughout these events, internal and external pressure groups played an important role. The Uganda Law Society (the bar association) and the Uganda

---

[14] AllAfrica, Inc. from the *East African* accessed April 11, 2006, through LexisNexus.

Human Rights Commission both issued statements critical of the government throughout the episode, publicized the issues externally, and got people into the streets to demonstrate. The newspapers ran editorials that were reasoned, not shrill, but were nonetheless strongly critical. Although the government imposed bans on coverage at several junctures, several papers kept up the drumbeat in their opinion columns. Another theoretically "independent" body, the Inspector General's office, also began to ask questions in the later phases.

The international community weighed in as well. A group of foreign envoys paid a visit to the court on the day of the first bail hearing. They were prevented from reaching the containment cell by the Black Mambas, but their presence sent a clear signal to the crowd. The Danish ambassador, chief of Uganda's development partners, tried to attend the court martial but was ordered out by the generals. The human rights groups issued reports and monitored events closely. The International Commission of Jurists sent representatives to monitor the trials, creating reputational pressure for the judges and lawyers. By mid-December, the governments of Sweden, the Netherlands, Norway, Ireland, and Britain had cut their bilateral aid programs in protest. Tony Blair spoke publicly against the actions at the opening of the Commonwealth Conference. The EU demanded a fair trial and expressed concern about the charges. The U.S. State Department issued a statement expressing concern about events.

Judicial independence is never won once and for all. It is constantly renegotiated. In the first quarter of 2007, two years after the initial incident that touched off Uganda's separation of powers crisis, the court martial reasserted its authority to try the accused, although it excluded Besigye himself. The Constitutional Court reiterated its holding that the military had no jurisdiction. Security forces once again swept into the High Court to prevent some of the men arrested three years earlier from accepting a grant of bail. A group of armed commandos entered the High Court and re-arrested the accused. An investigative team from the International Bar Association, which visited the country some months later, reported that the executive had started to infringe judicial independence in other ways as well, including refusal to abide by court orders, increasing personal criticism of particular judges, failure to appoint senior judges and consequent interference with the appeals process, deliberate under-funding of the judiciary, and use of military courts to hear cases against civilians accused of illegal weapons possession. (International Bar Association 2007)

The government's actions met with a response. The Uganda Law Society issued a statement that rebuked the government and suspended the membership of the Attorney General, the Director of Public Prosecutions, and several other officials for a six-month period. Several senior judges decried the government's actions as well, and the judges and lawyers joined in a one-week strike, although they later apologized to the country for this gesture of protest. In June, the donor community asked the government for assurances that it would desist from further efforts to undermine the courts and donors announced a significant contribution to the judiciary improve the ability of the courts to carry out their work. Judges and lawyers continued to articulate their concerns in public over the following months.

By January 2008, it remained unclear whether the government would take further action against the courts, or whether it would agree to improve respect for the separation of powers. It took no definitive measures against particular judges it considered unfavorable, however, and it did not urge a general uprising against the courts, a step Robert Mugabe pursued in Zimbabwe. Although politics entered the selection of new judges, there were no full-scale efforts to oust those already in office. At the same time, some judges reported pressure to decide cases in favor of the government, and the president and his associates insisted that the courts had no authority to adjudicate matters that were part of a broad reading of executive powers. Again, for at least a brief period, a fragile entente appeared to set in. In local newspapers, a few citizens began to wonder in print whether the courts were being asked to do too much, to carry responsibility for the country's fate when the separation of powers ought more reasonably to be preserved by actions of parliament and of opposition politicians, who clearly had a stake in preventing executive abuse of authority and had a greater ability to speak out.

Zimbabwe: Unhappy Outcomes

In 2000, the judiciary in Zimbabwe had an especially strong reputation for independence on the African continent. A series of impressive judges had led the court; some were non-African citizens of Zimbabwe, and some, like Enoch Dumbetshena, were important Zimbabwean insiders. The court had stood firm in the face of executive branch resistance on a variety of issues, from suspension of habeas corpus (ruled out) and reasonable time to trial to freedom of speech. Members of the public had come out on the streets in support of the courts when the government sought to interfere with their operation. However, chief justices in neighboring countries occasionally expressed worry that their Zimbabwe counterparts were too public, too visible – that they provoked the ire of the executive and would eventually find themselves closed down. They knew too well the difficulty of dealing with authorities unversed in law who were often highly self-interested and very intolerant of criticism.

After many years of institutional independence, the Zimbabwe judiciary lost its protected status in the wake of several controversial, anti-government rulings beginning in 2000. Although the initial focal point was a decision about land reform, political contestation was the underlying concern, as it would be a few years later in Uganda. President Robert Mugabe, then in his late seventies, had held office since 1980. Serious opposition had developed, led by the Movement for Democratic Change, a political party, and its leader, Morgan Tsvangirai. The Mugabe government had tried various ways to constrain the power of the party, a group that was well organized and large by African standards. It had also tried to draft a new constitution that would make the government and the military immune from prosecution for illegal acts, allow confiscation of farms, and concentrate more power in the president's hands. The new constitution had failed at referendum, as Zimbabweans chose to vote against the wishes of their president.

With parliamentary elections scheduled for June 2000, Mugabe's supporters reached for every tool they could find to build support. With the economy on the ropes, there were few options. One of these was the confiscation of land held by white farmers and the distribution of that land to ruling party members. A militia group led the effort, causing severe disruption and taking land from black farmers as well as white.

Land had long been a sensitive issue in Zimbabwe. Its white settlers, many of them former British air force personnel who had trained in the area during World War II, had made a unilateral declaration of independence, ushering in minority white rule. An armed struggle ensued, ending in an internationally brokered settlement and Mugabe's accession to the presidency. Yet, much of the best land remained in white hands. An internationally financed program was put in place to finance the gradual purchase of these farms on a "willing buyer, willing seller" basis. The program was mismanaged, however, and few purchases by small buyers occurred, although some larger tracts were transferred to powerful Mugabe supporters. In 1997, Tony Blair took the lead in ending the financing arrangement for this program. As the election of 2000 loomed and Mugabe's popularity ratings fell, the ability to pass out land in return for votes looked increasingly attractive.

The courts interfered with the electoral maneuvering. In April 2000, the Zimbabwe Supreme Court upheld a lower court ruling ordering squatters and veterans off farms seized under Mugabe's chaotic land reform program.[15] Mugabe had ignored the earlier decision, and openly admitted that he had not

---

[15] "Zimbabwe court orders veterans, squatters off white-owned farms," *The Associated Press*, March 17, 2000 accessed through LexisNexis.

ordered police to enforce it.[16] He ignored this ruling too, aided by a furious response from the Harare branch of the Zimbabwe Law Veterans Association, who demanded the judiciary step down or be removed by force.[17] At the time there were suspicions that the executive was actively encouraging the veterans to protest against the decision. This suspicion was confirmed by events like that which occurred in November 2000, when war veterans stormed the Supreme Court. Although police were present, they merely stood by and watched while the judges hid in their chambers.

The judiciary did not retreat from controversy. The June 2000 parliamentary elections were riddled with fraud. The new Parliament enacted a law that would strip the courts of a role in deciding challenges to the election results, thereby preventing the likely invalidation of thirty-seven parliamentary constituency races won by ZANU-PF, the ruling party.[18] In early 2001, the Supreme Court ruled this law unconstitutional. ZANU-PF lawmakers responded by passing a vote of no confidence in the Supreme Court. Minister of Information and Publicity, Jonathan Moyo, chief ZANU spin doctor until his fall from grace a few years later, accused the judiciary of favoring the Movement for Democratic Change (MDC) and whites, saying. "There can be no judicial independence without judicial impartiality, and as such the Supreme Court has lost its independence, it is because and only because the court has failed to be impartial."[19]

The government then began to use an array of tactics to infringe judicial independence. In February 2001, the government forced the chief justice, Anthony Gubbay, to resign, claiming that it could not guarantee his safety if he stayed in office.[20]

Two other justices – Ahmed Ibrahim and Nicholas McNally – were also asked to resign, but refused. Justice, Legal and Parliamentary Affairs Minister Patrick Chinamasa responded by saying that they could continue practicing and "would not be harmed."[21] Chinamasa also said that the government will "continue reforming the judiciary until it reflects the racial composition of the

[16] "Zimbabwe; Mugabe crosses the Rubicon," *Africa News*, April 13, 2000, accessed through LexisNexus.
[17] "Law Society Condemns Threats to Zimbabwe," *Zimbabwe Independent*, November 17, 2000, accessed through LexisNexus.
[18] "Zimbabwe judiciary biased in favor of whites, opposition: minister," in *Agence France Presse*, English, February 12, 2001, accessed through LexisNexus.
[19] Ibid.
[20] "Zimbabwe's Judges Are Feeling Mugabe's Wrath," *New York Times*, February 4, 2001, accessed through LexisNexus.
[21] "Zimbabwe minister says judges who refused early retirement "will not be harmed," BBC Monitoring Africa, February 23, 2001, accessed through LexisNexus.

country."[22] South African Constitutional Court judge Kate O'Regan remarked at the time, "It is with grave regret . . . that we observe what appears to be a grave threat to judicial independence developing in our neighboring state."[23]

In short order, Mugabe expanded the Supreme Court bench to include three additional judges. He appointed a new chief justice, Godfrey Chidya-usiku, who was widely perceived as a government supporter, and who chaired the 1999–2000 Constitutional Commission.[24] It was unsurprising then, in October 2001, that when asked to reconsider the rulings from the previous year, the new Supreme Court ruled in favor of the government's land claim program. In the 4–1 ruling, three of the judges had been appointed just two months previously ruled in favor. More senior judges, such as Wilson Sandura, Simba Muchechetere, and Nicholas McNally, were excluded from the hearing.[25]

Other changes in personnel followed. Michael Gillespie, a senior judge of Zimbabwe's High Court resigned and wrote in his final judgment that his departure was due to the "the breakdown to mob rule" as the government "renounces its commitment to the rule of law . . . [through] . . . controlling acts of violence and intimidation throughout the country." He went on to say, "A judge who finds himself in the position where he is called upon to administer the law only against political opponents of the government and not against government supporters, faces the challenge to his conscience, that is whether he can still consider himself to sit as an independent judge in an impartial court."[26] Minister of Information Jonathan Moyo responded by describing Gillespie as "an unrepentant racist former Rhodesia," with his departure being "really good riddance to bad rubbish."[27] Justice Ishmael Chati-kobo also resigned, and moved to Botswana after one of his judgments, allowing an independent radio station to broadcast, was countermanded by Moyo.[28]

Some within the judiciary tried to resist intimidation, and in February 2002 Justice Ahmed Ebrahim ruled against an electoral law passed by parliament.[29]

---

[22] Ibid.

[23] "South African judge expresses concern at threat to Zimbabwe judiciary," *Agence France Presse English,* February 23, 2001, accessed through LexisNexus.

[24] "Zimbabwe's judiciary no longer independent: farmers' lawyer," *Agence France Presse English,* October 2, 2001, accessed through LexisNexus.

[25] "Zimbabwe; Chinamasa Slammed for 'Simplistic' Remarks On Judges," *Africa News* from *Zimbabwe Independent,* October 5, 2001, accessed through LexisNexus .

[26] "Top former judge says Mugabe 'engineered lawlessness,'" *Deutsche Presse-Agentur,* October 6, 2001, accessed through LexisNexus.

[27] Ibid·

[28] "Zimbabwe; US Judge Slams Interference," *Africa News* from *Zimbabwe Standard* December 16, 2001, accessed through LexisNexus.

[29] "UN Experts Criticize Mugabe over Judicial Defiance," Panafrican News Agency (PANA) Daily Newswire, March 8, 2002, accessed through LexisNexus.

Mugabe simply ignored the ruling and published an edict reinstating the act.[30] Ebrahim resigned, making him the last of seven Supreme Court judges to step down since Anthony Gubbay's forced retirement.[31] UN Special Rapporteur on the Independence of Judges and Lawyers, Dato' Param Cumaraswamy, maintained at the time, "This action is a blatant violation of the UN Basic Principles of the Independence of the Judiciary, which expressly provides that states should guarantee the independence of the judiciary and that decisions of the courts should not be subject to revision save by lawfully constituted appellate courts."[32]

Former High Court judge Fergus Blackie (who is white) was arrested in the early hours of the morning and held in jail for three days – during the first day of imprisonment he was allegedly denied contact with his lawyers and family, not fed, and denied access to his heart medication. He was charged with attempting to pervert the course of justice, after he acquitted Tara White, a white accountant charged with theft, in one of his last rulings. Chief Justice Chidyausiku had ordered the investigations into Blackie, saying that he had acquitted White in order "to prevent a white person from going to jail." What seemed a more likely reason for the investigations was that another of Blackie's last judgments before his retirement in July was to order the arrest of Justice Minister Patrick Chinamasa for ignoring a summons to appear in court to answer charges of contempt of court. Chinamasa responded by saying that the judge's orders "should not be tolerated," and the police did not carry out Blackie's order.[33]

The attacks also reached the lower levels of the court. Walter Chikwanha, a magistrate in Chipinge, Manicaland, was assaulted and dragged out of court by a group of "war veterans." The attack occurred after he refused to place five members of the MDC into custody. The veterans then assaulted the lawyer who represented the MDC officials, and vandalized his car. Magistrates and prosecutors in Manicaland launched a week-long strike in protest.[34] Godfrey Gwaka, the magistrate for Zaka district, Masvingo, was stabbed shortly thereafter. It was suspected that the attack was related to judgments Gwaka had made on political parties. He was hospitalized after the attack.

By April 2003, the state had built up an impressive record of noncompliance with court orders. Zimbabwe Lawyers for Human Rights (ZLHR) documented

---

[30] Ibid.

[31] Ibid.

[32] Ibid.

[33] "SA Chief Justice Deplores Treatment of Zim Judge," SAPA (South African Press Association), September 19, 2002, accessed through LexisNexus.

[34] "UN Expert Calls for Rule of Law in Zim," SAPA (South African Press Association), September 2, 2002, accessed through LexisNexus.

at least twelve cases since 2000 in which the state has ignored court rulings. In a statement to the *Zimbabwe Independent* newspaper, the lawyers said failure by the state to enforce court orders would lead to a breakdown of the rule of law. "The state has systematically abrogated its responsibility to enforce or comply with court orders whether favorable to the state or not," said ZLHR director Arnold Tsunga.[35] Police and the army detained citizens without bringing them to court and ignored *habeas corpus* rulings. Orders issued by courts to police to arrest suspects with ZANU-PF ties were routinely ignored. Mugabe directed that it was acceptable to defy a judgment of any court in Zimbabwe if the affected party considered the outcome to have been the result of bias by a judicial officer.

Further evidence of the lack of judicial independence, and of a general breakdown in the legal system, was in evidence at Tsvangirai's treason trial. Judgment in the trial was "indefinitely postponed" after Judge Garwe failed to consult his two assessors on the verdict he allegedly proposed to hand down. The assessors blocked the judgment until they could review transcripts of the trial. Part of the problem was that fourteen hours of Tsvangirai's testimony were unrecorded because the court's audio equipment was faulty, and it took at least three days for the court to discover that they had no record of the accused's testimony. Garwe offered his own handwritten notes to be used as the transcript.[36] The state's two witnesses, Ari Ben-Menashe – whom Tsvangirai allegedly contracted to assassinate Mugabe – and his employee Tara Thomas, were singularly unconvincing, with Thomas even referring to notes during her testimony.[37]

Tsvangirai was eventually acquitted in what Justice, Legal and Parliamentary Affairs Minister Patrick Chinamasa said was evidence that the country's judiciary was independent and second to none: "Its judges act and decide on cases put before them independently and without fear or favor or interference. This is as it should be. The government believes that genuine democracy and rule of law dictate an unselective and unconditional application of the law. Where there is prima facie evidence of unlawful conduct, law enforcement agencies will and have a duty to act within the confines of the law."

As court packing and attacks on the judiciary progressed, self-dealing and lack of discipline became a problem within the judiciary. For example, the Judge President of the High Court, the second highest judge in the country

---

[35] "Justice System Eroded by State Non-Compliance, *Zimbabwe Independent* – AAGM, April 18, 2003, accessed through LexisNexus.

[36] "Zimbabwe's judicial system is on trial," *Business Day* (South Africa), August 16, 2004, accessed through LexisNexus.

[37] "Zimbabwean opposition leader's acquittal evidence of judicial independence: govt.," Xinhua General News Service, October 15, 2004, accessed through LexisNexus.

and the presiding judge in the government's treason case against opposition leader Morgan Tsvangirai, seized a white farm and installed members of the ZANU-PF.[38] Demands for better emoluments became the stock in trade, in lieu of challenging judgments.

As in the Uganda case, civic groups voiced opposition to the government's actions. In April 2002, the president of the Law Society of Zimbabwe (LSZ), Sternford Moyo, released a statement, questioning the competence of the Supreme Court. He suggested that the "government may have stuffed the Supreme Court with its sympathizers, thereby undermining the independence of the judiciary," and commented, "We have observed a significant departure from the culture of upholding the Bill of Rights in the Supreme Court. . . . We have seen a number of judgments which have caused us some anxiety, but we are still monitoring judgments to see whether a firm trend can be discerned from them." He also said, "The allegation that all white judges do not protect the rights of ordinary Zimbabweans is unfair, defamatory and contemptuous . . . and that "conditions of service for judges in Zimbabwe were among the worst in the southern African region."[39] University legal scholars joined the chorus. Constitutional lawyer and University of Zimbabwe lecturer Lovemore Madhuku told the *Financial Gazette*, "There is a pattern that is there for all to see. . . . ZANU PF complains and castigates the AG in cases in which political players from the opposition MDC are involved as well as individuals perceived to be enemies of the status quo."[40] The MDC voiced calls for change, causing its leader to be charged with treason.

POINTS OF DIFFERENCE AND THEORY-BUILDING

It may be premature to consider the Uganda tale to have ended differently from Zimbabwe's story. For the purposes of theory-building, it is worth pondering the points of difference and similarity, however.

External Leverage

In fairly authoritarian semi-democracies, domestic constituents for democracy or greater adherence to the rule of law may be organized and vocal, but they are also likely to lack the leverage to force a change in policy. Thus, as Robert

---

[38] "Zimbabwe judge secretly grabs white-owned farm," *The Daily Telegraph* (London), April 19, 2003, accessed through LexisNexus.
[39] "Zimbabwe; Lawyers Attack Supreme Court Judgments," *Africa News*, April 16, 2002, accessed through LexisNexus.
[40] Ibid.

Bates once wrote in an essay, policy change may be domestically demanded but externally supplied (Bates 1992). Pressure from international investors or donors will have more significance during such times in a country's history.

In both Zimbabwe and Uganda, domestic actors took to the streets to protest the executive's behavior toward the judiciary. In neither instance was this vocal opposition sufficient to alter the policies of the head of state or parts of his government. Those who objected to the actions of the executive branch had few critical resources with which to bargain. Heads of state and their entourages sometimes salt so many resources away in countries outside Africa that demonstrations and boycotts have little impact on their financial positions or they are simply unaffected by the economic downturns that may result, having built their own sinecures. Further, declining popular legitimacy may be of no consequence if leaders' time horizons are relatively short and the game is all about who can control jobs and money tomorrow, not about the views of citizens at the ballot box several years hence.

In these circumstances, international actors may prove helpful. However, external pressure is a fickle tactic. Its effectiveness varies across cases and often diminishes over time. Where an incumbent faces significant electoral pressure and has been unable to amass a personal fortune outside the country's boundaries (and thus create a destination to which he can exit), securing a continuing flow of international aid may be important for holding office and the executive branch will be more inclined to listen to donors. Similarly, where there is some sort of regional economic or political organization in which membership confers considerable benefit, heads of state may be more inclined to pay attention to the views of outsiders. These conditions vary across African countries. Even where they are favorable to the effective exercise of donor influence, diminishing returns may prove troublesome. The withdrawal of aid itself produces a loss of leverage. A donor can use the ploy once, but it then lacks the local assets to exercise leverage as effectively a second or third time. Furthermore, it is all too possible in resource-rich Africa to push a leader to choose short-term plunder, evisceration of state capacity, and escape rather than remaining in power as a stationary bandit, to borrow Olson's (1993; 2000) terminology. And of course, there is a risk that heavy external pressure will lead the government in power to associate things like rule of law with the foreign or international community, a ploy that may bring some leverage over local opinion.

Members of the international community expressed their concern about the government's actions in the Zimbabwe case, as well as in Uganda. Because of the earlier collapse in donor aid to Zimbabwe, however, leverage may have been more limited there than it was in the Uganda case a few years later.

(By contrast, Uganda was an international community poster child until the late 1990s.) Although one suspects that Museveni and his entourage have provided well for themselves, there is no question that Mugabe has lined his pockets through activity in the disrupted Democratic Republic of the Congo. Whether his country survives economically is not important to him. Further, the statements from the International Bar Association and other groups in Zimbabwe were powerful but may have aggravated Mugabe's sense of having come under assault from the West, a constant refrain in his speeches well before the clash with the courts in 2000.

Factions and Ideas

There were some other differences between the two countries that may partially account for the differences in outcomes. Division of opinion within the two governments may have varied in intensity. There is suggestive evidence that the Museveni government harbored people of quite different views on separation of powers questions. A stronger rule-of-law mentality prevailed in some parts of the civilian administration than in the military. Some of the better-positioned members of this elite appear to have offered at least muted criticism at least of the first infringements of judicial independence. They were not immediately dismissed for their divergent opinions. They may have succeeded in shaping the president's response or their actions may have helped illuminate just how far the executive could go before dissenters would leave and form their own parties. By contrast, in Zimbabwe, at the time of the events in question, there was little evidence of diversity of opinion and the president appeared to have the capacity to crush dissent on this subject.

Second, historical legacies may have played a role in shaping norms. In Uganda, there was no effort to decentralize violence against the judiciary, as there was in the Zimbabwe case. Although Ugandan ministers complained about the courts, they did not generally incite violence against them and most said nothing. There is no evidence that the military ever tried to empower others to attack the judiciary, and violence against judges themselves did not seem part of the repertoire, although certainly the judges themselves were very nervous. Some members of the military might have condoned the kind of action that had occurred in Zimbabwe, but they either thought it would attract an unfavorable reaction or they could not get others to go along with them.

Although the actions of the Ugandan Attorney General and the army were insupportable, they drew fairly heavily on elements of the language of law. They used the law as a weapon, but with some notable exceptions they tended to use law and not the street. They were guilty of abuse of process, among other things, but very often they simply exploited gaps and tried to use broad standards to their advantage in the absence of bright-line rules and clear precedents. In contrast, there was little attempt to use the language of law as a cloak in Zimbabwe.

Both countries had a thoughtful independent press in the mid-1990s, and judicial independence was a subject of reportage and editorial remark. Whereas the Mugabe government cracked down on opposition and closed presses, however, the Museveni government neither aimed to end press freedom nor succeeded in imposing limitations. Ugandans remained outspoken, and the country's independent newspapers ran considered editorials opposing the government's actions throughout the events described earlier. The brief ban on publishing imposed after the Black Mamba incident did not win compliance.

Arguably, even the effort to create a court martial in Uganda could be seen as mimicking the behavior of the Bush administration's legal team. If the Black Mambas and their patrons were indeed part of the Antiterrorism Task Force, funded by the U.S. government, and if they watched U.S. debates on the legality of special tribunals and courts martial, they may well have considered most of their actions acceptable. The outcome of *Padilla v. Rumsfeld* followed the Ugandan decision to try Besigye in the civilian court on criminal charges, however, suggesting that there may not have been a close mirroring.

The different lessons and legacies of the past may have distinguished the countries in this regard. It is possible that the miserable history of Idi Amin and Milton Obote and the near-experience of a very orderly rebel struggle induced a modicum of restraint and helped more moderate factions gain slightly more influence as the Ugandan conflict proceeded. By contrast, Zimbabwe's history has made it possible to invoke white domination as a specter to justify a wide range of abuses. Much of the population appears wise to the victimhood ploy, but the government views the tactic as useful nonetheless.

The Court

The two judiciaries, both independent at the start, also differed in telling ways. At the conclusion of Zimbabwe's struggle, many of the country's lawyers were white or Asian, as was true of a number of African countries. Although most of those remaining shared nationalist sympathies and a preference for one person/one vote, by and large they were not among those who had been imprisoned or who had fought alongside Mugabe. In Uganda, by contrast, several respected members of the court whom Museveni had brought back from exile or jail had been advisers or critics since the beginning of the struggle. They had nationalist credentials. The difference in experience may be significant not so much in the preferences or perspectives created but in the channels of communication that existed between the court and the government in the Ugandan case compared to Zimbabwe.

The way in which the judges conducted themselves differed too. One might not be entirely happy with the intellectual elegance, or lack thereof, of some of the Uganda opinions. No doubt there are times when a judge might be criticized for having given a party too much latitude. But there is sometimes wisdom in issuing messy judgments that create a principle or set a standard, on the one hand, and set aside immediate and drastic action, on the other. Some of the Uganda judgments had that character. By letting cases go ahead despite ambiguous charges while issuing a passport to the defendant, drawing out proceedings until election tempers cooled, allowing a result to stand while condemning violations of the law, etc., the Ugandan courts may have been able to build strength gradually, develop public understanding and norms, and induce some parts of the government and opposition to trust their actions, even if the results were far from perfect from the standpoint of justice. Although certain government actions provoked condemnation from senior judges, many of the statements were coupled with phrasing designed to calm tempers. The Zimbabwe judgments, which were often elegant, tended to be more hard-hitting, and sharp public statements by judges in the years before the clash may have aggravated relationships. Human rights lawyers might disagree with this assessment, but it is always well to remember that the U.S. Supreme Court issued the murky *Marbury* in a charged atmosphere and exercised restraint subsequently, gradually building a reservoir of trust.

TENTATIVE IMPLICATIONS

Social scientists often draw a distinction between "institutional origins" questions and much of the rest of the intellectual territory at the heart of political science – policy choice, political behavior, etc. How an institution gets started may be highly idiosyncratic, based on contextually specific distributions of preferences and bargaining choices. The early years in the life of an institution may have a similar character, though the underlying conditions we often use in explanations may shape an organization's longevity. The broad-coverage laws that are the stuff of much political science provide intellectual leverage mainly when institutions are stable. Thus, in accounting for the rise of independent judiciaries, the talents of game theorists and historians may prove more helpful than any resort to general explanations.

Nonetheless, it is possible to offer a few adages that arise from reflection upon the two cases described in this chapter. The first is clearly that infringements of judicial independence are likely to increase before and during elections in semi-democracies or new democracies. When it is not clear that opponents will reflect the rules of democratic alternation in power, the temptation to try to circumscribe contestation is great. The longer time horizons that make delegation of power to independent bodies a sensible proposition come only after years of successful alternation of parties in power.

Second, some countries may provide more fertile ground than others for the success of *Marbury*-like stratagems. The more viewpoint diversity within the executive and legislative branches, the lower the likelihood that the party in power will infringe the independence of the courts. Why? For the overtures of judges to receive a hearing, there must be people open to alternative perspectives in the president's inner circle or among his or her advisers. One might expect to see greater respect for judicial independence in countries where coalitions govern or where the chief executive shows some aptitude for listening to alternative perspectives. Similarly, where a high proportion of the senior members of the judiciary share important background traits with those in government, the likelihood of infringement may be lower, simply because communication is better and the judiciary is less likely to be viewed as foreign.

Third, although it is not possible to manufacture "Marbury moments," some kinds of institutional designs or personnel practices might make them more likely. For example, constitutions that grant clear powers of judicial review and are themselves strongly entrenched, making quick amendment more difficult, may provide more scope for such decisions. Constitutions that grant courts very narrow powers or allow legislatures to alter the language of fundamental documents very easily give judges neither the power nor the incentive to act as Marshall did in similarly trying times in U.S. history.

Finally, one must ask whether there are situationally specific reasons why the executive may be disinclined to fight back when a court rules in a way that limits the leader's power. 1) Do the leaders simply share the view that what the courts say deserves respect? Apartheid South Africa did not have a liberal, democratic leadership, but infringement of judicial independence was still considered unacceptable. 2) Does the leader see himself or herself as a citizen, likely to remain in the country? If so, popular protests in support of the judiciary may have more teeth than they would otherwise. 3) Can popular protest in support of the judiciary trigger serious armed insurrection or injure critical economic interests? If so, the threat of popular protest may prove effective. 4) Can the leader and key members of the entourage remain in the country and continue to earn incomes if displaced from power? If so, the incentive to infringe the independence of the judiciary may be lower. 5) Do the court rulings empower people who may, in turn, limit or channel the activities of more dangerous opponents? If a court ruling opens up elections and a militarized opposition must compete and put its popular legitimacy to the test, the more serious threat to the corporate interests of the leader's entourage may diminish. 6) If the leader's entourage is aid-dependent and donors threaten to withdraw assistance in the event the court is threatened, the executive may refrain from infringing judicial independence. 7) If the leader sees respect for the court as a prerequisite for his own acceptance by a global community of leaders, and he values membership in that community, then the risk of infringement may be lower. 8) If the leader and his entourage can support themselves through private business activities and do not need to control the government to earn a living, the incentive to infringe the independence of the judiciary may be lower, at least in political cases.

10

Judicial Power in Authoritarian States: The Russian Experience

Peter H. Solomon, Jr.

Like their democratic counterparts, authoritarian rulers need effective courts to perform the basic functions of courts – to resolve disputes, to impose social control, and to regulate at least aspects of public life (Shapiro 1981). At the same time, these rulers are often reluctant to endow courts with significant power in the form of politically sensitive jurisdiction and the discretion to make far-reaching choices. Yet, the record shows that some authoritarian regimes – for example, well-established or liberalizing ones – do entrust their courts with such responsibilities for holding public administration accountable, managing major commercial conflicts, and even maintaining quasi-constitutional order (Moustafa 2005; Ginsburg 2006). Under what circumstances authoritarian rulers opt for judicial power and with what risks, consequences, and compromises are questions ripe for comparative study.

This chapter examines the experience of three Russian states – Tsarist Russia (from the Judicial Reform of 1864); the USSR (including the late period of liberalization); and post-Soviet Russia (a hybrid regime that moved from electoral democracy to electoral or competitive authoritarianism). The chapter begins with two theoretical issues – (1) judicial independence and its relationship to judicial power and (2) distinctions among types of authoritarian regimes.

THEORETICAL PERSPECTIVES

At least in authoritarian states, judicial independence is not a given. Traditionally, European autocrats retained for themselves the right to dismiss judges whose decisions they disliked (until the seventeenth century, judges in England served "at the pleasure of the King"; Shapiro 1981: 91). Modern authoritarian rulers may also have ways of ridding themselves of offending judges (as was the case through most of Soviet rule), but they may also adopt security of tenure for most of their judges. Security of tenure, good salaries, good financial support of the courts, and judicial control of key aspects of court administration are recognized as necessary conditions for judges to render impartial decisions (Russell 2001). But they may not be sufficient, especially when judicial bureaucracies create strong incentives for judges to conform to the wishes of political masters and informal institutions support this behavior.

Yet the appearance of judicial independence is essential for the legitimacy of courts. Rather than keep all courts and judges in a state of obvious dependence on the executive, an alternative approach is to place matters of importance to the regime in separate tribunals, leaving the courts with only routine civil and criminal law disputes. Under these circumstances there is little risk in granting to regular judges the protection of tenure, especially if their performance is carefully monitored and only loyal and compliant judges are given promotions. At the same time, the judges serving on the special tribunals hearing the important cases may be carefully screened and lack the protection offered by tenure. This approach was adopted in Spain in the late Franco period. The "Spanish solution" comprised giving courts considerable independence but little power (Toharia 1975).

When rulers decide to enlarge the jurisdiction or discretion of courts, they are, as Shapiro stressed, yielding power to judges. If the rulers do not like the results, they may react in various ways; for example, taking back some of the jurisdiction or discretion already given. They may also be tempted to limit judicial autonomy, if only in the name of "accountability." This can be done by strengthening the filtering procedures of the judicial bureaucracy to ensure that only cooperative judges have good careers. Or powerful actors, government or private, may try to influence what decisions judges render. Another approach on the part of rulers and elites is to ignore court decisions or fail to cooperate in their implementation, which in turn deflates the authority of courts. The Russian experience provides examples of all of these methods of limiting the autonomy of judges. Based on that experience, this chapter argues that *when rulers empower courts that were not previously independent, the results will usually be ambiguous and contested as judges face new challenges to their independence, power, or both.*

What kinds of authoritarian regimes opt for stronger courts? What distinctions can be made among non-democratic states more generally?

Empowered and autonomous courts are unlikely to appear in totalitarian states, like the USSR under mature Stalinism. Where rulers seek to control and manage the economy and limit social organization outside of the state, they are unlikely to decentralize state power away from the executive by empowering courts. Even in what Linz and Stepan call "post-totalitarian states" – that is, weaker versions of totalitarian regimes – the same generalization applies, although there may be exceptions (e.g. Hungary in the 1970s; Linz and Stepan 1996: ch. 3).

But what about the broad range of authoritarian regimes? Tamir Moustafa proposes that a subset of "institutionalized, bureaucratic-authoritarian states" turn to the courts to address problems associated with authoritarian rule (including holding officials accountable, attracting investment, and reinforcing regime legitimacy). This suggests that older and more established authoritarian regimes are more likely to use courts than new, personalistic ones. This may be so. But the empowerment of courts may also connect to significant policy changes that call for the protection of old elites (as was the case in Tsarist Russia) or to a strategy for modernizing the economy (as in China; see Chapter 2 by Ginsburg). It may connect to liberalization, as was the case in late Soviet Russia and Mexico in the 1990s. It may also represent a legacy of incomplete, failed, or reversed democratization and become an awkward institution in a competitive authoritarian environment (as is the case in post-Soviet Russia).

The awkward truth is that there are many states where rulers aspire to the legitimation that comes from democratic practices like elections and constitutionalism, but who are unwilling to face the risk of leaving office. States that scholars now call competitive or electoral authoritarianism are becoming more common, and they are marked, as critics insist, by façade institutions and parallel political realities (Levitsky and Way, 2002; Diamond 2002; Krastev 2006; Wilson 2005). In this context, courts may acquire power in the form of jurisdiction and discretion, but find that both their authority to compel enforcement (a third dimension of power) and their independence become compromised, at least in the real world of informal practices and institutions.

TSARIST RUSSIA: COURTS AND AUTOCRACY

The Judicial Reform of 1864 instituted a revolutionary change in Russian courts, legal procedure, and the judiciary, producing independent and partially empowered courts that were incompatible with the autocratic regime with which they coexisted. The resulting tensions illustrate the limits of judicial power in an authoritarian state. As we shall see, weak versions of both administrative justice and judicial lawmaking through statutory interpretation were involved, but the challenge of industrialization did not lead to the real empowerment of courts.

Before the Judicial Reform of 1864 Russia had weak (and corrupt) courts based on social class distinctions. Judges were local notables without legal education, serving at the pleasure of officials and whose decisions were reviewed by provincial governors. There were no public or oral trials, and judges examined criminal charges in their offices through a pure version of inquisitorial procedure. The reform established a single hierarchy of courts for the whole population and gave most judges life tenure with firing only for cause. It established as well full public and oral trials, at which the sides were to be represented by counsel, including the option of trial by jury for serious crimes. Moreover, judges gained new discretion in applying the law, including a duty to rely in part upon their conscience, and, at least in the highest courts, the right to interpret the law (Solomon 1997).

The development and adoption of the Judicial Reform of 1864 was an extraordinary event, possible only in unusual times. The context was the mounting of a whole series of reforms all emanating from and related to the emancipation of the serfs. But other ingredients also made the reform process possible. One was the presence of a small cadre of enlightened jurists in high places in the bureaucracy, individuals who promoted and helped write the reform legislation. Second, this group had the advantage of working against the background of a broad consensus that the old system of justice was an embarrassment to Russia among its European neighbors. Third, the reform was facilitated by the recognition among many of the gentry dispossessed by the Emancipation that the protection of their new property rights required strong law and courts. It was the articulation of this concern by nobles close to the Tsar that convinced Alexander II to proceed with the Judicial Reform of 1864 (Wortman 1976). This motivation is consistent with what Tamir Moustafa calls the "power preservation" explanation of judicial empowerment (Moustafa 2005: 6–9).

The 1864 reform produced a judicial system that was bound to challenge the unlimited power of the tsar. No doubt the officials who drafted the reform saw things differently. They assumed that independent courts staffed by legal specialists not only were compatible with autocratic power, but would even strengthen it by ensuring the observance of the tsar's laws. In practice, however, some judicial decisions failed to meet the interests or expectations of the tsar or his advisors, and it became clear that the law was no longer a reliable instrument of autocratic power. As a result, over the decades of implementing the reform, the tsars and their ministers tried to minimize the loss of imperial prerogatives. They decided to remove political offenses from the regular courts and place them in military courts – especially after juries acquitted Vera Zasulich who assassinated a minister in cold blood – and to introduce special emergency regimes in parts of the country. In addition to narrowing the jurisdiction of regular courts, tsarist officials took measures to keep judges in line. Thus a law in 1885 gave the Minister of Justice the right to ask judges to explain any of their actions and to issue instructions about decisions in cases completed or procedure in future cases. The law also facilitated disciplinary proceedings against judges, increased the grounds for their removal, and allowed for the transfer of judges from one bench or court to another by the Ministry (Wagner 1976). Through these and other new powers of management, judges in Russia became subject to pressures to conform to the interests of their bureaucratic and political masters.

The 1864 reform introduced a pale version of administrative justice into Russia, and prompted many further attempts to strengthen it. Citizens gained the right to sue officials for material losses (albeit with the consent of the officials' administrative superiors), but the provincial commissions that heard these challenges consisted only of administrative officials (not judges) and since the state bore no financial liability, plaintiffs had to collect awards directly from the officials. Appeals might bring the conflicts to the First Department of the Senate, but this remained an administrative rather than a judicial body, to the dismay of Minister of Justice Zamiatnin, who in 1865 tried make it a formal site of an expanded judicial review of administrative acts. A recent study of the operation of the First Department, however, showed that its members acted as if they were judges (despite not having life tenure) and tried to keep government officials in line. It came to allow appeals from public organizations against decisions of governors that they believed infringed their rights. In 1897 Minister of Justice Muraviev tried without success to get this process disallowed. Between 1905 and 1917 the political parties of the center and right end of the spectrum sought reform of administrative justice. This provided the intellectual basis for the short-lived democratic Provisional Government of 1917 to legislate the creation of administrative courts (Pravilova 2000; Wortman 2005).

Underlying the resistance to strengthening administrative justice and the rights of citizens to sue officials was a strong belief shared by both top government officials like Pobedonostev and most legal scholars that judges should never be placed above officials of the executive (Pravilova 2000). This belief reflected both Russian experience and the civil law tradition, especially in its French version.

Officially, the civil law of the Napoleonic Code devalued and reduced to a minimum all forms of judicial discretion, and many of the new Russian jurists shared the preference for written law over legal doctrines developed by judges. But, as Martin Shapiro stressed, in applying laws, judges are forced to interpret their meaning, so that even in civil law countries top courts end up making law (Shapiro 1981: 136–143). Judges in France, according to John Merryman, developed the law of torts for that country, and, in like manner the top civil court of Tsarist Russia, the Civil Cassation Department of the Senate, in the 1870s and 1880s had a significant impact on the law of family, property, and inheritance (Merryman 1985: 73; Wagner 1994).

Almost immediately after the Judicial Reform of 1864, the Civil Cassation Department asserted that lower courts were obliged to adhere to its published interpretations of the law (whether in directives or cases) in all similar cases – this as a natural extension of its duty to interpret the law and to ensure uniformity. Many legal scholars objected that this principle was not based on law and was dangerous, but lower courts generally observed the precedents, if grudgingly, because they respected the department, recognized the need for uniformity, and feared the loss of time if forced to rehear cases after cassation reviews.

The Civil Cassation Department used this new power for the practical purpose of improving the situation of women who separated from their husbands. The law was heavily biased against them, with divorce very difficult to obtain and separation almost forbidden and imposing no obligation on the husband to support the wife. In a series of decisions in the 1870s and 1880s the Civil Cassation Department held first that spouses could agree to live separately as long as the courts held the reasons to be valid and there was no intent on permanence, and then that lower courts could award the wife support despite the husband's insistence that he wanted to live with her, as long as the courts found the conduct of the husband warranted such action. To be sure, the rulings were applied by lower courts inconsistently, and they were resisted by the Holy Synod. Only in 1914 was the legislation revised, despite many commissions and projects (Wagner 1994).

The last decades of Tsarist rule represented a period of intensive economic development in Russia, including the building of railroads, mines, metallurgy and metal plants, and arms production. Since part of the investment came from the private sector, including foreign sources, one might have expected some efforts to improve the protection of property rights through strengthening the role of courts in commercial disputes. It does not appear that this happened. As of the turn of the century commercial courts operated in Moscow, St. Petersburg, Odessa, and Warsaw. In addition, some disputes were also heard in regular courts; others in the large cities were handled through mediation. In 1903 a new Statute on Court Procedure in Commercial Matters was issued, but it is unclear with what intent or impact (Kleandrov 2001). Whatever the role of courts, high-ranking officials in relevant ministries did not respect laws and court decisions. They insisted, for example, on confirming corporate charters through separate laws that sometimes contradicted the general laws governing this matter. To the eminent jurist Petrazhitskii (writing in 1898) corporate law in Russia was marked by "bureaucratic arbitrariness." Many rules complicated the conduct of affairs, and officials had the discretion to decide when and how to apply them. The role of courts was so marginal that the major Western study of Tsarist law on corporations does not mention them! What it does record is a fundamental conflict between the Tsarist bureaucrats and the axioms of corporate culture (Owen 1991).

Overall, though, the story of courts in late Tsarist Russia is distinguished by the degree of independence achieved by judges despite the political system. The reluctance to establish administrative justice, the limited role of judicial interpretation in lawmaking, and the absence of a major role for courts in the commercial realm reflected the continuing suspicion of courts among Tsarist administrators and their unwillingness to cede significant power to anyone (Popova 2005).

COURTS IN THE SERVICE OF THE REGIME: JUDICIAL POWER IN THE USSR

For the most part the Soviet period in the history of Russia did not witness the empowerment of courts. Neither constitutional nor administrative justice developed to any significant degree – although versions of both existed in particular periods, and once the economy became largely state owned and administered, courts played a minor role in its regulation. Still, the period is not without interest. When an authoritarian regime aims at the monopolization of political and economic power, it still needs mechanisms for managing its officials and resolving conflicts among them. Major substitutes for courts – the Procuracy and state and agency *arbitrazh* – demonstrate this need. Moreover, even within a would-be totalitarian political order, there were places for limited versions of administrative justice and the use of constitutions in regime legitimation, albeit as a secondary matter. Of course, the last years of Soviet power under Mikhail Gorbachev stand out as a time of liberalization and democratization, and in this context the regime took major initiatives both to secure judicial independence and empower the courts. I deal with this period separately.

The Revolution of 1917 brought to the seats of power Bolsheviks whose attitudes toward law, courts, and lawyers were ambivalent if not negative. While many of them remained attached to the ideal of a society administered without the cumbersome and biased legal institutions of capitalism, most Bolshevik leaders, especially Vladimir Lenin, quickly accepted the utility of law as an instrument of rule and sought to develop law and courts to serve the new regime. A crucial part of this project was ensuring that judges would be loyal, if not also committed to the new order. What progress had been made under the tsars toward the entrenchment of judicial independence was for the most part reversed by the new Soviet regime, and the traditional autocratic subordination of law to political power was restored. Judicial appointments involved approvals by party officials, and terms in office for judges at all levels were of limited duration, thereby making the question of reappointment (at times in the form of denomination for uncontested election) also subject to political vetting. The system of financing courts mainly from local budgets rather than a central one further reinforced the dependence of judges upon politicians in their bailiwicks and helped assure their cooperation with their political masters. Finally, the strong instrumental conception of law left little place for attachment to the ideal of judicial independence, even though it was declared in the 1936 Constitution. Judges were expected at all times to pay heed to the political demands of the moment (expressed in criminal policy or in recommendations from party officials), while maintaining a public face of impartiality to enhance the court's prestige.

A defining feature of the Bolshevik approach to the administration of justice was the preference for cadres who were loyal over those who were expert. Throughout Soviet history the leaders preferred party members to nonparty members for appointments as judge or procurator, and until the mid-1930s saw little virtue in legal education for legal officials. In fact, most legal officials in the 1920s and 1930s lacked even general secondary education, let alone advanced legal training. In the mid-1930s Stalin and his colleagues decided that competency in law did matter after all and planned an expansion of legal education to produce jurists for the courts, but the fulfilment of this new policy came only after World War II. Even then, the norm was to provide first secondary and then higher legal education by correspondence to the investigators, procurators, and judges of the day; only a small number of well-trained jurists became legal officials. This pattern helped assure that officials who made careers in the legal agencies in the postwar years would not be infected with legal ideals that might threaten their inclination to conform with the expectations of their superiors.

Courts and judges retained the core jurisdiction that they had had under the tsars – that is, over criminal and civil disputes – and in these matters were given considerable discretion. Increasingly, the regime channeled this discretion, and through Supreme Court directives and policy statements outside the law told judges how they were expected to behave. Especially in the years before World War II, judges did not always comply with expectations, but instead made decisions in accordance with their sense of justice. Authorities sometimes viewed this conduct as resistance, and punished judges accordingly (Solomon 1996).

At times courts in the USSR did possess politically important jurisdiction. Thus, during the 1920s the Supreme Court of the USSR was responsible for handling constitutional disputes between republican governments and the central government; that is, the regulation of Soviet federalism. The 1924 Constitution of the USSR gave full jurisdiction for most areas of law and its administration to republican governments, and did not allow appeals from republican supreme courts to the USSR one. The USSR Supreme Court was empowered to assess, at the request of governmental authorities (e.g., the presidium of the Central Executive Committee, a parliamentary body), whether particular laws of the republics conformed with All-Union law, including the Constitution; at the initiative of republican governments (or on its own initiative), it could consider the legality of administrative orders issued by central agencies. In both instances, the role of the Supreme Court was only advisory. It was up to the Presidium of the Central Executive Committee to act on the Court's interpretations. Between 1924 and 1929 the Court issued eighty-six judgments about the legality of agency acts and eleven relating to laws of the republics. In most instances the politicians accepted its advice (Dobrovolskaia, 1964; Bannikov 1974; Solomon 1990).

The chairman of the USSR Supreme Court, Aron Vinokurov, sought to enhance the constitutional review powers of his Court, and in a new draft statute for the Court proposed in 1928 that it gain the right to review All-Union legislation and republican legislation at its own initiative. These proposals raised objections from many quarters and a discussion in which some politicians sought to take away from the Court some of the powers it already possessed. Vinokurov was forced onto the defensive, stressing that there was no violation of "separation of powers" when the Court's role was advisory, and how vital its role was for maintaining the hierarchy of laws. For the most part, Vinokurov won the battle (the Court even gained the right to review republican legislation on its own initiative), but lost the war. The very functions he had defended lost their relevance when the regime launched its war against the peasantry (collectivization) and legal standards and norms were all but abandoned for a time (Mitiukov 2005).

While eventually (in 1934) losing its albeit limited constitutional role, the USSR Supreme Court gradually gained the right to supervise lower courts, and with the Constitution of 1936 its appellate jurisdiction became unlimited. Because any case could be appealed to the top, the Court played a large role in assuring that the priorities of the centre took precedence over local ones.

This centralization of power within the judiciary was itself a reflection of the decision taken by Stalin and his circle in the mid-1930s to revive the traditional authority of law, so that it could serve as an instrument of rule and better perform the function of social control. In this context law meant nothing more than the laws and regulations promulgated by the state, and there was no pretence that they might constrain the leader. But reviving the authority of law did entail ensuring that judges and other legal officials had legal education and encouraging the pursuit of legal careers (the bureaucratization, if not also the professionalization of the judiciary). The official explanation for embracing law and giving a new priority to the administration of justice was that, with the building of socialism completed, the new economy and society needed the stability and order that strong legal institutions could provide. On the practical level, Stalin wanted criminal justice that would check the plague of disorder in the overcrowded cities, including drunken rowdy behavior and the activities of juvenile gangs (Solomon 1996: ch. 5).

The leadership also recognized the utility of law as a source of legitimacy for the regime and its practices. To begin, one group of judges on the USSR Supreme Court, members of the Special Collegium, assumed the task from 1934 to 1938 of hearing prosecutions for political or counterrevolutionary crimes characteristic of the era of purges and terror. While most such charges were reviewed summarily by the infamous three-person boards known as *troiki*, a small percentage of these charges were brought to the Supreme Court, in order to legitimate the repression. Thus, a panel from the Special Collegium heard the three famous show trials held from 1936 to 1938, in which leading politicians, past and present, confessed to participation in the most outrageous conspiracies that script writers could imagine.

At the same time, the new USSR Constitution was promulgated in December 1936, in large part to legitimate the political order that had been created through the collectivization and industrialization drives with both domestic and foreign audiences. This political order was characterized by the extreme centralization of power within the government and by the continued mobilization of the law to suit the regime's political purposes. In contrast, the 1936 Constitution emphasized the rights of citizens and democracy and called for courts that appeared normal and independent, even as they implemented regime policies. But there was no mechanism for enforcement of the constitution, considerable parts of which bore little relation to reality. In short, the Soviet Constitution of 1936 represented an entrenchment of neither rights nor judicial power, but rather a further twist in the manipulation of law and courts for political purposes, which now included regime legitimation (Solomon 1996: chs. 6 and 7).

Administrative justice also had a chequered history under Soviet rule. The Bolsheviks continued discussion of the establishment of administrative courts (which the Provisional Government had endorsed), but by the mid-1920s decided against this step. They preferred to empower the Procuracy (and for a time the Workers Peasants Inspectorate) with the task of reviewing complaints against the legality of acts of officials and ordering illegal actions corrected. Under the Bolsheviks the Procuracy combined its late Tsarist function of prosecution with its earlier mandate (pre-1864) of supervising the legality of public administration. This mandate involved not only responding to complaints but also undertaking fishing expeditions ("raids") on state enterprises and agencies. Over the years, in parallel with the Procuracy complaints procedure, courts did gain the right to review a short list of specific complaints, including seizures of property to cover unpaid taxes, fines and license suspensions imposed by the police, actions of judicial enforcers engaged in debt collection, and certain complaints against housing officials (Solomon 2004; Starilov 2001).

Observers of the Soviet scene were surprised to discover that the 1977 Constitution in article 58 confirmed that citizens had a right to complain to courts about illegal actions of officials and thus opened the door for the development of this right in legislation (Sharlet 1978). Although issued in the Brezhnev era, the new constitution had its origins in a drafting commission established under Khrushchev in 1962, and the provisions for administrative justice may date back to that time (Lukianova 2001). By the mid-1970s there was considerable support for this idea. From the late 1960s Soviet jurists discussed the matter vigorously, and versions of administrative justice began appearing in Communist countries of Eastern Europe (culminating with the establishment of the Supreme Administrative Court in Poland in 1980; Oda 1984). Whatever its origins, article 58 of the 1977 Constitution did not bear fruit until the Gorbachev era. As we shall see, it was only in 1987 that judicial review of administrative acts was significantly expanded.

From 1931 when the nationalization of productive property in the USSR was almost complete and the state-administered economy fully established, disputes among state economic units (enterprises, agencies) were handled not by courts but by tribunals of the state *arbitrazh* (disputes among units of different agencies) or agency *arbitrazh* (disputes among units of the same agency or ministry). Disputes often revolved around the allocation of blame for failures in contract performance that affected a unit's ability to fulfill its annual plan (especially deliveries). Although the Russian word for these tribunals suggests bodies that arbitrate rather than adjudicate, the panels of the *arbitrazh* system came to act as courts, albeit with an obligation to follow the interests of state administrators. The 1977 Constitution elevated the status of state *arbitrazh* by separating its tribunals from the executive branch of government and treating them as an "independent branch," analogous to courts (Kleandrov 2001: 25–28; Hendley, 1998).

As *arbitrazh* tribunals gradually became more court-like, so the underlying basis of economic disputes changed in ways that did not encourage losers to turn to the court. During the 1970s and 1980s an increasingly large share of economic activity in the USSR came to be performed in the parallel or underground private economy. While many of the same state firms became embroiled in disputes relating to their second-economy activities, the semi-legal or illegal status of this business made it hard to use the courts to resolve the disputes. As result, there developed a set of informal mechanisms for resolving disputes with a second- (illegal private) economy connection, informal mechanisms that carried over in the post-Soviet era (Pistor 1996)

LIBERALIZATION, DEMOCRATIZATION, AND THE COURTS

As of 1985, courts in the USSR remained weak, dependent bodies that lacked public respect, and the career of judge had low status and few rewards. Jurisdiction in matters of political import was limited. Judges were subject to multiple lines of dependency, including to local party leaders, and both judicial salaries and court budgets were miserly. All of this would change, sooner or later.

The decision of Mikhail Gorbachev and his confidantes like Alexander Iakovlev to embark on the liberalization of Soviet authoritarianism led quickly to pressures for democratization, and eventually to the erosion of the authority of the Communist Party of the USSR. This process also had profound implications for the courts, setting in motion attempts to make courts in Russia both independent and empowered. Between 1987 and 1990 the government of the USSR adopted a series of measures to accomplish these goals, which taken together represent a breakthrough from the Soviet past. Yet, before these measures could be fully implemented, they were overtaken by politics. In 1990 and 1991 the government of the Russian republic, still formally a constituent part of the USSR, began asserting its autonomy and in this context moved ahead of the USSR in judicial reform, making this an arena of competition between these two governments and their respective leaders, Yeltsin and Gorbachev. When the USSR fell apart at the end of 1991, the new Russian government had already committed itself to radical judicial reform, and during the next two years approved legislation to implement it. As of the end of 1993, most of the formal institutions of judicial independence and power were in place in Russia (although not in other post-Soviet states like Ukraine and Belarus).

The core plank of Gorbachev's liberalization was the policy of *glasnost*; that is, the opening up of the media and public discourse to allow long overdue criticism of misguided policies and abuses of power. The purpose was to develop public support for the regime's moderate reform policies, for example in the management of the economy, but the effects were more far-reaching. Muckraking journalists rose to the challenge and with the help of legal scholars exposed not only historical injustices but also recent abuses of the administration of justice and the accusatorial bias in the courts. Pressure mounted quickly for judicial reform, and by 1988 the political leaders had committed themselves in a party resolution (part of the platform for "democratization") to the creation of a "socialist *rechtsstaat*" or law-based state (Solomon and Foglesong 2000: ch.1). While some members of the Soviet leadership (including Iakovlev himself) envisaged a mild rights revolution, most thought they were simply endorsing a state where officials obeyed the laws (Iakovlev 1993). Moreover, the qualifier "socialist" implied that the Communist Party would remain above and beyond the law. All this notwithstanding, the resolution opened the door for the adoption of a series of measures to enhance judicial independence and power.

To curtail the vulnerability of judges to the whims of politicians, the system of appointment and tenure was changed, so that judges would serve for terms of ten years instead of five and for reappointment would face approval not by the party secretary of the same level in the administrative hierarchy but by the regional soviet (legislature) at the next level. Even more important, all appointments required preliminary screening by judicial qualification commissions made up solely of judges, and no judge could be fired during term except for cause and with the approval of the appropriate commission. In addition, interference in the work of the courts (e.g., trying to influence a court decision through an approach to the judge) was made a criminal offense (Solomon and Foglesong 2000).

The first empowerment of courts under Gorbachev came in the area of administrative justice. Reviving the struggle to realize article 58 of the Constitution, jurists succeeded in getting a significant expansion in judicial review of administrative acts introduced already in 1987. While the new law opened up the right of complaint to almost any subject matter, it did not apply to decisions taken in the name of a collegial body (like a city council), and complainants had to exhaust all administrative remedies before going to court. A second law on the subject in 1989 eliminated the first of these restrictions (Solomon 2004).

The commitment to a law-based state called for the establishment of a hierarchy of laws and new attempts to ensure that laws of different levels of government were consistent. The government of the USSR opted for a weak form of constitutional review, and entrusted this function in a new "Constitutional Supervisory Committee," approved in December 1988 and starting operation in May 1990, after a new union treaty revamped the relationship between the republics and the central government. Empowered to review the constitutionality of republican and All-Union legislation, this body was attached to the legislature (technically, it was not a court), and its decisions were advisory except with regard to Union laws violating human rights. (Decisions of the Constitutional Tribunal founded in Poland in 1985 also required confirmation by Parliament to become valid). In practice, almost all of its rulings were issued at the initiative of the Constitutional Supervisory Committee itself; the USSR government did initiate suits, whereas most of the republican ones did not. The period of the Committee's operation coincided with the separatist movements and the pressures that led to the breakup of the USSR (Trochev, 2005, 75–79; 118–122; Brzezinski 1998; Mitiukov 2006).

Constitutional review represents a subject on which Yeltsin's Russian government moved ahead of the Soviet one. Already in 1990 discussion of a new Russian constitution began, and the Yeltsin team decided to outdo the Soviet government by establishing a full-fledged Constitutional Court. The decision was formalized in an amendment to the 1978 Constitution of the RSFSR in December 1990 and in the Law on the Constitutional Court of May 1991. The initial membership of the Court was approved by the Congress of Peoples Deputies in October 1991 (Trochev 2005a: 97–104). This was a proper Constitutional Court, with jurisdiction modeled on its German counterpart, including the review of petitions from citizens (concrete review) and decisions on the constitutionality of any law that were to be authoritative and binding. As it happened, by the time the Constitutional Court began work in 1992, Russia was already an independent "democratic" country.

During 1991, while the leaders of the USSR struggled to keep the country together, the Russian leaders under Yeltsin moved ahead with a reform agenda on many fronts, from economic to legal. Thus, in July 1991 the Russian government took the lead in converting the system of state *arbitrazh* into *arbitrazh* (or commercial) courts, this in recognition of the emerging legal private economy and its needs (Hendley 1998). More dramatic was the approval by the Supreme Soviet in October 1991 of the *Conception of Judicial Reform of the RSFSR.* Written by nine legal scholars, among them the leading criminal procedure specialists, the Conception (a 100-page critique of the justice system) called for a revamping of courts, prosecutions, and investigations to eliminate accusatorial bias and make the administration of justice fair. *Inter alia*, the *Conception* endorsed life appointments for judges, even broader judicial review of administrative acts. and a new role for courts in supervising pre-trial investigations, including approval of pre-trial detention; it also recommended improved funding of courts and the conversion of trials to an adversarial process, including the revival of trial by jury (Solomon and Foglesong 2000: 10–11). All this was to come on top of the achievement in 1990 of the right to counsel during the pre-trial phase.

Much (but not all) of the *Conception's* agenda for reform was realized during 1992–1993. Under the lead of Sergei Pashin, reform-oriented jurists in the presidential administration secured passage of legislation that gave judges life tenure (after a three-year probationary term), while retaining the system of judicial qualification commissions with the exclusive right to remove judges; established judicial review of pre-trial detention decisions by procurators; established trial by jury; and eliminated the remaining restrictions on judicial review of administrative acts, so that prior administrative remedies did not have to be tried before approaching a court (Solomon and Foglesong, 2000: Solomon 2004; Solomon and Foglesong 2000).

As a result, when the first Russian republic ended in December 1993 with the passage of a new Russian Constitution, Russia had courts designed to encourage judicial independence and empowered to deal with important issues of concern to powerful persons.

RUSSIAN COURTS IN AN AGE OF COMPETITIVE AUTHORITARIANISM

In the new millennium, the Second Russian republic – that is, the Russian government operating under the Constitution of 1993 – moved from an electoral (or perhaps delegated) democracy in the mid-1990s to a regime best described as "competitive authoritarian" or "electoral authoritarian." Throughout the period, the state has been weak, and from 1994 to 1999 there was considerable decentralization of power to the regional level, at which regional cliques (even clans) dominated the scene and the transfer of revenue to the center for redistribution became difficult. As president since 2000, Vladimir Putin has made every effort to reconstitute the power of the federal government and make the Russian Federation an effective state. However, in the process he chose to sacrifice democratic elements, such as competitive elections for governors and presidents, which in his view interfered with the creation of a reliable chain of political command, so essential in an age of clans and terrorism. Moreover, power in the centre became fully concentrated in the hands of the president and his staff, with the federal legislature coming under his control and the checks provided by federalism weakened.

In short, most observers of Russian politics in Russia and the West agree that Russia has rejoined the ranks of authoritarian states, albeit one with competition for some posts and some media freedom. At the same time, Russia possesses a court system that was designed for a democratic political order in the making. That is, it is a judicial system meant to produce independent courts and impartial adjudication, and one invested with responsibility for important decisions. As was the case in Tsarist Russia, so again the fit between the courts and the polity is imperfect, and there is every basis for tension and strain.

As of 2006 all attempts to reduce the power of courts had failed, and courts handled constitutional, administrative, and commercial cases. Moreover, some of the remaining obstacles to judicial independence, such as inadequate financing, have been removed. Yet, through a combination of new measures to hold judges accountable and the operation of informal institutions, most judges are held in check, and at least some observers argue that the independence of the courts remains compromised.

During the late 1990s, courts throughout the country were taking supplementary payments from local and regional governments to make up for financial shortfalls from the federal budget, which was meant to cover judicial salaries and court expenditures (Solomon and Foglesong 2000: 38–42). To President Putin, taking these payments threatened not just to make courts dependent, but dependent upon the wrong politicians and business leaders. In addition, judicial caseloads, especially of civil cases, were expanding rapidly. To his credit President Putin made funding of the courts a priority, and from 2001 the Russian government has provided large new sums to support expansion of the number of judges (including new justices of the peace), more staff support (new clerks, media officers), repair of court buildings, computerization of the court operations, and the development of Web sites and posting of court decisions. It has also supported expansion of the number and improved training for the bailiffs charted with implementing civil and commercial decisions. In announcing in 2001 and again in 2006 programs for the improvement of the courts, Putin cited as a prime rationale the need to provide a basis for secure property rights and encouragement for potential investors! (MERiT 2006; Solomon 2002).

This same rationale underlay efforts to reduce the appearance (and reality) of judicial corruption through enhancement of accountability. In 2002 the composition of the Judicial Qualification Commissions was changed to require that one-third of the members not be judges (so that judges would not protect their own), and in 2004 there was a serious proposal to increase that requirement to one-half (Solomon 2005: 329–331). The screening of judicial appointees by the presidential administration, especially to *arbitrazh* courts and positions of chair of court, was strengthened, with the unforeseen consequence that the appointment process took longer than a year (Trochev 2005b). In 2006 there were efforts to require judges to submit full financial disclosure, and possibly to disallow employment as judges to persons whose close family members worked as lawyers (Kornia 2006; Sterkin 2006).

Whether this barrage of measures would succeed in reducing the responsiveness of judges (especially on the *arbitrazh* courts) to powerful persons in regional governments or in private firms was uncertain. The situation in which chairs of courts were part of local and regional government circles, as well as beneficiaries, both personally and institutionally, of largesse from local sources, continued, as did the role of chairs as intermediaries between outside interests and judges heading particular cases. Judges depended upon their all-powerful chairs not only for perks and benefits (scheduled to be replaced by higher salaries) but also for good references in the promotion process. Moreover, chairs could always find pretexts for pursuing disciplinary requests, even firing, through the Judicial Qualification Commissions, which were usually responsive to their requests. Thus, if the head of a powerful firm in a region needed the cooperation of an *arbitrazh* court, his friends in the regional government might inform the chair of the court what was needed in the interests of the region (Solomon 2006).

If firms could not influence *arbitrazh* courts directly, in some cases they could nullify the impact of court decisions by ignoring them or failing to cooperate in their implementation. Voluntary compliance with debt collection judgments appears to be a rarity, and many executives know how to hide assets so that bailiffs charged with collection do not find them (Kahn 2002). For a decade or more, some businesses have relied on specialists in private enforcement, whether from the criminal world or (later on) legal firms. Such bodies often rely on intelligence connections to obtain information that would be potentially embarrassing to debtor firms and so gain their cooperation in an effort to avoid publicity or denunciation (Volkov 2002).

Not only *arbitrazh* courts but also the Constitutional Court has had difficulty ensuring compliance with its decisions. The Court keeps records of implementation of its decisions, and sometimes turns to the president or government for help in securing compliance. Part of the problem lies in the civil law tradition, whereby even court decisions holding all or part of a law unconstitutional may not be applied directly, but require a change in legislation. According to Russian law, decisions of the Constitutional Court are directly applicable by officials and other judges, and do not require legislative changes as an intermediate stage of implementation, but many officials and judges in Russia act as if this were not so. In addition, there is competition among different courts and court systems in Russia, as other courts dislike deferring to the Constitutional Court. Then, there is the simple assertion of raw power. The Mayor of Moscow, Yuri Luzhkov, ignored a series of decisions of the Constitutional Court of the Russian Federation that deemed his efforts to restrict residence in Moscow unconstitutional. It required intervention by

President Yeltsin to get the president of the republic of Udmurtia to respect a Constitutional Court decision invalidating a recently enacted procedure for choosing, as opposed to electing, mayors of cities. By 2006, most regional governments were yielding to Constitutional Court decisions on matters relating to federalism, but officials throughout Russia resist rights-related decisions, unless ordered to observe them by political superiors (Trochev, 2005; Solomon and Foglesong 2000: 76–80). The flow of appeals to the European Court of Human Rights in Strasbourg (where nearly 25 percent of cases come from Russia) seems to have had some impact.

Of course, one way to avoid irritating rulings of the Constitutional Court is to eliminate the power of constitutional review, which some enemies of the court tried to arrange in 2001. The origins of the attack lay, paradoxically, in proposed amendments to the Law on the Constitutional Court to ensure compliance with its decisions, especially by regional authorities whose legislation the Court had ruled unconstitutional, sometimes stipulating what changes were required. As the changes were being debated in the State Duma, individual legislators (Valery Grebennikov, Oleg Utkin, and Boris Nadezhdin) and the Committee on State Development as well (under Lukianov) began attacking *the very right of the Court to issue rulings binding upon other branches of government*, not to speak of creating legal norms. Some Duma deputies defended the Constitutional Court's prerogatives, but the play of politics produced a dangerous situation, whereby in November 2002 the Duma Committee actually approved proposals that would deprive the Court of its essential power and convert it into an advisory body!

Members of the Constitutional Court (Baglai, Sliva, and Morshchakova) were forced to campaign against the threatened changes in both public forums and directly with the president. Any limit to the binding force of Constitutional Court decisions, they explained, would represent the end of constitutional justice in Russia. Morshchakova warned that, should the changes be introduced, they might be challenged in the Constitutional Court, which was likely to invalidate them. The resistance to potential undermining of the Constitutional Court proved successful, and the relevant Duma factions forced the authors of the offending amendments to withdraw them (Trochev 2002). What happened behind the scenes, including the role of the president in this process, is unknown. But this was not the first time in its young life that the Constitutional Court had to fight for its existence; in October 2003 the work of the CC was suspended for a year and a half after the Court attempted to stop Yeltsin's seizure of power (Sharlet 2003; Trochev 2002).

The Constitutional Court has a reputation as the most independent of all Russian courts, at least from the direct influence of interested parties (Russian

Axis 2003). But its members are keenly aware of the political context in which they operate, including the power of the presidency and the challenge of securing implementation of their decisions. There is every indication that they think strategically, looking beyond individual cases to the larger matter of their court's and judicial authority. In recent years the court has not opposed the president on important issues, such as the constitutionality of the elimination of gubernatorial elections, although a couple of dissenting judges articulated the case against it. (Back in Yeltsin's time the court approved the legality of the first Chechen war). Still, for a Constitutional Court to stand back from engaging in hot political issues does not mean that it is impotent. Arguably, any successful court involved in constitutional litigation must pick its fights with the other branches of government carefully, and not move too far ahead of political or public opinion (McCloskey 1994). Political tact aside, the record of the Russian Constitutional Court overall is admirable, especially given the conditions under which it works. The Constitutional Court of the Russian Federation has done far better than its counterpart constitutional courts in most post-Soviet countries.

Administrative justice must be counted one of the great success stories of post-Soviet judicial reform. In 1993 the requirement to use administrative alternatives before going to court was removed, and in 1995 the definition of officials against whose actions one could complain was broadened. The result was a wide open right to challenge the actions of officials, along with the right to challenge most regulations as well. By 2002 there were hundreds of thousands of complaints against the actions of officials heard in various courts, including military ones, and complainants won in some 70 percent of their attempts! This rate of success was much better than obtained by persons who complained to the Procuracy, who registered around a 25 percent success rate (Solomon 2004).

In addition, after a string of court decisions and legislative changes to boot, most normative acts below legislation were subject to review by some court. Not only regulations from ministries but also resolutions of the cabinet ministers (as long as they do not represent delegated legislation, so that the Constitutional Court has jurisdiction) and even presidential edicts are subject to review by the Supreme Court (though none of the latter has ever been overruled; Konstitutsionnnyi sud RF 2004). Between 1999–2002, the Supreme Court satisfied challenges to the legality of regulations, in whole or in part, in one-third of cases. According to Anton Burkov (2005), the actions of the Supreme Court in reviewing the legality of regulations had come to constitute a source of administrative law (Solomon 2004: 570–571). While the impulse to develop broad judicial review of administrative actions and regulations reflected a

progressive concern with limiting arbitrary actions by officials, the practice
also served the interests of the political leadership. The current efforts (from
2005 on) to establish a separate hierarchy of administrative courts, including
the power of higher ones to hold governors and mayors to account, appealed
directly to those interests (Starovoitov 2005).

One institution of post-Soviet Russian judicial reform that some authorities
find hard to tolerate is trial by jury. Started in 1993, and spread to all regional
courts for use in serious criminal cases like murder and rape and even political
charges a decade later, jury trials take away from authorities the near certainty
of conviction, and hence an element of power. In contrast to judges sitting
alone who render acquittals in such cases in 0.4 percent of trials, juries acquit
in 15–20 percent of trials and insist on leniency (as their right) in others.
Many of the acquittals stem not from prosecution of the wrong person but
from weak gathering and presentation of evidence, and at least a third of the
acquittals are reversed on appeal by panels of the Supreme Court. All the
same, law enforcement personnel including procurators get frustrated at their
loss of control (power) over the trials, and in some cases (especially political
ones) have allegedly arranged to have juries stacked with the right people or to
influence individual jurors. A public debate in 2005–2006 about the wisdom of
retaining juries reveals much about the misfit between democratic institutions
and the larger authoritarian political environment (Solomon 2005; Roshchin
2006; Kommersant 2006; Iakovlev 2006; Nikitinskii 2006; Brabii 2006.)

Overall, though, as of fall 2006, Russia has courts that are empowered in
significant areas and sufficiently independent at to act impartially in most cases.
At the same time, especially through the operation of informal institutions,
judges do sometimes experience pressure and come to conform to the wishes
of powerful persons in cases that matter to them (the Khodorkovsky trials are
a case in point). The result is a public perception that the courts are not
sufficiently independent. Through public relations efforts the reputation of
the courts may improve, but the vulnerability of judges to pressure will not
end as long as the political order remains authoritarian.

Another dimension to judicial power in Russia relates to its government's
membership in the Council of Europe and its consequent vulnerability to suits
brought to the European Court of Human Rights (ECHR) in Strasbourg. As
of summer 2006 the ECHR has ruled in a couple of dozen cases from Russia,
but often against the state in favor of private litigants, and there were literally
thousands of cases from Russia waiting to be examined, numbering close to
one-quarter of the cases submitted to the Court (Sova, 2006; Grigoreva 2006;
Matveeva 2006). Some of the cases from Russia were products of the work
of NGOs, notably the talented group of young lawyers who constituted the

Ekaterinburg-based firm Sutiazhnik (Sutiazhnik, 2005; Burkov 2006). Embarrassed by the results, the Russian government asked the courts to reduce their vulnerability to Strasbourg appeals, and already in 2003 the top courts issued a resolution calling for wide distribution of Russian translations of Strasbourg court decisions and for judges to pay heed to their lessons (Verkhovnyi sud, 2003). At the same time, Russian authorities see the Strasbourg Court as a resource for its enemies (excessive legal mobilization is not part of Russian tradition), and they are trying to change the ground rules for Strasbourg appeals in their favor.

To the extent that Russia's submission to Council of Europe norms stems from its desire for full membership in the international community, especially economic bodies like the WTO, an interest in foreign investment is at play. What will be the ultimate consequences of the Strasbourg court connection for Russia's legal and political systems is a question for future analysis.

CONCLUSION

Russian experience, under three different regimes, confirms that authoritarian rulers not only need courts to perform their basic functions but also choose at times to empower courts with sensitive jurisdiction. However, unless judicial independence is well established, the empowerment of courts (in whatever form) may lead to efforts to manage or control their handling of the new jurisdiction, often at the expense of judicial independence. Perhaps, some authoritarian rulers avoid these tensions by willingly giving up their power to the courts. But the alternative scenario of attempts to seek to influence how judges handle the new jurisdiction, in general or in specific cases, is equally if not more likely.

Both Tsarist Russia and post-Soviet Russia provide illuminating stories of the limits of judicial power and independence in authoritarian settings – in the first instance, a classic, though liberalizing, autocracy; in the second instance, a "competitive authoritarian" regime, in which democratic forms are prominent, but the urge of rulers to keep or regain power remains strong. In Tsarist Russia the desire of key officials to bring Russian government up to European standards, along with the Tsar's readiness to respond to the gentry's demands for courts that would ensure that they received full compensation for the emancipation of the serfs, led to the establishment of independent and empowered courts, which in their initial form were incompatible with the system of rule.

The post-Soviet story, of course, is ongoing, and how the tensions between a form of authoritarian rule and courts shaped for democracy will play out is far from certain. It is possible that the core of judicial reform will remain in place, and that sensitive jurisdictions will remain in the hands of the courts, if only to maintain legitimacy of the regime (which has no ideological alternative) and to give investors the impression of secure property rights. At the same time, as long as the dominant style of rule is authoritarian, it is hard to imagine real change in the informal practices and institutions that keep courts responsive to powerful interests and prevent judges from acting impartially in all cases.

11

Courts in Semi-Democratic/Authoritarian Regimes: The Judicialization of Turkish (and Iranian) Politics

Hootan Shambayati

Turkey is not a typical authoritarian or democratic regime. For much of the past six decades Turkey has held regular multiparty and reasonably free and fair elections. Power has changed hands numerous times, and governments have come to office and left as a result of elections. Furthermore, even though the Turkish military has intervened in the political process on a number of occasions, unlike in most other developing countries, the periods of direct military rule have been relatively short (1960–1962 and 1980–1983). Finally, for much of the past half-century, Turkey has had lively social and political societies that have acted with relative freedom, although major shortcomings continue to plague both. There is much to suggest that Turkey should be classified as a democracy.

At the same time, however, it is widely recognized that the Turkish political system displays authoritarian tendencies and that the military continues to play an important role in Turkish politics. The Turkish military has formally intervened in politics on four occasions (1960, 1971, 1980, and 1997). In 1960 and 1980, the military officially assumed the reins of power, while in the other two instances it limited itself to issuing a series of ultimatums that eventually brought down the governments of the day without formally interrupting the democratic experience.

The 1960 and 1980 military coups were followed by attempts to restructure political and social life through new constitutions. The military's desire to redesign the political and social life of the polity is, of course, a common feature of many military interventions. Military interventions are frequently reactions to what officers believe to be the shortcomings of the political system and are often followed by attempts to fundamentally alter the basis of the political system. In the Turkish case, the short periods of military rule have meant that the military has had to limit itself to altering the formal rules of the game while leaving the implementation of more deep-rooted changes until after the return to civilian rule. Consequently, creating a constitutional setup that allowed it to continue to influence civilian politicians and intervene in the political process was one of the major goals of the military leadership in both the 1960 and the 1980 military coups.

On each occasion the military regime imposed a new constitution on the nation before formally returning power to civilian politicians. Despite some major differences in the area of rights and liberties, the military-inspired 1961 and 1982 constitutions both display the fundamental distrust of the state elite toward politics and politicians (Özbudun 2000: 53–60). As I discuss below, both constitutions recognized the legitimacy of elections and elected officials, but at the same time tried to limit the effectiveness of elected institutions by subjecting them to control by a network of unelected institutions. In the view of military officers and high-ranking bureaucrats, including many jurists, self-interested politicians could not be trusted with serving the national interest. Accordingly, both constitutions were designed to limit the powers of the parliament and elected institutions by subjecting them to control by unelected state institutions.

In their attempts to restrict the powers of the parliament, both constitutions not only provided the military with formally recognized mechanisms to intervene in day-to-day policymaking but also empowered the judiciary to review the decisions of the parliament and the elected governments. As I discuss below, this division of sovereignty between elected and unelected institutions has contributed to the judicialization of Turkish politics and has led to the emergence of Turkish courts, particularly the Constitutional Court and the Council of State, as important political institutions that have often used their powers to counteract the parliament.

The division of sovereignty between elected and unelected institutions, of course, is not unique to Turkey and can be found in many regimes. Nor is it the function of a particular ideology. The prototype of such regimes is the Islamic Republic of Iran where the powers of the elected parliament and the president are subject to review by a web of institutions controlled by a religiously empowered Supreme Leader. As I discuss at the end of this chapter, in Iran too this political structure has contributed to the judicialization of politics.

Since the bulk of this chapter deals with the Turkish case, I begin with a brief discussion of the main characteristics of military-inspired judicial empowerments. I will argue that military regimes might be particularly interested in empowering the courts to become active in the political arena after the military's return to the barracks. I will then proceed to discuss the specifics of the Turkish political system and the role of the judiciary in Turkish politics. The final section of the chapter briefly discusses the Iranian case.

MILITARY-INSPIRED JUDICIAL EMPOWERMENT

Both Bruce Ackerman and Tom Ginsburg have argued that judicial review is associated with weak militaries (Ackerman 1997; Ginsburg 2003: 83). A similar conclusion can be reached based on Ran Hirschl's "hegemonic preservation thesis." According to Hirschl, waning political actors will choose to empower the courts to maintain hegemony in the event they lose control of the Parliament (Hirschl 2004). While a strong military, or for that matter any other strong actor, need not rely on the courts to protect its interest while in power, a military regime might have strong incentives to empower the courts before leaving office. Furthermore, political systems based on competitive elections with unelected "guardians," such as those found in Turkey and Iran, require a network of institutions that often include the courts to control elected institutions without undermining the stature of the guardians as allegedly above politics.

The military does not face the same dilemmas faced by civilian political institutions when empowering the courts. When civilian executives and legislators create constitutional tribunals, they are creating organizations that limit their own powers. When the military empowers the judiciary it creates an institution that limits the powers of civilian institutions without necessarily affecting the position of the armed forces. First, the military's core internal concerns, such as training or promotion, are likely to be outside the competence of the civilian judicial institutions, including constitutional tribunals. In the Turkish case, for example, the 1982 Constitution forbids the civilian courts from reviewing decisions of the Supreme Military Council.[1]

Second, the military is not equally interested in all policy areas. The military is likely to be much more interested in security and order than in public health or price controls, for example. Not only have the courts generally accommodated security needs but also an outgoing military regime can put in place rules and regulations that are exempt from review by judicial authorities. Until its amendment in 2001, for example, the 1982 Turkish Constitution prevented the courts from reviewing the constitutionality of laws and regulations put in place by the military regime.

Third, particularly in civil law countries, the military might see the judiciary as a natural ally in the post-transition period. Like the military, the judiciary in the civil law tradition is a hierarchical organization performing a "technical" role. Judges enter the judicial service shortly after completing their legal education and spend their entire careers within the judiciary. Like military officers, judges see their role as technical and believe that they are merely

---

[1] Article 125.

applying the law. Judges are trained to view law and politics as two completely distinct arenas. Furthermore, as in the military, the promotion of judicial personnel in the civil law tradition has historically been controlled by the more senior judges, producing an ideologically homogeneous institution with a strong *esprit de corps* that identifies strongly with the state and sees politics and politicians as divisive and corrupt. In short, the military and the judiciary might share a number of common values and assumptions about politics and politicians (Correa Sutil 1993; Galleguillos 1998; Guarnieri and Pederzoli 2002: 49; Hilbink 1999, 2001; Tate 1993).

Finally, an outgoing military regime can create constitutional tribunals and other judicial institutions that will be inclined to give the military's point of view the most favorable of hearings. Self-interested political actors adopt judicial review as an "insurance policy" to protect their interest in the event of future electoral losses (Ginsburg 2003: 25). The institutional design of the judiciary and the high courts, like those of other institutions in a democracy, depends on the relative strength and the interest of the political actors (Ginsburg 2003; Magalhaes 1999: 43; Smithey and Ishiyama 2000, 2002). Their ideal institutional design will produce judicial actors who will be partial to their interest whether they are in or out of power.

Two aspects of judicial institutions are of particular interest to political actors. First, judicial appointment procedures affect the ability of dominant political actors to appoint like-minded judges or to prevent the appointment of judges whose preferences they do not like. Second, the rules governing judicial careers and the institutions that manage those careers determine the judiciary's responsiveness to political actors. As Magalhaes, Guarnieri, and Kaminis (2007) conclude, "The control of a system of punishments and rewards associated to judicial careers (promotion, assignment, recall) . . . can be used to condition judicial behavior, independently of the actual composition of courts and the policy preferences of judges."

Civilian political actors' preferred institutional design depends on their estimate of their own political prospects under the democratic regime (Magalhaes 1999; Smithey and Ishiyama 2000). In East European countries where the outgoing Communist parties expected to hold onto power by winning the upcoming free elections, they were willing to increase the oversight powers of the political branches over the judiciary. Where they expected to lose the elections, however, they tended to isolate the judiciary from the political branches. Where the incumbent rulers were uncertain of their prospects under the democratic regime, they were more likely to provide a role for the opposition in appointing judges and less likely to introduce sweeping institutional changes (Magalhaes 1999: 47–48).

Transitions from military rule follow a similar logic. However, in these cases the picture is more complex. As a unit of the state, the military will be reincorporated into the state apparatus after the transition and can be certain of its continued participation in the state under the democratic regime. However, the military, unlike civilian authoritarian institutions such as Communist parties, cannot reorganize itself to compete in democratic elections. An outgoing military regime is an actor with no expectation of winning elected office, but certain of the military's continued influence under the new regime. As the Turkish case demonstrates, in such cases the tendency will be toward the creation of politically powerful judicial institutions to act as guardians of the military-sponsored constitutional order without directly involving the military. At the same time, however, the outgoing military regime will try to minimize the influence of the political branches in the affairs of the judiciary, including appointments to the high courts.

THE TURKISH POLITICAL SYSTEM

In 1998, when veteran politician and many times prime minister Süleyman Demirel occupied the presidential office, he was asked to comment on a growing crisis between the then-prime minister Mesut Yilmaz and the military leadership. According to published reports Demirel replied with the following story:

> In an English zoo there was an experiment to have wolves and sheep live together in one cage. Someone asked the director if the experiment was working. The director replied, yes, but occasionally we have to replace the sheep (Bila 1998).

Mr. Demirel should know. As prime minister he had been removed from office by the military in 1971 and 1980; as president he had presided over the military-engineered downfall of the Islamist Welfare party government in June 1997 and the party's eventual closure by the Constitutional Court in January 1998.

As the story above suggests, Turkey is an example of what Daniel Brumberg has called "dissonant institutionalization." According to Brumberg "dissonant institutionalization occurs when competing images of political community and the symbolic systems legitimating them are reproduced in the formal and informal institutions of state and society" (Brumberg 2001: 33–34). As a consequence, systems based on dissonant institutionalization are likely to produce high levels of political tension.

In the Turkish case, dissonant institutionalization has led to a bifurcated political system, where parts of the system aim at transforming the society, while others try to maintain the status quo. The consequence has been a high level of tension between what the Turks refer to as the State (*devlet*), consisting of the security establishment, the presidency, the judiciary, and parts of the civilian bureaucracy, and the government (*hükümet*), consisting of the elected Parliament and cabinet. The management of the resultant tensions is a fundamental concern of the political system.

At the same time, however, the system's continued survival depends on maintaining a high level of tensions between the competing institutions. While the continued coexistence of the wolves and the sheep in the same cage requires mechanisms to keep the two separate from each other, it also needs constant justification. As I have discussed elsewhere, "a regime based on divided sovereignty must prevent social and political tensions from boiling over and threatening the stability of the system, while at the same time generating enough tensions to justify the continued presence of both heads of the executive" (Shambayati 2004).

Regimes such as that found in Turkey are particularly vulnerable to societal challenges. Dissonant institutionalization is an indication that the ideological basis of the regime is weak (Brumberg 2001). In the Turkish case, the state is officially based on Kemalism. Kemalism, however, has never evolved into a full-fledged coherent ideology.

Kemalism aims at transforming society, particularly in areas such as secularism and nationalism, or, in the words of Ataturk, to bring the people to "the level of contemporary civilization."[2] The Turkish state elites see the state and the law as mechanisms for the transformation of society and often find themselves at odds with powerful societal actors whose interests are threatened by the civilizing mission. Furthermore, as the emergence of a modernist Islamist movement and Kurdish nationalism suggests, state policies have had unintended consequences and have led to the emergence of new social and political movements that are not easily incorporated into the existing political structure. From the perspective of the state elite, including many judges, the proper function of the courts is to defend the civilizing mission against potential threats from society, even if at times that means acting against the will of the nation as expressed through elections.

Dissonant institutionalization also contributes to judicialization at another level. As the story of the wolves and the lambs demonstrates, the division of

---

[2] This oft-repeated phrase is from a speech delivered by Ataturk on the Occasion of the Tenth Anniversary of the Foundation of the Turkish Republic (29 October 1933). See http://www.allaboutturkey.com/ata_speech.htm

sovereignty between elected and unelected executives is public and formally sanctioned. Both the Constitutions of 1961 and 1982 and other laws provided for a military-dominated National Security Council as an important part of the decision-making process and gave the military considerable power in the formulation and implementation of policies through a variety of nonpolitical regulatory and supervisory boards, such as the Higher Education Board and the Board of Radio and Television. The Turkish military is not merely the "guardian of the system," but is an active participant in the political decision-making process.

Nor is the military shy about its political role. In fact, suggestions that the military might not be interested in a given political issue are often met with a statement from the high command denying the lack of interest. For example, a few months prior to the selection of a new president by the Parliament in 2000, the chief of the general staff declared that it was "inconceivable that the military would not have an opinion on who will be the next president" (*Hürriyet*, 15 April 2000). Similarly, in 2003 when a meeting between the Commander of the Land Forces and a group of university rectors who opposed a government proposal to reform the Higher Education Board and the university entrance requirements caused a public controversy, the general staff circulated a formal statement that read "it is natural that developments pertaining to the national education system, which is of vital importance for Turkey, are followed by the General Staff" (*Turkish Daily News*, September 16, 2003)

Furthermore, the military's role is accepted as legitimate by a large segment of the political leadership and the public in general. For example, the military statements quoted above were immediately justified by the political leadership as "natural." In the first instance, as the then-prime minister Bülent Ecevit put it, "it is only natural that the military will be interested in these elections especially when the president is also the commander in chief of the armed forces and the head of the National Security Council" (*Turkish Daily News*, 16 April 2000). Similarly, the main opposition party (the Republican People's Party) characterized the rectors' meeting with the generals "as very normal" (*Turkish Daily News*, 16 September 2003)

Despite its influence, the fact that the military has to share power with popularly elected politicians means that it can only be effective if it can maintain its above-politics stature in public's mind. The framers of the Turkish constitutions tried to achieve this objective by transferring potentially contentious policy debates away from the Parliament and entrusting them to the so-called neutral institutions such as courts. As Haggard and Kaufman have argued, regimes with guardians create "insulated decision-making structures that can be counted on to pursue [the guardian's] policy agenda" (Haggard and Kaufman 1995: 121).

Judicial Empowerment in Turkey

The empowerment of the judiciary in Turkey dates back to the military-inspired Constitution of 1961, when "the judiciary was given a considerable share in the exercise of sovereignty" (Aybay 1977: 24). This so-called liberal constitution was a reaction to what many believed to have been serious abuses of political power by the elected Democratic Party governments (1950–1960) that had necessitated the 1960 military intervention. Like their counterparts in some other developing countries, the Turkish military turned to the legal community to legitimate the military intervention. As Rona Aybay notes, "one of the most interesting aspect of the May 27 [1960] coup is its legalistic tendency" (Aybay 1977: 21). Within hours after the coup the junta asked for and received the endorsement of a group of law professors who issued a rather lengthy statement in support of the coup. The statement in part read as follows:

> It is not right to regard the situation in which we find ourselves today as an ordinary political *coup d'Ètat*. The political power which should represent the conception of State, law, justice, morality, public interest and public service and should protect public interests had for months, even years, lost this character, and had become a material force representing personal power and ambition and class interests.
>
>   The power of the State, which before all else should be a social power bound by law, was transformed into an instrument of this ambition and power. For this reason this political power lost all its moral ties with its army . . . with its courts and the bar, with its officials who wanted to be loyal to their duties, with its universities, and with its press which represents public opinion, and with all its other social institutions and forces, and fell into a position hostile to the State's genuine and main institutions, and to Ataturk's reforms, which are of extraordinary value and importance if Turkey is to occupy a worthy place among the nations of the world as a civilized State (cited in Ahmad 1977: 162–163).

The experiences of the 1950s and the coup had convinced the military leadership and their civilian allies that the new constitutional structure should impose limits on the powers of the Parliament and prevent any single party from dominating the government. To meet this requirement, the 1961 Constitution adopted a new concept of sovereignty. Article 4 of the Constitution declared,

> Sovereignty is vested in the nation without reservation and condition. The nation shall exercise its sovereignty through the authorized agencies as prescribed by the principles laid down in the Constitution.

These words were repeated in article 6 of the 1982 Constitution and, as the official history of the Constitutional Court interprets them, were meant, "to put an end to the principle of the supremacy of the parliament."[3]

The 1961 Constitution took two steps to operationalize this provision. First, it increased the internal autonomy of some institutions such as universities and the radio and television authority and imposed severe limits on the ability of the Parliament to interfere in their internal affairs. Similarly, in an attempt to increase the independence of the judiciary, the newly established Supreme Council of Judges was given the responsibility to administer all judicial personnel matters (Devereux 1965). Furthermore, to further protect the autonomy of the universities and the judiciary, the constitution authorized the two institutions to petition the Turkish Constitutional Court (TCC), another new institution, in matters relating to their own functions.

Second, the 1961 Constitution divided sovereignty among a number of newly created institutions. Chief among these was the newly established National Security Council, which for the first time provided a formal venue for military participation in political decisions. In the judicial arena, the constitution enhanced the powers of the Council of State, an administrative court dating back to the Ottoman era and modeled after the French *conseil d'etat*, and created a Constitutional Court.

The establishment of the Constitutional Court was achieved with little controversy. The idea for a constitutional court with the power to review the constitutionality of legislative acts was first proposed in the mid-1950s by the Republican People's Party (RPP; McCally 1956), which as the main opposition party suffered the most under Democratic Party rule, and had little difficulty in passing through the RPP-dominated constituent assembly (Kili 1971: 139). Modeled after continental European constitutional courts, the Constitutional Court "was expected to counterbalance political institutions, especially the parliament, which would abuse their powers."[4]

The 1961 Constitution was "a last-ditch effort by the bureaucratic intelligentsia to set the substantive, as well as the procedural, rules of the political game in Turkey" (Heper 1985: 89). It tried to enhance the autonomy of the state by protecting it against interest-based politics. Although it granted the right of political participation, it also created bureaucratically staffed agencies to act as watchdogs over political institutions. Accordingly, in their structures and powers the TCC and other judicial organs reflected a constitutional design

---

[3] These words had originally appeared in a 1977 article by Rona Aybay (Aybay 1977: 23) and were repeated without attribution on the TCC's Web site.

[4] Official Web page.

that assumed a fundamental "mistrust of the organs dependent upon universal suffrage" (Aybay 1977: 24).

The consequence has been that the Turkish courts have not shied away from challenging the Parliament and elected officials. Between 1962 and 1980 the TCC reviewed 350 petitions for abstract review and annulled 37 percent of them (Shambayati 2008). In its attempts to the "tame the Parliament" the TCC was joined by the Council of State, which annulled 1,400 governmental decrees between 1965 and 1971 (Heper 1985: 92). The hyperactivity of the courts in the pre-1980 period led to charges that the courts were making it impossible for the governments of the day to govern and undoubtedly contributed to the political tensions and instability that finally resulted in the September 12, 1982, military takeover (Ahmad 1977; Dodd 1983).

Once again the period of direct military takeover was short, and power was returned to elected civilian officials within three years. Again, the military tried to restructure political and social life by introducing a new constitution. In the rising political polarization of the 1960s and the 1970s the internal autonomy of the universities and other institutions proved destabilizing, and the 1982 Constitution reversed the trend. This, however, did not result in an increase in the powers of the Parliament. Instead the 1982 Constitution relied on a number of so-called "neutral" institutions and commissions such as the Higher Education Board to administer the previously autonomous institutions.[5] A common feature of these institutions is that until the recent EU-inspired reforms they included a military representative on their boards.

The 1982 Constitution not only maintained the division of sovereignty introduced in 1961, but further limited the powers of the Parliament by stripping it of its appointment powers and transferring them to the president, an indirectly elected nonpartisan figure. This enhancement of presidential powers was designed to increase the military's influence. Under the new constitution, the leader of the military junta, General Evren, automatically assumed the presidency upon its formal adoption.[6] Furthermore, the framers hoped that the pre-coup practice of the Parliament choosing a retired military officer for the presidency would continue. Although of the four men who have occupied the office since 1983, Evren is the only one with a military background, the presidency, particularly under its current occupant Ahmet Necdet Sezer, a former president of the TCC, continues to be identified with the state and

---

[5] This controversial body is charged with supervising universities and was first introduced in the 1970s, but was ruled unconstitutional by the Constitutional Court because it violated the constitutionally guaranteed principle of the autonomy of the universities. It was given constitutional status in the 1982 Constitution.

[6] Provisional Article 1.

acts as a brake on the powers of the Parliament. As the next section shows, the changes in the powers of the president were also designed to reduce the influence of the Parliament over the judiciary.

The Judiciary After 1982

The 1982 Constitution maintained the basic division of sovereignty introduced by its predecessor and further enhanced the role of nonelected institutions in the decision-making process. The earlier constitution had relied on a number of institutions in which members appointed by the Parliament and those appointed by the various state agencies jointly exercised power. This cooperative structure, however, proved unsatisfactory as political tensions and violence continued to increase in the 1960s and the 1970s. Therefore, the 1982 Constitution abandoned the cooperative framework in support of a new structure that sharply reduced the role of the Parliament in determining the membership of the so-called neutral institutions and boards while increasing the role of state institutions. The most dramatic example was the National Security Council whose powers were greatly enhanced and in which the number of military members was increased at the expense of the civilian wing.[7]

A similar design was introduced for judicial institutions. Table 11.1 shows the appointment procedures for various judicial institutions. Under the 1961 Constitution the two houses of parliament appointed one-third of the members of the Supreme Council of Judges and Public Prosecutors and one-third of the justices of the Constitutional Court. The 1982 Constitution, however, under the guise of protecting the independence of the courts completely eliminated the role of the Parliament as either a nominating or an appointing body.[8]

Similarly, the 1982 Constitution reduced the number of judges on the Constitutional Court and drastically altered the appointment procedure. Under the original design, the Parliament appointed five of the justices while the other high courts and the president appointed the other ten permanent justices. Under the system in place since 1982, the Parliament and the cabinet have no role in the appointment process. Instead, the courts are the nominating bodies in the current system, while the president appoints all justices. For each seat the appropriate court submits a list of three candidates drawn from among its own justices and prosecutors to the president, who makes the final

---

[7] A series of constitutional amendments adopted since 2001 have increased the number of civilian members of the NSC in an attempt to "civilianize" the organization.

[8] The Minister of Justice and his deputy take part in the meetings of the council in an *ex officio* capacity.

TABLE 11.1 *Judicial appointment procedures*

Institution	1961 Constitution	1982 Constitution
Constitutional Court	Permanent 15 Substitute (5)	Permanent 11 Substitute (4)
Court of Cassation	4 (2)	2 (2) *nomination*
Council of State	3 (1)	2 (1) *nomination*
Court of Accounts	1	1 *nomination*
Military Court Cassation		1 *nomination*
Military Admin. Court		1 *nomination*
Higher Ed Council		1 *nomination*
Nat'l Assembly	3* (1)	0
Senate	2* (1)	NA
President	2**	11 (4)
Supreme Council of **Judges**	Permanent 18 Substitute (5)	Permanent 6 (Substitute 5)
Court of Cassation	6 (2)	3 (3) *nomination*
Judges of 1st rank	6 (1)	
Nat'l Assembly	3 (1)	
Senate	3 (1)	
Council of State	0	3 (2) *nomination*
President	0	6 (5)
Council of State		
Constitutional Court	All members	0
Supreme Council of Judges		$^3/_4$ of members
President		$^1/_4$ of members

* One has to be a member of the teaching staff of the departments of law, economics, or political science.
** One had to be a member of the Military Court of Cassation.
Figures in *italics* are nominations.

appointment. Finally, under the 1982 Constitution the military courts nominate two of the permanent justices of the TCC, a provision that is reminiscent of the Chilean Constitutional Tribunal in which the national security council appoints two of the justices.

The military was also given a role in the administration of justice through the controversial State Security Courts. The establishment of these courts had been a long-term military objective dating back to the coup by the memorandum of March 12, 1971 (Hale 1977: 187). They were established in 1973 through a constitutional amendment and special legislation to deal with the increasing political violence coming from both the right and the left of the political spectrum. In 1975, the Constitutional Court, acting on a petition from the Diyarbakir State Security Court, ruled that the tribunals were unconstitutional and ordered their closure.[9] The abolishment of these courts was given as a reason by the leaders of the 1980 coup as to why the 1961 Constitution was inadequate.

The framers of the 1982 Constitution revived the State Security Courts to deal with a wide range of crimes. Unlike ordinary courts, these courts were presided over by a panel of three judges, one of whom was a military judge appointed by the military courts. The Supreme Council of Judges and Public Prosecutors appointed the civilian judges and prosecutors. Until their final abolition in 2004 under pressure from the European Union and human rights organizations, these courts were one of the mainstays of the Turkish judicial system and used special procedures to try a wide range of crimes ranging from reciting politically provocative poetry[10] to acts of terrorism. Both their composition and their procedures were found to be in violation of numerous provisions of the European Convention on Human Rights and led to many rulings against Turkey by the European Court of Human Rights. At the same time, however, in the words of one prosecutor, they also "prevented many military coups" by satisfying the military's demands for harsh punishments for those accused of violating state security laws (*Turkish Daily News* February 20, 2001). Other judicial institutions have also contributed to fulfilling this function of the courts. As I discuss in the next section, the Constitutional Court and the Council of State have been particularly important in preventing direct military interventions. Through their rulings and public pronouncements both institutions have become important actors in the political arena.

The Courts in Action

The high wall between the judiciary and elected institutions erected by the 1982 Constitution and the judiciary's belief that it has a share in the exercise of sovereignty have turned Turkey into one of the most judicialized polities to be found in the modern world. On average the Constitutional Court issues a judgment for annulment in 76 percent of the cases that it receives for abstract review. As in other countries with abstract review procedures, most petitions for review are made by the opposition party, although Turkey's current president

---

[9] Although the original petition was partially based on the principle of the unconstitutionality of extraordinary tribunals, the TCC based its decision on procedural grounds.

[10] This was the charge against Turkey's current Prime Minister Recep Tayyip Erdogan, who served four months in jail after being convicted by the Diyarbakir State Security Court in 1999 (see Shambayati 2004).

Ahmet Necdet Sezer, himself a former president of the Constitutional Court, has also been very active in sending legislative acts to the TCC for review (Hazama 1996; Shambayati 2007).

The high success rate of the abstract review petitions is no doubt in part due to the fact that many provisions of the 1982 Constitution are no longer applicable to today's Turkey. Furthermore, both the process of integration with the EU and the privatization of the economy have required economic and political reforms that were not foreseen by the framers of the constitution. "Radical reforms," as Stone Sweet notes, "strain or tear the web of existing legal regimes, administrative practices, and case law" (Stone Sweet 2000: 52). Radical reforms, by definition, create tensions in the society and encourage an appeal to the courts. The law and the judiciary, however, are reactionary institutions that do not welcome reforms easily (di Federico and Guarnieri 1988: 168; Stone Sweet 1992: 39).

At the same time, however, the frequent rulings against the Parliament also point to a fundamental distrust between elected and unelected institutions inherent in the Turkish system. The distrust between the judiciary and politicians is evident not only in the frequent rulings of the Constitutional Court against the Parliament but also in its frequent public warnings to the ruling governments of the day not to violate the basic principles of Kemalism, particularly when it comes to secularism and national unity. Since the election of the Islamist Justice and Development Party (AKP) in 2002, for example, high-level justices have repeatedly warned the government not to try to lift the ban on the wearing of headscarves in the universities, an issue that is very important to the party's supporters. The strongest warning came from the president of the TCC in 2005, who used the anniversary of the Court's founding to warn the government that changing the law would be unconstitutional and that even a constitutional amendment would not suffice. He went on to remind the government that the Court has closed other political parties for violating the principles of secularism[11] (*Hürriyet* April 24, 2005). In effect, the president of the TCC was reminding the government that in a "militant democracy" like Turkey, the courts sometimes go beyond the text of the constitution to protect the regime.

An important aspect of protecting the Turkish democracy has been the frequent closure of political parties (Arslan 2002; Koçak and Örücü 2003; Kogacioglu 2003, 2004). Since 1983, the TCC has closed eighteen political

---

[11] This, of course, was a reference to the fate of the Justice and Development Party's predecessor, the Welfare Party, which was forced from office by the military in June 1997 and closed by the Court in January 1998.

parties. The Court has been particularly tough on Islamist and pro-Kurdish parties and has accused them of undermining secularism and the unity of the country. In closing these parties, as Dicle Kogacioglu has argued, the court has been participating "in shaping the boundaries as well as the content of the political process" (Kogacioglu 2004: 459).

The Constitutional Court is not alone in this task. Other courts, too, often use their powers to shape the content of politics. An example is a controversial ruling by the Council of State in October 2005 that argued that a kindergarten teacher could not be promoted because she wore a headscarf on her way to work. Although there are no laws that ban the wearing of the Islamic headscarf in public and the court recognized that the teacher in question had abided by the current regulations that forbid the wearing of headscarves in schools and government offices, it nevertheless argued that promoting her would set a bad example for the children in her charge and could undermine the secular basis of the state. Behind the Council's decision was, of course, the secular establishment's concern that the ruling AK party was systematically promoting its supporters into positions of influence in the state bureaucracy and was relaxing state regulations on religious practices.

This ruling caused a mini-crisis in Turkish politics when, in May 2006, a lawyer with ties to Islamist circles opened fire in one of the Council chambers, killing one of the justices and wounding four others. The shooting was greeted with much apprehension in Turkey, and both civilian and military leaders rushed to support the Council of State to show their solidarity with the judiciary. The president of the Council issued a statement that criticized the government's policies on secularism, blamed the attack on the government's criticism of the Council's original decision, and portrayed the attack as an attack on the secular state. The next day, large demonstrations were organized at Ataturk's mausoleum where representatives of various segments of the society including the political parties and the military gathered to defend the secular basis of the state. Public statements issued by the military, the president, and various judicial bodies emphasized the need to stay vigilant against religious reactionaries and pointed the finger at the ruling Islamist Justice and Development Party.

This tragic and inexcusable attack points to one of the shortcomings of attempts to resolve political differences through court rulings. Despite numerous rulings by the Council of State, the Constitutional Court, and the European Court of Human Rights, all of which have upheld the provisions banning headscarves in universities and state offices, the issue continues to play a prominent role in Turkish politics. Religious and center-right parties, particularly when in opposition, have repeatedly used the issue to rally their supporters. On the other hand, the secular establishment and center-left parties have continuously presented these campaign promises as evidence of disregard for the rule of law and as threats to secularism, hence justifying the continued vigilance of the military and the judiciary in protecting the "civilizing mission" of the state.

Similarly, the closing of numerous political parties, cultural associations, and publications and the frequent jailing of political activists have only had limited success in eliminating social and political movements that challenge the ideology of the state. Closed political parties, particularly those with Islamist or pro-Kurdish social bases, quickly reorganize and appear under a new banner to challenge the boundaries imposed by the state. The continued survival of these movements, and in the case of Islamist and pro-Kurdish political parties their ability to win elections, in turn is used to justify the need to vigilantly protect the civilizing mission of the state.

Even when the courts have ruled against the state, and there are many such instances, the rulings have tended to legitimate the continued division of sovereignty. In the mid-1990s, for example, when a number of prominent secular intellectuals were assassinated or attacked by terrorists with links to fundamentalist religious circles, the Council of State ruled that the state had failed to provide adequate protection to the individuals involved and therefore was liable (Orucu 2000: 694). Although on the face of it these rulings were victories against the state, they, of course, underlined the continued threat to secularism and the inability of the elected governments to deal with it.

In short, in Turkey's bifurcated political system the courts play an important role in protecting the civilizing mission of the state and maintaining the division of sovereignty between elected and unelected institutions. As the brief discussion of the Iranian case in the next section demonstrates, this situation is not unique to Turkey and is a function of the dissonant institutionalization in the political system rather than any particular ideology.

COURTS IN THE ISLAMIC REPUBLIC OF IRAN

The Iranian constitution of 1979 recognizes God as the only legitimate source of sovereignty.[12] Nevertheless, the dynamics of a mass revolution and the pluralism of the Shia political thought and religious establishment meant that the framers of the constitution also had to recognize the people as a source of sovereignty (Chehabi 2001). Accordingly, the constitution created a number of elected institutions, including a Parliament and a president. As in

---

[12] Article 56.

Turkey, however, the power of the elected institutions is subject to supervision by unelected institutions. Whereas in Turkey this supervisory role is played by the military, in Iran it is the Supreme Leader who as the highest religio-political authority supervises all institutions of the state, including the Parliament and the presidency.[13] While the Parliament and the president represent the will of the nation as expressed through elections, the Supreme Leader draws his legitimacy from representing the sovereignty of God based on the doctrine of the guardianship of the jurisprudent (*velayat-i faqih*). The Iranian political structure hence is based on competing notions of sovereignty and includes institutions that are often at odds with each other (Brumberg 2001; Buchta 2000). Consequently, high levels of tension are endemic in the Iranian political system.

Similar to Turkey, the Iranian political system relies on a number of extrapolitical and semi-judicial institutions to manage the tensions created by "dissonant institutionalization." The most important actor in this regard is, of course, the Supreme Leader himself, who is the final arbiter in all disputes. The Supreme Leader, however, like the military in Turkey, can only play this role if he can publicly maintain an above-politics posture. Consequently, the Supreme Leader relies on a complex web of institutions to control elected institutions. Courts and court-like institutions are an integral part of this system and play an important role in both managing and maintaining the tension-ridden political structure.

Iran does not have a proper mechanism for constitutional review. The initial attempts to establish a constitutional court based on the French Constitutional Council were rejected in favor of a system unique to Iran. In the Iranian system the power to review the constitutionality of legislative acts belongs to the Council of Guardians. The Council of Guardians is simultaneously an upper legislative house, a constitutional council controlling the constitutionality of laws, and a religious assembly vetting un-Islamic ordinances and candidates. As the upper house of the Parliament, the Council has to approve all pieces of legislations before they can become law. In reviewing legislation, however, the council does not limit itself to political considerations, but also makes a final decision on the constitutionality of proposed acts. The constitution further instructs the Council to also assure that all legislation meets requirements prescribed by religious law.[14] In addition to these functions, the Council also

---

[13] Technically, the Supreme Leader is an indirectly elected official, since a popularly elected Assembly of Experts, consisting of religiously qualified members of the clergy, selects him. He is, however, completely unaccountable and serves for life.

[14] Article 91.

has the controversial duty to determine the qualifications of the candidates for the various elections in the Islamic Republic, including those for the presidency and the Parliament.

The structure of the Council and its procedures ensure that it closely follows the ideological line established by the Supreme Leader. Six members of the Council are religious scholars directly appointed by the Supreme Leader. The Council also includes six nonclerical members selected by the Parliament. However, the Parliament's role in determining the composition of the Council is limited by the constitutional requirement that the Head of the Judiciary, an official appointed by the Supreme Leader, nominates the candidates. On matters concerning constitutionality, all twelve members take part in decisions, but the support of three-fourths of the members of the Council is required for a ruling on the constitutionality of legislative acts. In other words, at least three clerical members must support a decision on constitutionality. Only the six clerical members, on the other hand, conduct reviews based on Islamic law, and those decisions are made by a simple majority.[15]

Through the Council, the conservative factions within the Islamic Republic were able to stop the reformist government of President Mohammad Khatami from adopting many of its reform proposals. Between 1997 and 2005, the council rejected 37 percent of the laws adopted by the Parliament and disqualified scores of reformist candidates from standing in various elections, including those for the Parliament and the presidency (Secor 2005: 64).

The tensions in the Iranian political system are not limited to ideological differences between reformists and more conservative factions. They are an integral part of the system and are caused by the structure of the Islamic Republic. Soon after the establishment of the Islamic Republic, it became clear that the tensions between the Parliament and the Council of Guardians, and more generally between elected and unelected institutions, had the potential of paralyzing the political system. This realization led to the creation of another constitutional body, the Expediency Council.

The Supreme Leader appoints all members of the Expediency Council. In addition to the heads of the three branches of the government (the Speaker of the Parliament, the President, and the Head of the Judiciary), the council also includes the six clerical members of the Council of Guardians and other personalities of the regime appointed by the Supreme Leader. As the composition of the Expediency Council suggests, it is a forum for joint policymaking by elected and unelected institutions. Its main function is to arbitrate differences between the Parliament and the Council of Guardians and to establish the

---

[15] Iranian Constitution, Articles 91–99.

overall policies of the Islamic Republic. Its formation was a recognition of the high levels of tension endemic in the political system.

This system is complemented by a heavy reliance on courts and the judiciary. The Iranian judiciary is set up as a separate bureaucracy attached to the office of the Supreme Leader. The head of the judicial branch is directly appointed by the Supreme Leader and answers to him, rather than to the elected president or the Parliament. The head of the judiciary is responsible for the appointment of all judges and even nominates the Minister of Justice, who is a member of the president's cabinet. Furthermore, the Head of the Judiciary is an active participant in the policymaking process. He not only nominates the nonclerical members of the Guardian Council but he is also a member of both the Expediency Council and the National Security Council.

Despite constitutional guarantees of judicial independence, the Iranian judiciary is designed as a political institution that is responsible not only for the administration of justice but also for the implementation of the ideological/political line advocated by the Supreme Leader. The judiciary carries out its multiple functions through a complex system that relies heavily on specialized courts, such as the Press Court, responsible for matters related to the media, and the Special Court for the Clergy.

The judiciary emerged as an important political player during the presidency of Khatami (1997–2005). With the unexpected election of Khatami and the emergence of the reform movement as a viable political alternative, tensions in the Iranian political structure reached a new peak. As Eric Rouleau notes, "The cohabitation between the faqih Ayatollah Khamenei, the supreme politico-religious authority, and President Mohammad Khatami [came] to resemble a multi-faceted guerrilla war" (Rouleau 1999). Having lost at the ballot box, the conservatives, like their Turkish counterparts, relied on the courts to contain the reform movement.

During Khatami's tenure in office, political trials targeting his supporters became common, and dozens of politicians, activists, journalists, and intellectuals were convicted of a range of political crimes. In addition, the Press Court systematically closed many reformist newspapers (Khiabani and Sreberny 2001). Although the accused were often charged with undermining the regime, many of them were "children of the revolution" who not only had participated in the revolution but also had held high governmental positions in the Islamic Republic. Furthermore, the objective of these trials was not to punish the individual culprit, so much as to stop the political movement of the reformers.[16]

---

[16] See for example the remarks of journalist Akbar Ganji, one of the leading ideologues of the reform movement who was himself convicted for his writings, cited in Khiabani and Sreberny (2001: 206).

The press trials and the judicial crackdown on the reform movement closely resemble the activities of the Turkish courts, which have often used their powers to ban political parties and shut down civil associations and media outlets. Fighting social movements through the courts, however, has not always been effective. Many of the banned Turkish political parties, for examples, have often reappeared and shown themselves capable of winning elections. Turkey's present ruling party, the Justice and Development Party, emerged from the ashes of the banned Virtue Party. Virtue itself was the successor to the banned Welfare Party (banned by the TCC in 1998) that had succeeded the National Salvation Party (banned after the 1980 coup), which in turn was formed after the TCC had banned the National Order Party in 1971. Similarly, in Iran, banned newspapers often reappeared with a new title but with the same journalists and editors (Khiabani and Sreberny 2001). As the Iranian dissident Akbar Ganji notes, "In political crimes the court decision is not binding, if it is not accepted as binding by the people" (Ganji 2000: 80).

CONCLUSION

Despite their diametrically opposed ideologies, one being secular and pro-Western and the other theocratic and anti-Western, the Republic of Turkey and the Islamic Republic of Iran have remarkably similar political structures. Institutionally, both regimes are a mixture of democratic and authoritarian regime types. Whereas in Turkey, republican institutions, led by the military and the judiciary, compete with democratically elected institutions, in Iran it is the religious establishment and the Supreme Leader who oversee the elected Parliament and the president. As Volpi notes, "In organizational terms there is little that separates a body of religious overseers from a body of secular republican overseers" (Volpi 2004: 1071). What the two countries have in common is a bifurcated political system in which unelected institutions pursuing a civilizing mission share power with elected institutions that must be sensitive to existing societal interests.

Both the Turkish state and its Iranian counterpart pursue civilizing missions that aim to create new societies based on an ideology defined by the state elite. Since the creation of the Turkish Republic in 1923, the state has pursued a policy aimed at creating a secular and Westernized society. Similarly, the Islamic Revolution in Iran brought to power religious elites who rejected the existing society in favor of a utopian Islamic society ruled as a theocracy. In both countries, however, the state elites' vision of the future is not shared by important and powerful sectors. Consequently, even though the state elites have at least partially accepted the notion of popular sovereignty based on universal adult suffrage, they have created an institutional setup designed to defend the civilizing mission against its potential internal enemies. The hard-line secularists in Turkey and their religious counterparts in Iran share a common distrust of elected institutions that is reproduced in their respective political structures.

Whether one sees the cohabitation of elected and unelected institutions as the cohabitation of the "wolf and the sheep" or as "guerilla warfare," it is clear that in both countries the political system is tension ridden. Despite their enormous powers neither the Turkish military nor the Iranian Supreme Leader can guarantee the outcome of elections or the policymaking process. To manage the resultant tensions, such political systems empower so-called neutral institutions such as courts. The courts in these countries however, are not "impartial actors." Rather, their powers emanate from their partiality in favor of the state's civilizing mission and the continued domination of the political system by the unelected institutions.

12

Judicial Systems and Economic Development

Hilton L. Root and Karen May

INTRODUCTION: AUTOCRACY, LAW, AND DEVELOPMENT

A staple of the development policy literature is the idea that a better quality legal system will help generate economic growth, which in turn builds
constituencies for democratic reforms. Yet the causal linkages between the
judiciary and political liberalization have been difficult to demonstrate empirically. Legal reforms that are narrowly focused on better enforcement of property rights and contract law may be conducive to enhanced trade and investment, but we still have very little firm knowledge about those links and about
their ultimate relationship with democracy (Carothers 2003). Our investigation of the political role of the courts during economic transition describes
the different incentives for democracies and autocracies to strengthen the
role of courts as a framework for investment and trade, fiscal discipline, and
administrative centralization. We argue that this choice has different effects
on political rents, corruption, and aggregate economic activity in democracies
and autocracies. We ultimately conclude that there is little reason to believe
that judicial reform will lead to political transition.

THE ECONOMIC ROLE OF THE COURTS ACCORDING TO REGIME TYPE

A judicial system can be used as a tool to enhance the political survival of leaders within authoritarian regimes just as in democratic ones. Courts may help
reduce costs of commercial transactions for private citizens in both contexts.
However, the consequences of judicial independence for resource distribution
will vary according to regime type. Democratic leaders face incentives to provide such protection broadly, for example by guaranteeing broadly accessible,
functioning capital markets, stable monetary policies, nondiscriminatory contract enforcement and regulation, and transparent tax incentives for investment

to ensure a level playing field. In contrast, autocrats face incentives to provide selective benefits that maximize control over economic activity.[1] Instead of transparent, predictable, and accountable public policies, procedures, and institutions, autocrats may overlook or even encourage opacity, corruption, or inadequate capacity of the commercial law system to motivate investors to depend on government officials for the protection of their investments. In Indonesia, for example, Suharto had little interest in improving the outdated Dutch commercial codes because the ineptness of the court system made investors dependent on interventions by the head of state. This dependence provided regime officials with numerous venues for amassing rents and private wealth. In Latin America, according to the work of Paul Holden (1997), inadequate bankruptcy law reflects the social foundations upon which most Latin American regimes have been built. Without laws that facilitate the seizure of collateral, the assets of wealthy elites were protected from the risks of market competition.

An effective legal system depends on coordination with other state functions, which are also politically controlled. Impartial judgment by the courts depends on appropriate police work for evidence gathering, and enforcement of decisions after the court has ruled. Both political and administrative complexities can interfere with the court's independence and credibility in enforcing the law. Insufficient notification of procedural changes, inconsistent interpretation of regulatory requirements, and insufficient enforcement of licensing requirements are just some of the bureaucratic processes that can undermine the court's role in providing even protection of citizen rights.

The preferential or discretionary enforcement of property rights may still generate observable growth, but surpluses are not distributed evenly. This is a critical difference between the applications of jurisprudence in democratic societies versus autocratic ones: the more surplus an autocrat generates, the more she can pay off critical supporters that will maximize her tenure in office. Court functions that we associate with facilitating economic growth – attracting capital, enforcing contracts, helping to build a revenue base, and maintaining bureaucratic discipline – are applied selectively in order to reward the winning coalition.

In a democratic system, a large pool of citizens has input into the process by which leaders are chosen. This set is called the "selectorate" by Bruce Bueno de Mesquita et al. (2003). A subset of the selectorate actually chooses the leader,

---

[1] Control does not equate to central planning. Control may mean that the market is allowed to function freely in certain sectors, whereas in others economic activity is tightly controlled through licenses.

and this group is the "winning coalition," consisting of the ruler and allies such as the military and other instruments of power. The selectorate potentially has access to the benefits that are distributed by the leader. Both the selectorate and the winning coalition are large in democratic societies, in contrast to small winning coalitions in autocratic regimes. With a small winning coalition, the leader can exchange private goods (or targeted public goods) in exchange for political loyalty, at the expense of evenly distributed public goods. Inequality works to the advantage of the autocrat as membership in the winning coalition becomes more valuable. The most durable autocracies have a small winning coalition with a large selectorate, because members of the winning coalition have more to lose if they fail to support the ruler. The incumbency advantage grows over time as the ruler learns the price for which loyalty can be secured; the personal wealth of those with connections to leadership increases as loyalty becomes cheaper to purchase.

Growth in autocratic regimes therefore has a very different effect than growth in democratic systems. Democratic rulers have strong incentives to promote growth as a public good that is broadly distributed to the selectorate and general population. A democratic leader who fails to provide public goods may be removed from office. For the autocrat who has secured a solid base of support, the reciprocal arrangements between the state and the winning coalition do not require economic growth to be sustained. Sometimes better economic performance in certain sectors may work to the advantage of the winning coalition, but often corruption and economic inefficiency increase as the autocrat becomes more politically entrenched.

Contrary to Mancur Olsen's "stationary bandit" argument (1993) that an autocrat's political security is directly tied to growth, autocrats who promote broadly distributed economic development may actually see their tenure in office decline because the interests of society are at odds with those of the ruler. Instead of providing a larger revenue stream to an autocrat, growth may instead help enemies of the regime or weaken regime stalwarts. Either way, growth conceived as a public good can weaken the incumbent. The interests of leadership and those of the population are often not aligned, and autocratic regimes offer few mechanisms to correct that misalignment.

Court systems in authoritarian regimes, like other institutions in large selectorate-small winning coalition systems, are arranged to benefit a winning coalition and maximize the private wealth and political staying power of the autocrat. In this chapter, we explore the political motivations for leaders of authoritarian regimes to favor independent judiciaries according to the strategy for political endurance. Autocratic leaders often pursue expensive political agendas, which require substantial financial means. Such agendas can include conflicts with neighboring states, the desire to accumulate personal wealth, and the need to bribe elites to buy their support. In some circumstances, these agendas present economic, financial, and managerial dilemmas that motivate autocrats to create and empower court systems. For example, autocrats may face a need to attract investors, enhance revenue and credibility with regard to loan repayment, and reinforce central authority to overcome the inherent contradictions within hierarchical organizations caused by the private exploitation of information by regime representatives at lower levels.

INSTITUTIONAL SOLUTIONS TO AN AUTOCRAT'S MANAGERIAL DILEMMAS

Authoritarians face three peculiar managerial dilemmas by virtue of the status of the head of state as "above the law." That status limits the effectiveness of the state and its institutions because it implies the primacy of discretion over rules. Building a court system restricts executive discretion, but instead of weakening the regime it can actually help establish a stable framework for regime longevity. First, autocrats require investment and therefore must create a legal system to facilitate transactions. Second, they need to enhance revenue collection and credit; therefore, they need a legal framework that holds financial intermediaries accountable for their private debts and for dealing equitably with citizens. Third, they need to ferret out disobedience and noncompliance by subordinates; a legal system that discloses the abuses of officials enhances the leader's renown and ensures greater compliance from citizens. Administrative courts can make the state's administrative apparatus work more smoothly to ensure that information about performance and malfeasance is uncovered (see Chapter 2). Improved loyalty of administrative personnel is thereby attained, as well as a more contented populace.

Dilemma 1: Property Rights and Securing Investment Opportunities for Distribution to Loyalists

The first dilemma faced by autocrats is how to balance the protection of private property rights with the need to secure an effective coalition. The center of the legal reform agenda for liberalization is predictability in the enforcement of property rights and contracts more generally. Development practitioners and political economists often refer to the mandate for secure property rights as "policy stability" – investors should be confident that a country's policies regarding the protection of assets will remain stable, and that their assets will not be confiscated. For example, Hernando de Soto (2000) has emphasized the importance of property rights reform, assuming an empirical correlation between the rule of law and growth. We accept that clear property rights and rule of law reduce transactional friction and facilitate economic activity. Insofar as they effectively enforce property rights and contracts, courts serve as an institutional intermediary between commercial interests and the leadership of autocrat and democratic regimes alike.

On the surface, promoting a safe investment environment may appear to foreign investors and policy advocates as a progressive liberal improvement. The liberalization of foreign investment, however, may be linked to strategies of coalition building that increase economic inequality and limit local access to the political process. The links between economic and political liberalization are more difficult to establish than is generally understood in the literature on modernization.

Business surveys based on investor perceptions typically identify judicial reforms as a positive step toward advancing political stability and political openness. But perceptions can overstate the synchronicity of institutional reforms to outcomes. They disregard the prospect that judicial reforms may constitute a parallel system of regime legitimacy that rarely serves as an ultimate check on the power of the executive. Although an obvious advantage exists for investors to seek and support the building of effective systems of commercial law around the world, such institutions may have originated for entirely different political reasons, and may buffet authoritarian regimes by enhancing the tools available to the incumbent to buy loyalty.

A fundamental tension exists between the financial incentive of the ruler to attract foreign investment and the autocrat's political incentive to use property rights selectively. Growth is only indirectly linked to the ruler's revenue stream. From the autocrat's perspective, property rights are another tool to facilitate political and economic enrichment of regime followers in which loyalty, not consumer surpluses, is being optimized. Foreign investors may have valuable links to members of the winning coalition, or they may have resources that help leaders circumvent rivals. The ruler has an incentive to maintain a stable policy for enforcing property rights for financial elites because avoiding a financial crisis is essential to ensuring regime survival. But the autocrat may be less gracious with political opponents, and may direct the courts to practice selective enforcement. For example, Singapore's Lee Kuan Yew is alleged to have used the courts to bankrupt political opponents (Mauzy and Milne 2002: 132–136). The courts in Singapore were effective in processing commercial litigation and could identify the asset flows and resources of opponents, and then prosecute them with targeted tax enforcement. Coupled with effective administrative follow-up, the efficiency of the court system made threats to opponents more credible. The institutions that give Singapore a reputation for clean business practices also enable its leaders to intimidate political opponents (see Chapter 3).

In Indonesia, after export and import markets were freed from controls, the best contracts have often depended on partnerships with politically connected figures. Fisman (2001) has quantified this dynamic in Indonesia after liberalization and found that the value of political connections actually increased with liberalization. The distinction between broad growth and targeted economic interventions that reward political allies with investment opportunities is difficult to observe in aggregate growth statistics, which do not show the market distortions resulting from the reward of monopolies to political supporters and other forms of political rents collected in exchange for economic privileges. With their control over natural resources, Indonesia's leadership can establish narrow coalitional foundations by selectively distributing market access as private benefits to regime supporters. Control of these resources relieves it of the need to develop a clean business environment to attract adequate capital to sustain a broad-based governing coalition. Narrowing the winning coalition allows top leaders to keep the maximum returns for their own consumption and to ward off rebellion.

In short, some but not all autocrats will seek to empower courts to attract investment. The key variable is whether foreign investment capital – and judicial institutions that are useful to attract it – can be co-opted to ensure regime survival.

Dilemma 2: Financial Credibility and Debt Repayment

A second dilemma faced by relatively unconstrained rulers concerns the need to borrow to finance the regime itself. Institutions that promote rules over discretion provide political leaders with access to private capital at lower cost than would otherwise be the case. This insight is derived from the work of Kydland and Prescott (1977), who focused on the advantage of rules over discretion in monetary policy and the related role of central banks. In one extension of their model Root (1989) explores how the state can enjoy better credit terms, reflected in a lower interest rate, when able to borrow from intermediaries that are subjected to independent courts for enforcement of nonpayment of financial arrears. Such institutions reduce the costs of credit to the state by enabling leaders to draw upon the credibility of intermediary bodies that are themselves subject to a rule of law, even when the head of state may not be. Constraining sovereign discretion with regard to financial activity actually strengthens the ability of leaders to raise funds from private sources at more attractive rates than those available if the leader attempted to borrow directly from capital markets. Surprisingly, modern-day regimes with access to sources of external finance have a weaker incentive to develop effective commercial courts than did the kings of early modern European states.

The necessity to secure funds for war from domestic sources drove much of the legal, administrative, and fiscal institutional innovation that occurred in feudal France and England. Revenue collection required laws to strengthen collective identities and to define collective liability, effective administration was needed to implement the laws, and effective debt repayment was necessary to gain loans from the private groups that enjoyed legal protection and liability under the law. Many developing countries can substitute international sources of capital for domestic capabilities that require investments in state-building. With a much weaker technical capacity to track and monitor wealth, the kings of Old Regime France and England were able to collect a far greater percentage of their subject's wealth than can many emerging but weak states today (Root 1994).

When the French or English monarchs were above the law, they could not be compelled to repay their debts, and so had more difficulty finding sources of credit. As a result of royal discretion, monarchs enjoyed credit that was weaker than that of many of their subjects. The kings' onerous cost of capital could be mitigated by new institutional arrangements that benefited financiers and investors while ensuring a steady supply of government financing. Kings could not borrow against their own discretion, so they were compelled to create a legal regime that ensured repayment after they themselves left the scene.

In England the Crown needed to raise revenues from elites and designed a court system that gave rise to a constitutional monarchy, with strong protection of the property rights of the landholders and bondholders. North and Weingast (1989) have pointed out that the English kings benefited from the rise of Parliament, by allowing it to raise taxes to fund the kings' debts. The British Parliament had an interest in preventing the king from raising money through sources other than the Parliament itself. The Glorious Revolution placed limits on the Crown's ability to unilaterally change the terms of its financial agreements, which enhanced its credibility. In exchange for purse strings, the king gained a source of revenue at lower cost than was available to any other government in Europe, which allowed England to become the master of the oceans and eventually of international commerce. In addition, strong domestic commercial law was necessary to generate the funds for Parliament to tax. In England, the need for credibility led to the rise of constitutional monarchy and a liberal economy. Ironically, when international donors provide bilateral or multilateral funds to present-day autocrats, they reduce incentives for the government to provide strong domestic protection for commercial transactions.

In France the intermediary was not a legislative body, but rather a private body chartered by the king with the privilege of collecting royal taxes. The collectors often advanced their own funds to the Crown, knowing they could access the king's courts and army to draw upon the collective resources of the village communities, guilds, and provincial estates. The corporations were subject to the jurisdiction of the courts and could therefore offer credible financial commitments. In return for official recognition and privileges, these corporate groups acted as bankers for the king, providing funds at lower rates than the king could find on his own.

Taxing peasants also required that their collective village property be protected, which had corollary political benefits. By granting peasants access to the courts to protect the tax base, the king used the courts to build up constituent support from groups that might otherwise be marginal. His direct political objective was to supplant peasant allegiance from local seigneurs to the agents of the king. Indirectly the subordination of seigniorial authority to royal supervision may have had unintended revolutionary implications, creating a process that would lead toward the revolutionary events of 1789. The law of the king's courts became a venue in which a contest between peasant villages and their traditional seigniorial masters could be waged. The courts fanned the animosity toward seigniorial dues by hearing the grievances of peasant communities against their lords. The contests became more adversarial by virtue of the fact that the seigneurs enjoyed tax-exempt status, dating from the days they provided military service to the king. But by the eighteenth century, it was the taxes on the peasantry that financed the king's wars. In Great Britain, by contrast, the lords shouldered the burden of paying local taxes, and their authority grew in proportion to the burdens of national security that they bore for the entire community. Hence there was more justification for the English lords' economic status, and their enterprises gained protection in national law.

Today the heads of government rarely enjoy incentives to protect the enterprises of productive sectors of the population similar to those of the monarchs of eighteenth-century Europe because they can substitute international loans for capital drawn from sources of domestic taxation. This is true for both developed and developing countries. For developing countries, international financing often means an absence of a commitment to protecting the property rights of majorities, in favor of selectively distributed economic privileges that provide a loyalty premium to the head of state. If the ruler is lucky, natural resources such as oil or diamonds may be enough to finance the regime, and the messy business of negotiating tax revenue can be avoided. International financing from multilateral development banks and donors is another attractive source of funding, allowing the ruler autonomy from society.

If the regime does require tax revenue to survive, a unique set of incentives arise that can lay the groundwork for democratic transitions. This transformation can be seen in the practice of effective government by China's KMT after it lost the mainland. With a much smaller population and few economic resources on Taiwan, the KMT developed better governance systems, including higher quality courts, tax authorities, and administrators than they had operated on the Chinese mainland. There was not enough population or wealth on Taiwan for the KMT to maintain sufficient military capacity to ward off an attack from the mainland simply through corruption and extortion. After losing the mainland the KMT understood that wealth had to be husbanded by economic policies and incentives if Taiwan was to survive.

While the change process occurred at different rates, both France and England's innovations in the institutions of participatory governance were driven by the fiscal necessity of the state. With the advent of international financial institutions, domestic taxation is not the only option for securing government resources. Yet, foreign debt has caused further rifts between rulers and citizens, as foreign policy concessions made by dictators are often granted by developing countries to donors in exchange for extended credit.

Dilemma 3: Secrecy, Central Authority, and Administrative Discipline

The autocrat's third dilemma is driven by information. The secrecy inherent in the extremely hierarchical nature of autocratic regimes generates internal contradictions regarding the use and abuse of information by administrators at lower levels of the regime. Effective authoritarian governance requires that information be passed up and down the ladder of authority; however, there tends to be an overload of information at the top that creates opportunities to hoard information at the lower level, progressively diminishing the authority of the ruler. Low-level administrators can strip regime assets to create personal fiefdoms obscured from the purview of central government actors.

Layers of authority exist between the head of state and local administrators, creating ample opportunity for orders to be confused or mishandled. Judicial decisions and censures from senior officials are further constrained by protests, excuses, and appeals pitched to central authorities. Administrative complexity and overlapping responsibilities slow communication and result in the loss of timely information, facilitating the stripping of state assets for private gain.

Many autocrats depend on local notables whose resources constitute an independent power base. They must be co-opted into supporting the regime, but their loyalty can never be counted upon. Imbued with local biases, they seek to guard local or regional privileges, and their scope for hiding information and action is considerable. The policy decisions that are directed toward them are often construed in ways that fit their own needs. There is no easy way to solve this problem of local nonconformity; creating administrative law, and using central courts to watch over local communities, risks confrontation. Military force is always an option, but it complicates the prospects of future local cooperation. Inevitably when local big men are well entrenched, money spent locally will further perpetuate their control over local patronage networks. The leader can demarcate areas of local jurisdiction that fall under central control and slowly erode localized power, but the risks of hidden action and information will persist.

Kenneth Arrow's insights concerning "hidden information" and "hidden action" in corporate structures (Arrow 1979) offer useful parallels to the information asymmetries in authoritarian governments. As the agent of the stockholders, corporate management may pursue a project it knows to be unprofitable if it produces perks or salary benefits that management can enjoy. Likewise, an agent of the government may distort information (hidden information) about the performance of government policies and avoid passing along information about local economic conditions or the potential for governmental revenue generation. Agents can trade on information about planned government policies or projects (hidden action), striking black market side deals with other administrators or with private parties. Local officials become adept at stripping the value of the government assets at their disposal to earn private profits.

The autocrat may create or reinvent the courts to address this principal-agent problem – preventing the erosion of power and imposing supervision on agents in order to constrain their ability to conceal information for their private benefit. The administrative discipline administered by the courts helps build legitimacy for the regime because the visible effects of re-centralizing authority are perceived as reducing corruption to the benefit of society, recovering lost economic surpluses, and removing secondary officials who have distorted rule enforcement by distributing opportunities to their own local networks.

A significant literature has emerged that attributes the fall of the Soviet Union to the loss of hierarchical discipline at lower levels (Frye and Shleifer 1996). The corruption that was unleashed after the end of the Cold War was just the extension of a process that had already been underway. Local officials had been hiding information about the efficacy of policies from the central government and taking hidden actions that enabled them to gain control over government assets. Only the local officials knew about side deals among each other. Today, one of the most trenchant criticisms leveled at Communist Party officials in China is that lower ranking representatives are using their authority to collect rents through fees and licenses at the local level, which are then retained locally instead of being transferred upward. Resources are being diverted away from the center, making it difficult for Beijing to provide government services demanded by local populations.

It is well established that monitoring, such as that provided by court systems, can help solve information asymmetries and reduce the scope for corruption. Monitoring alone, however, does not contribute to the liberalization of the regime. Typically, monitoring is a way to exert central authority over the periphery. A side effect may be new avenues of contestation, but that is not the goal of such reforms.

It is also possible that the autocrat has no incentive to enforce administrative discipline. A weak court system and lack of transparency allow rulers more options for amassing private wealth. Although overall economic productivity and the social surplus may be compromised, the distributional impact may still be favorable to regime longevity. As mentioned earlier with the Indonesian example, autocrats may overlook opacity and corruption in order to guarantee that the state intervenes on behalf of favored investors, thus ensuring central economic control. If the autocrat does not need the courts to secure income or reward the winning coalition, resources will be diverted away from the courts and they will suffer accordingly. When courts are appended to stand-alone legal ministries, they rarely have funding to undertake their core responsibilities and are often prone to bribe-taking, ultimately undermining their legitimacy.

LINKAGES BETWEEN POLITICAL DISCIPLINE
AND COMMERCIAL LAW ENFORCEMENT

What is the incentive of an autocracy to adequately finance the courts? In some authoritarian regimes such as South Korea during the 1960s and 1970s, the courts were under the direct supervision and control of security forces, and in fact became an arm of the state security apparatus. Paradoxically, leaders who create judicial institutions that improve internal security for defense against enemies of the state can use these same institutions to establish effective courts that enjoy the respect of the population. In weak states, by contrast, legal institutions are viewed as protecting the private interests of the wealthy. Attaching the court system to the security function has a strong effect on the ability of the courts to function effectively. The security apparatus of the state is the most important disciplinary agent of an authoritarian regime. Ironically, a connection with the regime's security function may be the source of funding that allows the courts to disregard the power of external influence over contract enforcement, and to establish a reputation for professionalism. This relationship explains in large part the reputation for professionalism enjoyed by the judges of South Korea during the martial law period. The courts of Nazi Germany enjoyed the same high status. Court systems that are effective in disciplining political opponents are likely to be well resourced and efficient in enforcing property rights and commercial legislation. Judges who are directly responsible for the survival of the regime are likely to enjoy greater esteem than judges who are members of stand-alone judicial ministries that tend to be underfunded and prone to corruption. If judicial personnel are well paid, they have little incentive to hoard information and collect rents that divert economic activity.

The security connection also comes into play after court decisions are made, when credible enforcement is required to render court decisions effective. Enforcement is more easily provided if the courts are attached to the security apparatus, but when courts are stand-alone institutions, their authority can be circumvented.

Courts often seek to preserve their autonomy in some spheres by avoiding challenges to the regime on core issues, but such a strategy does not always work. For example, when Thaksin was elected prime minister of Thailand, the opposition questioned his eligibility to rule based on accusations of tax evasion. The Constitutional Court ruled in Thaksin's favor, arguing that the electorate already knew of these charges and elected him anyway, and it was not the mandate of the court to contradict the electoral mandate of the population. When Thaksin was deposed in a coup in 2006, the Constitutional Court was disbanded. In the Philippines, Marcos declared martial law, which the courts accepted on the grounds that he had been a democratically elected president. This initial rubber stamp became a turning point in the loss of independence for the courts, which had previously been perceived as meritocratic and professional. Celoza (1997: 82) explains,

> As he expanded the role of the military, Marcos limited the power of the judiciary. To ensure that his policies were implemented as he saw necessary, Marcos needed to curb the independence and review powers of the Supreme Court. Directly or indirectly, Marcos exerted pressure on the Supreme Court to give him a free rein; in turn, the court exercised a great deal of self-regulation to avoid confrontation with Marcos.

Frequently, a dual reality develops in authoritarian regimes in which a separation occurs between the regime's questionable moral legitimacy and its effective performance of routine daily civic functions, further reducing the court's capacity to effectively challenge the moral legitimacy of the regime. But the existence of judicial review may create a space in which the forces for contesting the regime will gather and in which they will learn how to coordinate using tools provided by the regime itself to later challenge the status quo.

THE LAW AND REGIME CHANGE

When considering how the courts can contribute to political liberalization, one must recognize that legal reform is part of a broader context of social reform. The courts mirror that larger process, whether they enhance or retard it. The courts can have a dual nature, providing legalistic justification for regime legitimacy and the ruler's arbitrary discipline of political opponents, while remaining more independent when dealing with contract or family law.

The evolution of institutions does not always optimize broad social welfare. Political and economic evolution is a process of adaptation and survival in the face of external pressure and competition, and the result is often policy volatility. In newly emerging states in particular, weak institutions can cost elites the opportunity to reap the rewards of power. Judicial institutions adjust to an equilibrium strategy, facilitating enough economic activity to optimize resources for the winning coalition while serving the ruler's political security.

The courts can play a stabilizing role by providing a mechanism for resolving administrative disputes, so as to release tensions and instabilities before they erupt. If the courts support the denial of citizens' right to assemble, mobilize, and organize for political purposes, open and inclusive administrative processes are unlikely to stimulate long-term political reform. Alternatively, in their role of reinforcing central authority, the courts may provide a venue to expose contradictions that can lead to disintegration of the regime. In such cases, the courts rarely initiate change, but rather provide a forum to voice changes already underway.

Political discourse may or may not evolve in an administrative court system that is primarily used to impose supervision on local leaders, as in China. At the base, citizens may perceive a dual court system as one in which grievances can be legitimately aired and potentially resolved, giving the appearance of inclusivity and effectiveness, which contributes to regime legitimacy and survival.[2] Autocrats who rule inclusively with a combination of strong political security and some access to arbitration to resolve local disputes may be able to cushion their rule from shocks in the economy or external environment.

---

[2] Jeanne Kirkpatrick subscribed to the notion that the most resilient autocratic regimes are the most totalitarian. This doctrine was clearly discredited after the fall of the Soviet Union.

In many of the case studies in this volume, the law furnishes a set of categories in which new ideas can be crafted and a vocabulary in which new concepts of civic responsibility can be described. But the creation of the vocabulary and the political options for mobilizing citizens to use that vocabulary for public criticism of the regime are two separate matters.

Dualism and Inclusivity as a Steady-State Equilibrium

As noted earlier, today's autocrats have several channels to circumvent reliance on domestic taxation to secure revenues for the regime. By far the most effective is the possession of valuable resources, such as oil or diamonds, that can be controlled by regime leaders. Without the fiscal incentive to protect taxable assets of regime citizens, the process of political liberalization will stall. Another channel that facilitates rule without domestic accountability is bilateral or multilateral bank lending to the sovereign. The loans most frequently benefit the incumbent leadership and the interests they represent, despite lending guidelines established by international law. The possession of revenues that come from sources that enhance an autocrat's independence from accountability to societal groups allows the leadership to shape those groups according to its own interests. Both the resource curse (Ross 1999) and the foreign aid curse give rise to large selectorate-small winning coalition systems in which political competition is stifled and some measure of judicial independence is lost.

Regimes that rely on peasants or other marginal groups for legitimacy do have an incentive to provide access to the legal system. The opportunity for poor farmers to appeal to the courts, however, does not imply that the autocracy will disintegrate; in fact it is more likely to contribute to stability by giving rulers ways to supplant the traditional powers of local elites. Thaksin in Thailand became well known for programs that benefited the poor. He did this expressly to circumvent local patronage networks that empowered local leaders. Thaksin had centralized political funding, letting big money politics overcome local political influence; once their power base was attenuated, local leaders had to support Thaksin or risk losing elections.

In China, the Communist Party has been strengthened by increased growth, but as a result of dynamic economic activity, the coalitional structure shifted toward a new class of financial elites, forcing a formal change in the party constitution. China scholar Hongying Wang discussed the CCP's adaptation strategy in a recent interview with Fareed Zakaria (Wang 2006):

> The CCP, the Chinese Communist Party has reinvented itself. That's the key; they're...not the Communist Party that you know about or people

idealize about. There's nothing communist about it except that it is a one-party system and it is determined to do everything, including changing its own nature to stay in power. The new principle as it is written in the Party Constitution now – the Party represents the most advanced production force, which means the capitalists or the capital owners; it represents the most advanced culture, which means professionals, intellectuals, and advanced "everybody's interests," which is just . . . covering every aspect.

The adaptation of judicial independence within a limited sphere of activity does not imply that political liberalization will ultimately result. Local dispute resolution may contribute to growth as a strategy to ensure continued centralized authority, but growth may also increase inequality, which works to the advantage of the ruler. Inequality can be exploited by the autocrat to further cement control by increasing the loyalty premium the ruler can extract from the winning coalition. When being cut off from the winning coalition means mediocre access to resources, the cost to the ruler of gaining loyalty is reduced. Thus, members of the winning coalition have more to lose when the society is more unequal – so loyalty can be purchased more inexpensively. The courts can become effective as vehicles for the activism of opposition only once the regime has already started to weaken. Hongying Wang continues as follows:

> People [are] looking at their neighbors, their urban cousins getting rich. . . . Some of these protests are about local environment issues, . . . unemployment . . . about half of [college students] them end up graduating not immediately finding jobs. . . . I think on the one hand it does represent a serious challenge to the legitimacy of the government; on the other hand I don't think in the near future it's going to generate the kind of collapse that people are sometimes talking about, because the Chinese Communist Party has been very smart from its own point of view in that you can protest as long as you guys don't get organized. You can talk all you want, so there is much more freedom now in China in terms of people's ability to express their discontent – just don't get organized. And the problem is if you are thinking of a revolution or any kind of meaningful upheaval without organization these protests are not going to cause any major change.

The Chinese example demonstrates that the granting of limited freedoms can be a strategy for legitimizing the regime without sacrificing central authority. As an instrument of that authority, the courts can still rule in favor of local plaintiffs in cases of low-level corruption without jeopardizing the political security of central leadership. Judgments that favor selectorate members reduce the threat of potential challengers from within to the winning coalition. In China, for example, Jiang Zemin rarely challenged the Shanghai Gang and his allies among the princelings, the children of revolutionary leaders, leaving behind a legacy of high-level corruption that his successor Hu Jintao is trying to erase. In effect, by becoming the party of the haves, the capitalists, and the bourgeoisie, the Communist Party has eliminated any meaningful and serious threats to it.

Revolution or Evolution

Further research on the nature of court cases in China is needed to determine the extent to which access to administrative courts is giving a voice to a new set of democratic challenges to the legitimacy of the CCP. Even if it is, this discourse is not initially dangerous until the regime starts to weaken due to other inherent contradictions or pressures. It is possible that the growing inequality in China constitutes such a contradiction. The courts could potentially be used to expose underlying instability in the coalitional structure that could lead to dramatic political change. Dualism may serve as an adaptation that provides regime stability, but because the incentives of autocratic rulers may diverge dramatically from the interests of society, courts that were originally designed to facilitate and lengthen authoritarian rule may actually become weapons against the regime (Moustafa 2007).

This occurred in Old Regime France, as de Toqueville argued. By supplanting the reciprocal bonds between lord and peasants with central bureaucratic codes, the monarchy initiated a revolutionary process that ultimately led to the regime's demise. In *The Old Regime and the Revolution* (1856/1998) de Tocqueville contends that it was the Crown's attempts at reform that "roused the people by trying to offer them relief." The shift to a rule-based system of centralized authority that weakened the Seigneurie created political space in which reforms became "practices thanks to which the government completed the people's revolutionary education." Inequality of status, symbolized by residual feudal dues owed to local seigneurs, became suspect. Seigneurial roles for the local community had become tenuous, and their tax-exempt status became more odious as their authority became more residual. The courts provided a venue to air long-standing grievances against seigneurial exactions and domination (Root 1985).

The White Revolution initiated by the Shah of Iran in 1963 provides a more contemporary example of reforms that highlighted deep-seated inequalities, thereby initiating a revolutionary process. The Shah hoped that economic growth would relieve pressures and ultimately provide a source of social coherence, but growth created conflict instead (Root 2006). Opportunities for capital accumulation were linked to a system of social exclusion. Meaningful policy participation was barred: democratic and meritocratic channels of access within the state were not built. In contrast to the anti-religious sentiment of the Enlightenment in the French Revolution, Khomeini's Iranian revolution in response to the Shah used the banner of organized Islam to provide a framework for the democratic political challenge. While the regime enjoyed early popular support and made social gains in terms of political participation, rules and regulations promoting access to capital for new enterprises not controlled by the government have been stiffly opposed by the incumbent leadership. The revolution's agenda did not emphasize eliminating corruption, or establishing an institutional and legal capacity necessary for a market economy. As a result, Iran's productivity declined after religious rule was established and has stagnated ever since.

Instead of economic conflicts, the courts in the Soviet Union exposed a different set of contradictions after the Communist leadership signed the Helsinki Accords. The Russians were subjected to human rights criteria that undermined the legitimacy of the regime and gave the United States a wedge to impose constraints. One unintended consequence benefited Russian Jews by allowing them to migrate to Israel, but the favoritism they enjoyed led other Russians to ask why they too did not enjoy similar rights; the Helsinki Accords had an unintended subversive effect that set the stage for Soviet decline as domestic discontent was empowered with a universal criteria with which to measure their own leaders.

The Iranian and Russian examples provide evidence to support the notion that a connection exists between the role of the courts and regime disintegration, but not that growth or democracy will necessarily result, or that a formalized democratic constitution will necessarily increase the welfare of society. For two centuries the revolutionary goal of responsibility and equal burden sharing was not met in France. Informal norms continued to reinforce structures of elite domination, including domination over entire sectors of the modern economy.

The celebrated case of England's transition to democracy, led by the rise of Parliament, could be described as more of an evolutionary process than a revolutionary one. The danger in moving reforms too fast is that the contradictions inherent in the regime and the incompatibility between formal and informal institutions can create a backlash situation in which resistance to reform increases, further entrenching authoritarian rule. An often overlooked aspect of this evolution is that for the Parliament to be effective it depended on the ability of the head of state to assert sovereignty over the entire kingdom. In England it was often said that the king was strongest in Parliament because it simplified getting the assent of the entire nation. The French king, who was ruling over a mosaic nation, had to employ much more cumbersome procedures to gain cooperation from his subjects. A considerable waste of resources resulted.

In systems with diminished winning coalitions and poor institutional infrastructure, resistance to reform of legal institutions is well focused and easy to organize. That opposition can come from entrenched social groups whose interests are threatened by judicial independence. Opposition can also come from within the bureaucracy. Legal ministries might resist the formalization of commercial law, as a rules-over-discretion approach would directly challenge the legitimacy of the regime. Finance ministries may be allied with reform, but they have no jurisdiction to promote it. In such cases, a common law approach may be much more effective at instilling viable procedures for enforcing contracts and mediating civil and commercial disputes. As individual cases are arbitrated, precedents are set and legal efficiency can slowly evolve. This reform strategy has been proposed as a possible mechanism to build up legal capacity in Africa, where legal ministries resist reform efforts because they would constitute a direct challenge to the legitimacy of the autocrat's rule. The French kings of the twelfth century astutely managed the diversity of regional legal institutions not by abruptly abolishing them, but by appointing a royal representative as local supervisor, facilitating a slower transition to a uniform legal code, which was less threatening to local interests.

The Law and Emerging Loyalty to the State

The institutionalist argument for legal reform that seeks to replicate formal structures with effective enforcement of commercial law must be combined with the political argument that takes the ruler's strategy for political survival into account. Building a rule of law is part of the political process in which the state acquires its legitimacy as upholder of the law, and in which the organs of state power are viewed as existing to enforce the law. The first national institutions were identified with the monarch, who embodied the nation morally and politically. The duty of the king to uphold the law became the moral justification for political leadership. Eventually the monarchs of Europe accepted that political power must be defined by law, so that by the eighteenth century, most administrative and legal matters were handled by professional administrators who acted independently of royal prerogative. Paradoxically, it was the strong political identification with the monarch that enabled the growing independence of government administration.

Qualitative studies of the origin of the rule of law in Western Europe have shown that the existence of courts does not necessarily lead to the acceptance of the supremacy of law, nor to the emergence of an authority that will enforce the law (Strayer 1970: 7). Rather change in judicial systems, as an adaptive process like evolution, does not produce an optimal and consistent outcome such as a recognizable liberal regime. The legitimacy of leadership must first be established before the courts will be viewed as upholders of a society based on law. In Western Europe the development of a society of law was an integral part of the political process of state-building. The courts emerged as institutions of law that strengthened the political identity of the group; local identity fused with loyalty to the state and ultimately with nationalism. This fundamental aspect of the European tradition – the emphasis on national cohesion embodied by a unifying national symbol – has been surprisingly embraced by the Chinese. In this case, the Communist Party functions as that symbol rather than the monarchy. The Chinese are only now just beginning to create law schools and to train judges, fifty years after the process of building a modern state began, and three decades after pro-market reforms were initiated.

For the courts to function in any society there must be an ability to distinguish between public and private –a distinction that is only beginning to take root in the habits and beliefs of the population in many emerging nations. In many developing countries basic security comes from pre-state organizations – family, neighbors, and the local strongman – not from the state. In many patrimonial African regimes that emerged after the colonialists departed, the strongest loyalties were to family and persons rather than to abstractions such as the national state. Instead of providing enduring institutions to deliver efficient administration, the strategy of political leaders was to gain control over existing governments or over residual colonial institutions for purposes of personal aggrandizement, and they accordingly used the courts to protect the income and prerogatives of the leadership. Latin America's courts functioned primarily to protect the private interests of the wealthy. In both examples the existence of courts does not lead to the acceptance of the supremacy of law.

Communist regimes, by comparison with African and Latin American legal systems, more effectively laid a foundation for broad public acceptance of the institutions of government. Communist societies deliberately avoided distinguishing between the private interests of citizens and the public concerns of the state. They elevated the interests of the state above all else and so dissolved primordial loyalties and networks of clientage and dependency that still exist in many former colonial regimes.

The desire of the poorer classes for security and good government in authoritarian countries has been constantly frustrated by the fact that leaders sought stability and longevity by appealing to the propertied classes. This process of mass identification with the symbols of state power has often failed to occur in many authoritarian regimes for both external and internal reasons. Many leaders during the Cold War cooperated with the geopolitical strategies of the major industrial powers in exchange for the resources needed to gain the approval of the privileged minorities. Governments could secure power without providing public services such as broadly available law, security, health, and sanitation that citizens demand in exchange for loyalty and resources. Necessary improvements in legal processes could be postponed. As a result loyalty to the state must vie with other loyalties. The state, without a real impact on the quality of people's lives, enjoys only limited respect.

The national leaders of many Third World nations have little in common with the citizenry. Local leaders, sometimes members of politically suspect groups who are involved with day-to-day security, are not recognized by government to create judicial institutions. Examples such as Hezbollah or the war lords of Afghanistan come to mind. In contrast, during European development the more competent local leaders were the first to establish courts and other instruments of state power. But many leaders today derive their fiscal capacity to rule from resources that are independent of the people who are being governed. Autocrats often survive because they have access to external resources and as noted base the stability of their regime on the support of the propertied and politically privileged groups; thus, their political survival strategies differ fundamentally from democratically elected leaders. External processes triggered by the Cold War that provided external funding for compliant dictators, and the resource curse that put resources into the hands of government elites, all interfered with the emergence of strong and accountable national states. External resources, generally available only to the incumbent leadership, lessen the efficacy of domestic political challengers, reducing the incentives for incumbents to be concerned with structural reforms and institution-building.

The larger process of building political legitimacy for the instruments of state power will ultimately determine if the courts emerge as upholders of the supremacy of law. The legitimacy of the state determines the legitimacy of its institutions, such as the courts. As part of the basis for state-building, the judicial system will not be truly effective until the other basic institutional components – both formal and informal – are already in place. The integrity of the courts and of the laws they uphold will flourish only once loyalty to the state becomes an item of faith for large majorities as opposed to small winning coalitions. To sustain such faith, legal reforms must be incentive-compatible across many dimensions – financing, credibility, security, and general welfare – with the ruler's strategy for survival and the interests of population at large.

As the case studies in this volume show, many of today's autocracies have court systems that are better organized than in the past. It remains an open question whether more effective courts will produce greater loyalty to the ruler and to the state or whether they will be a forum for opposition and for the replacement of the existing regime.

To assist policymakers, scholars must work toward mapping the characteristics of courts in regimes that have effectively implemented growth-enhancing institutions, those that have working democracies, and the rare cases in which legal and institutional reforms do in fact lead to growth *and* democracy. We must ask when these are two separate issues and when they converge.

For the courts to facilitate social change, they must be venues that encourage innovation and competition. This is rarely the purpose for which courts are created. Protecting innovation must be distinguished from the simple protection of property rights, which will inevitably focus on protecting elites to the exclusion of more marginal constituencies. The Coase Theorem that stresses reduction of transaction costs is not very helpful in the context of developing economies since the poor lack the resources to defend their property rights.

Finally, imposing formal institutional structures on a society with incompatible traditions is unlikely to succeed in bringing about lasting reform. Courts in the United States derive their authority from a constitutional mandate to interpret legislation. In most other societies the courts are an extension of the executive function. Without the balancing effect of the other branches, the scope for reform via the courts is limited. We tend to assume that court and legal reform along these lines form a healthy, inevitable pattern of evolution that contributes to human betterment – others see reform as a means to an end, an end for which there may be better alternative means.

CONCLUSION

The links between judicial institutions and liberalization are ambiguous at best. Even when the courts enforce property rights, contract, and family law, judicial power may block innovation and competition by selectively promoting the rights of established firms and technologies they control. Underneath the rules and procedures of formal constitutions and codes of conduct, the courts can be used to protect incumbent wealth. Governments may employ courts to improve contract enforcement, loan repayment, and bureaucratic discipline and still not allow citizens the right to assemble, mobilize, and organize for political purposes. As already noted, in autocracy the inclusiveness of legal rights and protection does not need to be any larger than the coalition that the leader cultivates to elevate his or her political power. Leaders who do not depend on broad coalitions have numerous ways to extend their tenure in office by manipulating judicial institutions. For this reason it is necessary for future analysis to distinguish between those functions of the court that advance or retard democratic change. It is not just the institutional framework that matters, but rather that legal reform is part of a broader context of social reform. The judicial system will lack legitimacy until the other instruments of national sovereignty win citizen acceptance.

Modern autocrats in contemporary Russia and Kazakhstan have learned how to prevent people from coordinating political activism or dissent while at the same time encouraging foreign investment. The key point for the literature to absorb is that the interests of leaders can be divorced from the national interests of the populations they lead. Modern autocrats can actually decrease the probability of revolt by being successful economically, so we must learn to distinguish between those who come to power in existing arrangements and those leaders who pose a revolutionary challenge that will alter the regime's coalitional foundations and expand the winning coalition by increasing the provision of public goods. Such leaders will inevitably undertake revolutionary transformations of the legal system. But so far we have not found any reason to believe that judicial institutionalization makes democratic reform more likely. Turkey provides an example of the judiciary working closely with the military that modernized the country, and the implication is clearly that judicial power conflicts directly with the emergence of democratic forces that contain strong anti-modern elements.

There may be particular institutional innovations that contribute to democratic reform, and we need to identify those and distinguish them from the general process of legal reform. It may be possible that leaders can reduce the likelihood of democratic revolt by providing courts that offer citizens redress to the performance of the administrative functions of government. We have also suggested that corruption in the courts can increase when the judicial system is underfunded so that, even if the judges have lifetime tenure, their credibility can be undermined simply by underpaying them. A weak financial base can make it possible for the courts to be intimidated by nonstate actors.

Our analysis indicates that the courts are part of the fabric of broader societal change, but can under restricted conditions precipitate change. Further research on what these conditions are will help define how reform of the courts is interwoven with larger social movements, and whether we can consider legal reform as a driving force, or an important incidental.

13

Courts in Authoritarian Regimes

Martin Shapiro

THE EXPANSION OF JUDICIAL STUDIES

This project represents something of a high watermark in the study of law and courts in general and judicial review in particular. Not so very long ago nearly every student of the politics of law and courts concentrated on the constitutional decisions of the U.S. Supreme Court. The very preoccupation with constitutional judicial review has led, in recent years, to more study of lands beyond the United States as constitutional courts and constitutional judicial review, or something very like it, spread to other democratic regimes, particularly after World War II. What once appeared to be a piece of American exceptionalism came into play in most European, continental, democratic states; and in the European Union and the European Convention on Human Rights; in more and more English-speaking countries; and in some Asian democratic states. Overseas realities eventually forced scholars to go beyond their American preoccupations.

At the same time, the very concerns with the politics of law and courts, or the judicial role in politics, that had so dramatically called our attention to the constitutional law of the U.S. Supreme Court and then to other constitutional law and courts eventually lead us to nonconstitutional courts of law, because it could hardly be denied that all sorts of American and foreign courts made significant public policy decisions in all sorts of cases involving all sorts of law.

For a long time the movement outward and downward from the constitutional judicial review of the U.S. Supreme Court remained concentrated on law and courts in democratic regimes. Indeed a strong argument can be made that courts can only make independent and effective public policy decisions in those polities that exhibit relatively high degrees of electoral, party-competitive democracy.

Again, however, global realities pushed scholarly attention onward. We confronted a growing number of "democratizing" states moving from more or less pure authoritarianism or one-party dominance to something like regimes of real party electoral competition. This made for some odd bedfellows: the former East Europe satellites, Mongolia, South Korea, Taiwan, Mexico, Chile, Argentina, some African and Middle Eastern states, and some states like Japan that might be taken as democracies rather than democratizing but had experienced long periods of one-party dominance. All this concern with democratizing naturally led to the twin questions: Was an independent, effective judiciary necessary to the achievement of democracy? Was the achievement of democracy necessary to the establishment of an independent, effective judiciary? On constitutional judicial review there was slightly less dualism. We had a number of examples, particularly in Europe, of democracy without much constitutional judicial review. So it appeared you could democratize without constitutional judicial review. But the question of whether you could have constitutional judicial review without democratizing remained open.

In the current world, concerns with political development or state-building or democratizing have become deeply entangled with economic development concerns. An international epistemic community of investment bankers and lawyers acting through entities ranging from American law schools to the World Bank has been busy trying to persuade the world that one key to national economic success is the "rule of law" enforced by independent judiciaries. Making the democratizing and even the authoritarian states safe for capitalism becomes a powerful incentive for studying courts in those places.

Finally, and a point to be turned to later, the religion of human rights that has so dramatically swept the world for the last half-century leads its believers to push for effective courts everywhere. No doubt in large part due to the American experience and its readings and mis-readings by others, courts, and in particular constitutional courts, have come to be seen by many as the premier protectors of human rights. Given that many of the students of courts, and of constitutional law in particular, are themselves true believers in the rights religion, or at least keen observers of it, they necessarily find themselves moving from the study of an American exceptionalism to the study of a hoped-for worldwide phenomenon.

Embarking on the study of courts in democratizing regimes almost inevitably pushes us on to where this project is – to courts in authoritarian regimes. The word "democratizing" itself suggests a *problematique*. Some authoritarian regimes moving toward democracy may not yet, and may never, pass over the unmarked border between the two. Others, having passed over, may or may not have fallen back. Others yet, such as Chile, having in relatively recent times moved across the boundary in each direction, are currently firmly on one side and offer courts and democratization as a historical subject rather than one of current concern. One way or another, however, the study of courts and democracy will inevitably entangle us with courts and authoritarianism.

So long as students of law and courts wore constitutional judicial review blinders, they could plausibly believe that even if their attention were drawn to courts in authoritarian regimes, there would really be no there there. As in the former Soviet Union constitutional judicial review would be merely a formal facade unworthy of study by those concerned with real politics. Once the blinders are removed, however, even in authoritarian regimes in which constitutional judicial review is insignificant, other aspects of law and courts may be politically relevant. Administrative judicial review – that is, the judicial oversight of whether administrative agencies have acted according to the statutory law – may be significant even, or especially, to regimes that have enacted statutes authoritarianly. The current Chinese fetish with courts and the rule of law is a dramatic example. Beyond judicial review, authoritarian regimes anxious for foreign investment may, à la the World Bank and IMF, support effective judiciaries for property, contract, and a wide range of other litigation of commercial concern. Once this floodgate is open we are reminded that imperial Rome, China, and Japan, and the numerous nineteenth- and twentieth-century European empires that were democratic at home and authoritarian in their overseas possessions, imposed relatively effective courts on their subjects. Indeed it can be argued that all political regimes, authoritarian and otherwise, will be inclined to institutionalize triadic conflict resolution arrangements simply because their private sectors will do better if such arrangements exist, and once they exist, courts necessarily will do some public policymaking.

This project actually reproduces much of the evolution of the field of study. There remains a heavy emphasis on constitutional courts and constitutional judicial review, but with a new alertness to administrative review. Inevitably, however, there is movement on to criminal, property, and contract law. "Inevitably," because human rights concerns are often expressed in terms of criminal prosecutions of rights violators and because economic development concerns are keyed to property and commercial law. The association of courts with rights protection is the central focus of most of these studies, but a few deal with constitutional division of powers questions and some with services that judges provide to authoritarian regimes that have nothing to do with or are antithetical to rights. Some of the studies are of polities that lie somewhere within the hazy border zone between authoritarian and democratizing, others of regimes that historically have passed back and forth over the boundary, and some of relatively long-term authoritarianisms.

Juridification and judicialization have become extremely fashionable terms in comparative law and courts studies. Those terms imply that courts did not do much politics yesterday, but do a lot today. And surely there was some real global spread of and increased significance of judicial interventions in public policymaking in the latter half of the twentieth century and beyond. Yet one is tempted to say that the word "juridification" applies more aptly to the study of comparative politics than to the actual politics being studied. To a very large degree it is not so much that courts do more now as that students of politics now see more of what courts do. It would be impossible to argue that common law courts and the civil law courts that for more than a century have been "interpreting" the relatively static language of the national codes have not been making a lot of public policy for a long time. It was just that comparative politics scholars chose to remain fundamentally ignorant of such lawmaking activity. The geographic spread of high-visibility, new constitutional courts, the global fervor over rights, and the central role of the Court of Justice in the development of the European Union, which comparativists could hardly ignore, have led to the judicialization of the field of comparative politics and the comparativization of the field of law and courts. This project, studying courts in what is usually perceived as their least favorable terrain, is a polar expedition in the new political geography of courts.

THE RULE OF LAW

Central to this polarism is a careful reexamination of the rule of law or due process of law. Vital to understanding why courts may be far more than a facade even in regimes that have no regard for rights is that we conflate two norms when speaking of the rule of law. The first is that the powers that be shall rule by, and themselves obey, enacted, general rules, and that they shall change their policies by changing those rules rather than by arbitrary deviations for or against particular persons. The second is that there is a core of individual human rights inherent in law itself, so that the rule of law must include the protection of rights. Central to this volume are two propositions. The first is that authoritarian regimes with no real allegiance to rights may, nevertheless, wish to pledge themselves, or at least their subordinate agents, to the rule of law in the first sense and to institutionalize courts as guarantors of that pledge. They may wish to do so because, quite apart from rights, they see some advantage to themselves in doing so. The second is that precisely because of the deep, long-standing, and universal association of the rule of law with individual rights, in authoritarian regimes that subscribe to that first sense of rule-of-law courts, such courts enjoy a certain potential for introducing at least some marginal protections for rights. Both of these propositions may be stated as hypotheses – the second probably far more problematic than the first.

THE DEVELOPMENT AND RIGHTS STORY

In a sense this volume is designed to test a story much touted by various purveyors of economic and political development strategies. The story runs as follows. Anxious to attract foreign investment, authoritarian regimes can be persuaded to institutionalize relatively independent and effective courts to assure investors of legal protections. Moreover written constitutions with some sort of bill of rights have become almost like national flags as an integral symbol of national sovereignty for all states, including authoritarian regimes that have no intention of doing anything other than waving them in the international arena. Because they provide an authoritarian regime benefits in terms of assuring international investors, such a regime will begin to tolerate, indeed encourage, judicial decisions protecting property rights. From that base the courts can and will move on incrementally to protect the human rights enshrined in the national constitution and supported by the international fervor for human rights. Even an authoritarian regime hostile to human rights will then let courts get away with an increasing level of even nonproperty rights protections because it wishes to maintain the competitive investment attraction advantages it receives from a property-protecting independent judiciary.

This project calls that story deeply into question. First, authoritarian regimes have a wide variety of tools, richly illustrated in our studies, for controlling judiciaries even while maintaining some facade of judicial independence for them. In particular, even courts seemingly devoted to defending the rule of law may faithfully serve an authoritarian regime that is making the law the rule of which the courts are protecting. In authoritarian regimes, either by compulsion or conviction, judges can independently and effectively pursue rule of law in the sense of government obedience to its own rules without acknowledging rights endowed with priority over those rules. In such situations an independent judiciary may not only be an ineffective rights protector against an authoritarian legislator but may even serve as an instrument of rights suppressions legislated by the regime.

Perhaps just as centrally, international investors may indeed be attracted by an independent, property-right-protecting judiciary but be quite content that the authoritarian state in which they are investing prevents courts from moving on from property rights to other rights. Indeed where anticipated returns on investment are high enough, or where a high enough risk premium can be extracted, foreign investors may plunge in with little or no assurance of legal protections, even in the face of considerable extortion, and without much concern about rights violations, property or otherwise.

OF INDIVIDUALS AND INSTITUTIONS

Like most efforts at the "new institutionalism" this project also points out that individual ideologies and skills as well as institutional design may be crucial to what actually happens. Even if we believe that there is a kind of inherent inclination of courts toward the protection of rights, and that belief is far from certain, independent judges may only defend rights if they want to. Here notions of formalism or positivism are often invoked. It is said that judges educated in a traditional positivist or formalist legal tradition, and thus seeing themselves as mere servants of the commands of the statutory law enacted by the legislature, will not intervene to protect individual rights against legislative incursion even if courts are quite independent. This argument arises in a number of our studies, but is somewhat problematic. Where there is a constitution with a bill of rights and formal provisions for judicial enforcement of that bill of rights, then positivist formalism would require that the judge enforce this command of the higher law to invalidate conflicting lower, that is statutory, law. The arch-positivist, Hans Kelsen, is as much a father of constitutional judicial review as is John Marshall. It is not positivism or formalism itself that intrinsically counsels judicial deference to statutes in legal regimes that formally command the courts to positively subordinate statutory to constitutional commands. Instead we must ask whether or why a formalist or positivist legal tradition has, in a particular national judiciary, turned into a perceived judicial duty to serve the legislature or the executive.

A large number of our studies involve transitions from relatively liberal democratic to authoritarian regimes and sometimes back toward democracy again. In some instances new constitutions and codes are written. In others the old ones are maintained as mere facades. Very often a kind of due process, rule-of-law constitutionalism is maintained in general, but special areas of military tribunals or simply "disappearances" are carved out. A relatively independent judiciary may be preserved but simply excluded from domains significant to the authoritarian regime. This strategy is one of the many authoritarian resources alluded to earlier. Where the strategy is not used, however, the issue of positivism or formalism does arise. How do judges who value their duty to the rule of law, or to judicial independence, or to staying out of politics and sticking to law, respond to changes from democratic to authoritarian regimes? This question may be more about the minds of the judges than the design of institutions.

At the most individual and least institutional level of all are questions of prudence and leadership. An authoritarian regime may choose to establish or maintain an inherited, relatively independent, effective judiciary. It may allow that judiciary some human rights leeway. The judges may define the judicial role to include some judicial review of government actions. Nevertheless, no effective judicial protection of rights may occur unless one or more judges combine significant leadership in moving their fellows in the rights direction with a sufficient sense of political strategy. This combination is well illustrated for nonauthoritarian states by John Marshall. A sense of when and where and how more or less incrementally a particular court can move to restrain a regime without triggering damaging or devastating reprisal is essential even in liberal democracies and all the more so in authoritarian states. And the ability to form winning coalitions among judicial colleagues becomes important precisely when and where the judges are relatively free of outside control. No matter what the institutional design, effective, rights-oriented judicial leadership and political prudence may or may not pop up in the courts of any particular authoritarian regime at any particular time.

JUDGES AND SOLDIERS

A number of the studies presented here highlight the relationship between courts and the military. It might appear obvious, and indeed is sometimes obviously true, that military, or military-backed, authoritarianisms will be hostile to judiciaries that attempt to restrain them and vice versa. Our studies also suggest, however, that a certain affinity or even alliance may sometimes arise between two professional corps, each respecting the other's professional integrity. That alliance may move the judges to greater tolerance of security rationales for government actions, or greater regime tolerance of judicial interventions, or both simultaneously.

CONVERGENCE

Not so much as a finding as an issue, convergence is a leitmotif of comparative studies. The responses of democratic states to terrorism almost automatically court convergence rhetoric when the topic is authoritarian states. Such rhetoric is all the more likely when the comparativists involved are law and courts specialists vitally concerned with human or constitutional rights but not particularly knowledgeable about matters criminal. So the convergence issue will simmer in any effort such as this one.

Scholarly specialists may be at the cutting edge of their own area of specialization, as I have argued the contributors to this project are. Often, however, they are prone to a certain uncritical acceptance of clichés when they borrow from adjoining fields. It is quite easy for those who are not criminal law specialists to readily accept the most conventional, received views of criminal due process or rule of law as defining the appropriate substance of constitutional rights in all circumstances.

The conventional model of criminal due process or rule of law has been elaborated from a particular prototype of the criminal. That criminal operates alone, lacks resources, and repeatedly commits the same crime until he or she is eventually caught, so that if not convicted at the first prosecution, will be by the second or third. Each of the individual crimes costs society relatively little, so that society can afford to wait until the odds on apprehension and conviction catch up with the criminal. Once apprehended, criminals necessarily cease criminal activity and lose any control they had over the prosecution's capacity to make the case against them.

In spite of our continuing allegiance to the conventional criminal due process model, we have learned that the model, unmodified, will not work when the criminal is not prototypic but instead consists of a large number of well-organized, high-resourced criminals who devote a large part of those resources to avoiding discovery and apprehension and can continue the organization's criminal activities, including denying the prosecution the evidence it needs, even after many of its leaders are apprehended. Such criminal organizations commit crimes so massive that society cannot easily contemplate their frequent repetition. Standard criminal due process does not work for organized crime, large-scale drug dealers, street gangs, and corporations. Standard search warrant requirements and uniformed-only police leave crack houses in operation. Prospective witnesses against incarcerated gang members are intimidated by unincarcerated gang members. Corporations hone their skills at deniability of knowledge and intent. Drug lords literally and otherwise fly under the radar. Whole neighborhoods become war zones.

We have acknowledged all this by RICO statutes, modifications in the law of criminal conspiracy, relaxations of the legal definition of entrapment, the employment of highly invasive surveillance techniques, no-knock search warrants, confiscation of property employed in alleged crimes under less than beyond reasonable doubt standards, suspended prosecutions of corporations on the condition that they accept court-appointed monitors, consent decrees, and many other devices that modify standard criminal due process where the defendant is not your standard burglar or convenience store bandit.

Terrorists are not your standard convenience store bandit. Modification of criminal due process to meet the deadly facts of terrorism is not well analyzed or evaluated under a convergence with authoritarianism banner. Indeed to pose the issue as a stark choice between conventional criminal due process or rule of law on the one hand or authoritarianism on the other would do enormous damage to the cause of constitutional rights in democracies. For there is little question of what choice the demos will make if they are forced to choose between a conventional rule of law ineffective against terrorism and a non-rule of law that is effective. Rather than rule of law and authoritarian banners and slogans, a careful, fact-oriented examination of exactly what devices and practices will achieve precisely what balance between individual rights and effective antiterrorism would best serve those interested in protecting constitutional rights. Nothing will serve authoritarianism better than greeting every attempt to deal with terror as authoritarian convergence.

THE LEGITIMACY PARADOX

A number of our studies also bring forward a catch-22 for courts in authoritarian regimes, particularly where such regimes have replaced more democratic ones and promise eventually to return to democracy. Usurping authoritarians may preserve the formal constitutional position, structure, and even personnel of the relatively independent courts of the previous, more democratic regime. An authoritarian regime may purport to establish an independent judiciary. Given the global appeal of "human rights," with its tendency to associate rights with courts, any set of supposedly or really independent courts is likely to enjoy a certain perceived legitimacy. If the courts challenge the authoritarian regime in which they are embedded to the extent that the regime openly ignores or controls them, they lose that legitimacy, which is about their only resource and defense against the authoritarians. If, however, they placate the regime excessively, they will undermine any public perception of their independence and thus lose their perceived legitimacy. If they manage things just right and maintain some perceived legitimacy, they lend that legitimacy to the authoritarian regime of which they are a part precisely because they are a part of it.

Faced with this conundrum many judges may feel that it is best to wait and fight another day. It may be particularly appealing to argue that "staying out of politics," even at the cost of passively lending a gloss of legitimacy to an authoritarian regime, may preserve a national tradition of judicial independence through an authoritarian interlude and assist it to flourish fully again upon the hoped-for coming transition to democracy. Or judges may conclude that avoiding the risks entailed in challenging government now, while providing independent conflict resolution in purely private disputes, is a first step toward democratization. Yet, particularly where constitutional judicial review is formally mandated, judicial passivity almost inevitably is read as judicial approval. While there are some devices for doing so, it is hard for a court that has a formal duty to say that something is or is not constitutional, or even just lawful, to refuse to intervene against allegedly unconstitutional or unlawful government acts without, at the very least tacitly, proclaiming the legitimacy of such acts. In this situation a court process risks either de-legitimating itself as an institution by challenging the government and then being crushed by it or legitimating their authoritarians.

COURTS AND REGIMES

Finally any reader of the detailed reports presented here is likely to be impressed by the fragility of courts and their dependence on regime-wide phenomena. The dynamics of courts in any particular polity are probably overdetermined, flowing from multiple and complex causes, many of which are neither directly nor obviously related to courts. In authoritarian regimes probably few political effects can be traced to particular judicial causes. In such regimes, of course, some particular judicial outcomes may be openly and brutally related to particular acts of the power holders. In at least some authoritarian regimes, however, the overall activism or passivity of the judiciary, or its level of activity in rights protection, may be complex and changing and depend at any given moment not only on institutional design but on a whole constellation of political forces and personal proclivities. In some authoritarian regimes at some times there would appear to be real judicial politics as opposed to total judicial subservience. If such a conclusion can be drawn from this project, then it has justified itself and further investigation of its subject.

References

Abrahamson, Eric, and Rosenkopf, Lori 1997. "Social Network Effects on the Extent of Innovation Diffusion: A Computer Simulation," *Organization Science* 8: 289–309.

Ackerman, Bruce 1997. "The Rise of World Constitutionalism," *Virginia Law Review* 83: 771–797.

Acuña, Carlos and Smulovitz, Catalina 1995. "Militares en la transición argentina: del gobierno a la subordinación constitucional," in Carlos Acuña et al. (eds.) *Juicio, Castigos y memorias*. Buenos Aires: Nueva Vision.

Ahmad, Feroz 1977. *The Turkish Experiment in Democracy 1950–1975*. London: Royal Institute of International Affairs.

Aliber, Robert 1975. "Exchange Risk, Political Risk, and Investor Demands for External Currency Deposits," *Journal of Money, Credit and Banking* 7: 161–179.

al-Jarida al-Rasmiyya, no. 124, June 17, 1971.

al-Jarida al-Rasmiyya, no. 40, September 30, 1971.

al-Morr, Awad. June 11, 2000. Personal interview, Moustafa.

Amann, Diane M. 2004. "Guantanamo," *Columbia Journal of Transnational Law* 42: 263.

Amnesty International 1986. "The Role of the Judiciary and the Legal Profession in the Protection of Human Rights in Chile." September.

Ancarola, G. 2000. "La función política de la Corte Suprema en los gobiernos de facto," in A. Santiago (h) and F. Alvarez (eds.) *Función Política de la Corte Suprema: Obra en Homenaje a Julio Oyhanarte*. Buenos Aires: Ábaco.

Andersen, Martin 1993. *Dossier Secreto*. Boulder: Westview Press.

Arab Republic of Egypt. 1977. *Legal Guide to Investment in Egypt: General Authority for Investment and Free Zones*. Cairo: General Egyptian Book Organization.

Arab Republic of Egypt. 1982. *Status of the Open Door Economy Investment Guide*. Cairo: Central Agency for Public Mobilization and Statistics.

Arab Republic of Egypt. 1984. *al-Mahkama al-Dusturiyya al-'Ulia*, Vols. 1–10.

Arab Republic of Egypt. 1998. *Report on the Reform of Judicial Functions*. Cairo: Ministry of Justice.

Arato, Andrew 2000. "Constitutional Lessons," *Constellations* 7: 316–340.

Arato, Andrew 2002. "The Bush Tribunals and the Specter of Dictatorship," *Constellations* 9: 457–476.

Arendt, Hannah. 1968. *The Origins of Totalitarianism*. New York: Harvest Books. Originally published in 1951.

Argentine National Commission on the Disappeared 1986. *Nunca Más: The report of the Argentine National Commission on the Disappeared*. New York: Farrar, Straus, Giroux.

Arnold, Wayne 2002. "Bloomberg News Apologizes to Top Singapore Officials." *New York Times*, August 27, section W p 1.

Arriagada, Genaro 1974. *De la 'Via Chilena' a la 'Via Insurrecional'*. Santiago: Editorial del Pacífico.

Arrow, K. J. 1979. "Pareto Efficiency with Costly Transfers," *Economic Forum* 10: 1–13.

Arslan, Zuhtu 2002. "Conflicting Paradigms: Political Rights in the Turkish Constitutional Court," *Critique: Critical Middle Eastern Studies* 11 (Spring) 9–25.

Aybay, Rona 1977. "Some Contemporary Constitutional Problems in Turkey," *Bulletin* (British Society for Middle Eastern Studies) 4: 21–27.

Ayubi, Nazih 1979. *Administrative Corruption in Egypt*. Cairo: National Center for Social and Criminal Research.

Ayubi, Nazih 1980. *Bureaucracy and Politics in Contemporary Egypt*. London: Ithaca Press.

Ayubi, Nazih. 1995. *Overstating the Arab State: Politics and Society in the Middle East*. New York: I.B. Tauris.

Baglini, Norman 1976. *Risk Management in International Corporations*. New York: Risk Studies Foundation.

Baker, Raymond 1978. *Egypt's Uncertain Revolution under Nassir and Sadat*. Cambridge, MA: Harvard University Press.

Baker, Raymond 1981. "Sadat's Open Door: Opposition from Within," *Social Problems* 28: 378–384.

Bannikov, S. G. 1974. "Verkhovnyi sud SSSR i sovershenstvovanie sovetskogo zakonodatelstva," in L.N. Smirnov (ed.) *Verkhovnyi sud SSSR*. Moscow.

Barkan, Steven E. 1985. *Protestors on Trial: Criminal Justice in the Southern Civil Rights and Vietnam Antiwar Movements*. New Brunswick, NJ: Rutgers University Press.

Barros, Robert. 2002. *Constitutionalism and Dictatorship: Pinochet, the Junta, and the 1980 Constitution*. Cambridge: Cambridge University Press.

Barros, Robert 2003. "Dictatorship and the Rule of Law: Rules and Military Power in Pinochet's Chile," in J. M. Maravall and A. Przeworski (eds.) *Democracy and the Rule of Law*. Cambridge: Cambridge University Press.

Bates, Robert. 1992. "The Impulse to Reform," in Jennifer Widner (ed.) *Economic Change and Political Liberalization in Sub-Saharan Africa*. Baltimore: Johns Hopkins Press.

Baum, Lawrence 2006. *Judges and Their Audiences: A Perspective on Judicial Behavior*. Princeton, NJ: Princeton University Press.

Beattie, Kirk 2000. *Egypt during the Sadat Years*. New York: Palgrave.

Belge, Ceren 2006. "Friends of the Court." *Law and Society Review* 40.

Bell, Daniel 2000. *The End of Ideology*. Cambridge, MA: Harvard University Press.

Benson, Miles and Wood, David 2002. "Terrorism Suspect's Detention by Military Faces Tide of Criticism," *Miami Herald*, June 16, p. 15A.

Bentley, John 1994. *Egyptian Legal and Judicial Sector Assessment*. Cairo: U.S. Agency for International Development.

Bermeo, Nancy 1986. *The Revolution within the Revolution: Workers' Control in Rural Portugal*. Princeton, NJ: Princeton University Press.

Bernhardt, Kathryn, Huang, Philip, and Allee, Mark 1994. *Civil Law in Qing and Republican China, Law, Society, and Culture in China*. Stanford: Stanford University Press.

Bian, Yanjie 1997. "Bringing Strong Ties Back in: Indirect Ties, Network Bridges, and Job Searches in China," *American Sociological Review* 62 (3): 366–385.

Bian, Yanjie. 1999. "Getting a Job through a Web of Guanxi in China," in B. Wellman (ed.) *Networks in the Global Village: Life in Contemporary Communities*. Boulder: Westview Press.

Bian, Yanjie, Shu, Xiaoling, and Logan, John 2001. "Communist Party Membership and Regime Dynamics in China," *Social Forces* 79 (3): 805–841.

Bidart Campos, G. J. 1989. *Tratado Elemental de Derecho Constitucional Argentino*. Buenos Aires: EDIAR.

Biddulph, S. 2004. "The Production of Legal Norms: A Case Study of Administrative Detention in China," *UCLA Pacific Basin Law Journal* 20: 217–277.

Bila, Fikret 1998. "Baba'dan 'kuzu' benzetmesi," *Milliyet* (Internet Edition), http://www.milliyet.com.tr/1998/03/22/index.html (accessed on February 18, 2007).

Bishop, W. 1990. "A Theory of Administrative Law," *Journal of Legal Studies* 19: 489–530.

Bishop, W. 1998. "Comparative Administrative Law," in Peter Newman (ed.) *The New Palgrave Dictionary of Law and Economics*, pp. 327–35. London: MacMillan.

Black, Henry Campbell, Nolan, Joseph R., and Connolly, Michael J. 1979. *Black's Law Dictionary: Definitions of the Terms and Phrases of American and English Jurisprudence*. St. Paul: West Publishing Co.

Brabii, A. 2006. "Kto podnial ruku na prisiazhnykh?" *Tikhookeanskaia zvezda*, April 15.

Braga da Cruz, Manuel 1988. *O Partido e o Estado no Salazarismo*. Lisbon: Editorial Presenca.

Bravin, Jess 2003. "Capital Charges Thrown Out In Moussaoui Terrorism Trial," *Wall Street Journal*, October 3, p. A6.

Brett, Sebastian 1992. *Chile: A Time of Reckoning*. Geneva: International Commission of Jurists.

Brooker, Paul 2000. *Non-Democratic Regimes: Theory, Government, and Politics*. New York: St. Martin's Press.

Brown, Nathan. 1997. *The Rule of Law in the Arab World: Courts in Egypt and the Gulf*. Cambridge: Cambridge University Press.

"Brown Quer Soltos Cinco de Guantanamo." 2007. *Folha de Sao Paulo*, August 8, p. A14.

Brumberg, Daniel 2001. *Reinventing Khomeini: The Struggle for Reform in Iran*. Chicago: University of Chicago Press.

Brysk, Alison 1994a. *The Politics of Human Rights in Argentina: Protest, Change, and Democratization*. Stanford: Stanford University Press.

Brysk, Alison 1994b. "The Politics of Measurement: The Contested Count of the Disappeared in Argentina," *Human Rights Quarterly* 16: 676–692.

Brzezinski, Mark 1998. *The Struggle for Constitutionalism in Poland*. London: Macmillan.

Buchta, Wilfried 2000. *Who Rules Iran? The Structure of Power in the Islamic Republic.* Washington: Washington Institute for Near East Policy.

Bueno de Mesquita, Bruce, Smith, Alastair, Siverson, Randolph M., and Morrow, James D. 2003. *The Logic of Political Survival.* Cambridge, MA: MIT Press.

Bueno de Mesquita, Bruce and Root, Hilton L. 2000. "When Bad Economics Is Good Politics," in Bruce Bueno de Mesquita and Hilton Root (eds.) *Governing for Prosperity.* New Haven: Yale University Press.

Burkov, A. L. 2005. "Akty sudebnogo normakontrolia kak istochnik administrativnogo prava." Aftoreferat kandidatskoi dissertatsii. Tiumenskii gosudarstvennyi univ.

Burkov, A. L. 2006. *Primenenie Evropeiskoi Konventsii o Pravakh Cheloveka v sudakh Rossii.* Ekaterinburg: Izd. Uralskogo universiteta. Available at: www.sutyajnik.ru/rus/library/sborniki/echr6/echr6.pdf

Butler, Judith 2002. "Guantánamo Limbo," *The Nation*, April, 1, pp. 20–24.

Calveiro, Pilar 1995. *Poder y Desaparición: Los Campos de Concentración en Argentina.* Buenos Aires: Ediciones Colihue.

Camp, Roderic 1992. *Generals in the Palacio. The Military in Modern Mexico.* New York: Oxford University Press.

Camp, Roderic 1995. *Political Recruitment across Two Centuries: Mexico 1884–1991.* Austin: University of Texas Press.

Cardoso, Fernando Henrique 1979. "On the Characterization of Authoritarian Regimes in Latin America," in David Collier (ed.) *The New Authoritarianism in Latin America.* Princeton, NJ: Princeton University Press.

Carothers, T. 2003. *Promoting the Rule of Law Abroad: The Problem of Knowledge.* Washington, DC: Carnegie Endowment for International Peace.

Carpizo, Jorge 1978. *El Presidencialismo Mexicano.* Mexico City: Siglo XXI.

Carr, David 1979. *Foreign Investment and Development in Egypt.* New York: Praeger.

Carrió, A. 1996. *La Corte Suprema y su Independencia.* Buenos Aires: Abeledo–Perrot.

Casar, Maria Amparo 2002. "Executive-Legislative Relations: The Case of Mexico (1946–1997)," in Benito Nacif and Scott Morgenstern (eds.) *Legislative Politics in Latin America*, New York: Cambridge University Press.

Catholic Church 1989. *Jurisprudencia: Delitos contra la seguridad del Estado.* Santiago: Arzobispado de Santiago, Vicaría de la Solidaridad.

Cavallo, Ascanio, Salazar, Manuel and Sepulveda, Jorge 1989. *La Historia Oculta del Regimen Militar.* Santiago: Antarctica.

Cayuso, S. G. and. Gelli, M.A. 1988. "Ruptura de la legitimidad constitucional. La acordada de la Corte Suprema de Justicia de la Nación de 1930," *Cuadernos de Investigación.* Buenos Aires: Instituto de Investigaciones Jurídicas y Sociales "Ambrosio L. Gioja," Universidad de Buenos Aires.

Cea, José Luis 1978. "Law and Socialism in Chile, 1970–1973." Ph.D. diss., University of Wisconsin-Madison.

Celoza, Albert F. 1997. *Ferdinand Marcos and the Philippines: The Political Economy of Authoritarianism.* Westport, CT: Greenwood Publishing Group.

Center for Human Rights Legal Aid. 1995. *"al-Qada' al-'Askiry fi Misr: Qada' Bighayr Damanat . . . Qada' Bidoun Hasana Mathamoun Bila Haquq"* [The Military Judiciary in Egypt: Courts without Safeguards, Judges without Immunity, and Defendants without Rights]. Cairo: CHRLA.

Center for Public Integrity 2004. *Global Access – Methodology Memo*. Washington DC: The Center for Public Integrity.

Chan, Cassandra 2003. "Breaking Singapore's Regrettable Tradition of Chilling Free Speech with Defamation Laws," *Loyola of Los Angeles International and Comparative Law Review* 26: 315.

Chaskalon, Arthur 2003. "From Wickedness to Equality: The Moral Transformation of South African Law," *International Journal of Constitutional Law* 1: 590–609.

Chavez, Rebecca Bill 2004. *The Rule of Law in Nascent Democracies: Judicial Politics in Argentina*. Stanford: Stanford University Press.

Chehabi, Houchng E. 2001. "The Political Regime of the Islamic Republic of Iran in Comparative Perspective," *Government and Opposition* 36 (Winter 2001): 48–70.

Cheibub, José Antonio 2004. *Political Institutions*. New Haven: Yale University Press.

Cheibub, Jose Antonio and Jennifer Gandhi, 2004. "Classifying Political Regimes: A Six-Fold Measure of Democracies and Dictatorships." Paper prepared for annual meeting of the American Political Science Association, Chicago.

Chen, Xueyi, and Shi, Tianjian 2001. "Media Effects on Political Confidence and Trust in the People's Republic of China in the Post-Tiananmen Period," *East Asia: An International Quarterly* 19 (Fall): 84–118.

Chng Suan Tze v Minister of Home Affairs, (1988) Singapore Law Reports 132.

Choi, C. 2005. *Law and Justice in Korea*. Seoul: Seoul National University Press.

Christopher Bridges v. Public Prosecutor, 1 *Singapore Law Report* 406, (High Court, 1997)

Chua, Mui Hoong, 1997. "PM: Precincts with Greater Support Get Upgraded First," *Straits Times*, January, 1, p 1.

Clarke, Donald C. 1995. "The Execution of Civil Judgments in China," *China Quarterly* 141 (March): 65–81.

Clarke, D., Murell, P. and Whiting, S. 2006. "The Role of Law in China's Economic Development" (January 27, 2006). GWU Law School Public Law Research Paper No. 187 Available at http://ssrn.com/abstract=878672

Cohen, Jerome A. 1997. "Reforming China's Civil Procedure: Judging the Courts," *American Journal of Comparative Law* 45 (4): 793–804.

Comisión Rettig (Comisión Nacional de Verdad y Reconciliación) 1991. *Informe de la Comisión Nacional de Verdad y Reconciliación. Texto Oficial Completo*. 2 vols. 2nd. ed. Santiago: La Nación and Las Ediciones del Ornitorrinco.

CONADEP (Comisión Nacional sobre la Desaparición de Personas) 1984. *Nunca Mas. Informe de la Comisión Nacional sobre la Desaparición de Personas*. Buenos Aires: EUDEBA.

Constable, Pamela, and Valenzuela, Arturo 1991. *A Nation of Enemies*. New York: W.W. Norton.

Constitutional Court of the Republic of Turkey. n.d. *The Turkish Constitutional Court*, http://www.anayasa.gov.tr/ (accessed on February 18, 2007)

Cooter, Robert and Ginsburg, Tom. 1996. "Comparative Judicial Discretion – An Empirical Test Of Economic Models," *International Review of Law and Economics* 16: 295–313.

Correa Sutil, Jorge 1993. "The Judiciary and the Political System in Chile: The Dilemmas of Judicial Independence during the Transition to Democracy," in I. Stotzky (ed.) *Transition to Democracy in Latin America: The Role of the Judiciary*. Boulder: Westview Press.

Cossío, José Ramón 2000. "Comentario al Artículo 105 Constitucional," en Miguel Carbonell (coord.) *Constitución Política de los Estados Unidos Mexicanos. Comentada y Condordada*, México: Porrúa/UNAM.

Cossio, José Ramón. 2001. "La Suprema Corte y la teoría constitucional," *Política y Gobierno* VIII (1).

Couso, Javier 2002. "The Politics of Judicial Review in Latin America: Chile in Comparative Perspective." PhD diss., University of California, Berkeley.

Cover, Robert 1975. *Justice Accused: Antislavery and the Judicial Process*. New Haven: Yale University Press.

Craig, Gordon 1955. *The Politics of the Prussian Army, 1640–1945*. New York: Oxford University Press.

Cúneo Machiavello, Andrés 1980. "La Corte Suprema de Chile: Sus Percepciones acerca del Derecho, Su Rol en el Sistema Legal y la Relación de Este con el Sistema Política," in Javier de Belaúnde Lopez de Romana (ed.) *La Administración de Justicia en América Latína*. Lima: Consejo Latinoamericano de Derecho y Desarrollo.

da Costa Filho, Milton Menezes 1994. *A Justica Militar no Poder Judiciário*. Brasília: Superior Tribunal Militar, DIDOC, Seção da Divulgação.

Dahl, Robert 1957. "Decision Making In A Democracy: The Supreme Court As A National Policy-Maker," Journal of Public Law 6: 279–95.

Damaska, Mirjan R. 1986. *The Faces of Justice and State Authority*. New Haven: Yale University Press.

"Death Penalty Ruled Out for Two British Detainees." 2003. *New York Times*, July, 23, p. A4.

de Matos, Marco Aurélio Vannucchi Leme 2002. *Em Nome de Segurança Nacional: Os Processos da Justiça Militar contra a Ação Libertadora Nacional, ALN 1969–1979*. PhD diss., University of São Paulo.

de Ramón, Armando 1999. *Biografías de Chilenos, 1876–1973, Miembros de los Poderes Ejecutivo, Legislativo, y Judicial*. Santiago, Chile: Ediciones Universidad Católica de Chile.

de Soto, Hernando. 2000. *The Mystery of Capital: Why Capitalism Triumphs in the West and Fails Everywhere Else*. New York: Basic Books.

de Tocqueville, A., Furet, F. and Mélonio, F. 1998. *The Old Regime and the Revolution*. Chicago: University of Chicago Press. Originally published 1856.

Del Carmen, Rolando 1973. "Constitutionalism and the Supreme Court in a Changing Philippine Polity," *Asian Survey* 13 (11): 1050—1061

Delupis, Ingrid 1973. *Finance and Protection of Investments in Developing Countries*. Essex: Gower Press.

"Detention Cases before Supreme Court Will Test Limits of Presidential Power." 2004. *New York Times*, April 18, p. 19.

Devereux, Robert 1965. "Turkey's Judicial Security Mechanism," *Die Welt des Islams* 10: 33–40.

Dezalay, Yves and Garth, Bryant 2002. *The Internationalization of Palace Wars: Lawyers, Economists, and the Contest to Transform Latin American States*. Chicago: University of Chicago Press.

Diamant, Neil Jeffrey, Lubman, Stanley B., and O'Brien, Kevin J. 2005. *Engaging the Law in China: State, Society, and Possibilities for Justice*. Stanford: Stanford University Press.

Diamond, Larry 2002. "Thinking about Hybrid Regimes," *Journal of Democracy* 13: 21–35.

Dickson, Bruce J. and Rublee, Maria Rost. 2000. "Membership Has Its Privileges: the Socioeconomic Characteristics of Party Members in Urban China," *Comparative Political Studies* 33: 87–112.

di Federico, Giuseppe and Guarnieri, Carlo 1988. "The Courts in Italy," in Jerold L. Waltman and Kenneth M. Holland (eds.) *The Political Role of Law Courts in Modern Democracies*. London: Macmillan.

Dobrovolskaia, T.N. 1964. *Verkhovnyi sud SSSR*. Moscow: Iuridicheskaia literatura.

Dodd, C. H. 1983. *The Crisis of Turkish Democracy*. Beverly, England: Eothen.

Dodds, Paisely 2004. "Arraignments on Tap for Cuba Detainees." *Times-Picayune*, August 23, p. A-10.

Domingo, Pilar 2000. "Judicial Independence: The Politics of the Supreme Court in Mexico," *Journal of Latin American Studies* 32.

Dow Jones v. Attorney General of Singapore, 1989. Singapore Law Reports 70; 2MLJ 385.

Drake, Paul 1996. *Labor Movements and Dictatorships: The Southern Cone in Comparative Perspective*. Baltimore: Johns Hopkins University Press.

Dubber, Markus Dirk 1993. "Judicial Positivism and Hitler's Injustice," *Columbia Law Review* 93 (7): 1807–1831.

Dyzenhaus, David 1991. *Hard Cases in Wicked Legal Systems; South African Law in the Perspective of Legal Philosophy*. New York: Oxford University Press.

Dyzenhaus, David 1998. *Judging the Judges, Judging Ourselves: Truth, Reconciliation and the Apartheid Legal Order*. Portland, OR: Hart Publishing.

Eisenstadt, Todd 2004. *Courting Democracy in Mexico*. Cambridge: Cambridge University Press.

Egyptian Organization for Human Rights. 1996. *Recurrent Detention: Prisoners Without Trial*. Cairo: Egyptian Organization for Human Rights.

El-Nazer, Gamal 1979. "The Legal Framework for Foreign Investment in Egypt," *Case Western Reserve Journal of International Lawyer* 11: 613–622.

Epp, Charles R. 1998. *The Rights Revolution: Lawyers, Activists, and Supreme Courts in Comparative Perspective*. Chicago: University of Chicago Press.

Etzioni, Amitai and Marsh, Jason H. 2003. *Rights vs. Public Safety after 9/11: America in the Age of Terrorism*. Lanham: Rowman & Littlefield.

Farhang, Michael. 1994. "Terrorism and Military Trials in Egypt: Presidential Decree No. 375 and the Consequences for Judicial Authority." *Harvard International Law Journal* 35: 225–237.

Ferejohn, John. 2002. "Judicializing Politics, Politicizing Law," *Law and Contemporary Problems* 65: 41–68.

Ferejohn, John and Weingast, Barry R. 1992. "A Positive Theory of Statutory Interpretation," *International Review of Law and Economics* 12: 263–279.

Fernandes, Octávio J.S. 1983. "O Superior Tribunal Militar e a Legislação de Segurança Nacional," *Revista do Superior Tribunal Militar* 7: 7–50.

Ferreira, Célia Lobão 1984/85. "Crimes Contra a Segurança do Estado," *Revista do Superior Tribunal Militar* 8: 23–88.

Fisman, R. 2001. "Estimating the Value of Political Connections," *American Economic Review* 91: 1095–1102.

Fontana, Andres Miguel 1987. "Political Decision Making by a Military Corporation: Argentina, 1976–1983." Ph.D. diss. University of Texas, Austin.

Fraenkel, Ernst 1969. *The Dual State: A Contribution to the Theory of Dictatorship,* E.A. Shils (trans.). New York: Octagon Books. Originally published in 1941.

Frye, Timothy and Shleifer, Andrei. 1996. "The Invisible Hand and the Grabbing Hand," NBER Working Papers 5856, National Bureau of Economic Research.

Fuller, Lon L. 1958. "Positivism and the Fidelity to Law – A Reply to Professor Hart," *Harvard Law Review* 71 (February): 630–672.

Fuller, Lon L. 1964. *The Morality of Law* (revised ed.). New Haven: Yale University Press.

"Further Talks on Guantanamo Britons." 2003. *Financial Times,* August 10, p. 2.

Galanter, Marc 1974. "Why the 'Haves' Come out Ahead: Speculations on the Limits of Social Change," *Law and Society Review* 9: 95–160.

Gallagher, Mary E. 2005. "Use the Law as Your Weapon! The Rule of Law and Labor Conflict in the PRC," in N. J. Diamant, S. B. Lubman and K. J. O'Brien (eds.) *Engaging the Law in China: State, Society, and Possibilities for Justice.* Stanford: Stanford University Press.

Galleguillos, Nibaldo H. 1998. "From Confrontation to Friendly Persuasion: An Analysis of Judicial Reform and Democratization in Post-Pinochet Chile," *Canadian Journal of Latin American and Caribbean Studies* 23: 161–192.

Gallo, Max 1974. *Spain under Franco: A History.* New York: E. P. Dutton and Company.

Ganji, Akbar 2000. *'Alijenab-i Surkhposh va 'alijenab-i khakestari: Asibshenasi gozara beh doulat-i demokratik-i tos'ehgara* [English title: *The Red Eminence and the Gray Eminences: Pathology of Transition to the Developmental Democratic State*] Teheran: Tarh-e no.

Garcia Villegas, Rene. 1990. *Soy Testigo* (Dicatdura – Tortura – Injusticia). Santiago: Editorial Amerinda.

Garrido, Luis Javier 1982. *El Partido de la Revolución Institucionalizada.* Mexico City: Siglo XXI.

Gathii, James T. 2003. "Torture, Extraterritoriality, Terrorism, and International Law," *Albany Law Review* 67: 335.

Geddes, Barbara 1994. *Politicians' Dilemmas.* Berkeley: California University Press.

Gee, Marcus 1997. "International Affairs: The Singapore Suits," *Globe and Mail,* March 12, p. A-15.

Gelli, M. A. 2000. "El papel político de la Corte Suprema en las crisis institucionales." In A. Santiago and F. Alvarez (eds.) *Función Política de la Corte Suprema: Obra en Homenaje a Julio Oyhanarte.* Buenos Aires: Ábaco.

George, Alexander, 1979. "Case Studies and Theory Development: The Method of Structured, Focused Comparison," in Paul Gordon Lauren (ed.) *Diplomacy: New Approaches in History, Theory, and Policy.* New York: Free Press 43–67.

Gerber, T. P. 2000. "Membership Benefits or Selection Effects? Why Former Communist Party Members do Better in Post-Soviet Russia. *Social Science Research,* 29: 25–50.

Gibson, James L. 1986. "The Social Science of Judicial Politics," in Herbert Weisberg (ed.) *Political Science: The Science of Politics*. New York: Agathon Press, 141–166.

Giles, Michael W. and Lancaster, Thomas D. 1989. "Political Transition, Social Development, and Legal Mobilization in Spain," *American Political Science Review* 83 (3): 817–833.

Ginsburg, Tom 2002. "Comparative Administrative Procedures: Evidence from Northeast Asia," *Constitutional Political Economy* 13: 247–264.

Ginsburg, Tom 2003. *Judicial Review in New Democracies: Constitutional Courts in Asian Cases*. Cambridge: Cambridge University Press.

Ginsburg, Tom 2007. "Law and the Liberal Transformation of the Northeast Asian Legal Complex in Korea and Taiwan," in Terrence Halliday, Lucien Karpik and Malcolm M. Feeley (eds.). *Fighting for Political Freedom: Comparative Studies of the Legal Complex and Political Change*. Oxford: Hart Publishing.

Ginsburg, Tom and Kagan, Robert 2005. *Institutions and Public Law: Comparative Approaches*. New York: Peter Lang Publishing.

Global Governance Indicators (2005) available at http://web.worldbank.org/WBSITE/EXTERNAL/WBI/EXTWBIGOVANTCOR/0,contentMDK:20771165~menuPK:1866365~pagePK:64168445~piPK:64168309~theSitePK:1740530,00.html

Goh, S. 1991. "Asia Has Much to Offer West – BG Yeo." *Straits Times*, August 13.

Gold, Thomas, Guthrie, Douglas, and Wank, David L., 2002. *Social Connections in China: Institutions, Culture and the Changing Nature of Guanxi*. New York: Cambridge University Press.

Goldberg, Suzanne 2006. "Pentagon Breaks with Bush on Detentions," *The Guardian* (UK), July 12.

Gomez, James 2005. "Free Speech and Opposition Parties in Singapore," *AsiaRights* 5, available at http://www.jamesgomeznews.com/article.php?AID=221

Gonzales, Albert R. 2001. "Martial Justice, Full and Fair," *New York Times*, November 30, p. A25.

González Compeán, Miguel and Peter Bauer. 2002. *Jurisdicción y democracia. Los nuevos rumbos del Poder Judicial en México*, México: Cal y Arena.

Graber, Mark 1993. "The Nonmajoritarian Difficulty: Legislative Deference to the Judiciary," *Studies in American Political Development* 7.

Graber, Mark 2001. "Thick and Thin: Interdisciplinary Conversations on Populism, Law, Political Science and Constitutional Change," *Georgetown Law Journal* 90: 233.

Grigoreva, Nina. 2006."Vperedi Evropy vsei: Rossiane lidiruiut po kolichestvu obrashchenii v Strasborgskii sud." *Rossiiskaia gazeta*, July 6.

Groisman, E. I. 1989. "Los gobiernos *de facto* en el derecho Argentino," *Revista del Centro de Estudios Constitucionales* 4: 35–45.

Guarnieri, Carlo and Pederzoli, Patrizia 2002. *The Power of Judges: A Comparative Study of Courts and Democracy*. New York: Oxford University Press.

Guseva, Alya, and Akos Rona-Tas. 2001. "Uncertainty, Risk, and Trust: Russian and American Credit Card Markets Compared." *American Sociological Review* 66:623–646.

Guthrie, Doug 1999. *Dragon in a Three-Piece Suit: The Emergence of Capitalism in China*. Princeton, NJ: Princeton University Press.

Hägerstrand, Torsten 1967. *Innovation Diffusion as a Spatial Process*. Chicago: University of Chicago Press.

Haggard, Stephan and Kaufman, Robert R. 1995. *The Political Economy of Democratic Transitions*. Princeton, NJ: Princeton University Press.

Hale, William 1977. "Turkish Democracy in Travail: The Case of the State Security Courts," *World Today* 33 (May): 186–194.

Hall, Bronwyn H., 2004. *Innovation and Diffusion*. National Bureau of Economic Research Available from http://papers.nber.org/papers/

Halliday, Terence, Malcolm Feeley, and Lucian Karpik (eds.). 2007. *Fighting for Political Freedom: Comparative Studies of the Legal Complex for Political Liberalism*. Oxford: Hart Publishing.

Hand, Keith J. 2006. "Using Law for a Righteous Purpose: The Sun Zhigang Incident and Evolving Forms of Citizen Action in the People's Republic of China," *Columbia Journal of Transnational Law* 45: 114–94.

Hart, H.L.A. 1958. "Positivism and the Separation of Law and Morals," *Harvard Law Review* 71 (February): 593–629.

Hart, H.L.A. 1961. *The Concept of Law*. Oxford: Oxford University Press.

Hazama, Yasushi 1996. "Constitutional Review and the Parliamentary Opposition in Turkey," *Developing Economies* 34 (September): 316–338.

He, X. 2006. "Notion of and Justifications for Gender Discrimination in Employment." LL.D. Thesis, Kyushu University.

Helmke, Gretchen 2002. "The Logic of Strategic Defection: Court-Executive Relations in Argentina under Dictatorship and Democracy," *American Political Science Review* 96: 291–303.

Helmke, Gretchen 2005. *Courts under Constraints: Judges, Generals and Presidents in Argentina*. New York: Cambridge University Press.

Hendley, Kathryn 1998. "Remaking an Institution: The Transition in Russia from State *Arbitrazh* to *Arbitrazh* Courts," *American Journal of Comparative Law* 44: 93–116.

Heper, Metin 1985. *The State Tradition in Turkey*. Beverly: Eothen Press.

Herb, Michael 1999. *All in the Family: Absolutism, Revolution, and Democracy in the Middle Eastern Monarchies*. Albany: State University of New York Press.

Hershbarger, Robert and Noerager, John 1976. "International Risk Management," *Risk Management* (April 1976): 23–34.

Hetherington, M.J. 1998. "The Political Relevance of Political Trust," *American Political Science Review* 92 (4): 791–808.

Hilbink, Elisabeth C. 1999. "Legalism against Democracy: The Political Role of the Judiciary in Chile, 1964–94." PhD diss., Department of Political Science, University of California-San Diego.

Hilbink, Elisabeth C. 2001. "Judges Like Soldiers: Lessons for Judicial Reformers from the Literature on Military Reform in Latin America." Paper presented at the 2001 Annual Meeting of the American Political Science Association, San Francisco.

Hilbink, Elisabeth C. 2007. *Judges beyond Politics in Democracy and Dictatorship: Lessons from Chile*. New York: Cambridge University Press.

Hinnebusch, Raymond 1985. *Egyptian Politics under Sadat: The Post-Populist Development of an Authoritarian-Modernizing State*. Cambridge: Cambridge University Press.

Hirschl, Ran 2004. *Towards Juristocracy: The Origins and Consequences of New Constitutionalism*. Cambridge, MA: Harvard University Press.

Holden, P. 1997. "Collateral without Consequence: Some Causes and Effects of Financial Underdevelopment in Latin America," *The Financier* 4: 12–21.

Huang, Philip C. 2001. *Code, Custom, and Legal Practice in China : The Qing and the Republic Compared: Law, Society, and Culture in China*. Stanford: Stanford University Press.

Huntington, Samuel P. 1991. *The Third Wave: Democratization in the Late Twentieth Century*. Norman, OK: University of Oklahoma Press.

Hutchinson, Allan and Monahan, Patrick 1987. "Democracy and the Rule of Law," in Allan C. Hutchinson and Patrick Monahan (eds.) *The Rule of Law: Ideal or Ideology*. Toronto: Carswell.

Iakovlev, Alexander 1993, January. Interview conducted by Todd Foglesong and Peter Solomon with Alexander Nikolaevich Iakovlev in Toronto.

Iakovlev, M. 2006. "Prisiazhnye opravdateli: Pochemy organy sledstviia ne polzuiutsia doveriem 'narodnykh zasedatelei,'" *Gazeta Versiia online*, March 3.

Iarayczower, Matias, Spiller, Pablo T. and Tommasi, Mariano 2002. "Judicial Decision-making in Unstable Environment: Argentina 1935–1998." *American Journal of Political Science* 46: 699–716.

Igounet (h.), Oscar and Oscar Igounet. 1985. *Codigo de Justicia Militar: Anotado, Comentado con Jurisprudencia y Doctrina Nacional y Extranjera*. Buenos Aires: Librería del Jurista.

Inglehart, Ronald 1997. *Modernization and Postmodernization: Cultural, Economic, and Political Change in 43 Societies*. Princeton, NJ: Princeton University Press.

International Bar Association. Judicial Independence Undermined: A Report on Uganda, International Bar Association Human Rights Institute Report, September 2007 accessed at http://www.ibanet.org/iba/article.cfm?article=129

Janos, Andrew 1970. "The One-Party State and Social Mobilization: East Europe between the Wars," in Samuel Huntington and C. Moore (eds.) *Authoritarian Politics in Modern Societies: The Dynamics of Established One-Party Systems*. New York: Basic Books.

Jennings, M. Kent 1998. "Political Trust and the Roots of Devolution," in V.A. Braithwaite and M. Levi (eds.) *Trust and Governance*. New York: Russell Sage Foundation.

Jiang, Z. 1998. "The Administrative Use of Law in China: The Baori Golf Club Tax Case," *Columbia Journal of Asian Law* 12: 191–249.

Kahn, Peter 2002. "The Russian Bailiffs System and the Enforcement of Civil Judgements," *Post-Soviet Affairs* 18: 148–181.

Kairys, David 1982. *The Politics of Law: A Progressive Critique*. New York: Pantheon.

Katyal, Neal and Tribe, Laurence 2002. "Waging War, Deciding Guilt: Trying the Military Tribunals," *Yale Law Journal* 111 1259–1310.)

Kaufmann, Daniel, Kraa, Aart and Mastruzzi, Massimo 2005. *Governance Matters IV: Governance Indicators for 1996–2004*. New York: World Bank.

Kelly, Margaret 1974. "Evaluating the Risks of Expropriation," *Risk Management* (January 1): 23–43.

Khiabani, Gholam and Sreberny, Anabelle 2001. "The Iranian Press and the Continuing Struggle over Civil Society, 1998–2000," *International Communication Gazette* 63: 203–223.

Kili, Suna 1971. *Turkish Constitutional Developments and Assembly Debates on the Constitutions of 1924 and 1961*. Istanbul: Robert College Research Center.

King, Gary, Murray, Christopher, Salomon, Joshua and Tandon, Ajay, 2003. "Enhancing the Validity and Cross-Cultural Comparability of Measurement in Survey Research," *American Political Science Review*, 97: 567–584.

Kipnis, Andrew B. 1997. *Producing Guanxi: Sentiment, Self, and Subculture in a North China Village*. Durham: Duke University Press.

Kirchheimer, Otto 1961. *Political Justice*. Princeton, NJ: Princeton University Press.

Klaris, Edward J. 2002. "Justice Can't Be Done in Secret," *The Nation*, June 10, pp. 16–20.

Kleandrov, Mikhail I. 2001. *Arbitrazhnye sudy Rossiiskoi Federatsii*. Moscow: Iurist.

Knight, Frank 1971. *Risk, Uncertainty and Profit*. Chicago: University of Chicago Press.

Knudson, Jerry W. 1997. "Veil of Silence: The Argentine Press and the Dirty War, 1976–1983," *Latin American Perspectives* 24: 93–112.

Koçak, Mustafa and Örücü, Esin 2003. "Dissolution of Political Parties in the Name of Democracy: Cases from Turkey and the European Court of Human Rights," *European Public Law* 9: 399–423.

Köch, Hannsjoachim 1989. *In the Name of the Volk: Political Justice in Hitler's Germany*. London: I.B. Taurus and Co.

Kogacioglu, Dicle 2003. "Dissolution of Political Parties by the Constitutional Court in Turkey: Judicial Delimitation of the Political Domain," *International Sociology* 18 (March): 258–276.

Kogacioglu, Dicle 2004. "Progress, Unity, and Democracy: Dissolving Political Parties in Turkey," *Law and Society Review* 38 (3): 433–462.

Kommersant 2006. "Vy prisizhnym doveriaete?" *Kommersant vlast*, April 10.

Konstitutsionnyi sud RF 2004. "Po delu o proverke konstitutsionnosti otdelnykh polozhenii punkta 2 chasti pervoi stati 27, chastei pervoi, vtoroi i chetvertoi stati 251, chastei vtoroi i tretei stati 253 Grazhdanskogo protsessualnogo kodeksa Rossiiskoi Federatsii v sviazi s zaprosom Pravitelstva RF," *Rossiiskaia gazeta*, February 3.

Kornia, A. 2006. "Advokat sude ne muzh. Sluzhiteliam femidy ogranichat lichuiu zhizn," *Vedomosti*, February 28.

Krastev, Ivan 2006. "Democracy's 'Doubles,'" *Journal of Democracy* 17: 52–62.

Krug, Barbara 2004. *China's Rational Entrepreneurs: The Development of the New Private Business Sector*. New York: RoutledgeCurzon.

Ku, Hok Bun. 2003. *Moral Politics in a South Chinese Village: Responsibility, Reciprocity, and Resistance*. Lanham, MD: Rowman & Littlefield.

Kydland, F.E. and Prescott, E.C. 1977. "Rules Rather than Discretion: The Inconsistency of Optimal Plans," *Journal of Political Economy* 85: 473–491.

Laitin, David 2002. "Comparative Politics: The State of the Subdiscipline," in Ira Katznelson and Helen Milner (eds.) *Political Science: The State of the Discipline*. New York: W.W. Norton and Company.

Landes, William and Posner, Richard 1975. "The Independent Judiciary in an Interest-Group Perspective," *Journal of Law and Economics* 18: 875.

Landry, Pierre F., and Mingming Shen 2005. "Reaching Migrants in Survey Research: The Use of the Global Positioning System to Reduce Coverage Bias in China," *Political Analysis* 13 (1): 1–22.

Lee, Kuan Yew 1990. Speech at the Opening of the Singapore Law Academy by Prime Minister Lee Kuan Yew. August 31, 1990. Available at http://www.sal.org.sg/

Lee, Kuan Yew 1999. *The Singapore Story: Memoirs of Lee Kuan Yew*. New York: Prentice Hall.

Lee, Kuan Yew 2000. *From Third World to First: The Singapore Story – 1965–2000*. New York: HarperCollins.

Lee, Tahirih V. 1997. *Contract, Guanxi, and Dispute Resolution in China, Chinese Law*; 3. New York: Garland Publishing.

Leuhrmann, L. 2003. "Facing Citizen Complaints in China, 1951–96," *Asian Survey* 43: 845–66.

Levi, Margaret 1998. "A State of Trust," in V. A. Braithwaite and M. Levi (eds.) *Trust and Governance*. New York: Russell Sage Foundation.

Levi, Margaret 1999. "The Problem of Trust," *American Journal of Sociology* 104 (4): 1245–1246.

Levi, Margaret, and Stoker, Laura 2000. "Political Trust and Trustworthiness," *Annual Review of Political Science* (3): 475–507.

Levinson, Sanford. 2006. *Our Undemocratic Constitution*. New York: Oxford University Press.

Levitsky, Steven and Way, Lucien 2002. "The Rise of Competitive Authoritarianism," *Journal of Democracy* 13(2): 51–65.

Lewis, Anthony, 2001. "Wake Up America," *New York Times*, Novemeber 30, 2001, p. A25.

Li, Lianjiang 2004. "Political Trust in Rural China," *Modern China* 30 (2): 228–258.

Lim, Li-Hsien 1998. "Singapore's Legal Framework Tops Again," *Straits Times (Singapore)*, May 16, p. 43.

Linz, Juan 1970. "An Authoritarian Regime: Spain," in Erik Allardt and Stein Rokkan (eds.) *Mass Politics: Studies in Political Sociology*. New York: Free Press.

Linz, Juan 1973. "The Future of an Authoritarian Situation or the Institutionalization of an Authoritarian Regime: The Case of Brazil," in Alfred Stepan (ed.) *Authoritarian Brazil: Origins, Policies, and Future*. New Haven: Yale University Press.

Linz, Juan 1975. "Totalitarian and Authoritarian Regimes," in Fred Greenstein and Nelson Polsby (eds.) *Handbook of Political Science*, Vol. 3: pp. 175–357. Reading, MA: Addison Wesley.

Linz, Juan 2000. *Totalitarian and Authoritarian Regimes*. Boulder: Lynne Rienner.

Linz, Juan and Stepan, Alfred 1996. *Problems of Democratic Transition and Consolidation*. Baltimore: Johns Hopkins Press.

Lobel, Jules 2004. "Winning Lost Causes," *Chronicle of Higher Education*, February 6.

López Dawson, Carlos. 1995. *Justicia Militar: Una Nueva Mirada*. Santiago: Comisión Chilena de Derechos Humanos.

Loveman, Brian and Davies, Thomas M. Jr., eds. 1989. *The Politics of Anti-Politics: The Military in Latin America*. Wilmington, DE: Scholarly Resources, Inc.

Lubman, Stanley B. 1996. *China's Legal Reforms*. Oxford: Oxford University Press.

Lubman, Stanley B. 1999. *Bird in a Cage: Chinese Legal Reform after Mao*. Stanford: Stanford University Press.

Lugosi, Charles 2003. "Rule of Law or Rule by Law: The Detention of Yaser Hamdi," *American Journal of Criminal Law* 30: 225.

Lukianova, E.G. 2001. "Znachenie Konstitututsii SSSR 1977 g. v razvitii istochnikov Rossiiskogo gosudarstvennogo prava," *Gosudarstvo i pravo* 4: 107–113.

Luo, Yadong 2000. *Guanxi and Business* (Asia-Pacific business series; vol. 1). Singapore: World Scientific.

Luque, María José 1984. "Consejos de Guerra: Justicia o Venganza?" *ANALISIS* (June 5): 26–29.

Luque, María José, and Collyer, Patricia 1986. "Proceso a la Corte Suprema," *ANALISIS* (July 1): 23–27.

Lydgate, Chris 2003. *Lee's Law: How Singapore Crushes Dissent*. Melbourne: Scribe Publications.

MacCormick, Neil 1993. "Constitutionalism and Democracy," in Richard Bellamy (ed.) *Theories and Concepts of Politics*. New York: Manchester University Press.

Magalhães, Pedro 1999. "The Politics of Judicial Reform in Eastern Europe," *Comparative Politics* (October) 32: 43–62.

Magalhães, Pedro C., Guarnieri, Carlo and Kaminis, Yorgos 2007. "Democratic Consolidation, Judicial Reform, and Judicialization of Politics in Southern Europe," in Gunther, Diamandouros, Nikiforos, and Sotiropoulos (eds.) *Democracy and the State in the New Southern Europe*. Oxford: Oxford University Press.

Magaloni, Beatriz 1996. "Dominancia de Partido y Dilemas Duvergerianos en las Elecciones Federales de 1994" (Party Dominance and Duvergerian Dilemmas in the 1994 Federal Elections) *Política y Gobierno*. 3(2): 14–32.

Magaloni, Beatriz 2003. "Authoritarianism, Democracy and the Supreme Court: Horizontal Exchange and the Rule of Law in Mexico," in Scott Mainwaring and Christopher Welna (eds.) *Democratic Accountability in Latin America* New York: Oxford University Press.

Magaloni, Beatriz 2006. *Voting for Autocracy: Hegemonic Party Survival and Its Demise In Mexico*. Cambridge: Cambridge University Press.

Magaloni, Beatriz and Sanchez, Arianna 2006. "An Authoritarian Enclave: The Supreme Court in Mexico's Emerging Democracy." Paper presented at the 2006 American Political Science Association Meeting.

Magaloni, Beatriz and Zepeda, Guillermo 2004. "Democratization, Judicial and Law Enforcement Institutions, and the Rule of Law in Mexico," in Kevin L. Middlebrook (ed.) *Dilemmas of Political Change in Mexico*. San Diego: Institute of Latin American Studies, University of California, San Diego.

Mahajan, Vijay, and Peterson, Robert A. 1985. *Models for Innovation Diffusion*. (Sage University Papers Series. Quantitative Applications in the Social Sciences; no. 07-048). Beverly Hills: Sage Publications.

Mahboubi, Neysun 2005 "How Administrative (Can) Constrain Chinese Officials." Paper prepared for conference on New Scholarship in Chinese Law, Center for Chinese Legal Studies Columbia Law School, April 15, 2005.

Mahmud, Tayyab. 1993. "Praetorianism and Common Law in Post-Colonial Settings: Judicial Responses to Constitutional Breakdowns in Pakistan." Utah Law Review 1993: 1225–1305.

Mahmud, Tayyab 1994. "Jurisprudence of Successful Treason: Coup d'Etat & Common Law," *Cornell International Law Journal* 27(1): 49–140.

Massadeh, Abdel-Mahdi 1991. "Disciplinary Actions under the Egyptian Civil Service Legal System," *Journal of International and Comparative Law*, 363–397.

Mathews, H.L. 2003. "Half of Spain Died." Available at http://www.rigeib.com/heroes/unamuno/franco.html

Matus Acuña, Alejandra 1999. *El Libro Negro de la Justicia Chilena*. Santiago: Editorial Planeta.

Matveeva, Anastasia 2006. "Rossiianie peregruzili Strasburgskii sud," *RBC Daily*, May 31.

Mauzy, D.K. and Milne, R.S. 2002. *Singapore Politics under the People's Action Party*. New York: Routledge.

McCally, Sarah P. 1956. "Party Government in Turkey," *Journal of Politics* 18 (May): 297–323.

McCloskey, Robert G. 1994. *The American Supreme Court*, revised by Sanford Levinson. Chicago: University of Chicago Press.

McCubbins, Mathew D., Noll, Roger G., and Weingast, Barry 1987. "Administrative Procedures as Instruments of Political Control," *Journal of Law, Economics and Organizations* 3: 243–277.

McCubbins, Mathew D., Noll, Roger G., and Weingast, Barry 1989. "Structure and Process, Politics and Policy: Administrative Arrangements and the Political Control of Agencies," *Virginia Law Review* 75: 431–482.

McCubbins, Mathew and Schwartz, Thomas. 1984. "Congressional Oversight Overlooked: Police Patrols vs. Fire Alarms," *American Journal of Political Science* 28: 165–179.

McNollgast 1998. "Political Control of the Bureaucracy," in Peter Newman (ed.) *The New Palgrave Dictionary of Economics and Law*. London: Macmillan.

McNollgast 1999. "The Political Origins of the Administrative Procedures Act," *Journal of Law Economics and Organization* 15: 180–217.

Melanson, R. A. 1991. *Reconstructing Consensus: American Foreign Policy since the Vietnam War*. New York: St. Martin's Press.

MERiT 2006. "O khode realizatsii federalnoi tselevoi programmy 'Razvitie sudebnoi sistemy Rossii,' na 2002–2006 gody," January 19. Available at www.economy.gov.ru/wps

Merryman, John Henry 1985. *The Civil Law Tradition: An Introduction to the Legal Systems of Western Europe and Latin America* (2nd ed.). Stanford: Stanford University Press.

Michelson, Ethan 2002. "How Much Does Law Matter in Beijing?" Paper presented at Law and Society Association Annual Meeting, May 30-June 1, Vancouver, Canada.

Michelson, Ethan 2006. "The Practice of Law as an Obstacle to Justice: Chinese Lawyers at Work," *Law and Society Review* 40(1): 1–38.

Migdal, Joel 1989. *Strong Societies and Weak States: State-Society Relations and State Capabilities in the Third World*. Princeton, NJ: Princeton University Press.

Migdal, Joel 1997. "Studying the State," in Mark Lichbach and Alan Zuckerman (eds.) *Comparative Politics: Rationality, Culture, and Structure*. Cambridge: Cambridge University Press.

Migdal, Joel, Kohli, Atul, and Shue, Vivienne (eds.) 1994. *State Power and Social Forces: Domination and Transformation in the Third World*. Cambridge: Cambridge University Press.

Mikhailovskaya, Inga 1999. "The Procuracy and its Problems," *East European Constitution Review* 8: 98–104.

Miller, Richard Lawrence 1995. *Nazi Justice: Law of the Holocaust*. Wesport: Praeger.

Ministerio Secretaría General de Gobierno de Chile 1991. *Informe de la Comisión Nacional de Verdad y Reconciliación.* Santiago, Chile.

Mintz, John 2002. "Rumsfeld Details Tribunal For War Captives," *Manchester Guardian Weekly,* March 28– April 3, p. 32.

Mitiukov, Mikhail A. 2005. *Sudebnyi konstitutsionnnyi nadzor 1924–1933 gg.: voprosy istorii, teorii i praktiki.* Moscow: Formula Prava.

Mitiukov, Mikhail A. 2006. *Predtecha konstitutsionnogo pravosudiia: vzgliady, proekty I institutsionalnye predposylki (30-nachalo 90-kh GG. XX v.).* Moscow: Formula Prava.

Moe, Terry M. 1990. "Political Institutions: The Neglected Side of the Story," *Journal of Law, Economics and Organization* 6 (December): 213–253.

Molinar, Juan. 1991. *El Tiempo de la Legitimidad. Elecciones, Democracia y Autoritarismo en México.* México: Cal y Arena.

Morgan, Bronwen. 2006. "Turning off the Tap: Urban Water Service Delivery and the Social Construction of Global Administrative Law," *European Journal of International Law* 17: 246–271.

Moustafa, Tamir 2003. "Law versus the State: The Judicialization of Politics in Egypt," *Law and Social Inquiry* 28 (4): 883–930.

Moustafa, Tamir 2005. "A Judicialization of Authoritarian Politics?" Paper presented at the Annual Meeting of the American Political Science Association, Washington DC, September.

Moustafa, Tamir 2007. *The Struggle for Constitutional Power: Law, Politics, and Economic Reform in Egypt.* New York: Cambridge University Press.

Müller, Ingo 1991. *Hitler's Justice: The Courts of the Third Reich.* Cambridge, MA: Harvard University Press.

Munck, G. 1998. *Authoritarianism and Democratization: Soldiers and Workers in Argentina, 1976–1983.* University Park, PA: Pennsylvania State University Press.

Munizaga, Giselle 1988. *El Discurso Público de Pinochet.* Santiago: CESOC/ CENECA.

Murphy, Walter 1962. *Congress and the Court.* Chicago: University of Chicago Press.

Nadorff, Norman J. 1982. "Habeas Corpus and the Protection of Political and Civil Rights in Brazil: 1964–1978," *Lawyer of the Americas* 14: 297–336.

Nathan, S.R. 1995. "Singapore: The System Works." *Washington Post,* September 20, p. A-19.

Nathan Associates, Robert R. "A Study of the Feasibility of a Private Investment Encouragement Fund for the Egyptian Private Sector." Submitted to U.S. Agency for International Development. Sept 1979.

Navarrete, B. Jaime 1974. "El poder del poder judicial," *Revista Chilena de Derecho* 1: 73–72.

Nef, Jorge 1974. "The Politics of Repression: The Social Pathology of the Chilean Military," *Latin American Perspectives* 1: 58–77.

Nehrt, Charles 1970. *The Political Environment for Foreign Investment.* New York: Praeger.

Ngai, N. P. 1997. "China's Youth Work in Rural Areas: Some Reflections on a Town and Two Villages," *International Social Work* 40 (1): 27–42.

Nicolet, Claude 2004. "Dictatorship in Rome," in Peter Baehr and Melvin Richter (eds.) *Dictatorship in History and Theory: Bonapartism, Caesarism, and Totalitarianism.* Cambridge: Cambridge University Press.

Nieer, Aryeh 2002. "The Military Tribunals on Trial," *New York Review of Books*, February 14, pp. 1–9.

Nikitinskii, L. 2006. "Biznesmen, kotoryi trizhdy ne vinovat," *Novaia gazeta*, March 2.

Nino, Carlos 1996. *Radical Evil on Trial*. New Haven: Yale University Press.

North, Douglass C. 1990. *Institutions, Institutional Change, and Economic Performance*. Cambridge: Cambridge University Press.

North, Douglass C. 1991. "Institutions," *Journal of Economic Perspectives* 5: 97–112.

North, Douglass C. and Weingast, Barry R. 1989. "Constitutions and Commitment: The Evolution of Institutions Governing Public Choice in Seventeenth-Century England," *Journal of Economic History* 49: 803–832.

O'Brien, Kevin J., and Lianjiang Li. 2005. "Suing the Local State: Administrative Litigation in Rural China," in N. J. Diamant, S. B. Lubman and K. J. O'Brien (eds.) *Engaging the Law in China: State, Society, and Possibilities for Justice*. Stanford: Stanford University Press.

O'Brien, Kevin J., and Lianjiang Li. 2006. *Rightful Resistance in Rural China*. New York: Cambridge University Press.

Oda, Hiroshi 1984. "Judicial Review of the Administration in the Countries of Eastern Europe," *Public Law* 29: 112–134.

O'Donnell, Guillermo 1973. *Modernization and Bureaucratic Authoritarianism: Studies in South American Politics*. Berkeley: University of California, Institute of International Studies.

O'Donnell, Guillermo and Schmitter, Philippe C. 1986. *Transitions from Authoritarian Rule: Tentative Conclusions about Uncertain Democracies*. Baltimore: Johns Hopkins University Press.

Ohnesorge, John 2007. "Chinese Administrative Law in the Northeast Asian Mirror," *Transnational Law and Contemporary Problems* 16: 103–164.

Oi, Jean 1986. "Commercializing China's Rural Cadres," *Problems of Communism* September–October: 1–15.

Olson, Mancur 1993. "Dictatorship, Democracy, and Development," *American Political Science Review* 87: 567–576.

Olson, Mancur 1996. "Distinguished Lecture on Economics in Government: Big Bills Left on the Sidewalk: Why Some Nations are Rich, and Others Poor," *Journal of Economic Perspectives* 10: 3–24.

Ong Au Chuan v. Public Prosectior [1980–1981] Singapore Law Reports 48.

Orden de Abogados 1980. *Antecedentes Histórico-Jurídicos: Años 1972–1973*. Santiago: Editorial Jurídica de Chile.

Örücü, Esin 2000. "Conseil d'Etat: The French Layer of Turkish Administrative Law," *International and Comparative Law Quarterly* 49: 679–700.

Osiel, Mark J. 1995. "Dialogue with Dictators: Judicial Resistance in Argentina and Brazil," *Law and Social Inquiry* 20: 481–560.

Ostrom, Elinor 2005. *Understanding Institutional Diversity*. Princeton, NJ: Princeton University Press.

Ott, Walter, and Buob, Franziska 1993. "Did Legal Positivism Render German Jurists Defenceless during the Third Reich?" *Social & Legal Studies (SAGE, London)* 2: 91–104.

Owen, Thomas C. 1991. *The Corporation under Russian Law, 1800–1917*. Cambridge: Cambridge University Press.

Özbudun, Ergun 1999. *Contemporary Turkish Politics: Challenges to Democratic Consolidation.* Boulder: Lynne Rienner.

Payne, Stanley 1967. *Politics and the Military in Modern Spain.* Stanford: Stanford University Press.

Peerenboom, Randall P. 2002. *China's Long March toward Rule of Law.* Cambridge: Cambridge University Press.

Peerenboom, Randall P. 2004a. "Out of the Pan and into the Fire: Well-Intentioned but Misguided Recommendations to Eliminate All Forms of Administrative Detention in China," *Northwestern University Law Review* 9: 991–1104.

Peerenboom, Randall P. 2004b. "Varieties of Rule of Law: An Introduction and Provisional Conclusion," in Randall Peerenboom (ed.) *Asian Discourses of Rule of Law.* London: Routledge.

Pei, Minxin 1997. "Citizens v. Mandarins: Administrative Litigation in China," *China Quarterly* 152: 832–862.

Pellet Lastra, A. 2001. *Historía Política de la Corte (1930–1990).* Buenos Aires: Ad-Hoc.

Pereira, Anthony 2005. *Political (In)justice: Authoritarianism and the Rule of Law in Brazil, Chile, and Argentina.* Pittsburgh: University of Pittsburgh Press.

Peretti, Terri Jennings 1999. *In Defense of a Political Court.* Princeton, NJ: Princeton University Press.

Perlmutter, Amos 1981. *Modern Authoritarianism: A Comparative Institutional Analysis.* New Haven: Yale University Press.

Pinkele, Carl F. 1992. "Plus ça change: The Interaction between the Legal System and Political Change in Francoist Spain," *International Political Science Review* 13 (3, July): 285–300.

Pistor, Katarina 1996. "Supply and Demand for Contract Enforcement in Russia: Courts, Arbitration and Private Enforcement," *Review of Central and East European Law,* 22: 1.

Popova, A.D. 2005. *"Pravda i milost da tsarstvuiut v sudakh" (Iz istorii realizatsii sudebnoi reformy 1864 g.).* Riazan: Idz. "Poverennyi."

Posner, Eric A. 2000. "Agency Models in Law and Economics," in Eric Posner (ed.) *Chicago Lectures in Law and Economics.* Chicago: University of Chicago Press.

Potter, Pitman B. 2003. *From Leninist Discipline to Socialist Legalism: Peng Zhen on Law and Political Authority in the PRC.* Palo Alto: Stanford University Press.

Pozo, Felipe 1983. "Momento Judicial: Presidente Habemus," *ANALISIS* (May): 9–10.

Pravilova, Ekaterina 2000. *Zakonnost i prava lichnosti: Administrativnaia iustitsiia v Rossii (vtoraia polovina XIX v–oktiabr 1917 g.).* St Petersburg: Obrazovanie-Kultura.

Precht Pizarro, Jorge 1987. "Derecho Material de Control Judicial en la Jurisprudencia de la Corte Supreme de Chile: Derogación Tácita e Inaplicabilidad (1925–1987)," *Revista de Derecho y Jurisprudencia* 1: 87–107.

Ramseyer, J. Mark 1994. "The Puzzling (In)Dependence of Courts: A Comparative Approach," *Journal of Legal Studies* 23: 721.

Ramseyer, J. Mark and Rasmusen, Erik B. 2003. *Measuring Judicial Independence: The Political Economy of Judging in Japan.* Chicago: University of Chicago Press.

Raz, Joseph 1979. "The Rule of Law and its Virtue," in *The Authority of Law: Essays on Law and Morality.* Oxford: Clarendon Press.

Rehnquist, William H. 1998. *All the Laws but One: Civil Liberties in Wartime.* New York: Alfred A. Knopf.

Rupublic of China, Constitution. 1946. Taipei: Government Printing Office.

Republic of Singapore, Parliament. Parliamentary Debates: Official Report (Singapore Government Printers) November 2, 1995: col 236

Republic of Singapore, Parliament. Parliamentary Debates: Official Report (Singapore Government Printers) January 14, 1998: column 93.

Rigby, Andrew. 2001. *Justice and Reconciliation: After the Violence.* Boulder: L. Rienner Publishers.

Robock, Stefan 1971. "Political Risk: Identification and Assessment," *Columbia Journal of World Business* (July–Aug): 6–20.

Rodan, Garry 2005. "Singapore 'Exceptionalism'? Authoritarian Rule and State Transformation" (Working Paper 131). Perth: Asia Research Centre, Murdoch University.

Rodan, Garry 2006. "Lion City Baits Mousy Opposition," *Far Eastern Economic Review*, May, pp. 11–17.

Rona-Tas, Akos and Guseva, Alya, 2001. "The Privileges of Past Communist Party Membership in Russia and Endogenous Switching Regression." *Social Science Research.* 30 (4): 641–52.

Root, Hilton L. 1985. "Challenging the Seigneurie: Community and Contention on the Eve of the French Revolution," *Journal of Modern History* 57: 652–681.

Root, Hilton L. 1989. "Tying the King's Hand: Credible Commitments and Royal Fiscal Policy During the Old Regime," *Rationality and Society.* 1: 240–258.

Root, Hilton L. 1994. *The Fountain of Privilege: Political Foundations of Markets in Old Regime France and England.* Berkeley: University of California Press.

Root, Hilton L. 1996. "Corruption in China: Has it Become Systemic?" *Asian Survey* 38: 741–757.

Root, Hilton L. 2006. *Capital and Collusion: The Political Logic of Global Economic Development.* Princeton, NJ: Princeton University Press.

Rosberg, J. 1995. *Roads to the Rule of Law: The Emergence of an Independent Judiciary in Contemporary Egypt.* PhD diss., Massachusetts Institute of Technology, Cambridge, MA.

Rose-Ackerman, S. 1995. *Controlling Environmental Policy: The Limits of Public Law in Germany and the United States.* New Haven: Yale University Press.

Roshchin, A. 2006 March 31. "Narod vinovat!" *Politkom.ru.*

Ross, Michael L. 1999. "The Political Economy of the Resource Curse," *World Politics* 51: 297–322.

Rossiter, C. L. 1948. *Constitutional Dictatorship: Crisis Government in the Modern Democracies.* London: Oxford University Press.

Rouleau, Eric 1999. "Iran: An Economy in Need of Reform," *Middle East Economic Survey* XLII (5 July).

Rubin, Edward 2002. "Independence as a Governance Mechanism," in Burbank and Friedman (eds.) *Judicial Independence at a Crossroads.* Thousand Oaks: Sage Publications.

Russian Axis 2003. "The Judicial System of the Russian Federation: A System-Crisis of Independence," Report available at http://www.russianaxis.org/files/10/judicial.pdf

Russell, Peter. 2001. "Toward a General Theory of Judicial Independence," in Peter Russell and David O'Brien, eds. *Judicial Independence in the Age of Democracy: Critical Perspectives from around the World*. Charlottesville, Va., and London: University Press of Virginia, 2001. pp. 1–24.

Russell, Peter and O'Brien, David 2001. *Judicial Independence in the Age of Democracy: Critical Assessments from Around the World*. Charlottesville, VA: University of Virginia Press.

Rustow, Dankwart. 1970. "Transitions to Democracy: Toward a Dynamic Model," *Comparative Politics* 2: 337–363.

Safire, William 2001. "Kangaroo Courts Betray Our Values," *Times-Picayune*, November 16, p. B-7.

Safire, William 2002. "Bloomberg News Humbled," *New York Times*, August 29, p A-25.

Safire, William 1997. "The Misrule of Law," *New York Times*, June 1, p. 17.

Sayed, Mar'ai 1980. Speech to the American Bar Association Convention, reprinted in *International Law* 14: 12–15 (1980).

SCC, 16 June 1984. *al-Mahkama* 3: 80.

Schattschneider, E.E. 1960. *The Semi-Sovereign People*. London: Wadsworth.

Scheuerman, William E. 2006. "Carl Schmitt and the Road to Abu Ghraib," *Constellations* 13 (1): 108–124.

Schmitt, Ç. 1985 (c1923) *La Dictadura*, José Díaz García (trans.) Madrid: Alianza Editorial.

Schulz, William 2003. *Tainted Legacy: 9/11 and the Ruin of Human Rights*. New York: Thunder's Mouth Press/Nation Books.

Secor, Laura 2005. "Fugitives: Young Iranians Confront the Collapse of the Reform Movement," *The New Yorker*, November 21.

Segal, Jeffrey and Spaeth, Harold. 1993. *The Supreme Court and the Attitudinal Model*. New York: Cambridge University Press.

Seow, Francis 1994. *To Catch a Tartar: A Dissident in Lee Kuan Yew's Prison*. New Haven: Yale University Press.

Seow, Francis 1997a. *The Media Enthralled: Singapore Revisited*. London: Lynne Rienner Publishers.

Seow, Francis 1997b. "The Politics of Judicial Institutions in Singapore." Lecture delivered in Sydney, Australia. Available at http://www.gn.apc.org/sfd/

Seow, Francis 1998. "Newspapers: A Ban is Not a Ban Unless Restricted." Paper presented at the conference, "The Limits of Control: Media and Technology in China, Hong Kong and Singapore," at the Graduate School of Journalism, University of California, Berkeley, April 2–3.

Shambayati, Hootan 2004. "A Tale of Two Mayors: Courts and Politics in Turkey and Iran," *International Journal of Middle East Studies* 36 (May): 253–275.

Shambayati, Hootan 2008. "The Guardian of the Regime: The Turkish Constitutional Court in Comparative Perspective," in S. A. Arjomand (ed.) *Constitutional Politics in the Middle East*. Onati, Spain: International Institute for the Sociology of Law.

Shapiro, Martin 1964. *Law and Politics on the Supreme Court*. New York: Free Press.

Shapiro, Martin 1975. "Courts," in Greenstein and Polsby (eds.), *Handbook of Political Science: Macropolitical Theory: Volume 5, Governmental Institutions and Processes*. Reading: Addison-Wesley Publishing Company.

Shapiro, Martin 1980. "Appeal," *Law and Society Review* 14: 641–642.

Shapiro, Martin 1981. *Courts: A Comparative and Political Analysis.* Chicago: University of Chicago Press.

Shapiro, Martin 1988. *Who Guards the Guardians? Judicial Control of Administration.* Athens: University of Georgia Press.

Shapiro, Martin 1989. "Political Jurisprudence, Public Law, and Post-Consequentialist Ethics: Comment on Professors Barber and Smith," *Studies in American Political Development* 3: 88.

Shapiro, Martin 1992. "The Giving Reasons Requirement," *University of Chicago Legal Forum* 179–220.

Shapiro, Martin, and Stone Sweet, Alec. 2002. *On Law, Politics and Judicialization,* New York: Oxford University Press.

Sharlet, Robert 1978. *The New Soviet Constitution of 1977. Analysis and Text.* Brunswick, NJ: King's Court Communications.

Sharlet, Robert 2003. "Constitutional Law and Politics in Russia: Surviving the First Decade," *Demokratizatsiya* 11: 122–128.

Shi, Tianjian 2001. "Cultural Values and Political Trust – A Comparison of the People's Republic of China and Taiwan," *Comparative Politics* 33 (4): 401sq.

Shirk, S. 1993. *The Political Logic of Economic Reform in China.* Berkeley: University of California Press.

Shklar, Judith 1986. *Legalism: Law, Morals, and Political Trials.* Cambridge, MA: Harvard University Press.

Shklar, Judith 1987. "Political Theory and the Rule of Law," in Hutchinson and Monahan (eds.), *The Rule of Law: Ideal or Ideology.* Toronto: Carswell.

Sieder, Rachel, Schjolden, Line, and Angell, Alan 2005. *The Judicialization of Politics in Latin America.* New York: Palgrave Macmillan.

Silva Cimma, Enrique. 1977. *El Tribunal Constitucional de Chile (1971–1973).* Caracas: Editorial Jurídica Venezolana.

Silverstein, Gordon 2003. "Globalization and the Rule of Law: A Machine That Runs of Itself?" *International Journal of Constitutional Law* 1: 405–426.

Sim, Susan 1995. "Shooting Star of S'pore a Legend in His Lifetime," *Straits Times,* December 13.

Skidmore, Thomas 1988. *The Politics of Military Rule in Brazil, 1964–1985.* New York: Oxford University Press.

Smithey, Shannon Ishiyama and Ishiyama, John 2000. "Judicious Choices: Designing Courts in Post Communist Polities," *Communist and Post Communist Studies* 33: 163–182.

Smithey, Shannon Ishiyama and Ishiyama, John 2002. "Judicial Activism in Post-Communist Politics," *Law & Society Review* 36: 719–742.

Snow, P. G. 1975. "Judges and Generals: The Role of the Argentine Supreme Court during Periods of Military Government," in Leibholz (ed.), *Jahrbuch des Öffentlichen Rechts der Gegenwart.* Tübingen: J.C.B Mohr. 24: 609–617.

So, Ying Lun, and Walker, Anthony 2006. *Explaining Guanxi: The Chinese Business Network.* New York: Routledge.

Solomon, Peter H. 1990. "The U.S.S.R. Supreme Court: History, Role, and Future Prospects," *American Journal of Comparative Law* 38: 127–142.

Solomon, Peter H. 1996. *Soviet Criminal Justice under Stalin.* Cambridge: Cambridge University Press.

Solomon, Peter H. 1997. "Courts and Their Reform in Russian History," in Peter H. Solomon, Jr., (ed.) *Reforming Justice in Russia, 1864–1996*. Armonk, NY: M.E. Sharpe, pp. 3–20.

Solomon, Peter H. 2002. "Putin's Judicial Reform: Making Judges Accountable as well as Independent," *East European Constitutional Review*, 11: 101–107.

Solomon, Peter H. 2004. "Judicial Power in Russia: Through the Prism of Administrative Justice," *Law & Society Review* 38: 549–582.

Solomon, Peter H. 2005. "Threats of Judicial Counterreform in Putin's Russia," *Demokratizatsiia* 13: 325–346.

Solomon, Peter H. 2006. "Informal Practices in Russian Justice: Probing the Limits of Post-Soviet Reform," in Ferdinand Feldbrugge (ed.) *Russia, Europe and the Rule of Law*. Leiden: Martinus Nijhoff.

Solomon, Peter H., Jr., and Foglesong, Todd N. 2000. *Courts and Transition in Russia: The Challenge of Judicial Reform*. Boulder: Westview.

Soto Kloss, Eduardo 1986. "Una Revolución Silenciosa," *Revista de Derecho y Jurisprudencia* 83 (1): 157–162.

Sova 2006. "Obzor reshenii Evropeiskogo Suda po pravam cheloveka po rossiiskim zhalobam (Mart 2006)." Available at http://osada-sova-center.ru

Squella, Agustín, ed. 1994. *Evolución de la Cultura Jurídica Chilena*. Santiago: Corporación de Promoción Universitaria.

Stansfield Business International v. Minister for Manpower 3 Singapore Law Report 742 (High Court, 1999).

Starilov, Iuryi N. 2001. *Administrativnaia iustitsiia: teoriia, istoriia, perspektivy*. Moscow: Norma.

Starovoitov, Aleksei 2005. "Razvitie sistemy administrativnoi iustitsii v Rossiiskoi Federatsii," *Sravnitelnoe konstitutsionnoe obozrenie* 2: 26–30.

Stepan, Alfred. 1971. *The Military in Politics: Changing Patterns in Brazil*. Princeton, NJ: Princeton University Press.

Sterkin, F. 2006. "Deklaratsiia sudei," *Strana.ru*, Februrary 21.

Stölleis, Michael 1998. *The Law under the Swastika: Studies on Legal History in Nazi Germany*. Chicago: University of Chicago Press.

Stone Sweet, Alec 1992. *The Birth of Judicial Politics in France*. Oxford: Oxford University Press.

Stone Sweet, Alec 2000. *Governing with Judges: Constitutional Politics in Europe*. New York: Oxford University Press.

Strayer, J.R. 1970. *On the Medieval Origins of the Modern State*. Princeton, NJ: Princeton University Press.

Suh, Sangwon and Santha Oorjitham, 1997. "No Holds Barred: After a Hard Fought Win at the Polls, Goh Plans for the Next Century," *AsiaWeek*, January 17.

Sullivan, Michael B. 1976. *Egypt: Business Gateway to the Middle East?* Geneva: Business International S.A.

Sutiazhnik 2005. *Otchet o vliianii sudebnoi praktiki OO "Sutiazhnik" na rossiiskoe zakonodatelstva i pravoprimenitelnuiu praktiku*. Ekaterinburg: "Sutiazhnik".

Tan, Hsueh Yun. 1997. "S'pore Gets High Marks for Being Well-Governed," *Straits Times (Singapore)*. June 9, p. 25.

Tan, Ooi Boon. 1998. "Top Marks for Justice System," *Straits Times (Singapore)*, September 14. p. 24.

Tang, Wenfang, and Holzner, Burkart 2006. *Social Change in Contemporary China: C.K. Yang and the Concept of Institutional Diffusion.* Pittsburgh: University of Pittsburgh Press.

Tang, Wenfang, and Parish, William L. 2000. *Chinese Urban Life under Reform: The Changing Social Contract, Cambridge Modern China Series.* Cambridge: Cambridge University Press.

Tate, C. Neal and Haynie, Stacia L. 1995. "Courts and Crisis Regimes: A Theory Sketch with Asian Case Studies," *Political Research Quarterly* 46 (June): 311–338.

Tate, C. Neal and Haynie, Stacia L. 1993. "Authoritarianism and the Function of Courts: A Time Series Analysis of the Philippine Supreme Court, 1961–1987," *Law and Society Review* 27(4): 51–82.

Tate, C. Neal. 1995. "Why the Expansion of Judicial Power?" in C. Neal Tate and Torbjorn Vallinder (eds.) *The Global Expansion of Judicial Power.* New York: New York University Press.

Tate, C. Neal and Vallinder, Torbjorn (eds.) 1995. *The Global Expansion Of Judicial Power.* New York: New York University Press.

Tavolari, Raúl 1995. *Habeas Corpus: Recurso de Amparo.* Santiago: Editorial Jurídica.

Taylor Jr., Stuart 2004. "Lawless in the Dungeon." *Legal Times,* January 12, p. 46.

Thelen Kathleen and Steinmo, Sven. 1992. *Structuring Politics: Historical Institutionalism in Comparative Politics.* New York: Cambridge University Press.

Thio, Li-ann 2002a. "Lex Rex or Rex Lex? Competing Conceptions of the Rule of Law in Singapore," *UCLA Pacific Basin Law Journal* 20: 1–76.

Thio, Li-ann 2002b. "The Right to Political Participation in Singapore: Tailor-making a Westminster-Modeled Constitution to Fit the Imperatives of 'Asian' Democracy," *Singapore Journal of International and Comparative Law* 6: 181.

Thio, Li-ann 2004. "Rule of Law within a Non-Liberal 'Communitarian'' Democracy: The Singapore Experience, in Randall Peerenboom (ed.) *Asian Discourses of Rule of Law: Theories and Implementation of Rule of Law in Twelve Asian Countries, France and the U.S.* London: Routledge.

Thompson, E.P. 1975. *Whigs and Hunters: The Origins of the Black Act.* New York: Pantheon Books.

Toharia, Jose 1975. "Judicial Independence in an Authoritarian Regime: The Case of Contemporary Spain," *Law and Society Review,* 9: 475–496.

Trochev, Alexei 2002. "Implementing Russian Constitutional Court Decisions," *East European Constitutional Review* 11: 95–103.

Trochev, Alexei 2005a. "The Zigzags of Judicial Power: The Constitutional Court in Russian Politics, 1990–2003." Unpublished Ph.D. diss., University of Toronto.

Trochev, Alexei 2005b. "Judicial Selection in Russia: Toward Accountability and Centralization," in Kate Malleson and Peter H. Russell (eds.) *Appointing Judges in an Age of Judicial Power.* Toronto: University of Toronto Press.

Truitt, Frederick 1974. *Expropriation of Private Foreign Investment.* Bloomington: Graduate School of Business, Indiana University.

Tsui, K. and Wang, Y. 2004. "Between Separate Stoves and a Single Menu: Fiscal Decentralization in China," *China Quarterly* 177: 71–90.

Tushnet, Mark 1999. *Taking the Constitution away from the Courts.* Princeton, NJ: Princeton University Press.

Ulbig, S. G. 2002. "Policies, Procedures, and People: Sources of Support for Government?" *Social Science Quarterly* 83 (3): 789–809.

'Ubayd. 1991. *Istiqlal al-Qada'*, pp. 290–305.

Unger, Roberto 1986. *The Critical Legal Studies Movement*. Cambridge: Harvard University Press.

U.S. Central Intelligence Agency 2004. *World Fact Book*. Available at https://www.cia.gov/cia/

U.S. Congressional-Executive Commission on China. 2002. *Taming the Dragon: Can Legal Reform Foster Respect for Human Rights in China? [Hearing before the Congressional-Executive Commission on China, 107th Congress, 2nd session, April 11, 2002*. Washington DC: U.S. Government Printing Office.

US Department of Commerce. 1981. "Investing in Egypt." Overseas Business Reports, OBR 81-08.

Uslaner, Eric 2002. *The Moral Foundations of Trust*. New York: Cambridge University Press.

Valenzuela, Arturo 1995. "The Military in Power: The Consolidation of One-Man Rule," in Paul Drake and Ivan Jaksic (eds.), *The Struggle for Democracy in Chile* (revised ed.). Lincoln: University of Nebraska Press.

Van Agtmael, Antoine 1976. "How Business Has Dealt with Political Risk," *Financial Executive* (January): 26–30.

Velasco, Eugenio 1986. *Expulsión*. Santiago: Copygraph.

Verdugo, Patricia 1990. *Tiempos de Días Claros: Los Desaparecidos*. Santiago: Ediciones ChileAmérica.

Verkhovnyi sud 2003. "O primenenii sudami obshchei iurisdiktsii obshcheprizvannykh printsipov i norm mezhunarodnogo prava i mezhdynarodnykh dogovorov RF" (October 10, 2003), *BVS*, 2003, No. 12, p. 3, *available at* http://www. supcourt.ru/vscourt_detale.php?id=1961 (last visited March 4, 2006).

Volkov, Vadim. 2002. *Violent Entrepreneurs: The Use of Force in the Making of Russian Capitalism*. Ithaca: Cornell University Press.

Volpi, Frederic. 2004. "Pseudo-Democracy in the Muslim World." *Third World Quarterly* 25(6): 1061–78.

Wagner, William 1976. "Tsarist Legal Policies at the End of the Nineteenth Century: A Study in Inconsistencies," *Slavonic and East European Review*, 54: 371–394.

Wagner, William 1994. *Marriage, Property and Law in Late Imperial Russia*. Oxford: Clarendon Press.

Walder, Andrew G. 1995. "Career Mobility and the Communist Political Order," *American Sociological Review* 60 (3): 309–328.

Walder, Andrew G., and Treiman, D. J. 2000. "Politics and Life Chances in a State Socialist Regime: Dual Career Paths into the Urban Chinese Elite, 1949 to 1996," *American Sociological Review* 65 (3): 191–209.

Wallace, Charles P. 1995. "Singapore's Grip," *Columbia Journalism Review*, November/December.

Wang, H. 2006. "Interview with Hongying Wang," *Foreign Exchange with Fareed Zakaria*. Show 229 Transcript edn.

Wang, Xixin 1998. "Administrative Procedure Reforms in China's Rule of Law Context," *Columbia Journal of Asian Law* 12: 251–277.

Waterbury, John. 1993. *Exposed to Innumerable Delusions: Public Enterprise and State Power in Egypt, India, Mexico, and Turkey*. Cambridge: Cambridge University Press.

Weber, Max 1946. "Bureaucracy," in H. H. Gerth and C. Wright Mills (eds.) *From Max Weber*. New York: Oxford University Press, pp. 196–244.

Weber, Max 1978. *Economy and Society*. Translated by Guenther Roth and Claus Wittich. Berkeley: University of California Press.

Wedgwood, Ruth. 2002. "Al Qaeda, Terrorism and Military Commissions." *American Journal of International Law* 96: 328–37.

Weingast, Barry R. 1995. "The Economic Role of Political Institutions: Market-Preserving Federalism and Economic Development," *Journal of Law, Economics, and Organization* 11 (Spring): 1–31.

Weldon, Jeffrey 1997. "The Political Sources of Presidentialism in Mexico," in Scott Mainwaring and Matthew Shugart (eds.) *Presidentialism and Democracy in Latin America*. New York: Cambridge University Press.

Whiting, Susan 2004. "The Cadre Evaluation System at the Grass Roots: The Paradox of Party Rule," in Barry Naughton and Dali Yang (eds.) *Holding China Together: Diversity and National Integration in the Post-Deng Era*. New York: Cambridge University Press.

Whiting, Susan 2006. "Growth, Governance and Institutions: The Internal Institutions of the Party-State in China." Paper produced for the World Bank Research Project on the Rise of China and India, available at www.ssrn.com

Widner, Jennifer 2001. *Building the Rule of Law: Francis Nyalali and the Road to Judicial Independence in Africa*. New York: W.W. Norton & Company.

Wilson, Andrew 2005. *Virtual Politics: Faking Democracy in the Post-Soviet World*. New Haven: Yale University Press.

Wintrobe, Ronald 1998. *The Political Economy of Dictatorship*. Cambridge: Cambridge University Press.

Wong, Y. H. and Leung, Thomas K. 2001. *Guanxi: Relationship Marketing in a Chinese Context*. New York: International Business Press.

Wood, Elisabeth Jean 2000. *Forging Democracy from Below*. Cambridge: Cambridge University Press.

World Bank. 2006. *Interactive Data Set*. Available at http://worldbank.org/data-query

World Economic Forum, 1997. *Annual Report*. New York: World Economic Forum.

Worthington, Ross 2001. "Between Hermes and Themis: An Empirical Study of the Contemporary Judiciary in Singapore," *Journal of Law & Society* 28: 4, 490–519.

Wortman, Richard 1976. *The Development of a Russian Legal Consciousness*. Chicago: University of Chicago Press.

Wortman, Richard 2005. "Russian Monarchy and the Rule of Law: New Considerations of the Court Reform of 1864," *Kritika: Explorations in Russian and Eurasian History* 6: 145–170.

Xu, Xiaoqun 1997. "The Fate of Judicial Independence in Republican China, 1912–37," *China Quarterly* 149 (March): 1–28.

Yang, Mayfair Mei-hui 1994. *Gifts, Favors, and Banquets: The Art of Social Relationships in China*. Ithaca, NY: Cornell University Press.

Zakaria, Fareed 1994. "A Conversation with Lee Kuan Yew," *Foreign Affairs*, March/April.

Zaki, Moheb 1999. *Egyptian Business Elites: Their Visions and Investment Behavior.* Cairo: Konrad-Adenauer-Stiftung.

Zaller, John 1991. "Information, Values, and Opinion," *American Political Science Review* 85 (4): 1215–1237.

Zhao, Yi 2003. *The Expansion of Judicial Power in China, Political Science.* New Haven: Yale University Press.

Zhong, Yang. 2003. *Local Government and Politics in China: Challenges from Below.* Armonk, NY: M.E. Sharpe.

Zink, Dolph Warren 1973. *The Political Risks for Multinational Enterprise in Developing Countries.* New York: Praeger.

Index

People's Action Party (PAP) (Singapore),
78, 92–97
See also Lee, Kuan Yew
People's Court (Nazi Germany), 39–41
People's Redemption Army (Uganda),
241
People's Republic of China. *See* China
Pérez, Hernán Santos, 173
Peron, Juan, 161
Peronists (Argentina), 160–161
Petrazhitskii, Leo, 266–267
Philippines, 5–6, 15–16, 315
Pinochet, Augusto, 102, 162
Placencia, Carlos Medina, 198
Plenary Criminal Courts (Portugal), 46
Police for Political and Social Defense
(Portugal), 45–46
police-patrol model of oversight, 142
political activism, 13, 20–21, 148, 151
political control, 158, 193–198
political dynamics, 2–3
political parties, 37–47
See also opposition political parties
political repression, 57, 162, 167–169, 170,
183
popular will controlled by judicial
systems, 5
Portillo, Lopez, 193
Portugal, 45–46
positivist legal tradition, 60, 118–120,
331–332
preemptive coups, 28
presidencialismo (Mexico), 183–184,
194
press, control of, 86–92
press, freedom of
in Chile, 110, 114
in Egypt, 149–150
Press Court (Iran), 301
PRI (Institutional Revolutionary Party)
(Mexico), 182, 183, 193–197, 199,
201–203
principal-agent problems
and authoritarian regimes, 312, 313–314
in China, 314
definition of, 59–65
in democracies, 62–63, 71
in Egypt, 139–146

and indoctrination, 60–61
and judges, 63–65
in the USSR, 313–314
See also hierarchies
Printing Presses Ordinance (Singapore),
86–92
private interests *versus* state interests,
322
private property. *See* property rights
Privy Council (Great Britain and
Singapore), 78–80
Procuracy (Russia and USSR), 62, 271
property rights
and authoritarian regimes, 8–9,
307–309, 330–331
in Egypt, 134, 135–136, 138–139
in Mexico, 192–193, 206
in Russia (Tsarist), 264
Provisional Government of 1917 (Russia),
265
Putin, Vladimir, 275, 276

Rahman, Sheikh Omar Abdel, 153
rape charges against Besigye
Raziq, Gasser 'Abd al-, 151
"recurrent detention" (Egypt), 154–155
recurso de protección (writ of protection –
Chile), 109–111, 114
regime change and judicial systems,
316–324
regime fragmentation, 24
Rehnquist, William, 54
Reid, Richard, 52
religion, freedom of, 110
repression, judicializing of, 27
Republican People's Party (Turkey), 291
Retamal, Rafael, 124, 128
right to assembly, 110
rightful resistance, 13, 69
Rights Revolution, The (Epp), 20
risk assessment and international
investment, 134–135, 147
Robles, José Cánovas, 176
rollback coups, 28
Rosende, Hugo, 114
rule of law
and authoritarian regimes, 167,
329–330